FIFTEEN YEARS

IN

INDIA

FIFTEEN YEARS

IN

INDIA;

OR,

SKETCHES OF A SOLDIER'S LIFE

BEING

AN ATTEMPT TO DESCRIBE PERSONS AND THINGS
IN VARIOUS PARTS OF HINDOSTAN.

ROBERT GRENVILLE WALLACE

GYAN

Published by

Gyan Publishing House
5, Ansari Road
Daryaganj, New Delhi-110002
Phone: 011-47034999, 9811692060
E-mail: books@gyanbooks.com

Distribution Network
gyanbooks.com
India, USA, Canada, UK, Australia, France

ISBN: 978-81-212-9298-6 (PB)
First Published,1822

2nd Impression 2023

Printed at: Gyan Press, Delhi.

FIFTEEN YEARS IN INDIA
Author: ROBERT GRENVILLE WALLACE

FIFTEEN YEARS

IN

INDIA;

OR,

SKETCHES OF A SOLDIER'S LIFE.

BEING

AN ATTEMPT TO DESCRIBE PERSONS AND THINGS

IN VARIOUS PARTS OF HINDOSTAN.

FROM THE JOURNAL OF

AN OFFICER IN HIS MAJESTY'S SERVICE.

Speak of me as I am — nothing extenuate,
Nor set down ought in malice. OTHELLO.

LONDON:

PRINTED FOR

LONGMAN, HURST, REES, ORME, AND BROWN,

PATERNOSTER-ROW.

1822.

TO

MY FATHER,

IN TOKEN OF FILIAL AFFECTION,

WHICH NO CIRCUMSTANCES CAN CHANGE,

THIS EFFORT OF MY PEN

IS INSCRIBED,

WITH

THE GREATEST RESPECT.

ADVERTISEMENT.

Arrowsmith's new map is now in such general circulation that it seems unnecessary to increase the expense of this work by adding a geographical sketch of India, containing the lines of march described by the author. All the principal places will be found in any of the large maps of Hindostan, by such readers as may be desirous of accompanying the writer through the different provinces he traversed.

In spelling proper names of places and persons in India, more attention has been paid to the common way in which they are written by the English authorities in the country, than to any prescribed rule of orthography. As much accuracy as possible is aimed at, but it is presumed to be a matter of little consequence, whether the name of a particular province be written *Guzerat* or *Gujrut*.

Native words are in general avoided, where English ones would answer the purpose. Of such as are used from necessity or for ornament, and not immediately explained, an alphabetical Glossary is given at the end of the work.

The natural productions of India are now so generally known in Europe, that it has been deemed unnecessary to give their scientific names.

PREFACE.

The gentleman who wrote the journal from which the following pages are chiefly drawn, went out to India in the beginning of 1805, and returned in 1819. During that period it was his lot to traverse a great part of the peninsula, from the Ganges to the Indus. He landed at Madras, and saw part of the Carnatic, joined his regiment in Malabar, and served with it in Mysore and Travancore; after which his fortune led him to Bengal, and a few years afterwards to Bombay, where he was employed with the army in Guzerat which invaded Kutch-booge for the first time, marched through Kattywar, and destroyed the fastnesses of the pirates in Okamundel. His corps being then called to join the Poonah subsidiary force, an opportunity was afforded him of seeing a considerable part of the Deckan during the late Mahratta war. The impressions made upon his mind by the scenes which he beheld in India, are now, with deference, offered to the public.

Much might be written on the excusable topic of prepossession; and, on the other hand, many arguments might be adduced to prove that all an author can say in behalf of his own book is *vox et prætcrea nihil.* These pages are therefore dismissed to their fate with a short anecdote.

A British officer, with a small detachment of *sepoys,* was stationed in a pass of the ghauts, for the purpose of intercepting the enemy's *hurkarus.* Among many other travellers, a man in the garb of a villager was stopped. By his own account he was merely going to a neighbouring town. He wore only a cloth round his loins, a blanket, which served him as a sort of tent, being contracted to fit his head while it covered his shoulders, and a pair of old sandals. This scanty dress and all other suspected means of concealment were carefully searched, and a stick, which he carried with little bells fixed to it, for the purpose of frightening away tigers and wild elephants on his journey through the forests, was broken lest there might be a letter enclosed. "Let him pass," said the officer. "*Saheeb*," replied an old *subadar* with a venerable beard, whose language being Hindostannee, I shall translate, "Sir, permit the voice of experience to penetrate the ear of understanding, and suffer me, thy servant, to examine these sandals." This hint, respectfully offered, was not scornfully rejected. The soles of the almost worn-out sandals were cut, and behold a letter in the Persian character, made up in the form of a small roll, was secured in a proper opening. It contained information that led to the surprize and defeat of the Mahrattas, with the capture of their treasure, camels, and elephants. The native officer knew what the European did not, that the old sandals were carried by the messenger on his march, lest the concealed communication should be injured by friction, and merely put on as a *ruse contre ruse*, when he was taken prisoner.

Thus reader, I wish with humility to insinuate that you should examine my book very attentively, for it comes before you without the recommendation of a literary name, a high sounding title, or a powerful patron; and therefore should it contain any interesting matter, it will resemble the *hurkaru*, you the officer, and I the old *subadar*, who assure you, with solemnity, that in it there is a great deal of truth.

INTRODUCTION.

THERE is nothing, it is presumed, in the following pages, contrary to good manners, received opinions, and social duties. It may therefore be asked, Why is the title page without a name? The writer may have a thousand reasons for anonymous publication; but, without enumerating them, he will give at once the history of this work, and his motive for declining immediate notoriety. On both subjects it is only proper to state, that he who now obtrudes himself on attention came home from India, after a long residence there, in a debilitated state of health, with a large family, under the well-founded expectation that solid independence awaited him; but so great and severe were his disappointments that he retired to a mountain, where he pasted on the fireboard of his humble parlour, the singular order of the day issued by Napoleon, when First Consul, against suicide: "A soldier ought to know how to subdue sorrow, and the agitation of the passions; there is as much courage in enduring with firmness the pains of the heart, as in remaining steady under the grape-shot of a battery. To abandon one's-self to grief without resistance, to kill one's-self in order to escape from it, is to fly from the field of battle before one is conquered."—At last, remembering the precept of Virgil, "*ne cede malis*," he sat down to write on India. A short prospectus gave some publicity to his intention, and the proposal was countenanced by his Majesty's librarian, by his Royal Highness the Duke of York, the Lord Lieutenant of Ireland, and two other distinguished personages. However so very few answered his letters, that one day while contemplating the fate of his undertaking, he scribbled thus in bad verse, for when sorrow touched his heart his understanding was in the habit of flying for aid to poetry :—

> Adieu! if patrons fail, thou sweetest charm
> O Education! to thy helping arm!—
> From Homer, Cicero, and Virgil's glow,
> My boys the force of truth will never know,
> And round my girls the Graces will not play,
> For maids of honour must have royal pay.

Casting his eye to the window which overlooked the road winding up the mountain, he saw a gentlemanly person, of the middle size, in a blue frock, leading a handsome grey nag, approaching, which was an unusual sight.

"I think I should know you," said the stranger, extending his hand, with a friendly and familiar aspect.

"Your face is that of an old Indian," replied the other, grasping the proffered hand;—"but the name—"

"Thoughtless," answered he; "the liver has altered us both; I should not have known you either, but for your Prospectus;—I came to see you, and put down my name;" and he pulled some bank notes out of his pocket.

"Not till the delivery," said the author.

"And I hope," said Thoughtless, after some preliminaries, "you have experienced much encouragement of a private and individual nature."

"Very little. I really fear I have mistaken the public taste."

"Your book is certainly addressed to the understanding, contrary to the modern system, which is to tickle the fancy, and occasionally become so pathetic that the heart almost breaks with a swell, and the soul rises towards the end into harmonic sublimity with the scene, till the curtain drops on a sort of ineffable felicity.—He who can effect this, may sport his curricle and livery, and breathe his nags at Brighton!"

"My own thoughts precisely, in better drapery than my wardrobe affords. I have often felt inclined to suspend my labours on the book in question. The risk of a light work would be trifling, and should the style and matter have merit to force their way, Messrs. Longman and Co. would not hesitate to make a proposal for something more scientific. But my own adventures in India are common-place:—joined my regiment an ensign, rose in gradation, and served a few campaigns not of an interesting nature."

"The circumstances of my life have been more diversified—I shall send you my journal—use it—'speak of me as I am—nothing extenuate;'—where fictitious names are used, add or diminish at pleasure; but where real actors are introduced, let no embellishment allure from justice and truth. You will perceive I wrote in the title page—'Fifteen Years in India, or, Sketches of a Soldier's Life.'"

"That strikes me as happy—simple—unostentatious—it pledges to no particular line. A tangent may at any time be formed in favour of merit or expediency, as the practice is at the Horse Guards, where no promise of a step is ever given. Had it been Memoirs, Travels, or any of the designations heretofore used, some known course must have been pursued at the jog-trot of a set of *palankeen* boys from one regular stage to another, instead of being as free as Pug in the wilderness to jump from the sublime to the ridiculous, and to chatter and grimace, just according to the romance of my disposition."

"Exactly—you will be in the situation of a prudent minister of state who reserves to himself perfect liberty; for what is there in fifteen years in India? In that time, it is true, a man may have seen much and observed little. It is sufficient, then, to excite curiosity, but it is by no means binding as to any particular mode of gratification. But there is a third addition, explanatory of the first and second, namely, 'being an attempt to describe persons and things in various parts of Hindostan.'"

"Equally guarded I protest; *parvis componere magna*, the three heads resemble those of Brahma, Vishnu, and Sheva, in the cave of Elephanta, which are curious to behold, but so difficult to understand, that learned *Pundits* and Christians deeply skilled in oriental lore cannot agree as to the interpretation.

"An author should consider himself as opening a game at chess. He who aims at success, whether he play a regular Philidor party or a Gambit, must well consider before he pushes his meanest pawn, for one move at the outset may so entangle his pieces, confine his field of operation, expose his king to check, and disorganize the combination of his queen, rooks, bishops and knights, that he may be mated under the very fire of his own towers, from taking up a position where his forces could not come into action."

But, gentle reader, I most conscientiously declare that I aspire not at sporting either curricle or livery, nor do I wish to breathe my nags at Brighton, though the desire of beholding the smile of my Royal Master is near my heart. The highest flight my ambition has indulged in is to have a *shigrampo* of such dimensions as to contain twelve persons, great and small, with an abundance of warm cushions, to protect from the penetrating winter air of my native hills in journeying to church. All that is desirable in the *shigrampo* of Malabar, the *hackery* of Hindostan, the bullock coach of the Carnatic, and the *palankeen* carriage of Calcutta, might be adopted; for a pair of mules or Scotch poneys, in plain clothing and harness, would transcend a couple of oxen, notwithstanding their delicious humps, silk housings, golden tassels, and silver bells; and a servant in clean drab surtout would be as ornamental as any *turbaned* driver. I would covet nothing more in the mansions of luxury, except a glass of good old Madeira or Port, instead of raspberry and ginger substitutes; yet the Vicar of Wakefield's wife was not better pleased with champagne of her own making, than my kind-hearted rib is when she mixes the ingredients in such just proportions that the acid does not prevail, or, as she technically says, "*predominate;*" nor the lusciousness hurt the vivacity or interfere with the transparency. Nevertheless, I am seriously inclined to think that with my *shigrampo*, and servant in clean drab surtout, I should not have "*les vapeurs noirs,*" or in native phrase "*the blue devils,*" at home so often when a sigh assails me. "To be sure, my dear, as you say, we must strive to be contented; but I wish I was once more on the sweet little island of *Colabah*, taking an airing to the light-house, the band playing, and all your brother officers promenading and saluting the ladies with such grace and spirit. Then you know we would have a little tea party this evening and a dance, but I must forget those happy times." Then a tear starts to that eye whose beam has pleased mine for near twenty years; and really, sympathetic reader, one at present fills mine to think that I cannot kiss it away so as to prevent another from springing up when that deceiver Memory mocks her by representing the past more fascinating than the present.

To conclude, trust me, I have more respect for your feelings, notwithstanding all the aforesaid trifling, and a better opinion of mankind in general (though I know human nature to be a curious mixture), than not to make it my ardent aim to afford you information and entertainment.

SKETCHES.

CHAPTER I.

To see an estimable friend depart
For Europe, agitates my pensive heart.
Adieu to scorching winds! Farewell, ye plains,
Long marches, camps, where war eternal reigns.
Welcome the comforts of his native soil,
In blest retirement sweet from by-gone toil.

THE prospect with which a man solaces himself who leaves his native land for the purpose of improving his condition, is to return home and enjoy the fruit of his enterprize. This fond hope, common to all speculators in India, makes it a subject of congratulation when any one is so fortunate as to realize the general expectation by taking a passage for Europe. But there is a struggle between joy and sorrow on both sides. Fifteen or twenty years must elapse before even a successful candidate for the favours of fortune can in progression be in the state to which he looks common forward with such anxiety. In the meantime his heart becomes linked to friends and associates, the anticipated separation from whom becomes more and more painful as the hour approaches. At that period he again experiences some of the emotions of an exile. He lingers fondly, and hesitates to bid adieu, perhaps for ever, to companions endeared to memory by long community of pursuits, and participation in toil and danger.

Adventurers to India would not be so frequently disappointed, if, soon after arriving there, each fixed for himself the object of independence at a moderate and rational distance, with determined resolution to march steadily towards it, and there to stop. In taking the first steps for the acquisition of fortune, the mind is humble and easily satisfied; but this calm and philosophic contentment gives place to ambition, when the career becomes more rapid and easy. New desires then arise, hopes expand, and an exertion is made to increase what was once thought enough. One boundary is passed after another till death either stops the march, or the traveller returns to his native soil, so much debilitated from long residence in a hot climate, as to be incapable of enjoying his hoarded wealth.

The Company's immense army is officered by young gentlemen of family, respectability, and good education. They go out at a tender age, and a few months places them at an apparently hopeless distance from the objects dearest to their affections. On joining their regiments in the interior, and becoming fit for duty, they are sent on detachments to small out-stations, where they have frequently to pass the dreary wet season without a possibility of enjoying the consolation of society or friendship. Placed in command of whatever number of Sepoys the exigency of the service may require, with merely the assistance of native officers, they are entirely left to the resources of their own minds. In the civil department, the Company's servants are generally replaced by youths of high connections, and very often of most finished education, which is carried on in oriental literature for a considerable time after their arrival in India; and although they have advantages as to society and comfort far beyond those of the military branch, still the attendance on college lectures, and the great labour required by such as are not blessed with natural talents to pass the examinations, make life very irksome. Another class consists of the young officers of the King's regiments in India, who generally experience much mental pain before they become reconciled by habituation to the country.

These three classes of fine young men at setting out in life feel the emotions so beautifully described by Campbell in his Pleasures of Hope. While surrounded by friends and the tender ties of kindred in their native land—while their young hearts feel the influence of that sweet affection which exists between brother and sister, and perhaps begin to warm with sensations of a still more tender nature for a sister's fair friend — they stand at summer eve, and behold the prospect glittering in all the enchantment given by distance ; but upon approaching the tempting scene, the rocky and barren projections of that mountain are perceived which fancy had conjured into those green spots on which the aching eye rests so seldom in life.

It has been suggested to the reader, by the lines at the head of this chapter, that an adventurer to India was regretting the departure of a companion for his native soil, while at the same time he rejoiced at the accomplishment of his friend's wishes, and the cause of this intermixture of sorrow and pleasure has been explained. Both were military men who had seen some service together; and these sketches of a soldier's life will open with a relation of the manner in which Lieutenant George True was enabled to return home.

This officer had the honour of holding a commission in one of his Majesty's regiments, and having been long exposed on very active campaigns to the utmost severity of the climate, his health was in a declining state. Strict temperance and a good constitution had enabled him to keep at his post, while many of his companions found an untimely grave instead of that distinction at which they aimed. His private affairs, however, were of a nature to preclude the prospect of returning to the renovating breezes of his native hills, and he persevered in his profession, in the hope of honourable fame and glorious independence.

The irruption of a predatory horde into the Company's provinces in the south of Hindostan Proper, had rendered the march of his corps from Baroda necessary, in the month of June. At this period all nature is parched. The thirsty earth throws back with sickly languor the burning rays of the sun, and the air, heated to a suffocating degree, sweeps along whirling clouds of dust. But the benevolence of Providence about this time intercepts the glare by spreading a thick canopy of damp clouds over this torrid part of the earth, which soon open their flood-gates and pour down a deluge of refreshing rain, that revivifies expiring vegetation and animal life. In the awful intervening space, however, burning fever drinks the juices of many a distracted brain. A major and twenty-three soldiers of this brave regiment fell dead under coups de soleil in one day. Death in this form is terrible to contemplate. The moment the system is affected by the atmosphere, the blood no longer circulates; and if immediate steps be not taken to remove the obstruction by copious bleeding, a relief often very difficult to be procured, life for ever ceases. No enemy being in the vicinity, the marches were made at a very early hour, to avoid the intense heat of the meridian sun. On the day previous to that in which a material change occurred in the prospects of Mr. True, the force had reached a village called Bowla, situated in the Run, a deserted tract of country so named, between the gulfs of Kutch and Cambay. Thence to the town of Limree extends a cheerless sandy plain. The villages were all in ruins, having been desolated by the dreadful famine of 1802. Indeed it is surprising that even the poor and miserable should have ever thought of seeking an asylum in this unfriendly region; for the earth is of such a thirsty nature that the deepest wells will not yield water, nor the best made *tanks* contain it. Nondoudra is the next halting place, and during the march thither the long looked for *monsoon* commenced.

At two o'clock on the morning of that eventful day, the moon was dimly seen at intervals, through dark clouds. The British camp was, however, often visibly revealed by vivid flashes of lightning that illuminated the zenith, and rushed with fiery broad course into the remote horizon, accompanied by awful and sublime peals of thunder. Natives, camels, elephants, and bullocks, pressed by their loads, were ready to move off with the line drawn up in front. Here the Sepoy's wives might be seen, tying their children on the backs of bullocks, or placing them, like poultry in baskets, to be carried on their own heads. There the numerous servants of the officers, some with lanterns searching where their master's tents stood, lest any thing should be left behind; others

2

with chairs and breakfast apparatus, conducting greyhounds in leash, carrying couches, or leading horses, and followed by grass cutters and water carriers — in short, there were at least seven native followers for every fighting man. But it was melancholy to see the numerous European sick of the force carried along on men's shoulders, some dying, and others in burning fever; and it would have produced a smile on the face of the most serious, to behold the convalescents mounted on bullocks, and laughing heartily at each other when left sprawling by the plunges of their horned supporters, unaccustomed to such obstreperous loads.

Two miles from Bowla the flood-gates of the heavens opened, and the rain fell in torrents. For some time the sandy expanse, which had not tasted moisture for six months, drank freely the mighty deluge; but as the line proceeded very slowly, being forced to halt frequently for the rear, this march occupied several hours, and the road at length became so soft and heavy, that the beasts of burden sunk to their bellies. Then were seen tents and boxes rolling in the mud, while the field pieces were dragged along with great difficulty. In short, order was changed into confusion, and as indescribable a clamour was produced by the crowd on the baggage flank, as if the enemy's cavalry had been dashing among them with their merciless spears.

Lieutenant True was the officer of the rear guard. During the march, finding himself so exceedingly faint as to be unable to keep his seat in the saddle against the pelting of the storm, he had sent his groom for a *dooly*, and discovering a little to the right a *pagoda*, near a ruined village, he alighted under its shelter, and stood leaning on the neck of his horse. The objects before him seemed to grow black, and the whole scene became of a shadowy tint. In fact, he felt as if the hand of death was upon his heart. "Gracious God," said he, "is this the end of my earthly hopes? Preserve me, for the sake of her I love, and the dear objects of our affection." He fainted and fell. At this moment, a profuse gush of blood from his nose relieved him. After bleeding copiously, he felt much better. His docile *Arabian* had stood near him. "Thank God," said he, regaining his seat, "I feel now able to proceed," and he soon overtook his guard, and reached the camp, where the surgeon having prescribed for him, he retired to his tent for repose.

"Saheeb," said his servant Ballo soon after, opening the tent door, "one soldier other regiment, master speak to want."

"Let him come in." He entered the marquee, and making a fine curve with his right arm, touched the polished front of his shining cap, and withdrawing the same gracefully, stood in the erect posture of "Attention."

"Ah! what do I see? Am I awake? As I live the face of Bob Gordon."

" I am indeed the identical Bob, and right happy to see your Honour in the land of the living."

" This is wonderful !—When did you leave home, and what forced you to turn soldier ?"

" Misfortune, Sir; I left Ireland only a year ago, and recognized you this morning passing with the rear-guard through our lines."

" Ah Bob ! Several years have passed away since I left my native land, and emerged from the joyous stage of school-boy. In all my wanderings I have not met a soul from the spot that cherished my childhood, nor have I received any account from home, having never written, for private reasons. But the sight of you has brought early associations feelingly to mind. I have many questions to ask ; but first, sit down and tell me the cause of your own misfortunes."

" Then you have not heard of your father's return to his native soil."

" Eh Bob ! — Is my dear father in Ireland, and has he overcome the persecution of fortune ?"

" He has indeed, Sir. — Rolling in wealth, he would give it all to witness the return of you, his only son."

" Wonderful ! And my uncle, what of him, is he alive and still the same ?"

" Alas, Sir, still so."

" How melancholy to think of him, and what he might have been. ' Oh that a man should put an enemy in his mouth to steal away his brains!' And the worthy Mr. Stanhope, what of him?"

"A distressing account, Sir. A villain, in the mask of a gentleman in holy orders, seduced his beautiful and only daughter. The father threatened to prosecute the clergyman, who was of the Catholic church, unless he changed his religion and married her. Dreading this, the horrible miscreant induced his victim to forget the strongest tie of nature, and to father her child on the author of her own being. The distracted parent died broken-hearted. His daughter, stung with remorse, confessed on her death-bed, almost immediately after, the horrible part she had acted. The priest fled, and her only surviving brother sold off his property, changed his name, and exiled himself for ever from his native country."

"Torturing thought, that the depravity of human nature should produce such a tragedy!"

"But say, Bob, how are the family of Rose Mount? Well, I hope."

"Ah no! The worthy old magistrate became a bankrupt, and his son-in-law, young Mr. Sinclair, who married the lovely Miss Fanny, lost his whole fortune in the crash, and is now a struggler in life with several children to support. There was a bill of exchange drawn and accepted by the old gentleman, who was in the habit of taking that freedom, on his son, then engaged in commerce. It happened that he was embarrassed and unable to honour the unexpected bill when presented, and to secure his credit disavowed the acceptance. The enraged holder lodged an information against the father for forgery. He withdrew till it could be explained and adjusted, but was soon after killed by a fall from his horse."

"And how is old farmer Glendinning? His pretty daughter, the gay thoughtless Mary, is, I hope, happy."

"The fate of poor Mary, Sir, is a sad one. She was seduced by a captain of yeomanry. She had received a religious education, and would have resisted the insinuating addresses of a suitor so much above her in rank and fortune; but the son of Sir Walter Sennit had married a miller's daughter, and made a lady of her by education, and poor Mary concluded that her own station in life was more respectable and less liable to objection. The circumstances of her fate were so affecting that I, who am poetically inclined, could not resist the temptation of endeavouring to immortalize her story in a ballad, for the instruction of every pretty girl."

"Let me hear it, Bob?—You had from your childhood a turn that way. I recollect hearing of one of your verses made at a singing school, and given out to the psalm tune."

"As I was coming here the night,
"I spied a merry joke,
"A young man courting wi' a lass,
"Rolled up in a big coat."

"Yes indeed, Sir, and what caused it to be taken notice of was, that the very young man, the subject of it, started up and exclaimed— 'Fine a bit, Bob, but that was me.'"

THE FATE OF MARY.

Beneath Rosstrevor's lofty side,
Glenallon cottage stood,
Whose front o'erlook'd the silver tide,
And kiss'd th'approaching flood.

A pretty garden near it smiled,
Perfumed by countless flowers;
These favourites of an only child,
Amused her leisure hours.

No snow-drop peeping from its bed,
Was more divinely fair;
The tints transparent blood had spread,
With roses might compare.

Her parents saw with fondest hope
Her childish years subside;
Each heart-endearing look bespoke
Their happiness and pride.

To win her love, full many a youth,
Soon bent with ardent aim,
And in the crowd professing truth,
A yeoman captain came.

His form was of the manliest kind,
Yet dashing spruce and neat;
With manners pleasingly refined,
His herds and flocks were great.

But ah! beneath each winning smile,
  Lurk'd treacherous intent;
For like the weeping crocodile,
  His wiles no pity lent.

Alas! that such a selfish heart
  Should animate a frame
Of symmetry in every part,
  Whose soul should be the same.

But soon credulity will find,
  External form pourtrays
No surer image of the mind,
  Than dress of worth displays.

Deep sighs from the distracted breast,
  Reveal'd to watchful art,
That Cupid's bow had banish'd rest,
  From an enamour'd heart.

Description! thou art much too faint
  The sequel sad to tell,
Conception must the struggle paint:
  Alas! poor Mary fell.

The dreadful news with mortal grief
  Her mother petrified;
" My Mary," tears refused relief,
  She strove to speak, but died.

Her father frenzied, sought to find
  His poor deluded child;
Religion sooth'd his placid mind,
  As summer zephyr mild.

She in despair and deep distress
  From her betrayer fled,
Soon as she found her wretchedness,
  For he had sworn to wed.

Her gentle frame, to want unused,
Droop'd like a tender flower,
By nature's cheering fount refus'd
The renovating shower.

Let Fancy's pencil represent
A cellar dark and cold,
For there she lay with sickness spent,
Sad lesson to behold.

The old man came ! heart-rending scene !
A daughter thus to see ;
" My God !" he cried, in anguish keen,
"Take not my all from me."

Her pallid cheek with many a tear
He bathed. " O Mary live,
" Dismiss each painful killing fear,
" My darling, I forgive."

But she dishonour could not bear ;
His grey head too lies low ;
Ye lovely girls beware ! beware !
And human weakness know.

" Very pathetic indeed ! I declare, Bob, your poetic strain deserves a compliment ; and I hope your verses will record poor Mary's fate when the present generation has passed away. But tell me of the worthy curate—how has fortune dressed his silver locks ?"

" He has found happiness on earth, Sir, which he so well deserves, as a foretaste of the felicity that awaits him in heaven. But the particulars require some detail. You know he was very poor, and had a numerous family to support. There is a parish that yields its rector an income of one thousand a-year, although the church never contains five persons in it as a congregation, for the parishioners are catholics. The rector, who lived at a distance, quarrelled with his bishop: his Grace ordered him to have divine service performed regularly, adding, it had only lately come to his knowledge that the contrary was the case. Knowing it was in vain to expostulate, he was forced to fix the curate's salary very high. Seventy pounds a year induced a young man to undertake the ludicrous task of preaching a sermon every Sunday to the clerk. He persevered for some time; but one day, instead of doing so, he lectured, and pointed out extempore the necessity of strict conformity to Christian doctrine. The bishop heard of it, and wrote a letter to the rector, informing him that his Grace was not only surprized, but utterly confounded at the irregular proceeding in his parish. That the Almighty only knew what his curate might say, in the latitude he was giving to the unrestrained flights of absurd and whimsical imagination. "If this practice," said his Grace, "which directly strikes at the root of every thing orthodox, be not visited with the utmost severity, the Lord only knows where it may end, even in the destruction of the Protestant church, and the overthrow of our venerable constitution." The rector was forced to dismiss his curate, being greatly apprehensive that he might be prohibited from having one, if he did not shew that he concurred with his Grace in thinking the irregularity seriously reprehensible. Upon this he offered old Mr. Meekly 100*l.* a-year to do his duty, who moved to that part of the country, to the no small regret of all our neighbourhood. But his situation and merit reached the ear of the Lord Primate, whose goodness is universally known, and Dr. Stuart wrote him with his own hand a letter notifying that he had heard of his great worth, and felt happiness in being now able to present him with a living of seven hundred per annum."

"And how are the loyal tenantry, Bob? Do they continue to commemorate the battle of the Boyne on the 12th of old July?"

"No, Sir, that custom is discontinued, for about five years ago there was an actual battle on that occasion, instead of a sham fight, which induced the magistrates to prohibit it. The Orange boys had, as usual, made great preparations, and assembled with flags and streamers: — they formed in two divisions, one of which, commanded by King William, marched down the slope to the tune of the Boyne Water; while the other, under King James, was drawn up on the opposite side of the Devarnagh river. A smart discharge of blank cartridges announced the attack. But lo! in the hottest part of the engagement, a body of Roman Catholic youths, from the mountains of Slievegullion and

Killeary, started up from an ambuscade with pitchforks, grapes, and scythes, and assailed the two Kings. The Duke of Schomberg was actually killed in the river, and the waters of the stream was reddened with the blood of both parties; for the Orange boys fought desperately in honour of the day with the butts of their firelocks."

" Unhappy country, where political wounds are not permitted to heal!"

" But tell me, Bob, are the manners of the credulous people about Mount Norris and Loughgilly changed? Do they believe in ghosts, witches, fairies, lougherymen, and banshees?"

" Yes, indeed, Sir, as much as ever; and it is believed as true as the gospel, that a lougheryman appeared to Farmer Jones, of Rathcarberry, only a short time ago."

" Pray, Bob, mention the particulars."

" The farmer was sitting in the parlour, which was also his bed-room. Being fond of music, he was playing some of his merry tunes on his Irish organ, as he calls the bagpipes, and occasionally talking to his wife, who was in bed. — He was enjoying his glass of warm native too at intervals, for it was a cold winter night. The door stood a little ajar, and in the middle of a favourite tune — 'I'm over young to marry yet' — a little slender figure, about two feet high, of exceedingly beautiful form and proportion, with laughing black eyes and a red cap, came skipping into the room. He danced with astonishing grace, swung in air, and kept such fine time, that the delighted musician played on with pleasure and surprize. At length he had to rest from fatigue. But the lougheryman nodded for more music, and kept nodding till he gained his wish. The farmer, who is a merry man, enjoyed the fun, and played several of his best tunes for the little dancer; and his wife, who is of the methodist persuasion, positively says to this day, that she heard her husband several times saying he was tired and could play no more, and that at last he raised his voice in anger — 'Get out of my sight, you little unreasonable brat; you would never be satisfied.'

"That very night the flames burst out of the house in the dead of sleep, and nothing but life was saved—and it is said the lougheryman set the house on fire in three different places, in revenge for not getting enough of music; and that if he had been gratified, he would have filled Mr. Jones's pockets with gold."

The lieutenant was amused and interested with these and other stories that reminded him of home. Such is the case, O reader, with every man absent for several years from his native place. As a bird, forced by want to quit the nest which contains the objects dearest to affection, flutters around and strains each pinion but to return, so does the adventurer to India, in all his wanderings, mentally circle like the mariner's needle to that north pole of his heart, the scene of his boyish days — when he regains it, he finds the hills, vallies, mountains, and rivers where they were; but those who gave life and rapture to the remembered scene, where are they? — Many of them gone, as we shall shortly be, to

> That undiscovered country from whose bourne
> No traveller returns.

CHAP. II.

HERE *Gunga's* banks terrific scenes display,
Idolatry stalks forth in open day.
Grim death like lightning human life assails,
And pale disease o'er banish'd health prevails;
Vice glares with specious aspect undismay'd,
While virtue hides her lovely face afraid!

THE Hoogly, on the eastern bank of which the city of Calcutta stands, is the western arm of the Ganges, and the natives call it, as well as many other rivers, Gunga, being the name of one of the three goddesses of waters. She is fabled to have been brought to light in the same way nearly as Minerva — from the brain of Brahma.

In going up this fine river, the observer, if he be a man of sensibility, is strongly affected with what he sees. The luxuriance of nature and the grandeur of the scene please his eye, while the customs and manners of men make his heart bleed. He beholds many an emaciated human being, worn away to the last gasp of lingering existence, brought from a distant residence to expire near the sacred stream; the pains of death are often embittered by forcing the muddy water down his throat; for when the recovery of any person is despaired of, his immediate friends hurry him off to the river, in the hope that the goddess will restore him miraculously to life, if they can force him to drink freely. Should any one die at home, near the Ganges, it would be lamented as a great misfortune. When the grasping dispositions of mankind are considered, and it is recollected that those about a dying person share his property, the various accounts of the numerous murders perpetrated by seeming attention to this shocking custom need not be discredited. The wealthy pitch a tent, partly in the water, to screen the sick from the glare of the sun; in this the patient is placed, sometimes on a low cot, and oftener on the ground, with his head in the stream, there to be restored to health by drinking plentifully, or to die with the certainty of immortal bliss. The poor are seen writhing in the pangs of suffocation, under officious, mistaken kindness of friends, and lying all night in the water.

At the same time he views the smoke ascending in curling volumes from many a funeral pile; and the useful stream bearing away the remains of those whose friends could not afford to burn them. On each bank his sight is shocked occasionally with dead bodies, rotten and torn by fishes, mouldering to kindred clay on the spot where the tide chanced to cast them, for no man will remove them, it being contamination to touch a dead body whose caste is unknown.

Very few Europeans remain long in vigorous health.

Were a country gentleman, in the full enjoyment of all his bodily faculties in this happy climate, to be suddenly transported to St. John's church, in Calcutta, during the performance of divine service in the month of June, he would fancy himself seated among ghosts. He would look upon their sallow countenances with fear, and see the big drops like tears coursing each other on the anxious brow, notwithstanding the large fans suspended overhead, and drawn briskly backwards and forwards, by means of ropes passed from them through the windows of the church, by natives outside, to produce an artificial circulation of air. If he followed any gentleman to his home, he would see him there throw off his coat, and put on a light white jacket, as a relief from his sufferings; and on passing the burying ground beyond Chouringhee, the stranger would there perceive, in the numberless tombs and monuments, ample evidence of the terrible mortality prevailing in the land of his sojourn.

The absence of health is more manifest here than in many other parts of India. Men who follow sedentary employments, that require close mental attention, are most numerous, and soonest decline, in a province which is peculiarly inimical to the European constitution; for such quantities of putrescent matter are left by the inundations of the Ganges and Burrumpootre, that they infect the air with malignant vapours, which prove more fatal to strangers than to the natives. This remark is indeed applicable to all Hindostan, in every part of which the European is prematurely wasted by slow but sure degrees, if not assailed by fever or acute hepatitis.

There is no doubt, however, that if a proper regimen were observed from the first arrival of an European in a hot climate, the preservation of health would be of much longer duration. It is probable that the great Creator in his wisdom has suited the constitution of man to that soil of which he is formed; but plants, with care, flourish where they were never intended to grow, and it is surprising that so many skilful naturalists seem not to consider the effect of a similar process on their own body and mind. Most young men live in India thoughtlessly and luxuriously, as long as they are able. Before they prepare for defence, they are taken by the enemy. Nature and instinct have directed the natives of different climates to adopt that course of living best calculated to preserve health, without which all other earthly blessings lose the power of conferring happiness. Should it not therefore be the object of every sojourner in a strange land to conform as much as possible to the mode of living adopted by the aborigines? Personal comfort soon induces a man, in a hot climate, to dress lightly; but the palate is a deceiver, for as the powers of digestion decrease, it requires and craves to be gratified with what is pernicious. The Hindoos live chiefly on vegetables — rice is the principal of their food; and the use of strong liquors may be said to be unknown. That diet preserves the fluids of the body free from inflammation on the part of the stomach, and they enjoy during the usual course of existence regular physical health, and many of them are long lived. If you adventure to India, do as I have done; dine often on boiled rice and goats' milk, and you will probably live to enjoy the *otium cum dignitate* to which you aspire, during the decline of life, in your native land.

According to Faithhorn on bilious disorders, the liver is an organ of the most general and universal importance and use in man: its acute or chronic affections often appear under the form hydrocephalus, cough, asthma, consumption, mesenteric disease, stomach complaints, headaches, melancholy, debility, flatulence, and costiveness. In our attempts therefore to preserve health, our success must depend on enabling this grand source of life and vigour to perform its due functions, by which alone the bowels are emptied, the blood cleansed, the strength recruited, and the mind invigorated. Now as there is some unknown atmospheric peculiarity in India which produces superaction of the liver, does it not follow, that an inflammatory mode of living must be pernicious?

The body and the mind are so intimately connected, that the one cannot perform its functions with out the co-operation of the other; and grief may therefore be the cause of much mortality in India. Disappointed expectations on arrival in that country, separation from every object held dear, and the very remote prospect of return home, produce the blackest melancholy in minds of great sensibility. In short, these emotions have driven several valuable young men to commit suicide, for nostalgia is not restricted to the Swiss.

At the head of this chapter it has been said, that vice glares with specious and bold aspect, while virtue hides her lovely head, in Hindostan. That the reader may fully comprehend the truth of this strong remark, it is necessary for him to reflect upon the idolatry of Brahma, which sanctions a general indulgence of the gross passions of human nature to such a degree, that it is asserted, on good authority, that there are mysteries in the celebration of some of its secret rites similar to those once performed in honour of Venus, at her temples in the Isle of Cyprus. But the facility with which atonement can be made for the commission of the most horrible crimes, is a demonstration that they are often perpetrated. Yet many people argue, that the Hindoos are an innocent and harmless moral race. Quite the contrary is matter of fact. The mass of the general population is in a state of monstrous depravity. Lying and perjury are so common, that an oath goes for nothing in a court of justice. In the city of Benares, the fountain of

Brahminical lore, when Lord Valentia visited it, there were four hundred natives, who supported themselves by giving false evidence in courts of law. Let the sceptical reflect upon the numbers that are sacrificed every year in pilgrimages to Badrinaut, Juggurnaut, and several other temples in India; let him think of what is before the public on the subject of Hindoo infanticide; the burning of wives with their husbands; and the encouragement of suicide, or voluntary sacrifice, so general in India; and surely he will change his doubts for abhorrence and detestation.

The state of concubinage, in which so many of the native females live, corrupts all morality and decency. Nearly every European private soldier has a family of half casts; and there have been officers of rank and civilians in the country not contented without seraglios, like other Nabobs, whom they learned to exceed in debauchery. But to resume our story.

"Well, George," said one of Mr. True's brother subs, dashing into his tent, followed by half a dozen of his friendly companions in arms, "my old boy, how are you after the *coup de soleil?* You must come to the mess to-night, we have thirty-seven guests."

The evening air was still and refreshing; for the storm with which the monsoon commenced had cooled the burning earth, and calmed the troubled atmosphere. Nature seemed to have sunk into repose from the violence of her late struggle, suggesting to the contemplative observer an idea of those calms that intervene as agreeable vicissitudes, in voyaging on the stormy ocean of human existence. The camp was all life and motion.

When the gun had announced the setting of the sun, and the drums, bugles, and trumpets along the line performed that fine point of war, "the retreat," Mr. True went to the mess. The guests now arriving, were received with frank politeness; they formed into circles before a spacious tent, the walls of which were thrown up all around for the circulation of every breath of air. Camp tables, calculated for seventy or eighty guests, occupied the centre of this grand hall of canvas. A double row of clear wax-lights stood at proper intervals along their surface, shining with increased lustre through Indian table shades. Here were servants with their masters' dinner apparatus, which the stewards took care to intermix, so that every guest might receive proper attention; and there a *Parsee* behind each chair ready to point out his master's place, and attend to his wants, as soon as Nuswangee, the messman, shrilly drawled out, — "*Gontlemun, Denere on table-e !*"

Excellent cheer and good old wines soon excited a flow of spirits, and the luxuries of the East having allayed the edge of appetite, conversation began to circulate.

"Where is Duval, that he has not joined the force with you?"

" He was obliged to remain behind from a sad accident. A tiger hunt was formed a short time ago; the party came upon a large female in the act of suckling her cub; she sprang with amazing force at the trunk of the foremost elephant, upon which Duval was mounted: the other elephants, struck with panic at the exertions of their companion to shake off such a dreadful foe, disregarded the drivers, and scampered away from the scene of action.

" In the meantime, Duval had lodged a brace of bullets from a double-barrel in the body of the tiger; she staggered and fell, but recovering, and feeling the smart, she sprang on the back of the elephant, and our friend was precipitated to the ground by the violent plunges of the animal to get rid of such a load as the tiger, whose maddened claws and teeth tore the flesh in ridges from his mighty body. Duval having recovered from the shock of his fall, lodged another bullet from a pistol in the body of the tiger, which brought her once more to the ground, but again recovering, she seized him by the back in her monstrous mouth. Even in this desperate situation his presence of mind did not desert him; he drew his remaining pistol from his belt, and placing the muzzle of it over the panting heart of the tiger, lodged its contents in that vital part. The death gasp of the monster relieved him from seemingly inevitable destruction, just as his companions came up to his assistance; though lacerated, he is doing well; and we all hope to see him join in time to have a dash at the Wagurs."

"Yes, indeed," said the political agent, seated near a young ensign, whose enquiries he kindly answered respecting the inhabitants of the neighbouring provinces, "some of the customs of these regions are as wonderful as the manners and habits of the people in general. Strange it is that a country, in which hospitals are endowed to preserve with care the old and maimed of every description of animal, should permit insanity, idiotism, ulceration, and leprosy to shock the eyes of humanity in the streets of its cities; yet to see this you have only to travel to Surat. And equally surprising it is, that men who are ready to tear an European to pieces for destroying the life of a peacock, a monkey, or a bullock, should notoriously put every female infant to death, and encourage beautiful virgins to sacrifice themselves on the funeral pile in the flames that consume the bodies of boys to whom they were betrothed when children, and whose lot it was to lose their husbands before consummation; yet the latter custom prevails throughout India, and the former is practised by the Ierajahs of the provinces of Kutch and Kattywar. Let me add, that if you continue thus curious, it will not be said hereafter of you

> "Cœlum non animum mutant qui trans mare currunt."
>
> HORACE, Epist. XI. Lib. I.

Which the surgeon translated—"The heaven, not

the mind, of those changes who cross the sea." — But some one corrected his error, in taking the wrong nominative case, and said — " I would construe it thus :"

" Qui they who, currunt go, trans over, mare the sea, mutant change, cœlum their climate, non not, animum their mind."

" Bravo, bravissimo!" exclaimed a student from the college of Armagh.

" You will do well, my dear Sir," said a young M.D. to an officer, who was complaining to him of the state of his health, " to continue the aperient plan, with the cooling medicines I have sent you, until the indications of the regularity and healthy action of the bowels appear. In short, the general cause of the frequent aberration from health in this climate seems to be the impediment offered to the due assimilation of the food by the absorption of the nascent principles of electricity in the circulating fluids of the body ; and as these principles are of an acid quality, those chemical agents which can neutralize them, and at the same time impart a vivifying stimulus to the system, are indubitably indicated. Nitre being a compound of nitric acid and potash, and nitric acid having an excess of oxygen in its formation, these circumstances point it out as an appropriate remedy. The aperient medicines are recommended to remove accumulation, and consequent congestion."

The cloth being removed, claret began to revel

in the exhilarated veins of all, while their ears were regaled by the harmonious tones of a full band. Spirit is excited by the well executed solo of the flourishing trumpet, emotion awakened by the soft round swell of the Kent bugles; and thrills of pleasure touch each heart on hearing the magic turns of the piercing clarionet and melodious flute, blending their tender, spreading or softened warblings with the deep relief of the duly attuned horns, bassoons, and kettle drums.

Other senses were refreshed by the perfume of bubbling *hookahs,* that from silken carpets gave their odorous vapour, circling through silver snakes to the pleased palate; or by the gently rousing application of the scented maccaba, that passed in a superb box.

And it should not be forgotten, that an attentive observer might have seen the worthy colonel commanding the corps, handing from off his plate a tart to the interesting orderly boy of the band, who stood behind his chair ready to communicate the calls for particular pieces to the master in an adjoining tent, and slipping his pleasing gift to the youth, as if unwilling that the affectionate benevolence with which he treated every one under him should be known.

Our aged King's health being drunk in silence; the Prince Regent's with noble animation; the Duke of York and the army's with three times three; and the Duke of Clarence and the navy's with a loud huzza and Rule Britannia, astonished the crowds of gazing Hindoos, collected to see the English, who shook their beards, and murmured their thoughts to each other in deep re-echoed ejaculations.—The president then called upon the major for a song, and he gave—" Let the glass pass, drink to the lass," with a "*je ne sais quoi,*" that made the table ring with " Encore ;" after which, " Auld lang syne" was sung by Dr. Robertson, with pathos that spoke to the heart of the guests, whose hands were linked around the table, while a tear stole to the eye as memory recurred to the scenes of boyhood.

The ghurries were now striking twelve, and the shrill voices of the Sepoy sentries challenging "Who com dere-e ?" " Rounds."—"Vat ouns?" " Grand rounds."—" Vans one give cant line."—" Ass an ouns, all is velle-e-e ;" upon which the band was sent to repose, and the prudent guests stole away to enjoy refreshing sleep ; but some thirsty souls remained enjoying their bottle and well-spiced devels, till the generale beat at four o'clock.

It will be obvious to the reader, how many things have been omitted in this brief sketch of a military camp dinner in India. The *curries, palows,* and *mullagatawnies* might have been described, and the ingredients which compose those eastern dishes specified, and more of the conversation might have been given. But enough has been said to demonstrate the importance of a mess to every corps. A well regulated one preserves harmony, polishes manners, and improves the understandings of the officers. Where this bond of society brings them every day familiarly together in friendly intercourse, under necessary restrictions, no divisions into parties take place. Like a well regulated family, their habits become assimilated, and an affection like that of brotherly love is necessarily produced.

There are in every regiment some well educated officers, who improve their early advantages to the utmost; and there is hardly a question which can arise on the subject of ancient or modern discoveries, but some one will be found capable of answering it. But it must also be acknowledged that there are others who form a direct contrast; and in the fine corps in which Mr. True had the honour of serving, this was the case; so that at one part of the table might be heard an animated discussion respecting the spirit of Miltiades, or a difference of opinion between Cæsar and Pompey; while at another, there was a description given of the Persians pouring "*Wollies*" into the Russians; and to the question — "Pray what fish is that before you?" this answer was returned, "Really I do not know; I am not *botanist* enough for that."

CHAP. III.

There, in Britannia's fertile verdant isle,
The cottage, garden, farm, and mansion smile.
No deadly serpent lurks beneath the rose;
But whispering love may in the shade repose.
No dreary forests cover useful space—
A gallant peasantry supplies their place.

Every inhabitant of Great Britain should exult in the security he enjoys in his own country, on comparing it with other regions of the globe. Were he to travel over the northern parts of India, and see its population cooped up within walled cities; were he to see hordes of Pindarries, with plunder in their van, desolating the plains; were he to look upon the ruined villages and towns that every where bring a tear to the eye of sensibility; and behold sometimes poor old men and women creeping from the ruins, as from the graves of departed happiness, near which they still lingered, with what grateful feelings would he afterwards view the smiling cottages that adorn the surface of his native soil, where a good lock and window-bolt are considered protection enough against those men, everywhere to be found, who are wolves to their fellow-creatures.

It must, however, be acknowledged that a different picture should, in truth, be given of other parts of India. In Malabar, a country diversified with beautiful hill and dale, and watered by crystal streams flowing to the sea from the neighbouring mountains; in the Carnatic, in Mysore, in the Koncan, and in every tract long under the controul of Britain, walled towns and forts are forsaken by the peaceful peasantry, whose cottages begin to clothe vast plains, where desolation and solitude reigned. The golden melon and pumpkin may be seen in all the full blow of native luxuriance, overspreading the roofs of their dwellings, surrounded by groves of cocoa-nut trees, through which the broad-leaved plaintain and climbing pepper vine peep at every opening, and smiling chubby children, and groups of laughing females, may be viewed going down to the wells, with all the simplicity of patriarchal days.

In establishing this security and happiness, throughout so large a portion of Asia, which is entirely owing to the impartial justice of our glorious constitution, many acts of oppression, no doubt, hidden from the research of man, were committed; for have ever armies traversed a country with hostile banners, without producing deplorable effects; or have ever men been found, who were so virtuous, that some of them in carrying plans into execution which had for their object the good of mankind, did not dishonour their cause by the gratification of their own passions? No man exists, who is further from being the sycophant of power than he who now addresses the public: for it is durably impressed upon his understanding, that all governments should be watched, and forced to observe the rules of equity, because they are composed of men, and it is the nature of man to encroach upon the rights of his fellow-creatures. If therefore he ventures to praise the constitution of England, it is from mature conviction that it is the best in the world, and that we who live under it enjoy the greatest share of rational liberty, consistent with political security. Therefore, in continuation of the poetical heading of our chapters, we would exclaim —

What! If the public service of the state,
Draw largely from the purse of poor and great;
For Britain's weal, to eternize her fame,
None should refuse his life that bears her name.
There lives no son of England's favoured land,
Who should not give his all with cheerful hand.
There breathes not one of Scotia's warlike race,
Or Erin's hardy offspring, but should face
Distress and poverty in every form,
To see the Albion triumph o'er the storm,
And sail superbly down time's ambient tide,
The Thistle and the Shamrock by her side.

But as this flight may be thought digressive from Sketches of a Soldier's Life in India, a sudden right about is made to the thread of our history.

Mr. True, having ascertained from Bob Gordon the particulars of his life, which are considered foreign to our subject, acquainted him with many circumstances in his own adventures in India, which we would accordingly narrate verbatim, had he not passed over some interesting matters, with the modesty becoming a brave man; it is therefore necessary to guard his honour, and an author's veracity, by relating in the third person what it is thought proper to make known respecting this gentleman.

It has already been indirectly intimated to the reader, that he was of an ancient and most respectable family in the north of Ireland; but early misfortune blighted his hopes in Europe, and it was with some difficulty he obtained an ensigncy in a regiment in India.

No situation can be more lively and agreeable than than that of a young officer on board an Indiaman, during his passage out. Hope presents to his youthful mind a bright picture. The captain and officers of the ship are generally attentive and gentlemanly, and a large party of ladies and brother passengers sit down every day to excellent cheer, and exhilarating wines, at the cuddy table, while the evenings are spent in dancing on the quarter deck, either to an organ or the ship's band. At the same time, the lee-side is occupied by the soldiers and their wives, whose unsophisticated steps form a ludicrous contrast to the graceful movements on the other quarter. Time flies, and his flight is unheeded amidst the diversions found in music, books, drawing, backgammon, chess, and piquet. It is most to be dreaded, in such a situation, that quarrels should arise, and disturb the harmony that ought to reign; but fortunately on this occasion there were so many old officers returning to their regiments, and such proper discipline exercised by the senior, who commanded the troops on board, that every aberration from concord was checked, and the whole kept in proper tune. Nothing was wanting but a few pretty girls, to make out a quadrille, or a love story; but it so happened that no Celia went to the land of husbands at this time, and our young adventurer therefore had no opportunity of losing his heart.

The monotony of a long voyage is always great, where there can be little but sea and sky to meet the eye, and the screams of aquatic birds to recreate the ear. Madeira, the peak of Teneriffe, the channel of Mozambique, the Island of Joanna, and the distant appearance of Ceylon, have been often described, and it need only be said, that a fine view of St. Thomas's Mount, near Fort St. George, was gained without having witnessed any very important occurrence; and the clear blue cloudless sky of the Coromandel coast shed its azure cheerfulness on the mind of Ensign True, while he surveyed from the poop those new objects which arose to his amused sight; for although he had read many descriptions of Madras roads, and of landing at Fort St. George, the reality as far exceeded what he had conceived, as the grandeur of nature surpasses the finest panorama executed by the ablest artist.

Before a distinct view was obtained of the shining white buildings of Madras, the bright sandy beach, and tall palmira trees that beautify the shore, the natives were beheld as if walking on the smooth glass-like surface of the serene ocean, whose bosom was only fanned by zephyrs that carried the ship imperceptibly towards her destination. These children of Neptune were known by the captain. Leaving their catamarans (which are little more than a log of wood and a paddle) fastened to the chains, they climbed the side like monkeys, and accosted him as an old acquaintance, but with such respect as is paid to a God. Nearly naked, having only a cloth round the loins, and a cap made of mat on the head, their slight and agile forms, their jetty bodies shining from being anointed with oil, and their intelligent countenances, formed an interesting spectacle, which was soon followed by groups of tall graceful figures rustling on the deck in long white muslin robes, and large gold ear-rings, looking more like fine Irish women painted black than men who were brought alongside by Mussoola boats, loaded also with a variety of fruits and refreshments. These boats are admirably calculated to meet the violence of the surf on the Coromandel coast, which is so great as to render it very dangerous to go on shore in any other. The rowers watch the approach of the first billow, and with great dexterity manage their long oars so as to raise the stem of the boat to receive the shock which dashes it forward to a great distance, while with loud shouts they receive the shower of foam and spray that follows them. Having just time to recover, another wave, still more mountainous, heaves the boat aloft and precipitates it headlong, groaning and spouting the salt fluid from its planks that bend like whalebone, for they are sewed together with the fibres of the cocoa nut, called *coir*, the boats being flat-bottomed, with high sides and no keels. Another surf sent Ensign George True high and dry on the beach.

Assembled on the shore to see the troops and passengers land, there were crowds of spectators, whose Asiatic costume and gesture imparted an indescribable novelty to the scene, while the bustle and competition among the natives for the advantages of carrying the luggage to the Fort, their solicitations to be employed as servants, the earnestness with which they presented their characters, and the extraordinary idiom of the English language through whose medium they endeavoured to set forth their former services, produced such busy confusion, that Mr. True stood for some time lost in wonder. The recruits for the regiments on the Madras establishment, who were generally Irish lads, expressed their astonishment in loud exclamations.

"Arrah, Pat, only look at the coaches wid the black ladies, carried, by my salvation, on the backs of naked human craturs. Och! man alive, hear the bells! and how they grunt and keep the time wid their legs and arms together. Fat would your moder and sister Juddy, at Ballyporeen, say to see dis, my jewel!"

What excited Paddy's surprize were the numerous palankeens, conveying the native clerks from the offices in the Fort to Black-town, for it was now evening in the month of July. One of these hackney conveyances soon after transported Mr. True to the tavern, a staff-serjeant having taken charge of the soldiers, and marched them off without delay to the depôt at Poonamallie. Next morning he paid his respects to the authorities at Madras, and was ordered also to the depôt, to await an opportunity of joining his corps on the Malabar coast. This did not happen till the month of October, during which time he made frequent visits to the presidency, and saw much of the society at Madras. The grandeur and pomp in which the governor, commander in chief, members of council, and principal civilians lived, naturally surprized a youth new to the luxury of the east; but the sensations of pleasure which these fascinations imparted, were counterbalanced by the torment he endured from the bites of musquitoes, and the distressing heat of the climate.

Poonamallie is situated a march inland from Fort St. George. To the different villages around Mr. True often rode, being curious to witness the idolatrous processions of the natives, and their veneration for the Brahminy Bull. At this season the Carnatic presents a barren and parched level aspect to the beholder, except in the vicinity of towns, where, by artificial irrigation, green spots are produced that smile with all the charms of vegetation, and meet the pleased eye amidst the brown sandy desert-like prospect. The buffalo is the animal in general use for all purposes of husbandry. Herds of these ferocious looking creatures were roaming over the plains. Frightened at the European costume, they would cock their ears and tails, raise their backs and noses, gaze a little, and then turn and run, shaking their slate coloured huge sides, to the nearest *tank* or river, and plunge in the water, just keeping their eyes, horns, and tails above the gratefully cool fluid.

No rain fell till September, when showers were frequent, and the monsoon began to threaten. It generally sets in with violence in the latter part of October, when the flag-staff of Fort St. George is struck, and ships are directed not to approach the roads for three months. During this period, while the floods of heaven deluge the plains of the Carnatic, no rain falls on the coast of Malabar, but a fine alternation of land and sea breezes prevails, for the monsoon commences in the beginning of June, and is over before it sets in on the Coromandel coast. This strange phenomenon is occasioned by the stupendous Ghauts whose height arrests the clouds that convey fertility from the ocean, and produce a peculiarity in a region where the climate is naturally the same as to latitude.

The earth, thus refreshed and renovated, yields one good crop of rice in the year; but where artificial moisture is procured, two harvests are reaped. Water is raised for this beneficial purpose in an ingenious way: on the bank of a well or river, much below the level of the fields, an upright strong post is erected, to the top of which a lever is fixed, that moves on a central fulcrum. To one end of the lever a rope is attached of such length as to drop, with a leather bag tied to it, into the water when the beam is depressed, but when raised the bag strikes against an embankment, and empties the contents into a channel which conveys it to fertilize the neighbouring plantations. The man who manages this machine runs up several steps cut along the lever, till he places his foot above the fulcrum, and turns it so that the bag falls into the water and fills; seeing which, and poising himself with nice dexterity, he runs up the opposite way till he comes to that part where his weight is sufficient to raise the object of his labour. In this manner he will continue running backwards and forwards as quick as thought, raising at every turn a considerable quantity of water, till a fine stream flows to every part of his plantation.

Nothing can exceed the address and ingenuity of the natives of the Carnatic. The Madras jugglers are the most expert in India, and rival those of China in astonishing feats of art, swallowing swords, vomiting fire, charming snakes, balancing weights, leaping and tumbling over sharp-pointed weapons, so as to amaze every beholder. All the inhabitants of the provinces under this presidency enjoy perfect security in their property and persons, and amidst their cocoa-nut and plantain groves taste perhaps as much real happiness as falls to the lot of man. Their virtues are industry, passive obedience, and contentment; but lasciviousness, falsehood, and selfishness are prominent traits in their character. All the peninsula of India from the river Kisthna may be said to belong to the government of Fort St. George; for the only native states which preserve the show of independence are those of the Rajahs of Mysore, Travancore, and Cochin, who are in fact merely tenants of the East India Company. The population of the presidency, exclusive of the subjects belonging to the three princes above mentioned, was estimated at twelve millions, but it will be found now to exceed fifteen; and if the whole be taken together, the mass would be above twenty millions of souls.

This vast extent of territory is divided into districts, over which the Company's civil servants preside as judges, magistrates, collectors, and assistants. Justice is administered according to the Gentoo and Mahomedan law; but there is a supreme court at Fort St. George, consisting of three judges, and a full establishment of barristers and attorneys, whose jurisdiction is very considerable. The population is controlled by upwards of

200 civilians, and an army of fifty thousand men, the expences of whose establishments exceeded £5,000,000, which was more than the revenue by £400,000 per annum, so that the government was upwards of £9,000,000 in debt; but this was counterbalanced by a surplus revenue in Bengal, and by the great improvement expected from the peace and security then fully established throughout the provinces subject to Madras.

The principal article of trade consists of piece goods which are paid for in specie, and the exports exceed the imports very considerably; but as a commercial establishment, this presidency is inferior to Bombay, although second only to Bengal in political consequence. That it is not subject to such extremes of heat as our more northerly possessions in India, will perhaps surprize the reader; the thermometer ranges at Madras during the whole year from 70° to 91°, so that with the assistance of *punkoes* and *tatties* the houses are kept agreeably cool even in the hottest day. The European families at Madras reside in garden houses, generally of one story high, but whose pillars, virandas and terraces might remind a beholder of the grandeur of Grecian temples; and the stucco made of shells with which they are finished has the beautiful polish of marble. The gardens, and the fine shady roads about Madras, are extremely agreeable to a new-comer: exercise is generally taken along these fine avenues before breakfast, for the morning is delightful in India. The forenoon is spent in paying and receiving visits, and in lounging with the ladies. *Tiffin* is served up at one, after which all idlers take a siesta, or spend the afternoon in reading. In the evening the fashionables sport their gay equipages on the mount road, and having shewn themselves off around the cenotaph erected to the memory of Lord Cornwallis, return to dinner, after which a ball and supper, or perhaps theatricals in the pantheon, by amateurs who aim solely at pleasing the ladies, close the daily scene.

One of his Majesty's ships having to go round to Bombay for repair, the opportunity was favourable for sending the recruits to the Malabar coast, and accordingly Ensign True embarked in charge of several detachments. The soldiers were distributed among the sailors, and he was invited to join the officers' mess, where he experienced an agreeable and cordial reception. There were two other passengers on board, a fine-looking old French gentleman and his adopted daughter, whom the captain very politely accommodated on their return from Pondicherry to Mahé, a beautiful settlement near Tellicherry.

The young lady was at first sea-sick, but she made her appearance at divine service on Sunday, when the quarter-deck was covered with a sail-cloth awning, and the sides screened round with the flags of the ship, for the comfortable reception of all on board, to whom the captain read prayers and one of Sterne's sermons. Mr. True entirely forgot his devotional duty that day, for his eye feasted by stealth on the most bewitching object he had ever seen. She was about twelve years of age, and had all the pleasing roundness and fascinating bloom of approaching maturity, which the female form displays about that period in hot climates. Her dress was a simple but tasteful white muslin robe; and the only ornament she wore was a half-blown artificial rose, which the eye rested upon, but rather to behold the beautiful virgin swell of the bosom in which it was placed. Her auburn hair was negligently but elegantly turned up with a comb, and shining ringlets played in natural curls on her temples of snow. Her face and figure were those of one of the most beautiful daughters of Eve, with soft but penetrating blue eyes, whose brightness forced the gaze of admiration to withdraw, but whose attraction quickly brought back the runaway. Her features were exquisitely regular, but it was the infantine sweetness playing upon them, combined with an archness coming from the soul, that gave the captivating expression to them, which the young ensign could not resist.

Having to deliver stores at Trincomallie, the ship lay-to in Back-bay under the flag-staff, from which point the fort and ridge on which it stands appear to advantage. Mr. True was sitting on the side sketching the scene, and he had introduced the castle of Osnaburgh in the distance, and shaded the whole, when Monsieur Fortier, who was standing behind looking over his shoulder, exclaimed —"Bravo, bravissimo! — Benè, benè, tres bien"— with a look of great complacency.— "It is very well — permit me to look — strengthen here de shade a little more, and the light dere will produce one grand improvemong. Pardonnez moi, — I will shew it to Nannette." So saying he skipped off, calling in a shrill tone—"Ma chere Nannette," and her sylph-like form came out of the round-house to meet him. She admired the sketch, and returned it with her own fair hand, and this slight accident led to a closer acquaintance. Monsieur Fortier said he would feel pleasure in hearing the youth read part of Charles the Twelfth, for the purpose of correcting his French pronunciation, and Mademoiselle most graciously lent him "Elizabeth," with "Paul and Virginia."

One day he was leaning over the railing of the poop, so that he looked into the open window of Miss Nannette's cabin, at which she was sitting, with drawings and books before her on a table, but at that moment she was braiding up her beautiful hair and looking in a dressing glass, seemingly with great pleasure. He forgot himself, or never suspected that she might understand Latin, for he ejaculated with much feeling from the 5th ode of Horace —

"Cui flavam religas comam,
"Simplex munditiis!"

"Je ne sais pas," said she, in the sweetest tone of playful delight, and added with naiveté, in a childish half-angry half-pleased way,—"Not for you to be sure."

The youth was confounded, his face burned, and he drooped his head and looked the picture of woe.

"Oh! I am not angry," said she; "it was only a little of my vanity. I wanted to shew you that I understand Latin."

He said something in a very low tone in reply, and she leaned over the window the better to hear it, seemingly unconscious that there was any danger in doing so, when, dreadful to relate, she fell overboard!

He shrieked,—and plunged after her.

It is a long way from the poop of a seventy-four to the surface of the sea. He made a great splash and sunk. When he recovered, he saw Miss Nannette floating a little way from him, seemingly kept up by her muslin drapery, and just caught her as she was sinking, and almost breathless from the effort she had made to keep her head above water. She twined her arms round his, and would have taken him down with her, but he succeeded in keeping her and himself on the surface.

"For heaven's sake," said he, "do not clasp me. You are quite safe, I can support you with ease; but if you cramp me, we shall be inevitably lost."

She soon recovered her presence of mind, and became heroically tranquil. "Oh! mon papa! mon papa!" was all she said on letting go her hold; after which with his left hand he supported her with the greatest ease. Upon looking round he discovered the ship at no great distance, and saw she was laid aback. Two life-buoys and some hen-coops were floating a little way off that had been thrown out to assist him, but he could not reach them, for there was a strong current at this time on the surface, running with the breeze into the gulph of Menar, that carried them away past the vessel, while a still stronger counter current beneath urged the vessel forward against the breeze towards him and the lovely nymph he supported, and at the same time the flow in the opposite direction transported them towards the wished-for point. A boat had been let down as quick as lightning from its stays on the quarter, but the officer who had leaped into it, in his hurry and anxiety, mistook one of the hen-coops for his object, and rowed off with all dispatch. The captain, who saw from the deck the alarming mistake, almost burst his lungs before he could rectify the error; but the oars had now to pull against the current, and made very little way. And now the scientific captain saw with pleasure, that the young ensign was an expert swimmer, and that he supported his fair charge with ease and skill.—"So, so," exclaimed he, from the quarter chains, where he stood managing with nice art and success the ship, in order to intercept the objects of his solicitude, and at the same time cheered Monsieur Fortier with hope, who was prevented, by two officers, from jumping overboard.

Mr. True was now within a few yards of the vessel. He heard all tongues applauding his skill, and saw the adventurous tars coming down the chains with ropes tied round their middle and hanging over the side, their hands extended to his assistance, when, horrible to relate, the cry was heard — "A shark! a shark!" "Oh God! the harpoon, boatswain,"— vociferated the captain. The men at the helm, panic struck with the terror of all on board, forgot their duty, and the ship hove on the swell away from the youth and lovely girl. But two experienced officers seized the wheel. In the meantime True looked round, and the sweet creature he supported exclaimed, "Mon Dieu! mon Dieu!" Hope sunk within his breast; for he saw the pilot fish approaching him, smelling and feeling the way before a large shark that followed timidly at a distance, whose monstrous length and bright green colour illuminated the blue waves.

How does a brave but raw young soldier feel, who for the first time marches up to storm a battery, and sees the flashing cannon vomiting grape, which mows his comrades down, while every moment he is forced to close to the centre, for the purpose of replacing a slaughtered friend? His heart for a moment faints, and his soul, loth to quit its tenement of clay, looks to retreat for safety; but indignant honour cries louder than the thunder of artillery "Shame!" and he rushes on to death. So did Ensign True feel in this awful moment of his life. His hand trembled, and the water just covered the pale lips of the beautiful Nannette when she had exclaimed "Mon Dieu! mon Dieu!" Love and glory forced the blood to rush again from his heart; he raised his struggling charge above the surface once more, turned her from the monster's course, and opposed himself to the danger, determined to thrust his right arm into the throat of the shark, and, if possible, to pluck out the heart of his foe.

The monster was just on the point of seizing his prey — the harpoon fell short — its splash made him turn; but having seen his object, he again darted towards it. Just as his jaws opened to lacerate the body of our young adventurer, Frank Stanley, one of the soldiers on board, who was standing on the hammocks, rose in the air, and with all his force leaped on the shark armed with his bayonet, which he strove to plunge in his body. A shout of admiration, mixed with awe, burst from all observers. The astonished monster, like lightning, cut his way into the bowels of the deep. The boat arrived and Stanley was caught up by the sailors, who also carried the ensign and Nannette, rising like Venus from the foam of the ocean, on deck, where she was embraced by her almost frenzied father, and her deliverer fainted, from his long-continued struggle, in the arms of the captain.

CHAP. IV.

While yet the ebbing flood that bears away
My friend, permits a pause of short delay;
We stand at Champaul Ghaut's refreshing green,
And contemplate the grandeur of the scene.
Aurora's hand had spread the genial feast,
Of golden morning o'er the silver east;
While crowds of Hindoos, at the dawn of day,
With Gunga's tears to lave their sins away,
Plunge in the Hoogly's deep majestic flow,
Whose curling waves move past sublimely slow.
A wood of lofty masts, Britannia's pride,
From ships well moor'd along Calcutta's side,
Extends to where Fort William's flag unfurl'd,
Proclaims our glory to the eastern world.
Far spreading thence the city's rich display,
O'er which appears the splendid car of day,
Of lofty structures, pleased we thus behold,
Like orient pearls that glow in burnished gold.

Artificial descents to rivers, wharfs, quays, and landing places, are called Ghauts in India. Many of these, on the banks of the sacred Hindoo streams, have magnificent flights of stone steps, leading from pagodas, whose structure, antiquity, and grandeur surprize every beholder. They are distinguished by the appellatives of gods and goddesses, as "Kallighaut," or, "Champaul Ghaut," the latter of which is an insignificant one, but it is the place where Europeans generally land, on arriving in Calcutta, and embark, on leaving it for their native soil. Thence along the left bank of the Hoogly, there is a fine promenade to Fort William, whose spreading trees, planted on each side, lend a refreshing shade, through which cool breezes from the broad bosom of the river wing their course over the esplanade, to meet the attraction of the heated atmosphere of the city. From this point of view Calcutta appears to great advantage, for the panorama embraces the river Hoogly and shipping, the buildings and docks on the right bank, the magnificent structures of the Government House, Town-hall, Supreme Court, Fort William, Kidderpore School, the Theatre, and the fine range of palaces along the Chouringhee side of the esplanade, together with the row at right angles, extending to the river, through which the monuments, mosques, pagodas, and churches of the city have a beautiful effect.

The aspect of morning is sweet and refreshing in the east. Night's damp shades having restored objects to an agreeable temperature, the eye rests and recreates upon them, in that short period during which they can be seen to advantage, as they lose the power of gladdening sight in the glare that overspreads them soon after sun-rise. Crowds of Hindoos approach the river during this delightful space, to bathe and pray. They bring with them small images representing some of their thirty thousand millions of gods, and such as have none, make little idols of the mud of the Ganges, which they set upon the bank and adore. The men and women go down into the water together, dressed as they come to the river, except that many of the former, who wear turbans, long gowns, and slippers, leave these articles aside, and bathe in their trowsers alone. On coming out they wring their wet garments, which dry in going home; and the women often strip in the river, wash their apparel, and dress there again; for the female dress is generally composed of one long piece of cloth, the end of which is rolled several times round the waist, whence it flows in graceful folds down to the ancle; the other end is drawn tastefully round their breasts, so as to cover the back also, and serve as a veil, flowing over their black hair, braided up in a knot behind, when they meet Europeans, on which occasions they often turn their backs, and stand till the strangers pass. They wear rings in their noses and ears, and on their fingers and toes, with ornaments encircling on their wrists, arms, and legs, of gold, silver, brass, ivory, glass, bone or horn, according to their circumstances. They have bright dark eyes, the glances of which they strive to increase, by painting their eye-lashes jet black, which colour is also thought beautiful for the teeth. Their forms are graceful, and of commanding deportment, from the erect and majestic step common among the females of Hindostan. The inhabitants of Bengal, like those of other flat and rich marshy countries, are of portly stature, and have those large joints, prominent bones, swelling muscles, and rough and elastic integuments, which have been called fine properties for a soldier. Their cast of countenance, with the exception of colour, is the same as our own, except that there is no variety in the eyes and hair, which are very nearly of the same colour every where in India, although the complexion varies from the deepest shade of black to a soft pale tint, which in some of the northern females might be termed *fair*. The aspect is penetrating and bold, and the movement powerful and vigorous. Bengal Sepoys are the finest looking in the Company's service, nearly all grenadiers, and individually very brave; but like other large men, they are not so hardy, nor do they stand change of climate so well as the natives of Madras and Bombay.

If the reader, not acquainted with Hindoo mythology, was startled by the mention of thirty thousand millions of objects of adoration among the Hindoos, it ought to be explained, that this is the number of gods mentioned as composing the fourteen heavens. But it appears that not one in a hundred of even tolerably well informed natives, have any correct notion of the nature of their religion. The peasantry are actually in a state of the grossest ignorance, and kept so by the Brahmins. Sometimes they offer adoration at the tomb of an European of rank, who had become popular for acts of generosity and grandeur of soul. A crowd of them has been seen by the author, at Seroor, making their offerings, paying their devotions, and invoking the shade of Colonel Wallace, to cure some disease, or avert some calamity, with candles burning round the monument erected to his memory, and a priestess performing his rites, and deriving a livelihood from the presents brought to obtain her intercession. Colonel Wallace, who distinguished himself on many occasions, commanded the Poonah subsidiary force, and died at the cantonment of Seroor. He was a fine, venerable looking soldier, and made this strange impression on the affections of the credulous natives, who firmly believe that he is still their patron and friend.

The Bore, an extraordinary swell during spring tides, which agitates the Hoogly, has rendered it necessary to lay down moorings before Calcutta. This phenomenon is not peculiar to the Ganges; it is felt in several other rivers, and is occasioned, no doubt, by the great body of water during the springs that rushes up their channels, and drives back the mass flowing to the sea, with an impetuosity proportioned to the resistance opposed by projections or straits in the course of the returning fluid. The navigable bed of the Hoogly is in some places very narrow, and often nearly choked up with shifting sand banks, so that the tide finding in some parts of its course ample space, and in others having to force its own way, its violent effects may be easily conceived. It rushes past Calcutta with astonishing fury, and what is curious, sometimes takes one side of the river and then another, but never visits its broad bosom. That side up which it rushes is raised to a frightful height, and the appearance is that of a monstrous billow of the ocean in a storm, or the dash of a foaming surf. Boats have been swallowed up by the Bore, and all in them lost. The *dandies* on the Hoogly, therefore, feel great terror at the idea of being caught, and take care to get out of the way in due time, which they know so well that immediately before its approach, all is uproar and seeming confusion. Hundreds of boats are seen rowing as for life and death towards the middle of the river, the crews of which urge each other on with shouts and wild shrieks, and seem to delight in the general exertion to surprize the beholders with noise and precipitancy, though at the moment no danger appears; but soon afterwards the spectator is sensible how necessary it was to take precaution, by seeing the Bore foam past with fearfulvelocity.

Fort William is superior to any other fortress in India. It is constructed on the most scientific principles of military architecture, and fortified in a manner which, with a British garrison, would bid defiance to all the powers of the East. Its foundation was laid soon after the Battle of Plassy in 1758, the old fort of Calcutta having been found unfit to sustain a siege. The barracks in it are superb; and the remarkable state of cleanliness in which its shady walks and fine parades are kept, together with the attraction of a military band, which plays almost every evening for public entertainment, draws all the fashion of the city to promenade within hearing, and causes it to be a continual scene of gaiety, except during the monsoon. In this fortress the Honourable Company have an excellent arsenal, and a gun foundery, with a large establishment for the preparation of the material of an army.

But to a contemplative mind the most curious object within the walls of Fort William at this time was Vizier Ally, once Nabob of Oude, who was confined in a room made to resemble an iron cage, for the murder of Mr. Cherry, where he lingered out seventeen years of his life, and died at the age of thirty-six. (Vide the Gentleman's Magazine for June 1818, page 84.) At the time he was seen by the author, in 1814, he was an emaciated wretched looking being, the vicissitudes of whose career are pregnant with interest and instruction.

The city of Calcutta now extends from Kidderpore to Cossipore, a distance of about six miles along the banks of the river Hoogly; and if the reader trace in imagination a half moon from that base line, about two miles in breadth, he will have a pretty accurate idea of its surface. About one hundred and ten years ago, nothing was to be seen on the space where a magnificent city and fortress now stand, but a few Indian huts, called the village of

Govindpore. As the human mind may be advanced to wonderful maturity at an early age, by being expanded under the influence of skilful masters of education, so this city, pushed forward by the able political architects that superintended its progress, has all the majesty of age with the vigorous flow of youth yet in full circulation.

Dr. Boughton, at a time when the Company's affairs were at a low ebb, and the factory on the Hoogly in its infancy, was so fortunate as to cure the daughter of the Emperor Shah Jehaun of a dangerous illness. This obtained for him much influence at court, and paved the way to advantages in trade for his employers that contributed essentially to their success.

In this way rose the city of Calcutta, which is now the metropolis of a mighty empire, co-extensive with that of the Great Mogul. It was surrounded by a mound of earth, called the Mahratta ditch, raised by the early settlers, when those marauders were plundering the province of Bengal. The Marquis of Wellesley had this ditch levelled, and on what was the fossé there is now a fine circular road, from one extent of the river-front of the city, to the other. The prospect around is a vast plain, unbounded by a single hill, whose soil is rich and exceedingly fertile. No stones are to be found near the city, therefore the houses are composed of brick, and the marble and free stone of the public buildings were brought from a distance. Chouringhee, Park Street, Durrumtollah, the Jaun Bazar and Esplanade, now form the European part of the town. On passing along these fine streets, the mixture of native huts with houses of the most noble appearance, like Grecian temples, spoils the effect, though, when at a distance, the detached state of the houses, giving them the character of palaces, insulated in a great space, is an advantage, and strikes the beholder with greater admiration. It would not be easy to describe the grandeur of the line of buildings that surround two sides of the Esplanade of Fort William, situated about a mile from the city; to which there is a fine broad road called the Course, watered every day, that it may be in an agreeable state for the society to exercise in their carriages, buggies, tandems, and palankeens, as soon as the declining sun permits such recreation. To pourtray the edifices of interest would be dry and tedious. Besides those before mentioned, the churches and chapels, and the college and museum deserve notice, with the numerous beautiful garden houses that ornament that part of the suburbs below Kidderpore, called Garden Reach, to the extent of more than five miles.

In this country, unless the reader reflects how grateful it is in hot climates to have large and airy rooms, remote from the glare or intrusion of the sun, and also how easy it is with plenty of funds to raise large structures, he will be unable to conceive the magnificence and extent of these dwellings, on some of which vast sums have been expended. Nothing can, therefore, be imagined finer than the approach to Calcutta. These houses rise upon the sight, like so many scenes of enchantment, one after the other; the vessel or boat glides on and sometimes touches the constantly verdant bank of the river, till Fort William, the numerous ships lying off Calcutta, and the seemingly interminable extent of the city, beautified with groves of evergreens, complete a climax, that to be properly felt must be seen. The city is upwards of an hundred miles distant from the Sand Heads, in a direct line, and the approach is much longer by the windings of the river. Very large ships seldom go up to Calcutta, but discharge and take in cargo at Kedgeree, Saugur, or Diamond Harbour, poor places and the only ones worthy of notice below Fultah Farm, where there is an inn for the accommodation of passengers. Here the grandeur of the city begins to appear; next the Company's botanic gardens please the eye, and then all is delightful till the stranger lands at Champaul Ghaut, and perhaps encounters a cloud of dust, which assures one of his senses that he has not landed on the Elysian Fields.

The river Hoogly is so dangerous, that the pilot service is very extensive. The Company have ten vessels, fast-sailing schooners, each commanded by a Branch, with masters, mates, and assistants, all Europeans, who cruize in turn off the Sand Heads, and conduct ships up the river.

About seventeen miles above Calcutta are the Governor General's country seat, park, and gardens, situated at Barrackpore, which is a military station, with a remarkably beautiful cantonment for two regiments of Sepoys. The officers have erected a very neat theatre, and often invite their friends from town to witness amateur performances of a very respectable and interesting description. Thither there is a fine road from the city; and in the governor's park there is a collection of the curious birds and quadrupeds of the East, which attracts the visits of strangers. Just opposite to it, on the other side of the Hoogly, is seated Serampore, a Danish settlement, where the Anabaptist mission has established a school, and a press for printing the Scriptures in the native languages. The French settlement of Chandernagore lies about twenty miles higher on the western bank also, and not far from it is the Dutch factory of Chinserah; and to these agreeable places of recreation parties of pleasure are often formed from Calcutta.

The police department in and around the city is finely conducted. It has a corps of natives called runners. These men are armed with cutlasses and round targets; and guard-houses are erected at convenient distances for their accommodation, where they are ready at all hours to run to that point whence a call is heard for their assistance. In consequence of this efficient police, and the opinion vulgarly entertained that the magistrate at the head of it is a magician, who can discover all stolen property, robbery and theft are seldom attempted by the natives; and the misconduct of European sailors and soldiers, nearly all addicted in such a hot climate to intemperance, is restrained. Such as have witnessed the fun of sailors on getting ashore after a long voyage, will easily conceive their excesses. But in India they are excited to the utmost display of folly, by the desire which many Europeans have of *shewing off* in great style before crowds of wondering Hindoos.

Europeans in Calcutta, exclusive of the civil and military servants of government, are clergymen, merchants, some members of the medical profession, shopkeepers, schoolmasters, tradesmen, and speculators, who come out under free mariner's indentures. The government shews a decided dislike to colonization; and permission to remain, in all cases, is refused to adventurers without authority from the Court of Directors; some who resisted an order to depart, have been forced on board a ship by the bayonets of a military escort. Though the government has the power of sending any European home, yet that arbitrary act has been committed only in a few very glaring instances, where individuals of restless ambition attempted to disturb the peace of the country; for it would be monstrous injustice first to permit a man to establish himself, and afterwards to arrest the course of his industry. There is, however, an European and half cast public in Calcutta that crowds two large protestant churches, a Presbyterian meeting-house, a large Anabaptist chapel, and three extensive Portuguese churches. With respect to the exact number, however, nothing like accuracy can be assumed, since no census has been taken; but in Hamilton's East India Gazette authorities are quoted upon which may be placed perfect dependence. In 1802, the police magistrates estimated the population of Calcutta at 600,000, and calculated that within a circle of twenty miles there were 2,225,000 souls. Sir Henry Russel, the chief justice, a few years ago, estimated the inhabitants of the city and its environs at one million; and General Kyd calculated the population of the town alone, at between 4 and 500,000. There are upwards of 78,760 houses belonging to individuals, viz. to British subjects 4,300, Armenians 640, Portuguese and other Christians 2,650, Hindoos 56,460, Mahomedans 17,700, and Chinese 10.

As to the native part of Calcutta, it is, like most other Indian towns, composed of narrow crooked streets, and houses some of brick and others of reeds, bamboos, wood, and mud, covered with tiles, or thatched with the leaves of the cocoa-nut tree; but the palaces or dwellings of many of the native rajahs and great men of large fortune are an exception. Some of the streets too, such as Rada Bazar and the Cossipore road, are tolerable; and the new and old China bazars present a fine display of Asiatic and European splendour.

The variety of costume and contrast of appearance to be seen in the streets are worthy of notice. Many a young Bond-street dandy struts with inconceivable self-satisfaction; and youthful British, Portuguese, and French half cast, with tawny face, and neck stiffened almost to suffocation, jumps from the sublime to the ridiculous in attempts at imitation. A stranger's eye would next perhaps rest upon a Capuchin friar, with the beard and costume of the 14th century; and soon remove to a British missionary, who, in deepest black and countenance of longest sorrow, musing on the state of man, marches against a grave Turk, who jostles a Persian, who discomposes a Seik, who insults an Arabian, who electrifies a Chinese, who contaminates a Hindoo, who upsets a dancing-master, and terrifies an Armenian. He would see the military staff, bucks with waving feathers and gorgeous agulettes, shading their fair country-women with silken *chattahs* from the glare of the sun, while handing them from some grand long room or attractive bazar to their carriage, chariot, phaeton, barouche, sociable, or palankeen; and he would try to have a peep into the covered *hackeries* or native carriages of the opulent Hindoos, drawn by bullocks richly caparisoned with silk, and jingling bells of silver, in which their wives are concealed from the eye of man when they visit their female friends. And what would he say in another part of the town, upon seeing a dozen of almost naked runners dashing down the street with drawn sabres and upraised targets to separate a group of British tars, fighting for no other purpose than to show the Hindoos the courage and blood of England?— But to resume our thread of narrative.

Frank Stanley, who at the imminent peril of his own life endeavoured so nobly to save that of his officer, was a promising youth of handsome exterior, with an air and address much above his humble station, to whom Ensign True had paid some of those little attentions during their passage from England, that win the human heart. He was a reduced branch of a very respectable house, and patronized by his relation Squire Worthy, whose niece, a beautiful young lady, was heiress to his large estate. The old gentleman took Frank from his mother to his own home, and seemed to feel much pleasure in the improvement of his mind; for he employed him to read aloud the battles of Marlborough and Prince Eugene, in which he greatly delighted. His old lady herself used to come into the library and sit with her netting for hours, hearing him. Miss Sarah Oliver would also lend an attentive ear, and her aunt at length conceived that she discovered in her pale cheek, love lurking for the handsome stripling, in whom she saw no merit because he was poor. Their reading and family intercourse was soon at an end; but Frank had imbibed not only the glances of Sarah's dark blue eyes, but the romantic notions of a soldier of fortune. He embarked in his arduous profession in the hope that he would reap laurels worthy of being laid at the feet of the girl his soul adored, and sailed for India full of high expectation. Among one hundred and twenty recruits, with whom he crossed that wide expanse of ocean which separates Europe from Hindostan, he found only one in whose society he felt the sympathy of congeniality. Kindred souls soon assimilate, and in the person of Charles Thoughtless, Frank Stanley realized the visions that youthful imagination had formed of friendship.

The infant years of Charles Thoughtless were passed in Dublin, the place of his birth, with every promise that his opening prospect would be delightful. But a change came over the scene. His mother died, and his father, a gentleman belonging to one of the learned professions, became unfortunate in his pursuits. When about five years old, Charles was removed to the country, and placed with his grandmother, then in slender circumstances, being much reduced by the extravagance of sons, to whom she had given a high education; but who, like many other young men, were not contented with such means as she could afford. His preparation for life received its finish at the school of Maghernahaly, in county Armagh, where the Dominie amused his pupils by performing the battle of Aughram. One of the mistresses' quilts was converted into a curtain for the stage; sheets and shawls were the scenery, and a blind fiddler filled the orchestra. The master acted the ghost, and Thoughtless strutted in the character of Sarsfield. But to be brief with matter not much in point, he became enamoured of the glorious profession of arms, and having neither interest nor friends to enter the army as an officer, he determined to hew a way for himself to distinction through the ranks, for he was left to manage his own affairs, his father having crossed the Atlantic in search of fortune in the new world.

These young adventurers, with the other recruits, upon coming ashore at Madras, were marched off, as has been mentioned, to the depôt at Poonamallie, having received two drams of arrack and some biscuit to support them on the way. The first river they crossed, they all plunged into it like ducks, to gratify their longing desire for water, which they thought, in consequence of being so long on a short allowance, the most precious gift of providence. To avoid the heat of the day, they had marched from Choultry plain a little before sun-set, for travelling by night is delightful in India. About twelve o'clock they arrived at the depôt, and slept for the remainder of the night on the parade, with their knapsacks for pillows, it being covered with soldiers who had brought their mats out to lie in the open air, rather than be bitten to madness by musquitoes in the barracks. But next morning they found that the white ants had attacked their knapsacks, and, *mirabile dictu*, had eaten a dictionary belonging to Stanley, and Brookes's Gazetteer, the property of Thoughtless. Their time passed not unpleasantly, however, at the depôt, for serjeant-major Luttrell, a most excellent and worthy man, paid them many marks of attention. But they had dangerous duty to perform in the fort, over three hundred French prisoners; two of whom were shot in an attempt to escape, after having killed the sentinel on the ramparts. These gallant fellows had been taken on board privateers belonging to the Mauritius; and from them, Charles and Frank picked up a smattering of the French language.

CHAP. V.

The monument we here behold with pain,
Is there a heart can from a sigh refrain?
Whose sculptured base commemorates the time,
When the brave Holwell suffered in this clime.
With seven score men it was his wretched fate,
In the black hole a *Soubah's* sleep to wait;
Though dying Britons strew'd the reeking ground,
And many a hero gasped for breath around,
The slavish guards, O horrible! avow,
None dares to chase sweet slumber from his brow!

When the black hole was pointed out to the author, it was almost full of coals; but he viewed it with strong emotions, and rejoiced that millions of people, who have now the watchful eye of our mild laws, guarding their rights as men, were rescued from the tyranny of masters who could strike such terror into their subjects, as to prevent pity from driving away slumber, on hearing the dying shrieks of 146 human beings! And when any man reflects upon the simple order of a Soubah, having the power to trample him under elephants' feet, to throw him to tigers or lions, to hang him up in an iron cage to waste away by slow degrees, or to have his life pinched out of him by exquisite and indescribable tortures, he will set the right value upon trial by jury, and freedom from tyranny.

The monument which commemorates the capture of Calcutta in 1756, by Surajah Dowlah, is hastening fast to decay, having been shattered by lightning. Being an obelisk of considerable altitude, it is one of the conspicuous objects upon which a stranger's eye rests, among the numerous spires, temples, and minarets of the city, which give a pleasing and magnificent variety to the prospect from the river. This noble sheet of water is full a mile wide before the town, and every day ships are seen in full sail on its bosom ; for seven hundred vessels take their departure annually from the Hoogly, with upwards of 150,000 tons of merchandize; and some idea may be entertained by the reader of the busy scene, when he reflects that the trade of Calcutta averages from thirteen to fourteen millions sterling per annum, and that upwards of 300,000 boatmen are employed on the Ganges, in conveying the productions of the upper provinces to the presidency, and circulating the commerce of Europe through the East. Formerly, no trade yielded a more certain profit to the speculator than the latter, and three voyages were usually considered as ensuring a fortune to the captain of an Indiaman. But since the opening of the free trade, the markets have been glutted, and in many instances adventurers were unable to realize prime cost. The imports of Calcutta average from two to three millions, and the exports from four to five annually, and the treasure imported amounts to six or seven millions a year. With the inland trade, which averages five millions per annum, the government reap a revenue from the commerce of Calcutta, of £108,000. The whole revenue of the Bengal Presidency is very nearly ten millions sterling, and the annual charges about eight, with a debt of twenty millions, against which there are assets to a far greater amount, for the dead stock belonging to the Honourable Company in India is enormous. There are about four hundred civilians on this establishment, who receive salaries of from five hundred to four thousand pounds a year. The Bengal army is about sixty thousand strong, and is organized and inspirited by sixteen hundred European officers; and, besides the settlers in Calcutta, there are upwards of two thousand British subjects residing in the interior of this province, as indigo planters, shop-keepers, and speculators.

Much might be said respecting the fertility of Bengal, and especially of the district in the vicinity of Calcutta. The latter is, in short, a perfect garden, and the former the most productive province in the world, yielding not only rice and wheat in abundance, but valuable crops of indigo, cotton, tobacco, sugar, and opium, with silk, saltpetre, and a variety of other valuable productions. There have been various calculations with respect to the population of Bengal, Behar, and Benares, which have been ascertained to give 162,000 square miles, and about 30,000,000 of souls.

But, owing to the extensive deserts and forests, and to the inundations of the Ganges, there is not an acre of arable land for each person.

In a garden house, near Calcutta, the sons of Tippo Sultan reside, with as much freedom as is consistent with the security of their persons. The reader will recollect that they were removed to Bengal soon after the massacre at Vellore, and the eldest has since put a period to his own existence. Although there is a faithful account of the tragedy at Vellore before the public, yet I am sure the reader will be pleased to learn further particulars from a letter to a friend, written by Mrs. Fancourt, whose husband was commandant of the garrison.

This unfortunate lady commenced her account, by describing the happy and tranquil evening she and the colonel had spent, amused with the Hindostannee prattle of their little daughter, a child about four years old. They had retired to repose at a late hour, and some time after were alarmed by hearing a continued firing in the direction of the barracks. Colonel Fancourt started up, and opened the venetians round the bed-chamber, but all was quiet near the house, though the noise of a distant struggle was loud. The long roll beat at the main guard, and a quick firing continued there. The colonel, leaving his lady greatly alarmed, went out to ascertain the cause of the uproar. Soon after, Mrs. Fancourt heard the firing much nearer, and the doors of her house were burst open. She rushed down the back stairs with her child in her arms, and jostled against a man in the dark passsage. "My God!" said she, "who are you?"—"Do not be alarmed, madam," replied the unknown, "I am an officer."—"And, good heavens!" continued the lady, "what is the matter?"—"The Sepoys have risen on us, and are murdering every one. Fly, madam, and save yourself, if possible;" and he burst open the back door, through which the lady escaped unobserved; but at the same moment he fell himself under the bayonets of the Sepoys, who had now made their way through the house. Mrs. Fancourt concealed herself behind a mat in a poultry shed in the compound, the roof of which was broken, and the door almost eaten away by white ants, where she endeavoured to soothe her little girl, who clung to her breast in a state of terror. The firing had ceased, and she now saw the Sepoys carrying her plate and property away tied up in sheets.

Next morning the scorching beams of the sun fell on her through the broken roof, and her little girl began to cry aloud from hunger and from thirst, with which she was herself extremely faint. Soon after a Sepoy, placed as a sentry over the house, heard the child, and discovered her. Struck with pity, he covered the roof of the shed with mats, and brought her a loaf and some milk. Towards evening she heard the approach of cavalry, and soon after the galloppers of the 22d dragoons from Arcot burst open the gate of the fort. Then followed the clashing of sabres, the trampling of horses, the shout of victory, the groans of dying men ; and she was handed from her concealment by the commanding officer of that gallant regiment, who carried her child in his arms into the house. To her anxious inquiry for her husband, she was answered, that he was wounded severely ; but there was hope. "Oh ! take me to him," said the lady, and she was conducted to another room, where, almost lifeless on a couch, the surgeons of the cavalry stood in affliction over him, having dressed his numerous wounds, without the smallest chance of preserving his valued life. Let the curtain drop on the rest, for imagination to paint and sensibility to feel.

After the miraculous escape of our ensign and the fair Nannette, the majestic ship soon weathered Cape Camorin and glided along the beautiful coast of Malabar. The captain of the vessel and his officers paid marked attention during the remainder of the voyage to Mr. True, and his deliverer Frank Stanley. Nannette looked her gratitude, and Monsieur Fortier danced for joy. From the former George learned that she was not the daughter of the latter, but the only child of a British officer killed at the storming of Seringapatam. At that time she resided at Pondicherry, and a close intimacy existed between Madame Fortier, who then lived there, and her mother, who died soon after, leaving her unprotected, with only a small sum of money at interest in a house of agency at Madras. Monsieur Fortier had taken her home. He had no children of his own, and became so fond of her, that she called him with all filial affection, Papa. He and Madame Fortier were amiable. In his youth he had been in the French army; but having acquired some property at Pondicherry, and also a plantation at Mahé, he resigned his commission, and preferred passing the remnant of his life among his palms and pepper vines, to a return to Europe, where the links of early association were all broken. Nannette was, therefore, perfect mistress of her mother tongue, with all those accomplishments which Madame Fortier was so well qualified to impart; and the vivacity and romance of a French education grafted so well on the vivid imagination of an Irish girl, that the fruit produced was of the most delicious flavour.

The scene was now sublime. On one side the blue ocean formed the horizon, while on the other the stupendous ghauts seemed to scale the azure sky. The country appeared in the most beautiful diversity of hill and dale — here covered with thick groves of tall cocoa-nut trees — there laid out in fields and pepper plantations — while the silver streams were seen meandering from the mountains, and the spires of many a church, peeping from the eternal verdure with which they were closely embraced, met the roving eye.

Captain Osborne had orders to land the recruits at Tellicherry, but he lay-to for half an hour near Mahé, and sent Monsieur Fortier and Nannette on shore. While the vessel was nearing that charming spot, George carried the French books he had to their cabins.

"Keep vat I lent you, mon fils," said Monsieur, with a friendly grasp of his hand, "as une petite reminéscence of me, and come and see my garden at Mahé."

He then approached Nannette, and trembled as he entered her cabin door; with much difficulty he said he had come to return Elizabeth, and Paul and Virginia, and he attempted to express his admiration of their contents, and his regret at parting with their owner.

Two crystal drops stood in her eyes, and she said, "Oh then keep these two little volumes which I love, and they will remind you of me."

"Ah," answered the young enthusiast, "can you imagine that I require a remembrancer? But since you bestow on me what you love, I shall strive to prize the valued gift as it deserves, and never shall these dear books leave me but with my latest sigh."

"Since such is your determination," said she, laughing, "I must give you a more portable keepsake; take this," and she offered him a penknife; but drawing it back playfully, added in a girlish tone, "Nay, that would cut off remembrance; here is my picture; and there," continued she, lopping off one of her ringlets with the knife, "is something more, to remind you that when I braid my hair, I shall think on him who risked his life so fearlessly to save mine from certain destruction," and she turned away and wept. But perceiving that George was about to be very tender in his reply, she brushed away the tears and added, "Nay now, *je vous entends* — there is my hand — fare thee well."

He pressed the rosy fingers of Nannette to his quivering lips that could not articulate adieu, and casting a longing, lingering look, retired.

CHAP. VI.

The muse of history wipes the tear away ;
Thy battles, Clive, she shows in bright array.
We trace our empire from where Ganges laves
Bengalia's eastern coast with her blue waves,
To where wide Indus cools the western shore,
And hears the surges of Arabia roar.

Mr. Clive beginning that course of success which afterwards ennobled him, backed by an English fleet under Admiral Watson, retook Calcutta the year after its capture, conquered the armies of Surajah Dowlah, and deposed him from the soubahship; placing his prime minister, Ally Kaun, in his stead, who soon after put his former master to death. But the limits assigned to these sketches will not permit the author to enter into the extensive fields of the history and geography of Hindostan. A very brief notice must therefore suffice.

The whole of this vast region may be said to extend in length, from latitude 8° N. to 35°, and from longitude 72° E. to 92° in breadth. This has been estimated at 1,020,000 geographical square miles ; and the calculation is, that it contains 101,000,000 of inhabitants. Taking in the late acquisitions in the Deckan, Konkan, and Kutch, the British actually possess 400,000 square miles of this territory, with a population of full 60,000,000 of souls; and the East India Company directly controul upwards of 776,000 square miles of India, containing 86,000,000 of men, for the only parts of Hindostan now independent are Nepaul, the territories of the Seiks, and those of Scindea, Holkar, and the Rajah of Berar; but late events have placed these powers so completely under the British government in the East, that our empire may now be said to extend from the Indus to the Burrumpootre, and from the Hemaleah mountains to the island of Ceylon. The western and northern boundaries are defined by the river Indus, and that prodigious chain of mountains that runs almost from China to Persia, eternally covered with snow, and forming a bulwark in many places 22,000 feet high between Hindostan and Tartary. On the south, the Indian Ocean washes the shores, and towards the east, the forests of Tipperah and mountains of Chittagong mark the frontiers. Having thus trespassed as little as possible upon the patience of the reader, the *jog-trot* is again resumed.

Our young adventurers soon joined their regiment at Cannanore, and, after due submission to preparatory discipline, were pronounced "fit for duty," and embodied with as brave a corps as ever charged bayonets. The adjutant, who was a gentleman of Devonshire, of polished manners and good education, seemed from the first moment to distinguish the trio. He shared his bungalow with the ensign, and finding that Thoughtless and Stanley wrote tolerably well, he employed them as his clerks, and invited them to live near him in the office; for, said he, "Your youth may be corrupted by bad company and example in the barracks."

George soon observed that his regiment was full of life and spirit, the effects of harmony and brotherly love. Colonel Mars, who commanded it, had seen much service. Although he was fond of frequent field days, early parades, health marches, and sea bathing, and required the officers and men when out of their quarters constantly to appear in full regimentals, yet he was beloved by high and low; for impartial justice and the public good were the objects he had in view. In attaining which, he blended the *suaviter in modo* so agreeably with the *fortiter in re*, that his conduct was a model for the study of all under him. The mess was finely regulated, and never had George met more generous and gentlemanly companions. Frank and brave, his spirit was congenial with theirs, and he was soon considered a most promising young officer. His high opinion of Stanley and Thoughtless being known, procured for them much regard in the corps, and his brother officers frequently came into the office and noticed them with those winning little condescensions that are so pleasing to soldiers.

It may be presumed, that the admirer of Nannette was not unmindful of Mr. Fortier's invitation;

and the approach of the period for holding the races at the French settlement presented to his ardent mind a favourable opportunity. On the evening previous to the appointed day, he rode with a gay heart, accompanied by the bucks of Cannanore and Tellicherry, to Mahé, which is beautifully situated on a rising ground, skirted with gardens and plantations,on the south side of a river navigable for a considerable distance higher than the town. A comfortable inn afforded accommodation for the night to such as had not pitched their marquees on the esplanade; and at dawn, next morning, the course exhibited the fashion and beauty of Malabar and Canara, while crowds of natives gave life and interest to the surrounding groves of lofty palms. It was a grand sight to see the fleet Arabian steeds, of noble form and mettle, struggling proudly and with arduous emulation towards the goal.

Monsieur Fortier was near the stand, mounted on a grey charger. Nannette beside him in a white muslin riding habit, hat and feather, on a black Pegu poney. "I rejoice to see you, Mr. True," said she, presenting her hand. "*Tres bien, j'espere,*" cried Monsieur, giving him a friendly grasp; — "You breakfast with me, *allons donc.*" "You see what a fine prospect we have from our viranda," said Nannette, upon entering the house through a charming plantation of pepper vines, and a garden —

"Where creeping shrubs of thousand dyes,
Waved in the west wind's summer sighs."

This fine viranda, in fact, went round the spacious apartment to which he was conducted, from the silken ceiling of which a tastefully painted punko was suspended, and the whole had the appearance of a grand canopy, supported by small green pillars of the Ionic order. Green venetian blinds separated the inner square from the viranda, to which there were four folding doors, leading down a magnificent flight of stairs. Gauze screens prevented the admission of dust into the viranda, and gave that nameless charm to the scene that a veil bestows on exquisite beauty. In the rear appeared the majestic ghauts and lovely country; from the left, hill and dale, adorned with groves and interesting villages; to the right, a winding river and the town of Mahé, while the front embraced the placid blue ocean. The sun was at this moment illuminating the whole. A ship, with every sail set, was standing down the coast. The tide was rippling over silver sand to bathe the marble steps leading down the *ghaut* from this delightful garden house. George was lost in contemplating the sweet prospect.

"How lovely! what a romantic spot this is," said he to Nannette, with whom he was left, while Mr. Fortier went to see Madame, for a slight indisposition had confined her at home.

"It is, indeed, a lovely and romantic place," replied she; "and there is a story that gives it real interest in the latter point of view."

"Do, pray let me hear it," said George, with vivacity, for he had a strong tendency to romance.

"When we resided at Pondicherry, a young lady lived here with her father, who was beloved by a gentleman at Tellicherry; in every point an eligible match except in fortune, which the old people admired. The youth often ventured down the coast in a canoe, to serenade her, and attracted her attention from this viranda, where, after the family had retired to rest, she used to sit to see the moon-light, as she poetically said, dancing on the water to the silver tones of her guitar. The bed-chambers are at a considerable distance from this sitting-room, therefore her musical lover in the canoe was never overheard; and at length being fascinated, she descended the stairs, stepped into his boat, which conveyed her to a Syrian church situated in the bosom of a cocoa-nut *tope*, where the marriage ceremony was performed by the venerable high priest."

George could not have articulated a syllable in reply; but he was relieved from embarrassment by the entrance of Mr. Fortier, who conducted him to breakfast.

After an elegant dejeuné, and much agreeable conversation on general subjects, in which Madame Fortier evinced extensive acquaintance with French and English authors, and also with the Persian and Hindoo poets, our ensign, running his fingers over the keys of a piano-forte, said to Nannette, "Do you ever sing my favourite, the Sentinel, now? Memory has often recurred to the pleasure I felt during our voyage in hearing it. The idea strikes me as beautiful."

"Indeed," replied she, "it is a great favourite with me also;" and with an evident inclination to gratify him, she seated herself at the instrument.

THE SENTINEL.

FROM THE FRENCH.

THE evening star in beauty chaste,
Shone mildly o'er the camp of France;
Near which a youth on guard was plac'd,
Who sung thus, resting on his lance:—
Haste, refreshing zephyr, go
And to my friends my story bear;
Say, I watch those fields to shew
That love and glory are my care.

By the foe's dull glimmering light,
In silence see their guards advance;
While to abridge the tardy night,
The Frenchman sings upon his lance:—
Haste, refreshing zephyr, go
And to my friends my story bear;
Say, I watch these fields to show
That love and glory are my care.

The day-star will the fight recall,
When victory shall my fame enhance;
But should it be my lot to fall
And die upon my trusty lance,
Then in pity, zephyr, fly
And to my friends my story bear;
Say, until my latest sigh,
That love and glory were my care.

"I have no doubt," said Mr. Fortier, in the French language, "that such sentiments animate the hearts of many British soldiers as well as French."

"Elevated feeling," answered George, "must be more general in your army than in ours. Merit and bravery under the French government are sure passports to the highest promotion, and therefore great numbers of adventurers, whose education and family are highly respectable, enter the ranks as soldiers of fortune. In our service the army is recruited from the dregs of the people, and it is sometimes difficult in a regiment to find a sufficient number of intelligent tolerably well educated men for non-commissioned officers; and although the road is open to the superior ranks for every deserving man, yet not one in a hundred is ever so fortunate as to get a commission."

"There is something in the organization of the British army," said Madame Fortier, "which is very extraordinary. It appears to me strange that its discipline can inspire such men as compose it with the conspicuous bravery and fortitude in the hour of trial which characterize the English among the nations of Europe."

"The institutions of the British army," replied Mr. Fortier, "are admirably suited to the moral and physical habitudes of its component parts: its discipline inspires passive obedience in the soldier, and haughty superiority in the officer: its dress engenders pride, and gradually raises every man, however low, to self-estimation and consequence in his own eyes — feelings that necessarily produce habitual courage, far preferable to the enthusiasm of our troops, that constantly requires a strong stimulus to rouse it into action. The punishment in your army is well calculated also to awe vulgar minds, not accustomed to reflection ; but it would destroy all energy and public spirit in ours. But, in short, there is a national intrepidity in the British, a constitutional boldness, something like what we admire in a game-cock, that gives you a just claim to be ranked with the most warlike nations that ever existed."

" I am quite sure," said Nannette, " that Mr. True's gallant deliverer, Frank Stanley, is not of vulgar origin." And both she and Mr. Fortier made enquiries respecting his health and welfare.

" There are," said George, " in every regiment in our service, some young men in the ranks of superior connexions, whose extravagance or misfortune ruined their early prospects. In short, the brother of the Earl of Winterton, the Honourable Charles Tunmour, was a private soldier the other day at Bombay."

The conversation then took a general turn ; and George became acquainted with many interesting particulars respecting the manners and customs of Malabar.

CHAP. VII.

The page where Wellesley's glorious name appears,
Is rich with martial deeds of former years;
With mighty plans which from his genius rose,
And crushed or neutralized Britannia's foes.
To Minto then we turn with rapid glance,
And see him wrest the eastern isles from France;
While Russel gains his native land applause,
By shielding millions with her equal laws.

According to Sir John Malcolm, at the conclusion of the Marquis Wellesley's government, the following was the state of India:—The Emperor of Delhi was under the British protection. Secunder Jay, the Subadar of the Deckan, was completely confirmed in our alliance, and maintained a subsidiary force of one regiment of Europeans, two corps of native cavalry, six battalions of Sepoys, and a proportion of artillery.

The complete reduction of the Mahratta Chiefs, Scindea, Baggogee, Bhoonsla, and Holkar, had been effected. The government of Tippo was annihilated, and that of the Mysore family established. Our authority had been completely introduced into the Carnatic. The conquest of Cuttack had connected the territories of Madras and Bengal, and the cession of Guzerat, Malabar, and Canara, combined almost the whole coast from the Ganges to the Indus. The whole of the Duab was in our possession, and the right bank of the Jumna, with a line of petty states, from the mountains of Cumaoun to Bundlecund.

It is not my intention to enter into the rise and progress of this extensive power. One or two observations must suffice. The decline of the Portugese nation facilitated the elevation of the British; and the ability of Lord Clive, Mr. Hastings, and the Marquis of Wellesley, consolidated our conquests into a fine empire. No portion of history is more pregnant with interesting matter. The British had not merely to fight the native powers, but to conquer the French; and instances of valour and self-devotion might be adduced, from the pages of Orme and others, worthy of the most warlike periods of Greece and Rome; for is there in ancient or modern times, an example of greater skill and intrepidity than that recorded of Major Laurence, who in 1753, at Golden Rock, near Tritchinopoly, with 380 Europeans and 500 Sepoys, charged the French battalion under Monsieur Astruck, and routed it, though superior in numbers to his own, and backed by the whole Mysore army and Mahratta cavalry, who made repeated charges up to the very bayonets.

French power, though it continued formidable in the islands of the Mauritius and Java at the end of Marquis Wellesley's administration, had been entirely destroyed, by his amazing talents, on the continent of Asia, and it was left for Lord Minto, during his mild and equitable government, to wrest these last possessions from that enterprizing nation, whose privateers traversed the Indian seas, and captured the pilot vessels at the mouth of the river Hoogly. No British governor general was ever the object of such general admiration among the natives as Lord Wellesley. The vulgar thought him a god; and I have heard some of the classically educated half casts call him the Pericles of England. It is said that such was the activity of his mind, during his important administration, that he hardly ever sat down to breakfast, but walking thoughtfully round the table, recruited nature, and returned to business. He caused the magnificent government house to rise on a scale worthy of his country's glory. To him is due the praise of establishing the college of Fort William, and of discovering those military talents in his brother, which the battle of Assaye made known to England, and which have since astonished the world, and conferred on Ireland the honour of having produced the greatest captain of the age.

British prosperity in India appears, in a great measure, to depend on the ability of the governor general, who is armed with almost despotic power. His talent and conduct may be said to ensure the loyalty of the native forces, and the secure confidence of the inhabitants, that their persons, property, institutions, and customs are held sacred. But, besides the Hindoo and Mahomedan population, there is a numerous class of subjects, called half-casts, who require particular attention. They are excluded from the military and civil service, although many of them are men of talent and education. It may gratify pride, to consider their energies inferior to those of their fathers, because there is a shade of difference in their colour; but man is every where essentially the same, and national superiority seems to be produced by artificial causes. Now, they profess the same creed as we do — our laws are theirs — their passions are warmed by the same education, and their souls expanded by similar references to those land-marks of antiquity that urged their sires to aim at immortality, but they are sunk in their own estimation, by seeing the road to ambition shut against them. Their situation excites pity, which is a dangerous feeling when directed to a formidable and increasing body.

The regular army of India has, during the late war, been considerably increased, and at present it consists of about one hundred and fifty thousand men, thirty thousand of whom are Europeans, chiefly king's troops; for the Company, beside their civil and military servants, have only about five thousand European soldiers formed into five battalions of artillery and three of infantry. Their native cavalry consists of about ten thousand men, remarkably well mounted and appointed, with experienced and active European officers, who have organized and disciplined them precisely on the British system. The infantry is in like manner in a most efficient state. The whole is formed into regiments, each having two battalions, with about the same establishment of European officers as a single regiment in his Majesty's service. Promotion proceeds according to seniority in each corps as far as captain, but the higher steps go by army rank on the presidency to which each regiment belongs. The native part of this fine army, as was proved in the rebellion in 1809, may be employed by designing men for the destruction of government; and principles of a very dangerous tendency were then circulated among the Madras troops by their officers. There seems, however, to be a radical defect in the native organization of the Indian army. The highest rank in it for a native officer is that of subadar, to which he rises from the ranks through the grades of naik, havildar, and jemidar. But a subadar is subordinate to an ensign placed in the company with him. It is the nature of the human mind to look forward to some object; but hope in the breast of a subadar stagnates and produces dissatisfaction, which is communicated to the sepoys; and several instances might be adduced of this feeling in the massacres that have occurred whenever the prospect of change excited them to turn their bayonets against their European officers.

In the European part of the Company's army there is also an illiberal defect: non-commissioned officers cannot rise to the rank of ensign. This exclusion, which is contrary to the spirit of British equality, of course affects the sense of proper pride, and retards the expansion of spirit which would otherwise take place. Many very comfortable situations, however, are open to them, such as those of conductors of ordnance; and several of them having amassed a little money, are permitted to settle as shopkeepers in the interior, where they wear out life with comfort and independence.

Nearly all the native soldiers, with the exception of the Mahomedans, are raj-puts, which term means "offspring of the royal race." This tribe is a subdivision of the grand class *khatri*, of which it is said there are one thousand sects. Bravery, glory, fortitude, generosity, and princely conduct are the characteristics of this cast. They affect the nominal termination of *singh*, which in Sanscrit is "the lion;" an apt symbol of the ferocious courage of this race of warriors.

The natives of India, with respect to the administration of justice, are in the same state as their forefathers under the Mogul emperors, with the additional protection afforded to them by the supreme court at Calcutta, in which they can prosecute any European judge or magistrate for an unlawful exercise of his power. Hindoo and Mahomedan laws are in full operation all over the country. The

Nizamut Adoulut of Calcutta superintends the criminal courts, and the Sudder Dewany Adoulut governs the proceedings in the civil ones. The supreme court consists of a chief justice and two puisne judges, with an establishment of six barristers and fourteen attornies, under the same formalities which exist in this country. Its jurisdiction as an admiralty court extends over the high seas between India and the Cape of Good Hope; and the measure of its operation by land is guided by the limits assigned to the presidency of Bengal, and by native rights and customs. The Hindoos admire our laws, but complain of the attornies as the greatest sharks in the universe. Nevertheless each office may be seen full of Hindoos every day, being the most litigious people in the world; and perhaps there is more moral depravity to be witnessed about the seat of justice in Calcutta, than in any other place on the face of the earth. Sir Henry Russel was for many years lord chief justice of Calcutta, and his impartiality and benevolence secured the affections of the natives to such a degree, that many thousands of them presented him a most grateful address upon the occasion of his departure for Europe; but this great and good man had often to deplore the perjury and profligacy of native witnesses.

One great defect in the judicial establishments in India, however, is, that the supreme criminal courts have such a vast extent of jurisdiction over

Europeans, and the perpetrators of crimes have to be brought from such a distance for trial, before punishment can be inflicted, that the salutary effect of it in prevention is in a great measure lost. A short anecdote will illustrate this. His majesty's 17th regiment of foot was for a long time stationed on the northern frontier, upwards of one thousand miles from Calcutta, and many of the soldiers began to despair of ever more seeing the presidency. From this feeling, seven of them entered into a conspiracy to murder a black man, under the impression, that only one of them would be hanged for the crime; and that in the meantime they would all have a pleasant trip to Calcutta. Accordingly, a musket was loaded, and lots were drawn, and they proceeded together a little way from the cantonment in search of their victim, who was ploughing his field, when he received a bullet through his heart, from the hand that had been armed for his protection. Five of the seven were executed in Calcutta for the murder; and, it is probable, that if a criminal court, having jurisdiction over Europeans, had been near the spot where it was committed, six lives would have been saved to the community, and an enormity prevented, which must necessarily have produced disgust and horror among the native population of the place. There is another defect, a hardship, perhaps an injustice, under which those natives labour who are amenable to the British courts of law. The jury, by which they are tried, is composed entirely of Europeans, and the reader will easily conceive how objectionable this regulation is in several points of view. Every facility is, however, afforded to the inhabitants of Calcutta, in recovering debts from Europeans. Commissioners are appointed, who sit daily, and in whose court a process is followed up, similar to civil bill in this country, but more expeditious in its operation.

When Ensign True returned to Cannanore, he told Frank Stanley the romantic story with which Nannette had amused him; but, added he, "I suspect my fair young lady has embellished a plain tale with a little poetical fancy."

"Confusion to me," said Frank, "but I would offer Miss Nannette a seat in a canoe."

"That is my intention," replied George; "confusion to me, but it is. I shall buy one directly, and get a fisherman to paddle us down the coast. Your flute and my violin will sound delightfully on the water."

"There is Moote," rejoined Frank, "our cook, whose father is a boatman, and the lad was brought up to catch pamphlets and bombaloes, till he thought he could better his prospects by frying them. I am sure he will answer your purpose exactly."

"Come hither, Moote," said George, "and tell me — can you paddle a canoe well?"

"That my business, master," answered Moote.

"Then go quick, Moote, and purchase a large one," said the ensign. "For what will you get one?"

"A gold mohur very large tree canoe will buy, master."

At this moment, a furious rustling was heard between the mats of the ceiling and the *cudjans* that covered the office; and a piercing cry of some animal, in great pain, seemingly throttled by another. Soon after, the mat burst, and a large rat tumbled to the floor, followed by a prodigious snake, as thick as a man's leg, and of great length. George, Frank, and Charles jumped on the cots to avoid the snake, and with their weapons of defence, they began to slash away at the unwelcome intruder; but the rat escaped under the door, and the snake pursued it and was lost in the long grass of the compound.

A beautiful *teerettee*, belonging to the adjutant's establishment, hearing the uproar, came running to the door, followed by her two maids. She was dressed in fine Indian muslin, and gorgeously decorated with jewels, having clusters of pearls in her ears, rings of rubies on her fingers, chains of gold round her neck, and bracelets sparkling with gems on her wrists, while from her nose hung a bunch of precious stones.

Moote, having satisfied her curiosity, coolly observed, "Rat snakes very good, master — thank God, you no kill; master would die, if snake die."

"Confusion to me," exclaimed Frank, "but this is a queer country, where such superstitious notions prevail."

In the stillness of a beautiful night, George's canoe, managed by Moote, was seen gliding down the coast of Malabar, and approaching the charming residence of Nannette. The silver tones of a fine rondeau, by Kreutzer, crept along the dark blue waves, while a moon-beam discovered her seated in the viranda, attentive to the recognized musicians. George's fingers expressed on his violin the emotions of his soul; and Frank's flute formed a fine accompaniment to a symphony, when it ceased, and they sung the following ballad, while George's cremona produced a charming bass.

THOMAS AND SARAH.

Young Thomas, a soldier both gallant and true,
Loved Sarah, bewitchingly fair,
And he made her his bride, for she loved him too,
And they were a most happy pair.

FIRST VAR.

Sweet's the light of the silver moon,
Mild and soft as my Sarah's eye:
Sweet's the zephyr that plays at noon,
Across the bowers where roses lie;
Yet there are joys I more delight in,
For pleasures like these, ah! why should I rove,
True bliss my footsteps to home inviting,
The smile of welcome from her I love.

Kind were those who with smiles would greet me,
Bounteous ever their friendly board,
Roofs where splendid pomp would meet me,
Ne'er the comforts of home afford.
O thou dear spot, my humble dwelling,
My heart beats for thee wherever I rove,
'Tis truly a treasure, all wealth excelling,
The smile of welcome from her I love.

SECOND VAR.

But duty forc'd him from his home to go,
Across rough seas to face Britannia's foe.

THIRD VAR.

While yet I linger on the strand,
Before I quit my native land,
I pen these lines, with trembling hand,
To thee, Sarah.

Brief is the time I have to stay,
Our ship will sail e'er close of day,
And I must then be forc'd away
From thee, Sarah.

Oft times when darkness shades the deep,
And seamen nightly watches keep,
The thoughts of thee will banish sleep
From me, Sarah.

May He who rules this earthly ball,
Whose bounty is bestowed on all,
Let no distressing troubles fall
On thee, Sarah.

In tender mercy he will spare
Our babe, and make him good and fair,
To smile away all anxious care
From thee, Sarah.

Let not my absence give thee pain,
Though I'm compell'd to cross the main,
Soon, soon, I will return again
To thee, Sarah.

Th' unwelcome boat is now in view,
To bear me from my babe and you,
I've only time to say — adieu!
To thee, Sarah.

FOURTH VAR.

Then, with her baby on her knee,
She oft would sing this lullaby:

FIFTH VAR.

Since duty bade my soldier go,
My heart with anguish burns,
In silence will I hide my woe,
'Till he again returns.

From all that used to yield delight,
I now with sadness turn,
And seek the gloomy shades of night,
Then pray for his return.

Both seas and mountains do us part,
He cannot hear me mourn;
Yet well I know his constant heart,
Will languish to return.

The lovely pledge he left with me,
To lisp his name shall learn,
And say, "Dear mother cheerful be,
Papa will soon return."

Then haste my Thomas, quit the shore,
On which you now sojourn,
And make your Sarah blest once more
By greeting your return.

SIXTH VAR.

To love the Fates for once were kind,
He clasps his Sarah to his breast,
And now he guards the infant mind,
And sings his darling thus to rest.

SEVENTH VAR.

The stream of time with rapid motion,
Hath swept a fleeting year away
Into eternity's vast ocean,
Since on thee beam'd the light of day.

May each return of this glad season,
Find thee with health and plenty blest,
And virtue pure, and sober reason,
The inmates of thy youthful breast.

To me thou art the greatest treasure,
That heaven could send to crown my joy;
And no amusement yields such pleasure,
As playing with my darling boy.

I love to see thy brown locks, flowing
Adown thy forehead, soft and sleek,
To mark thy blue eyes, brightly glowing,
And pat thy pretty dimpled cheek.

To see thee like a cherub sleeping,
Secure on thy fond mother's breast,
While she a careful watch is keeping,
That nought disturb thy balmy rest.

Oft from the noisy world retiring,
My tranquil hours thou wilt beguile,
And more my peaceful home admiring,
Since there I meet thy welcome smile.

May God continue thy protector,
Through every period to old age;
And may his law be thy director,
When anxious cares thy mind engage.

May no calamity distressing,
  Thy health or happiness destroy,
But every morning bring a blessing,
  To comfort thee, my darling boy.

After which the boat paddled in silence towards Monsieur Fortier's ghaut, but Nannette waved her hand in token of disapprobation, and having struck with much feeling a few notes of "O say, simple maid," on her piano-forte, disappeared.

"Is not that from Incle and Yarico," said Frank Stanley; "and does not the fair lady say to her lover, that she would follow him all over the world? Confusion to me but she does, and it is an answer to your serenade."

George replied with great spirit, on his violin, "Voulez vous dancer, mademoiselle?" in which he was joined by Frank; and Moote, dropping his paddle, began to dance, and skipped into the ocean, where he swam about for some time, singing "*Tazzee be tazzee, tazzee ta*," while his legs and arms splashed in cadence to the music.

CHAP. VIII.

Now Hastings! England looks to thee for fame,
Time has enrolled thy well established name,
And soon thy worth and wisdom forth will blaze,
With splendour equal to the highest praise.
Were all the great philanthropists like thee,
The dreary world a paradise would be;
For very few are now disposed to aid,
Unless by strongest motives they are sway'd.
O pregnant thought! my friend his silence broke,
And thus his sentiments at parting spoke:
" How true! with surly gesture nearly all
" Receive the needy on this earthly ball;
" O task severe, for indigence to raise,
" A little store for life's declining days,
" Tho' traits of modesty may line the face,
" And education the deportment grace."

The Marquis of Hastings, from the days of his childhood, displayed an ardour for glory. When young, in America, he bravely marched from his entrenchments to meet an enemy vastly his superior in numbers, and with success, which his ability and valour ensured, conquered and maintained his position. Amidst the congregating masses of French columns, in his riper years, he nobly advanced into the heart of the Continent, and safely conducted reinforcements to his prince in the moment of imminent danger; and when his country required his personal exertion at an advanced period of life, he relinquished the ease and luxury of a palace, and the joys of domestic felicity, to expose himself beneath the burning sun of a pestilential climate in the heart of Hindostan. The greatness of his character will thus be recorded in the scroll of time, while its amiable qualities are treasured in the bosom of thousands of his poor fellow-creatures, who owe their prosperity to him; for every man, however humble, who can lay claim to merit, is sure to find in him a friend, ready to hear, and prompt to serve.—

> While memory holds her empire o'er my brain,
> Thy bounty on her tablet shall remain!

Whoever has read his lordship's reply to an address from the inhabitants of Calcutta, on his return to that city, after his glorious campaign, which ended in the overthrow of Holkar's army, and in the destruction of the power held by two most treacherous chiefs, the Nagpore Rajah, and Peishwa, will admit that the late Mahratta war was fraught with perils of fearful magnitude. Had it not been for the transcendant talent and wisdom with which his lordship met them, the effects might have been very different. Scindea would have thrown his whole power into the scale against us. Instead of the combination being destroyed in detail, the united forces of the northern parts of India would have been directed against the Company's possessions, and the war carried into their finest provinces.

The horrible irruptions of the Pindarries into the territories of our allies forced his lordship into this war, which has happily terminated in the extirpation of that horde of plunderers, and in a vast accession to the former stupendous resources of the Company. The origin of the Pindarries is involved in obscurity. They are first mentioned by an authentic historian in the operations of Aurungzebe in the Deckan, in the year 1689. They served under Peishwa Bajeit Row in his invasion of Malwa in 1730, and with Sadishee Row at the battle of Paniput in 1761. After this they established themselves on the banks of the Nerbudda ; and, in the British war of 1803 with the Mahrattas, almost attained to independence on the fall of the latter. When the Mahrattas began to recover strength, and their restless spirits prompted them to look forward with hope to conquest, great attention was paid by them to the Pindarries. These freebooters were in fact considered as constituting a military school favourable to their own purposes, and encouraged by them. Acting secretly by their management, they were divided into two grand corps called "Scindea Shahee" and "Holkar Shahee," and trained to make very long marches. Incredible things have been stated of their movements ; but it is well known that when pressed they marched at the rate of 100 miles in two days, 300 in a week, 500 in a fortnight, over hills, &c., and that their ordinary rate was from 30 to 40 miles a day. They were all mounted on Mahratta horses, many of which were of a small and feeble breed; but their utmost animal energies were excited by doses of opium proportioned to their fatigue. Out of every five Pindarries, two were well armed with spears, swords, and targets and matchlocks, and mounted on strong large horses; the other three were *looterers*, and sent into the villages, while the well organized body remained in array to cover and protect their plundering operations. These two grand divisions of the Pindarries were subdivided into battalions of from 500 to 1000, commanded by an officer called "Thookar," who had under him subalterns called Mohullodars and Targee Walls, commanding smaller divisions of from 100 to 500, or from 10 to 100, according to the exigencies of the service.

Much need not be said respecting the latter part of the poetical head of this chapter. The man who has travelled through life, without being introduced into it by the powerful hand of patronage, and who has had to struggle against that coldness to all the duties of humanity which, as Dr. Gregory assured his daughters, pervades mankind, will perfectly understand those lines that deplore "worth by poverty oppressed." Long is it before a youth, deprived of parental aid, and wandering among strangers, can rise to rank and independence. Every one, even if we give him credit for more than ordinary feeling, has duties to perform nearer home, and says, "I must be just before

LOVE AND DUTY.

O lady fair! the trump of war
Hath summoned me from thee afar;
When honour calls he must away,
Whose faithful heart would never stray
  From love to ought but duty.

  When the battle's o'er,
And by valour we have conquer'd,
  May there be in store,
The girl I love, for me.

  Then will joy be mine,
Remote from care and sorrow:
  Eager to be thine;
Hard fate to march to-morrow.

  Fortune, how unkind
Thou art to mar my wooing;
  Cupid be not blind,
But guard her heart with care.

O lady! let a thought on me,
Whose bliss will be to think of thee,
In absence touch thy gentle breast,
For mine perturb'd will feel no rest,
  Far, far from thee, on duty.

The canoe was put about by the skilful Moote, and the sweet voice of Nannette, accompanied by her piano-forte, was heard:—

Malbroug s'en va-t-en guerre,
Mironton ton ton mirontaire, &c.

Then her lily hand waved the signal of departure, and her faultering tongue uttered —

"Vale! vale! iterum vale! non longè vale."

The dawn of the next day discovered eight hundred gallant hearts in full march. Colonel Mars's grey charger pawed the turf in front; the adjutant on a bay arab in rear. Two six-pounders, a pair of light howitzers with their tumbrils, and a proportion of artillerymen and pioneers were in the centre. In two days the camp was pitched on the bank of the stony river, at the foot of the Poodicherrum ghaut. The rains had subsided on the coast; but this region of mountains was still capped with clouds, that occasionally burst in vivid flashes of lightning and explosions of thunder. Torrents of rain had recently fallen, and masses of water were now precipitated over precipices, forming majestic cataracts. The river was swollen, and it was found necessary to halt next day, in the hope that the floods would be carried off to the sea; for the rocky bed of the river was unfordable, and it was impossible to cross, except by a swinging bridge for foot passengers, constructed by the villagers of Viatore with bamboos. It was thrown over from two high cliffs, between which the roaring floods had forced their way. The bamboos were fastened together with the fibres of the cocoa-nut, and swung upwards of one hundred feet above the foaming torrent. This bridge, just wide enough to admit one man between two coir ropes that ran along its edges, supported at intervals by upright bamboos, danced in air beneath the tread of the dizzy passenger. Here Frank and his friend Charles stood and gazed with awe at the stupendous wonders of nature, proclaiming, as loudly as the thunder on the mountains, the majesty and omnipotence of the Creator.

No breath of air ruffled the leaves of the forests about Viatore. At night, the hisses of snakes sighed fearfully through the stillness of the glens near the camp, and the howls of tigers, wolves, and leopards were heard echoing along the mountains, while perspiration oozed from every pore, under the oppressive closeness of the atmosphere. But next morning the furious torrent had subsided into a silver stream, over which the guns and elephants crossed with ease. The advance-guard was seen winding round the ghauts, tottering up frightful abruptions, and creeping down fearful declivities, where a false step was certain destruction. Then five hundred naked natives were beheld bounding like goats from crag to crag. These mountaineers had been sent by the Coorg Rajah, to assist in getting up the guns and tumbrils; and with pioneers, and working parties of the soldiers, they at length succeeded in hoisting the artillery from tree to tree, letting them down with similar caution, from one perpendicular to another. Seven miles the mighty struggle continued against the difficulties which nature presented in this frightful pass over the ghauts, of which some idea may be formed when it is remembered that the Bombay army, which first entered Mysore through it, were three weeks in transporting fourteen pieces of heavy cannon from the bottom to the top. The ghauts are higher than any mountains in Europe, and justly called the Indian Appenines. They are clothed nearly to their summits with lofty trees.

George reached the end of the pass, and while the head of the column halted for the rear to come up, he sat down on a rock, with his naked breast exposed to receive the cool air that now played upon his heated frame. He saw from this elevation the sea that washed the dwelling of Nannette, and kissing her portrait, that hung near his heart, said to Frank —

> "Place me beneath the burning ray,
> Where rolls the rapid car of day;
> Love and the nymph shall charm my toils,
> The nymph who sweetly speaks, and sweetly smiles."

And Stanley answered,

> "O could I hope that war's ennobling toils,
> Would clear away what now the prospect spoils;
> That time would grant the girl I love to me,
> How fortunate and happy I should be."

"But confusion to heroics, and all sorrow, and thinking," added he, and he sunk into his usual tranquillity of soul.

They now saw the elephants winding up the ghauts, loaded with tents, and beheld their sagacity and caution with wonder, in situations where a single false step would have precipitated their vast carcases some hundred yards from the road into an abyss below. Their attention was also directed to the bullocks, loaded with trunks, creeping with surprising success up places where a beholder would suppose it impossible for them to climb, and sliding down other steeps almost perpendicular, while the officers' horses, conducted by their grooms, could scarcely keep on their legs. An Indian hermit, who lives in a cave in this pass, was an object of curiosity to every eye. He was naked. His body and face were painted with chalk of different colours, while his eyes glared from their deep emaciated sockets. A long brown beard hung down over his breast, clotted and matted with ashes falling on it from his head, the reddish hair of which almost reached to the ground. His habitation appeared to be a cavity formed by the fall of an immense fragment of rock, dislodged from an overhanging part of the stupendous mountain, under whose threatening brow he resided. It had bedded itself partly in the earth, and on other rocks, and the old man had made a door of wattles, and a fence of thorns, to keep off wild beasts. A clear stream ran through the cave. The hermit lived on the contributions of travellers, in return for which he performed his devotional exercises, counting a string of large wooden beads that hung round his neck, and scattering wild flowers, red paint, and oil on an idol cut out of the rock, while he prayed aloud for the success of their journey.

From their rocky seats, Frank and his friend Charles saw the clouds flashing lightning and bellowing forth peals of thunder far beneath them. The air then becoming clearer, a vast prospect opened of green waving trees, successively receding from their view, in a gentle undulation, instead of that abrupt steep which they expected to contemplate from the head of the Poodicherrum. Nothing could be more beautiful than the silvery appearance of the rivers, winding through the provinces of Malabar and Canara towards the sea, and disclosing themselves like veins on the transparent bosom of loveliness.

" Can it be the deception of distance," said Charles, " that makes azure masses of light and shadow of the huge ghauts over which we have crept, and gives the sea-girt shore that charming and varied appearance, which imagination never before formed to my mental eye."

" Yes," answered Frank ; " and a similar delusion delights us in the prospect of human life."

" Do you think," added Charles, " if our friend Mr. True had Nannette, you Sarah, and I my own simple Mary, in some delightful rural spot at home, with competence and health smiling upon our happy dwellings, that a wish would remain, or that distance would seem pregnant with greater felicity."

His reflecting English friend shook his head, and, with the characteristic solidity of his countrymen, replied,

"Intellect says, that weak man looking forward to felicity in an immortal state, cannot find on earth what is in heaven. When surrounded with every terrestrial charm, the restless soul, therefore, creates imaginary wants, and, according to our favourite Roman author, 'to wish is to be still a slave.' Nevertheless, with the aid of the pure religion of our fathers, and the kindness of the God to whom our mothers called in the pains of our birth, we might experience as much happiness as falls within the sphere of human enjoyment. We expect too much, and generally think we receive too little. In short, how could we avoid drawing a bill upon futurity to ensure the possession in another world of those fascinating forms which we are sure must become as lifeless and cold in this as the clay of which they are formed. To lose irrecoverably an object dearer than self, seems almost beyond the balm that religion administers to the sorrows of life."

At this moment approached a group of native horsemen, armed with matchlocks, targets, spears, and swords, and wearing turbans and long quilted gowns. A stout copper-coloured personage, with whiskers and large mustachios, was in front: his legs were cased in military boots that reached half way up his thighs, and a large sabre in red velvet scabbard glittered in gold mountings at his side, while a miniature of Marquis Wellesley set in diamonds and pearls decorated his breast. He was met by Colonel Mars, and surrounded by the officers, whom he welcomed to the Coorg, in broken English. This was no less a person than the Rajah of that country, the firm friend of the Company, and an imitator of our costume and manners. Many of the officers accompanied his highness to his palace, for the purpose of enjoying a profusion of excellent claret and champaign, with a good substantial dinner, in a pavillion which he had erected on the model of one at Brighton, where a fine company of dancing girls were in waiting to amuse his guests.

In the meantime some of the young soldiers who had taken off their shoes and gaiters, were suffering much from the bites of leeches, which had crept up their legs. At first they were not felt, because not much thicker than a hair, but when filled with blood, they became as large as one's finger, and felt as cold as ice. Such men as permitted them to drop off when satiated, scarcely felt any pain, but those who tore them off groaned in torment and bled profusely. This was the cause of much noise and laughter in camp; but some terror was excited upon finding that thousands of black scorpions and snakes were lurking under the stones in the tents, and in the long grass around them.

"Well, confusion to me," said Stanley, "but this is a wonderful country." "Confusion to me, but it is," said Thoughtless; "look here," and a number of naked *coolies* approached, carrying wild hogs, buffaloes, antelopes, tigers, leopards, and mountain goats, tied to bamboos on their shoulders, which had been sent by the Coorg Rajah, as a feast for the soldiers.

The object of the force was to reduce a refractory chief in Wynaud, who, aided by the Nairs, Poligars, and Moplas, had refused to pay tribute, and attacked the collector. Colonel Mars turned to the right, therefore, on passing Rajapet, and entered the immense *jungles* that extend along the back of the ghauts. Although the country lying eastward of these mountains is called the table land, it is not a plain, nor is the surface on a level with the tops of the ghauts. On the contrary, in their vicinity, the country is mountainous, and the plains of Mysore are approached through chains of fine hills and forests of noble timber. From this region of *Tiek* the Company draw their supplies for the manufactory of gun-carriages at Seringapatam. The quarter-master often found it difficult to pitch upon an open space for encampment, such impenetrable clumps of bamboos grew among the trees, each as thick as a man's leg, and as tall as the mast of a ship. Some of the vallies and open tracts in these forests are cultivated, and the wild inhabitants make extraordinary habitations, like nests, in the clumps, consisting of many hundreds of bamboos growing together so closely as to touch, whence by cutting out the centre ones a secure dwelling is easily made, to which they ascend by steps cut in the clump. From these nests a watch is kept over the cultivated spots, and the beasts of the forest are assailed with noise and arrows. The warriors and chiefs of this country, as well as a great part of Malabar, are called Nairs. Hyder Ally was the first Mahomedan that subdued them. After the overthrow of his son Tippo, they were restored to power by the British government; but such was their tyranny over the inferior casts, that it could not be tolerated on principles of humanity. A Nair may approach a Brahmin; but if a Teir came near a Nair, the latter would cut him down; and the murders committed in this way were formerly deplorably great. They are exceedingly expert in the use of the bow, and discharge several arrows at the same time, by means of their feet and hands.

As the force approached the hills of Pollinjol, the advance guard, flankers and rear, were annoyed by showers of these arrows whizzing from invisible enemies. Had an inexperienced officer commanded, the casualties would have been very great; but Colonel Mars advanced with such caution that he baffled every attack. Advantage was taken of the wind, and the jungles were set on fire. The scene was awfully grand, for the flames flew like lightning through the dry underwood and long grass. Wild elephants and tigers were heard crashing the forest in their flight; while the yells of such Nairs as were overtaken in the nests from which they fired their arrows were appalling; but the Poligars and Moplas, who were making common cause with the Nairs, seized every height, and fired rockets upon the force. These are tubes of iron filled with combustibles, and tied to a long bamboo with thongs. A charge of powder carries this through the air, in the direction it receives, to a prodigious distance, and it bursts with awful noise, while the bamboo forms circles when the rocket lights, and destroys every thing in its way. Fortunately, its fiery course through the air, where it forms a beautiful bow like a falling star, and the noise of its approach, are such, that soldiers can easily get out of the way. Nevertheless, great confusion was produced on the baggage flank by these frightful weapons. All opposition on the part of the enemy was, however, unavailing; one position was assailed after another, and such destruction was caused by grape-shot and shrapnel-shells, that the chief of the table land gave up the contest, and Colonel Mars re-established a strong post in a fine stockade near Mamentoddy, the beauty of whose situation, though deformed by war, was striking.

The force, therefore, having succeeded in its operations above, now descended the ghauts, through the Cooteady pass, which was obstinately defended by the Nairs and Moplas, who had a strong mud fort at the bottom. Acquainted with the difficulties the force had to encounter, the enemy occupied every rock and tree, firing upon the line incessantly, as it was creeping and winding slowly along. Several brave fellows had their arms pinned to their sides, and their bodies and limbs pierced; but the military skill and perseverance of Colonel Mars overcame every thing. He had foreseen the nature of the service, and provided plenty of doolies; and the collector had such influence over the coolies, that very few of them deserted. Night, however, overtook the force about the middle of the pass, and it was obliged to bivouac till morning. The scene was tremendous. Showers of arrows and rockets fell around the out-posts during the whole of this struggle, which the darkness of night did not interrupt. The ghauts appeared in a blaze, and the roar of artillery and musketry among such masses of mountains may be conceived, but cannot be described. Camp fires were lighted, and the commissariat being in fine order, the soldiers received their drams and rations with the utmost regularity; and Colonel Mars, with his own eyes, after securing his position near the river in a sort of valley, saw that the wounded received all possible attention. Next morning he reached Cooteady and invested the fort, which he determined to take by escalade.

Ladders of bamboo were accordingly constructed, and the force went down to storm the place at daylight next morning, the defences having been all destroyed by the six-pounders. The guns opened on the great entrance, as if the main attack was intended to be made there against the gates and sally-ports. But Colonel Mars had in the meantime formed the regiment into three divisions, one of which now made a false attack with a howitzer on the opposite quarter, and an alarm was given that the English were mounting the walls. The *gingals*, bowmen, and matchlocks were all hurried by the killedar to that face, and opened a tremendous fire on some stone pagodas, and thick hedges, behind which the colonel had ordered Captain Steel to post his men, with a discretionary power to act according to circumstances. Major Forward, with the second division, wheeled to the left under the wall, and placed his ladders against a weak angle, the loop-holes of which were destroyed; while Colonel Mars, with the grenadiers and light infantry, carried an out-work on the right. The killedar, upon discovering the major's position, hastened thither distracted in his mind; but before he could reach that point, Frank Stanley and several grenadiers had mounted the parapet; and Colonel Mars, who was one of the first on the wall, waving his sword, exclaimed, "My brave comrades, follow me;" and he hastened to turn the garrison from the second division, that would have been otherwise exposed to a murderous fire. Captain Steel observing that the killedar had withdrawn numbers of the garrison from his face of the fort, determined upon co-operation with his commanding officer, and Ensign True was one of the first that mounted the ladders. Major Forward had now gained the ramparts, having been nobly aided by Charles Thoughtless, who volunteered to lead the forlorn hope; but the Nairs, seeing that they were attacked on all sides, were struck with panic terror, and, throwing themselves over the walls, were either dashed to pieces or escaped into the woods.

The Moplas, having now become sensible of the hopeless part they had espoused, made the best terms possible with the collector, and the whole country was in a few months restored to obedience and tranquillity. Colonel Mars returned with the force to Cannanore, after making a demonstration through the province; and in marching past Mahé, George perceived the well-known lily hand of Nannette waving from the rear viranda, as she recognized him passing mounted on his bay Arab, for he, Frank, and Charles had escaped unhurt, or in poetical language, the shield of love and friendship had protected them from arrows, Nairs, Poligars, Moplas, and rockets.

Panama and her two *ayahs* ran out to express their joy at seeing the adjutant return rosy with health and toil; and Moote, as soon as he had prepared some fish, rice, and coffee for Charles and Frank's breakfast, made his *salam*, and went to see if the canoe was in safety.

CHAP. IX.

Ye palaces, where *bobberchees* excite,
For luxuries, the languid appetite;
Say, why Dame Fortune fills a tailor's sail,
While science is the inmate of your jail?
Say how attorney's wives can ape the great,
Loll in barouche or sociable in state?
How coachmakers can hoard up *crores* of wealth,
And dancing-masters chariots keep for health?
How auctioneers and stable boys can lay
A *lack* up safe to cheer a rainy day?
While oft the book-taught skill of Greece and Rome,
Finds in this burning clime nought but a tomb!
Nay, e'en the dregs of Gunga's sable race,
Gratuitously false with callous face,
Who lend their gold at ninety-nine per cent,
And pocket half the *mohurs* which they lent,
Soon cease on fickle fortune to depend,
While learning pines without a single friend.

A GOOD table is not considered enough in Calcutta; it must groan beneath the weight of every thing in season, and the native cooks are very expert ticklers of the Epicurean palate. The usual routine of living in Bengal is similar to that at Madras, but much more gorgeous. After morning exercise breakfast is taken, which consists not only of tea and coffee, and the light accompaniments usually served up in this country, but of highly spiced meat, fish and fowl, with all the varieties of fruit produced in that garden of the East, and preserves, ices, and jellies in endless profusion. Perhaps there is not in the world a greater delicacy than the mangoe fish of the Hoogly, which is as beautiful to the eye as it is delightful to the taste. With the flavour of the mangoe, which is an uncommonly fine fruit, it combines the colour and richness of the trout, and has a fine large roe which cannot be compared to anything, being a perfect original. For two months in the year this charming fish is caught in plenty, and the roes are preserved, and always appear at table. The mangoe fish is as large as a trout, and in the estimation of a gentleman who would have done honour to the court of Heliogabalus, is worth a voyage of fifteen thousand miles. "The mangoe fish," said he, with a smack, "ah! the mangoe fish! the mangoe fish is worth coming to India for." Tiffin consists of heavy joints, and numerous dishes and stews, and pies and minces, with capital Madeira, Hodson's pale ale, and Maxwell and Key's claret and cherry-bounce. The carriage, buggy, or *palkee*, parades the course after siesta, and dinner is a grand display of all that can be conceived of eastern luxury. *Tatties* produce air, and *punkoes* circulate it, while chandeliers and table shades, reflecting wax lights, convert night into day. Bengal is the region of hospitality. There is something in the sun of the East that warms and opens the heart. Large parties generally sit down to dinner. Every thing that can be conceived is put on the table, with *curries*, *palows*, and *mulligatawnies*. Claret and champagne circulate, and song and good humour prevail. But ambition among the ladies to give the tone to society pervades the higher ranks to such a degree, that all over India Europeans form into parties, as if the institution of Brahma's casts produced a change in their nature. There are numberless exclusions from society in Bengal, and perhaps rank, precedence, and etiquette are not so much attended to at Carlton palace as in the Chouringhee.

Luxury prevails in Calcutta certainly to a greater degree than at Madras or Bombay. The Bengal officers are called "Qui hies," from the number of servants they keep, it being usual when they want attendance to say, "Qui hy — who's there;" but the Madras bucks are nick-named "Mulls," from a poor broth common in the Carnatic, which the Bengal gents pretend to despise, though it imparts a very pleasing flavour to rice, under the name of mulligatawney; and the Bombay officers are called "Ducks," in allusion to an insipid kind of fish, very plentiful on that coast, which is known by the name of bombalo, and much used as a relish at breakfast throughout India. These may be always seen swimming near the surface of the sea on the Malabar coast, and they are called "ducks," which has been transferred to the Bombay officers by the wits of the supreme presidency.

It may be supposed, from the lines at the head of this chapter, that the humble stations of life are sneered at by the author; but far be it from him to despise any honest man. Has not the tailor cause to be contented with his lot, and who should mock his calling? Seated cross-legged on his board, he may sing and stitch away, with not a fear but that of pricking his finger. His seam will keep his thoughts fixed at home; and if they wander in moments of relaxation, they may rest upon what gratifies pride and ambition every where, namely, that the habit he is making will surpass all others in elegance of cut, and raise his fame above every other tailor in the land. When industry has elevated him to wealth, he may place his needle, thimble, and sheers in his coat of arms, and instead of exclaiming, "Sink the tailor, father," he may rejoice, and let folly nick-name him "the seventh part of a human creature," for

> "Worth makes the man, the want of it the fellow,
> "The rest is all but leather and prunella."

The lower conditions of life are pregnant with considerations which produce contentment. As the modest primrose peeping beneath the fragrant thorn feels not the angry winds of heaven, but on the contrary is sheltered from the storm so it is with the humbler classes of society. While our sovereign, on his glorious throne, feels ten thousand anxieties for the repose of his dominions, the artisan has nothing to fear but that his business may suffer if his mind wanders to the political affairs of Europe.

In short the author's own profession may be adduced as an illustration of the happiness to be found in the lowly walks of life. Every peasant in this free state enjoys more individual liberty than any officer in the British service, all of whom, from the general to the ensign, are subjected to the summary punishment of death, by military law, for even the disobedience of an order. They strut about in times of relaxation, with all those glittering trophies of dress, which, while they feed vanity, produce self-respect and proper pride; they feel the dignity resulting from acquired valour, and are from appearances viewed by many as most happy fellows. But how few can contemplate the reverse of the picture, and see these men under the rigour of command, forced to bear the whims of immediate superiors, who are, like all other mortals, a mixture of good and bad, weak and wise, vain, ridiculous, proud, and haughty; invested by the nature of military service with almost despotic sway; see them obliged to march to-day and to halt to-morrow; now to encounter the scorching rays of a tropical sun, and again to freeze under wintry skies; here flying to the rear to repel the charge of cavalry, there rushing to the front to meet the blaze of masked cannon; and, after war and climate have tried their mettle, sitting down in some town in idleness, under all the temptations of vicious pleasures, from which poison more victims sink than from the fire of the enemy. If we were seen thus, we should not be objects of envy even to a citizen's apprentice.

What has been said is applicable to attornies, coachmakers, livery-stable-keepers, and dancing-masters:

> " Honour and fame from no condition rise,
> " Act well your part, there all the honour lies."

The Hindoos flock to the attorneys of Calcutta, some of whom are thus enabled to live in a style that a nobleman would not despise in this country. Barristers in India, who become popular, generally make a moderate fortune in seven years; but some successful attorneys have feathered their nests in three short annual revolutions. It will easily be conceived how profitable the business of an auctioneer is in Calcutta, where a constant transfer of property to a prodigious amount is taking place every day. Some of the partners in the firm of Tulloh and Co. have come home with princely fortunes. Coach-making in such a luxurious settlement is also very lucrative. But, in short, no profession is more so in India than that of a dancing-master, on account of the great numbers of half casts, among whom, particularly in Calcutta, there is a rage for this amusement. There are eight or ten schools for young ladies in the city, at which exhibition balls are given sometimes twice a month; and as many seminaries for boys on a large scale, at each of which the dancing-master receives £2 per month for every pupil, so that he soon makes a fortune. Two hundred and fifty scholars yielded Mr. M'Donnel £6000 per annum; he built a palace and kept his carriage; while several very learned and ingenious Europeans pined in the jail of Calcutta for debts contracted to save them from starving. There is not in the world a worse field for an adventurer out of the civil and military service, who has no profession, than India; all situations in public offices being occupied by natives, except those which can be procured only by interest or length of service in some department under government.

There are no Jews in Calcutta, because, as has been often jocosely said, a *shroff* or *sircar* would out-Isaac Isaac; and therefore, without detracting in the least from the respectability of many Hindoos, it may be said, with great truth, that the dregs of the people are in the most deplorable state of moral and civil degradation; truth is not in them; and they are so addicted to gratuitous falsehood, that an inferior is generally cautioned, "*Such bola.*" — A witness may swear with the *veidan* on his head, and his right hand in the water of the Ganges; but no judge would believe him who had experienced the perjury common in every court of justice. When a young civilian arrives from Europe, he generally falls into the hands of a shroff or sircar, who supplies him with money, in the hope of touching the perquisites when his debtor shall attain political power. Many an inexperienced youth has been involved in embarrassments by the cunning of these sharks, so as never to get extricated without disgracing either himself or his country by winking at the most flagitious practices. Formerly the evil was deplorable; but it has met with a considerable check in the regulations recently adopted by government: still it continues, and probably will, although in the world there are not civilians of more integrity and elevated feeling than the Company's servants. The trial of Mr. Bristoe at Bombay is well worth the reader's attention, not merely for the eloquence displayed by the advocate-general, but on account of the picture of human nature which the proceedings discover.

That passion which the poet calls the "*amor sceleratus habendi,*" stimulates the inferior orders in Hindostan to the most wicked ways of acquiring riches, as an all powerful means of propitiating the Brahmins, whose influence over the vulgar is incredible. With them heaven may be purchased for money, and all the pains of pilgrimages to ensure happy transmigrations avoided, by endowing pagodas with the fruits of extortion and knavery.

A golden key opens the way directly to the celestial sanctum sanctorum of the Hindoos. All their gods are accused of the most flagitious crimes, and their worshippers scruple not to follow examples so seductive to human nature. But it is amazing that man's intellect can be crazed and bewildered to such a degree as to believe the most palpable absurdities, which are respected as genuine truths by the mass of Brahma's followers. These credulous people are in the same state of mind as Perriwinkle when conversing with Colonel Feignwell. The old virtuoso believed that the traveller knew to the breadth of a hair what quantity of combustibles the sun burns in a day, and how much of it turns to ashes, and how much to cinders. A Hindoo, when his Goru tells him a monstrous thing, may shake his head and say,

"This is marvellous strange."

But the fat Brahmin shows him the polufloisbois, and the moros musphonon, and becomes as invisible as if he wore the ring of Gyges. The Hindoo account of creation may be cited as an illustration of this credulity.

In the beginning there was a woman created by the thirty thousand millions of gods in the fourteen heavens: she was called Paraxacti, and became the mother of three sons, Brahma the creator, Vishnu the preserver, and Sheva the destroyer. Brahma produced the four casts; the Brahmins from his head, the Khatris from his arms, the Vyases from his body, and the Soodres from his feet. He formed fourteen worlds, equal to the considerable parts of his body, and in imitation of the number of heavens. The three brothers agreed to marry their mother; but Brahma afterwards fell in love with his own daughter, and endeavoured to persuade her to become his wife. She was unwilling to comply; but he transformed himself into a stag, followed her into a forest, and effected his purposes by violence. His brothers, in an assembly of the thirty thousand millions of gods, accused him of the crime; it was determined that he should be punished by the loss of one of his five heads, and Sheva tore it off with his nails.

The reader will recollect that at the head of the Poodicherrum ghaut Charles Thoughtless had talked fondly of "his simple Mary," which no doubt produced some surprize, no mention having been previously made of that fair maiden. A few words will, however, make what seemed mysterious perfectly intelligible. Charles, upon rising to the rank of pay-serjeant, had found his society courted by the European shopkeeper of Cannanore, who had an eye to the sale of heel balls, shirts, and nankeen for the use of the soldiers, and he was invited to a party at his house. Mr. Morris was a very agreeable young man, and lived in good style on the bright sandy beach, having the cool ocean in front, the fort of Cannanore to the right, and cocoa-nut groves to the left, while the town was seen from the rear. The evening was serenely beautiful, and they sat in the front viranda with telescopes, watching the distant objects. "There," said Morris, "are the ladies. That elderly dame is the deputy commissary's wife of Mangalore, and that young creature tripping by her side is an orphan whom she has educated, having no children of her own; the other is Mrs. Victory, the conductor's wife; and that dandy is a Mr. Rodriguez, who plays well on the violin, and has a situation in the pay-office at Tellicherry." The graceful form of the young female had fixed the attention of Charles, whose telescope gave her the appearance of an angel, and she was immediately surrounded by all the graces and loves that the warm imagination of boyhood confers on a pretty girl. She wore a turban, beneath which her dark tresses played upon a fine complexion, while the infant swell of a lovely bosom gave to her tripping step the interest of maturity, with the playfulness of childhood. In her eleventh year, she was just displaying that fine expansion which the female form in India then discovers, and her modest retiring look seemed to avow some consciousness that she was a half-blown rose. Before Charles heard the music of her voice, or saw the pearls that seemed to enhance the lusciousness to her lips, his fancy had endowed her with every accomplishment. A sweet temper beamed in her smile, chearfulness lodged in the dimple of her cheek, and he discerned mirth lurked in the arch glance of her eye, yet restrained by the charming timidity of virgin simplicity and confined education; for knowing she was merely on a visit here, he considered her as just emerged from the solitudes of Mangalore. — Such is the delusion of a youthful mind.

Nothing could surpass the harmony of the evening. Conductor Rogers, with his Irish wit, and no brogue "*at all at all*," delighted the company, while the young Portugueze shewed his shape and played the fiddle, and Charles spouted the battle of Aughran, "Behold, brave Sarsfield, in our camp we lie;" — Morris sang, "When the heart of a man is oppressed with care;" — Rogers gave, "My sweet pretty Mog, your'e soft as a bog, and wild as a kitten;" — Victory amused the ladies with "Poor Miss Bailly;" — Charles, upon being pressed, quavered "Love and glory;" — and the pretty young Mary, after several hems, warbled "While pensive I thought on my love," which electrified the dandy, as he burst his stays in making her a bow to the ground. In short, Charles asked Mary how she liked Cannanore. "It is a charming place," said she. — "Then, perhaps, you would like to remain here," observed Thoughtless, half angry with himself for being so bold. — "That may not be," replied Mary. — "It entirely depends upon yourself," continued the rash boy. — "How, pray?" enquired she, quite unconscious of his purpose. —

" Will you marry me?" answered the young dog, with characteristic abruptness. She blushed — but with the frankness of an unsophisticated heart, said, " You may ask my mother;" for she called her parent by adoption that tender name. After escorting " his simple Mary" to the fort, he returned home to build castles in the air, and write verse about genuine love and connubial felicity.

What rapture must pervade two honest hearts,
If fond affection sympathy imparts?
When Hymen's golden chain unites those hands,
Whose souls are linked by nature's stronger bands.
And oh! if offspring bless the happy pair,
What dear delight with them each joy to share;
To see the darlings smile, to hear them talk,
In half-form'd sweet words, and attempt to walk;
The father clasps the prattlers to his breast,
The mother smiles to see her dears caressed,
And feels those joys that cannot be expressed,
Hangs round his neck, and gazes on each face,
Where strong resemblance her affections trace;
Such scenes as this from genuine love must flow,
That none but they who love can feel or know.

Poor Charles was now a smitten deer. He consulted with his friend Frank, after he had made up his mind on the subject. To his benefactor, the adjutant, he also imparted his intention, begging his advice on a subject of such importance. " I expect my company shortly," said that worthy man, " and shall then go home on leave. I have your interest much at heart, and it is my intention to recommend you for an ensigncy to a friend who is high on the commander-in-chief's staff. Marriage at your age seldom turns out well, and it may ruin your prospects in the army. However, it would be injustice on my part to throw any obstacle in your way. My wish is to forward your views, consistently with your own plan of happiness, which I wish with all my soul you may realize." Full of gratitude, Charles made but a feeble reply. Seeing however that his intention of marriage was displeasing to his benefactor, he formed a resolution of conquering love, and intimated his determination to the adjutant. He was not aware how futile his endeavours were against such an opponent:

> *For* he who stems a stream with sand,
> And fetters flame with flaxen band,
> Has yet a harder task to prove,
> By firm resolve to conquer love!
>
> *Lady of the Lake, Canto* 3*d.* 28.

He was obliged to succumb. Proposals were formally made and accepted, and there being no delays of law, the day was fixed, the turkey killed, and the ham boiled, the wedding dinner being provided by Mr. Rogers, who was bride's man, when the aforesaid order to march against the Nairs of Wynaud retarded the completion of happiness for some time. On the return of the force therefore to Cannanore, arrangements were made without delay, and the Reverend Mr. Dunsterville performed the ceremony with gravity, and drank the bride's health with spirit. The kind adjutant had built a neat bungalow for the young pair ; and after dinner, it was warmed with a dance, and a profusion of excellent old Madeira, sent by Captain Solomon, with a note to Charles, expressing his wish that the union of that day might be crowned with felicity during a long life.

CHAP. X.

They may dig *Tanks*, plant *Topes*, and *Lingums* raise;
Pay servile Brahmins for base fulsome praise;
Champo the body into sleep profound,
While *Nantchees* dance in wanton maze around,
And *Punkoes* wake the dozing atmosphere,
And *Bheesties* cool the *Tatties* for more air.
But on his fate with pity I look down,
Who sells the smile of conscience for her frown;
He blinds internal evidence of right,
And glooms his bosom with the shades of night.

In such a hot climate as India, to lay out wealth in constructing reservoirs for water is considered pleasing in the sight of God, and enjoined by the Brahmins as a propitiation for sin. The *Gorus*, to whom the Hindoos confess, never fail to urge them to the erection of charitable monuments, from the execution of which the Brahmins derive great profit, without the appearance of actually receiving money; for the sums devoted by repentance are laid out by the priests of some pagoda in general, who therefore make it their study, first to inflame the passions, and then to rouse the terrors of remorse. Many of the tanks in India are magnificent sheets of water, with fine flights of stairs leading from the embankments to the bottom. To plant shady groves is, in like manner, a delightful exercise and a sacred duty for the wealthy; and fine topes of fruit trees give a beautiful aspect to the parched surface of Hindostan. The erection of pagodas is deemed another propitiatory act of great efficacy, and some of these structures are so noble and gorgeous as to astonish Europeans, who have seen the finest specimens of ancient and modern art. Those temples, in which the ceremonies are performed for barren women, are called Lingums. In Hindostan the greatest misfortune is to be childless; the second, not to have a son to perform certain rites after death. Ladies, therefore, not blest with children, being sure of losing the affection of their husbands, who are at liberty to supplant them by other wives, perform pilgrimages to celebrated Lingums, and enrich the Brahmins, in the hope of prevailing on heaven to take away their reproach. Powerful indeed must be that feeling in the female breast, which could induce Sarah to give Hagar to her husband, could urge Rachel to say, "Give me children or I die," and Leah to rejoice, "Happy am I, for the daughters will call me blessed." But in India the same natural desire is greater, for the agony of husbands is rendered by custom even more intense than that of Abraham, when he said, "Lord God, what wilt thou give me, seeing I go childless." It is said that the Lingum temples conceal scenes of the grossest moral depravity.

The practice of champoing, previous to the

afternoon siesta, is very general among the Hindoos and Mahomedans. It is done by kneading and rubbing with the hand the limbs and body. Sensations are produced something a-kin to those ascribed to a warm bath. The nerves become relaxed, and a pleasing something, like the soft vapour of sleep, steals over the person under its operation. Many of the Hindoos of luxurious habits get this performed by the soft hands of females, who sit beside them on rich carpets, while they lie reclined on silken mattrasses. The idea of these attendants rubbing an old man's legs and arms, cracking the joints of his fingers and toes, and pulling his chin, ears, and nose, may cause the reader to smile, but the custom is thought no more of in India than that of a maid washing her master's feet in this country. During the operation, *bhauts* entertain the opulent Hindoos with stories, and nantchees with song and dance, so that the luxury of a nabob, lying thus under a punko, producing artificial air, while the apartment is cooled by tatties, surrounded by bards, musicians, and dancing girls, may be easily imagined. It is a melancholy fact that the moral degeneracy consequent on this custom, communicates itself to Europeans, some of whom have had their seraglios, bhauts, and nantchees; there being rooms covered with quilted silk mattrasses, wainscotted or inlaid completely with pier glasses, and decorated in a style too characteristic of their destination. The sensualists of India have innumerable songs, and stories, and plays of an unhallowed tendency. The whole Hindoo mythology is filled with details as offensive to decency as the vile representations that disgrace the walls of their temples; and in the great annual processions of the idols, the object of the Brahmins is, by ceremonials of the same evil tendency, to amuse the people, and corrupt their minds. Volumes might be filled from the popular and absurd accounts of the thirty thousand millions of Hindoo gods, but I shall only venture to abridge the incarnations of Vishnu.

A devil carried away the *Veidam*, and plunged with it into the profound depths of the ocean. The Brahmins were in despair, but Vishnu became a fish, and after a long chase through the caves of Neptune, restored the sacred volume to the priests of his temple. The Hindoos believe there are seven seas in the world, one of which is composed of butter. Upon a particular occasion the gods determined to feast on this, and caused the golden mountain which supports the fourteen heavens to be brought near its shore, over which a snake with one hundred heads was laid to serve them as a sort of ladder by which they could reach the butter. The giants of the earth seeing this, while the deities were descending on one side, caught the snake, and drew it towards them so violently, that the frame of the universe would have given way, had not Vishnu changed himself into a tortoise, and taken the world on his back. In the meantime the snake, pulled by the nose on the side of the giants, and by the tail on that of the gods, was unable any longer to endure the pain, and, contrary to all rules of good breeding, vomited in the face of the former, many of whom were so shocked at his vulgarity that they died. But those who survived fought the gods, and gained possession of the sea of butter. Upon which Vishnu changed himself into a perfect Venus, and distracted their hearts so completely with love, that the gods were enabled to finish the feast with comfort.

Some time after the creation of the world, the three brothers, Brahma, Vishnu, and Sheva, the latter of whom is often called Rutrem, quarrelled respecting the extent of their power. "Gentlemen," says Sheva, "listen; to end our dispute I shall hide my head and legs where I please; if either of you be able to find them, to him I shall submit; but should you both search in vain, I am to be acknowledged as supreme." Brahma changed himself into a swan, and put his long neck into every hole in the universe, but all to no purpose, till the thistle flower discovered to him where the head was. The feet were, however, still to be found, and in search of these Vishnu became a hog, and rooted up the bowels of the whole earth without success. His next metamorphosis was into a monster. He had formed a friendship with a giant named Iranian, and granted him the favour that no one should be able to kill him by night or by day. The giant thinking himself invulnerable, became a horrible tyrant; but Vishnu rushed upon him in the evening under the shape of a lion, half man, and not only tore him to pieces, but drank his blood. After this he became a dwarf, to punish a giant named Magapelixacravanti, who had abused his power by grinding the faces of the poor. Vishnu requested three feet of ground to build a house for himself and family; but the giant's prime minister, the morning star, suspecting that the dwarf had some treasonable project in view, by the force of magic, glided down the throat of his master when he was going to pour the water of possession on the applicant's hand: this feat cost him dear; for instead of preventing the grant, the king feeling a tickling in his throat thrust a sharp instrument into his gullet, by which his prime minister suffered the loss of an eye. The dwarf being now in legal possession, became so large that the kingdom could not contain the little toe of his foot, and he kicked the head of Magapelixacravanti to hell. Having seen the wickedness of the giants he determined upon punishing them all, and assumed the form of a man named Rameni, who went about the world washing his hands in the blood of tyrants. The last incarnation of Vishnu was into a negro. A king named Campsen had a sister called Exuda, and a magician had predicted that he would be dethroned by one of her children. To prevent this, he put them to death as soon as they were born; but Vishnu was her eighth child, and escaped by being brought up as a shepherd. On arriving at the years of maturity, he raised an army and put his uncle to death. He then married several wives; but remembering the charms of rural life, he furnished himself with sixteen thousand shepherdesses. His next incarnation is expected in the form of a horse; and he is now supposed to be wallowing in a sea of milk reclined on a snake, which serves him for pillow and bed.

These fables are ridiculous in our eyes; but nothing should be esteemed so that has the effect of bewildering the human mind, and upholding such a delusion as the system of Brahminical idolatry. It may amuse the reader, who has never dipped into Hindoo mythology, to hear part of what is related of Rutrem.

He married a princess named Parvardi, daughter of the king of the mountains, with whom he lived a thousand years. His brothers were displeased, and dragged him from his wife, dooming him to an exile on earth, during which time he went about practising all kinds of lewdness. Parvardi went in search of him, and one day while bathing wished for a child, upon which one rolled off with the dew from her forehead, and she called him Vinayaguin. Her husband was greatly surprized upon his return to see this child, but believed his wife's story, and adopted the boy as his son. But his trouble was not over; for his father-in-law, having heard of his debaucheries when in exile, would not admit him to his presence. He however entered the banquetting-hall, where he and the gods were regaling themselves, and tore them by the hair, from the fragments of which a giant rose that disfurnished the sun's mouth of teeth, and left those bruises on the face of the moon which are seen to this day. He killed several of the guests, and threw the head of young Vinayaguin to the dogs; but Rutrem replaced it by fixing an elephant's head on his shoulders so precisely that the veins united. The next transformation of Vishnu proved extremely embarrassing to Rutrem; but it would afford no amusement on recital.

The moral depravity to which the Brahminical idolatry leads, during the early part of life, engenders the keenest stings of remorse in age; and every where may be seen the most wonderful efforts to reconcile memory with conscience. Devotees will perform pilgrimages of five hundred miles on the broad of the back, never rising during the whole time from that position. A penitent will stand on one leg so long as to cause it to swell to a prodigious size. Knives are thrust through the cheeks, so that the blades cross each other out of the mouth, and thus mangled, the penitent lies on thorns exposed to the sun, with his face smeared with sugar to attract flies. Others swing suspended from the rim of a very high wheel by an iron hook run through the tendons of the back for a long time, while the wheel is turned violently round. Many throw themselves under the wheels of the great car in the processions to be crushed to death; and others drown themselves in the sacred rivers, that their bodies may feed alligators, held in veneration for that purpose.

It may be said that the object of these sacrifices is to ensure happy transmigrations; but many of them are made as atonements for sins remembered with an agonized spirit.

That appearance of despising the gifts of fortune so common in India is not always real. Diogenes may be seen every where in his tub; that is, *sanyasees* are numerous, who voluntarily deprive themselves of what are esteemed the comforts of life. They sit every day naked in the sun's glare, covered with ashes, seemingly unmindful of every earthly thing. But many of them have enjoyments at night in the recesses of pagodas, that are enriched by the tributes paid to their self-devotion.

Soon after the marriage of Charles Thoughtless, Ensign True was promoted to a lieutenancy. No young officer had ever passed through this noviciate more respectably. He was esteemed by his superiors, respected by his equals, and beloved by the soldiers. No quarrel nor midnight brawl had sullied his reputation as a good-natured companion and perfect gentleman; for when ruffled by the petulance of others, he had always shown that he wished neither to offend nor be offended; and his intimacy with the worthy adjutant secured him from the company of those who drank *brandy pawny* after their return from the mess. Indeed his common-place book was a proof how much he respected the understanding of his friend and instructor; for he had enriched it by transcribing from his choice collection of books every passage marked by the adjutant's pencil, and had fingered the leaves of Cowper, that gentleman's favourite poet, so much, that he evinced the congeniality of his taste. And it is suspected that an article under the letter E. was an extract from the adjutant's memorandums, the writer not having met with it in any of the works on the art of war. It ran very nearly thus:

As ensign, you have power over the happiness of the soldiers under your command greater than any magistrate possesses for controlling the subjects of our sovereign. Your authority extends directly or indirectly to every man in the regiment; for you may punish to an extent that exceeds the jurisdiction of any justice of the peace without an information before him on oath. If your own liberty be taken away by the articles of war, you gave it up voluntarily, and have no right to murmur; but the sweeping clauses that govern the very manners of an officer, and render him at every moment accountable to a court of propriety for ungentlemanlike conduct, have vested him with tremendous privileges over the soldiers. If you confine them unnecessarily; if you irritate brave spirits by sending them to drills merely to gratify your own peevishness, without any view to the public good; if you brow-beat them, and sink them in their own estimation, or provoke them to forget fear; a word may escape which a court-martial will deem insolent, and your eyes behold the blood of a gallant fellow whipped out of his veins; while such is his firmness of soul, that he bites through a bullet placed between his teeth to enable him to endure the pain, without permitting the escape of a sigh from his heart. But what must be the anguish of his soul in reflecting that a boy was invested with such murderous power over a man. Remember for what General Ziethen was beloved by the soldiers, and why General Wolfe almost adored. They were idolized for generosity, charity, valour, mercy, virtue, and religion. Remember, too, that "every quality which is enjoined by Christianity as a virtue, is recommended by politeness as an accomplishment; gentleness, humility, deference, affability, and a readiness to assist and serve on all occasions, are as necessary in the composition of a true Christian as in that of a well-bred man. Passion, moroseness, peevishness, and supercilious self-sufficiency, are equally repugnant to the characters of both." Remember also to guard against dissipation, into which many a youth is led more by idleness and ennui than by disposition. It destroys the sensibilities of the heart, and debases all the generous and exalted feelings of the soul. Many young men in India delight in what are vulgarly called mid-night-rows, to frighten the poor natives; but this custom will be more honoured in the breach than the observance. Hear how the enlightened Sir James Macintosh addressed Lieutenants Macguire and Cauty at Bombay.

"A soldier has taken up arms to protect the rights of his fellow-citizens, and to preserve the public quiet. He is an armed minister of the laws, and we expect from him a peculiar affection and veneration for those unarmed laws and magistrates for whose protection he has girt on his sword. Every true soldier must have too great a reverence for the noble virtue of courage to sully and degrade it in the wretched frays of sottish ruffians: it is reserved for nobler objects; he will not prostitute it on such vile and ignoble occasions. True fortitude is too serious, too grave, too proud a quality to endure such degradation. Such vices are most unofficer-like, because they are most ungentleman-like. As long as courage continues to be one of the distinctive qualities of a gentleman, so long must the profession of arms be regarded as the depository and guardian of all the feelings and principles which constitute that character. A gentleman is a man of more refined feelings and manners than his fellow men. An officer is, or ought to be, peculiarly and eminently a gentleman. But there is nothing so low and vulgar as the fame of a bully, and the renown of midnight brawls; they imply every quality of a highwayman but his courage, and they very often lead to his fate."

Every officer should also bear in mind that whenever he forgets to control himself, and to keep down those offensive qualities of the mind that rouse resistance to authority, he injures the gracious sovereign his master, and wounds the interests of his country, by circulating complaint and dissatisfaction amongst the men, who lose all *esprit du corps* under mismanagement. Men naturally dislike their superiors. Liberty and freedom are inherent in our animal constitutions; but the understanding submits to what reason pronounces a benefit, and gratitude swells the hearts of soldiers with affection towards officers who can penetrate sensation, and govern according to the principles that guide and win them. Clearchus restored order when confusion reigned in his army, by seeming to join with his soldiers in revolt from the standard of young Cyrus, and the latter secured their co-operation in his projects by knowing how to touch the master-key of their passions. Like a skilful musician, he placed his finger on that stop which produced the desired effect. This shows the necessity of learning in youth how to command in age. Nothing can more finely inculcate the importance of study than many parts of Santa Cruz. "Alexandre appelloit les œuvres d'Homère, qu'il portoit toujours avec lui, 'le recueil de toute la discipline militaire, et des actions de valeur.' " "Il vous est fort avantageux," dite Tite Live, "de voir dans des personnes illustres des examples de toute façon, qui vous apprennent à imiter ce qui peut vous être utileet à la république, ou à éviter ce qui n'a eu qu'un commencement et un succès honteux." Aristote dit, "que l'histoire sertinfinement dans les déliberations; parceque pour l'ordinaire les choses futures sont fort semblables aux choses passées." In short, think while you have leisure, that you may know how to execute with promptitude, and let the following books receive your particular attention:—The Bible, Homer, Thucydides, Xenophon, Cæsar, Plutarch, Q. Curtius, Polyænus, Frontinus, Vegetius, Appian, Arrian, Folard's Polybius, Livy's Tacitus, Machiavelli, Gustavus's History, Charles the XII., Campagne du Prince de Condé en 1674, Philip of Macedon, Histoire de Scipio et d'Epaminondas, Turenne's Maxims, Turenne's two last Campaigns; Puysegur, Art de la Guerre; St. Rémy d'Antoni, Santa Cruz, Guichard, Guibert, Mazeroy, Mém. de Fenquire, Reverie de Saxe, Le Père Daniel, King of Prussia, Templehoffe, Lloyd, Histoire de la guerre en Bohême; Military Miscellany, Life of Marlborough, Cambridge; Dirom's wars in India, Dundas; Instructions for Hussars, Seldern; Pleydel's Field Fortification, Mém. de Mouluc, Mém. de Surlaben, Jackson on Armies, Life of Buonaparte, and of Wellington, with the French Bulletins, and the Duke of York's Regulations.

George serenaded Nannette no more, for he was so frequently in her society, and his attentions were received with such frank cordiality by Madame and Monsieur Fortier, that he had golden opportunities of fanning the lively spark of prepossession in her tender breast into a flame of affection, which nothing but the chill of death could extinguish; and the noble generosity of her soul attempted not to conceal that the ardent love he evinced for her was pleasing to her heart. He admired the elegant simplicity in which Mr. Fortier's accomplished little circle lived. Instead of the heavy gorgeous dinners at Cannanore, from which the ladies made their exit soon after the cloth, to leave the gentlemen at liberty to enjoy their claret, the dishes at Mahé were light and proper for a hot climate, cooling fruits were in great plenty, only a few glasses of excellent wine were drank, after which coffee was introduced, and music, drawing, or interesting conversation supplied the place of drowsy libations. The admirable moderation recommended by Horace in the second satire of his second book is well understood by the French in India. They never rise pale and sated from the gross indulgence of pampered palates; on the contrary, their frames are animated by a constant flow of healthy vivacious spirits. There were a few very agreeable families at Mahé. An accomplished Major resided there on his parole, having been taken with his wife and daughter on their passage to Java, who aided Nannette in the scientific parts of music and drawing; and a Monsieur Panouilliers, professor of languages, who attended her in acquiring a knowledge of Latin and Italian, was a most gentlemanly person, and extensively acquainted with general literature. But Nannette was also studying the Persian tongue under a Moonshee, and receiving lessons in Sanscrit from a Pundit belonging to the judges court of Calicut. George was charmed to find Nannette's taste so congenial to his own; her reading was more extensive than his; but such was her delicate attention to the feelings of the human heart, that she concealed her superiority, and permitted one half of the beauties in their morning amusements to be pointed out to her. He joined in all her studies with the ardor of an enthusiast, and Mr. Fortier would often say, while they were devouring the pages of French, Italian, English, and Persian authors, "My children, hæc studia adolescentiam alunt, senectutem oblectant, secundas res ornant, adversis solatium et perfugium præbent, delectant domi, non impediunt foris, pernoctant nobiscum, peregrinantur, rusticantur." He was sincerely attached to the interests of the Bourbons, and having left France before the revolution, he abhorred its excesses; and although he admired the wit of Voltaire, and the eloquence of Rousseau, he detested their impiety and abhorred their principles. Yet as a Frenchman he exulted in the glory of his country, and the fine traits of Napoleon's character had captivated his admiration; but though the conversation often adverted to this interesting topic, no offensive comparison was ever made by either him or the Major; on the contrary, all their praise was bestowed upon British intrepidity, our national generosity, our noble constitution, and the freedom ensured to the press by our glorious laws.

"Ah!" said the old gentleman, "had the Emperor granted liberty to the French nation, which their generous confidence in his conspicuous virtue deserved, he would have surpassed all that was excellent in the character of Alexander as depicted by Rollin; but he is insulting the affection that idolized him, and breaking the spirit that depended upon his kindness."

"His good genius left him," said Madame Fortier, "when he sacrificed to ambition his conjugal affection for Josephine."

"During his rise," said the Major, "virtue was the god of his idolatry; but having never appreciated 'the uses of adversity,' he is infatuated with good fortune, and forgets the moral truth that it is the interest of a king to live in the hearts of his subjects."

"Much might be said," replied George, "by way of apology for your magnificent emperor. In short, major, he might answer you in the words of Dido, '*Res dura, et regni novitas me talia cogunt.*' And perhaps he may yet do all that is expected, when the memory of the past will gild the joy of the future; for it must be acknowledged that he is one of the most singular men that ever lived,—a genius in war, eloquence, and government. In Italy, his rapid combinations astonished all; can any thing be more beautifully pathetic than his letter from Egypt to Madame Bruire on the death of her husband, or more sublime than his allusion to the pyramids just before the battle in their vicinity; and what can exceed the grasp of his intellect in combining the powers of Europe in one centre of co-operation with his projects?"

"Ah!" said Nannette, "as a military man, you are naturally an admirer of the hero, rather than of the sage."

"However," replied the Major, giving George a kind grasp of his right hand, "I honour the man who can see the merit of an enemy, and look forward with anxious hope to those happy days when unrestrained intercourse may subsist between your generous country and ours."

Many traits in this charming society pleased George, and one was the tender attention constantly paid to their wives by Mr. Fortier and the Major, who never went out, even for a short excursion, without kissing their ladies on the cheeks and forehead, which some people may laugh at as a ridiculous custom, and signifying no more than "my love," and "my dear," so common between many a pair who have their private quarrels; yet nothing is ridiculous that contributes to happiness and keeps up harmony and respect, where unceremonious familiarity would be so apt to engender neglect.

George was at first greatly amused with Nannette's Moonshee, who was an old Mussulman with an exuberant beard and of a polished address, but who generally fell asleep while his pupil was learning her lesson. Her good-nature never permitted her to use any expression to rouse the aged preceptor, now beginning to sink under the infirmity of years; but when she encountered any letter so cramply written as to baffle her conjecture at the word, she paused, and the Moonshee, struck as it were by the harshness of silence, would start, and by an explanation enable her sweet voice to proceed, when shaking his head, like the figure of a Chinese mandarine in a toy-shop, he would relapse into slumber, and Nannette would, with a look of compassion, gently reprove George, for being disposed to laugh at the oddity of the contrast between the lovely girl and the dozing grey beard, incapable of enthusiasm in the presence of such beauty, by saying, "You there behold the change wrought by time on mortality, and such will be our portraits in a few years."

"But not with such beards, fair lady, I hope," said he, smiling.

"Your chin may be shorn, fair gentleman," replied Nannette, with a sigh; "but your brent brow will exhibit those wrinkles, and my cheeks that ashy paleness."

"The thought is too melancholy for a jest," answered George, and a tear started to his eye.

But at other times the Moonshee was talkative and well-informed; and the Pundit was such a great astronomer and mathematician, that while Nannette was decyphering the Sanscrit characters, he would lean his head so far back over the chair, calculating eclipses on the ceiling, that his turban would generally fall off and expose his unconscious and closely-shaved pate to the excitement of George's suppressed mirth; for his black beard in that position protruding so much, gave to his sharp features a lengthened appearance irresistibly comic. But when not absorbed in reverie, he was very intelligent, and spoke tolerably good English. He often played chess with George while the Moonshee was attending to Nannette's improvement; but at other times he sat as before described, and the group would really have made an admirable subject for the pencil of Hogarth.

George felt the greatest anxiety to be united for ever to Nannette, and yet he hesitated to make any direct proposal on the subject. Endowed with a more reflecting mind than Charles Thoughtless, he often ruminated upon the importance of marriage, and the prospect of having a family to support on subaltern's pay. In the meantime another monsoon had passed. The rainy season sets in on the

Malabar coast more awfully than in any other part of India. Were it not for the interposition of the ghauts, the whole country would receive renovation by the S. W. monsoon, which brings with it the vapours of the Indian ocean. Its approach is announced by the most tremendous peals of thunder that imagination can conceive, and lightning so vivid and frequent, that night is converted into day by the almost continuous blaze of the rushing electrical fluid. After this awful announcement, which is generally at night, the flood-gates of heaven open, and it rains in torrents for ten or twelve days and nights together, so that the rivers from the Ghauts swell prodigiously, and course with grand precipitation to the sea, sweeping all before them, so that Bartolomeo supposed that the numerous large snakes observed on the Malabar coast were washed from the ghauts by the torrents. The rain having thus continued for some time, there is an interval of showery weather, followed by another dreadful hurricane; and at the end of the monsoon, which continues three months, there is a frightful thunder storm called the Elephanta. No rain falls afterwards for the remainder of the year, except in the vicinity of the ghauts, where showers sometimes occur before the commencement and after the termination of the monsoon on the coast. The monsoon travels at a regular rate northward, and therefore in that direction one climate receives it later than another, and with less violence. When it reaches the Hemaleah range, it turns eastward; so that at Calcutta it appears to approach from the north, and sets in with violent north-westers, which are seen travelling with clouds of dust in the van towards the city, in such an appalling form as to turn day into night, and to prevent all communication during the time of their fury.

CHAP. XI.

Behold the *Sircar* sly, inured to guile,
Mark the persuasive cringe and ready smile;
The blackest vice is easy to the knave;
Bribe him, he sits as silent as the grave;
Lure him with gold, he swears that black is white,
A plunge in Gunga sets his conscience right.

Sircars are the native agents of Bengal, who collect debts and cash drafts for the *shroffs*, in whose establishments they sit on mats with their bags of money, and scales to weigh it, and their books, made of the leaves of the palm, on which with a *style*, the entries are written. Their sons are brought up as *crannies*, and every European gentleman has one of them to keep his accounts. Exposed to temptation, and accustomed from childhood to lying and cheating, almost every sircar is of the character described in the above lines. Such as are intended to go into the service of Europeans, make prodigious exertions in learning to speak and write English. Some of them are sent to school for that purpose; but many pick it up by ear, with the assistance of other natives and a dictionary. It is wonderful how accurately a Hindoo can copy English, without knowing a word of what he is writing. We find how difficult it is to transcribe

Hebrew, Greek, Latin, or French, without being able to read those languages; but many *crannies* will write in our character, which is as different from their own as Hebrew is from English, and copy proceedings in council, correspondence of government, and papers containing intricate researches in science, without knowing the meaning of one word in the whole, or how to spell a syllable. Some of their attempts at fine English, when they advance so far as to become conceited, is truly ludicrous. A volume of malaprop letters might be produced; but one specimen, from Captain Williamson's East India Vade Mecum, may suffice.

The cranny who composed it was left by his master in charge of his bungalow for a few days; during that time a high wind arose and blew down one of the window shutters. He determined upon apprizing him of this, and inwardly rejoiced at the opportunity afforded him of shewing his proficiency in English. Let the reader conceive an office-desk with a cranny seated at it; a dictionary placed before him, with a slate and pencil, and self-exultation in his countenance. He turns over the leaves with a finger and thumb, and an earnestness of countenance that would have done honour to Dr. Sangrado, upon the occasion of feeling the canon's pulse. He shakes his head — rubs the globe of memory — erases the word he had written as fit for his purpose, and chooses another of more learned and fulminating sound. Then he takes his pen and paper, and dispatches to his master what he thinks will truly surprize him :

HONOURABLE SIR,

Yesterday vesper arrive great hurricane, valve of little apperture not fasten ; first make great trepidation and palpitation, then precipitate into precinct. God grant master more long life and more great post.

I remain, honourable Sir,
In all token of respect,
Master's writer,
BISSONAUT MAITRE.

P. S. No tranquillity in house since valve adjourn ; I send for carpenter to make re-unite.

Yet some of the sircars make a very considerable advance towards an accurate knowledge of the grammatical construction of English, and learn to speak and write it well enough for business. The following is an actual letter from a native house of agency, and a specimen of middling composition :—

SIR,

We have pleasure acknowledge yours, 18th instant. Have sent goods cording you order, and hope you find all first quality. We madam supply with money whenever she send us. Your remittance last month received in course, and placed your account. Have looked all place here for white cloth, such you want — none can find — soon as we get shall send next supplies with,

Remain, Sir,
With prayers for health,
Your obedient humble Servants,
HURRUMBO, DASS, SONS, & Co.

But some of the letters received from natives are written in perfectly grammatical language; yet the above is about the standard of general correspondence with Europeans in every part of India where the Hindoos, Mahomedans, and Parsees conduct their business in our language.

The sircars of Calcutta are employed by the shroffs, it is said, to inveigle the young civilians to borrow money. But in most cases every one acts on his own account, though he impresses on the mind of the borrower that he is very poor, and would not for the world, if he had money of his own, charge twelve per cent. compound interest. These sharks watch on the banks of the Hoogly for the arrival of strangers, and introduce themselves with much address. Should a young man have no friend at hand, he inevitably falls into the clutches of a sircar; for being surrounded and assailed by crowds whose language he does not understand, he feels the necessity of employing some one of that cast to whom he can communicate his wants without hesitation. He who overcomes the rest by his powers of persuasion, places his young master in a palankeen, and guides him and his luggage to that tavern whence he receives pay for bringing custom. Then he hires servants, each of whom pays for his place; and having ascertained by enquiries the nature of the youth's prospects, if money be wanting, he can get some from a shroff on *master's note*, on account of which, perhaps, some time afterwards, *master* is lodged in gaol, should unpromising circumstances occur. In short, if a young adventurer have not some friend to take him by the hand on his arrival in India, he remains at the mercy of his sircar, who gets any English money the stranger may have brought for half its value, astonishes him with bills, and induces him to enter into the pleasures of the town.

Throughout Hindostan every youth intended for business is well instructed in accounts. Most of the natives can speak and write several dialects. The system of education is on the plan that was adopted from the Hindoos by the Rev. Mr. Bell at Madras, and improved upon by Lancaster. Teaching is generally conducted in an open viranda, upon the floor of which sand is spread, where the children learn to trace the characters of the alphabet. While reciting their lessons they make a great noise, and stand in a ring round the master, who corrects any error in tone, gesture, or emphasis, and manages them as the conductor of a band does the musicians under his charge. After completing their studies at a native school, some of them are sent to the European seminaries at the three presidencies, where they learn to read Virgil and Horace, become versed in mathematics, and are taught how to solve quadratic equations and curious problems in fluxions. In short, their capacity as calculators is very great; for vegetable food is so friendly to clearness of head, that all their faculties, retentive powers particularly, are in full animal perfection. Abstraction is with the Hindoos a practical virtue, and they can fix the mind with intensity on a particular object, so that it is not uncommon in every city to meet with men who can play successfully at chess without seeing the board. But in reasoning on moral or political points, their understandings seem to be tinged with prejudice. They are like the blind men spoken of by Locke and Burke, who could not distinguish colours without actual contact. In short, where any thing is tangible, can be regularly analysed, or touched with the finger, they are unrivalled. The eldest son of Gopez Mohun Tagore was so expert in contracted arithmetic, that he could multiply and divide in half the time required by any process known in Europe, and he wrote a hand as swift as speech, and yet with such geometrical precision, that it surpassed copper-plate.

The native agency of India is carried on with admirable regularity. Money may be transferred from one part of the country to another in all directions with ease. The shroffs *hoondies* are as good as bank of England paper. Posts are as regular through all the Company's provinces as they are in this country. The letter-bag is carried by a man called tappal, who runs as fast as a post-horse for one stage; he is then relieved by another runner in waiting; and thus communication is kept up nearly at the rate of the mail coach with us. During the night the tappal carries a torch and bells to frighten away wild beasts, so that his course is seen afar off like a meteor, and heard by the tigers and elephants, which crouch for fear.

Nevertheless, masters and servants so often misunderstand each other, that many ludicrous blunders happen every day, and a young man new from Europe may be seen stamping and raging with disappointment at a grave Hindoo, who is too dull to comprehend his meaning, although the sircar who engaged him had protested that he could speak English quite well. A volume might be filled with anecdotes on this fertile subject. Two short ones may be adduced as examples.

An officer told his servant in Hindostannee to go to a friend with his salam and borrow his saddle. In explaining this, he used an article which made the boy conceive that he wanted quite another thing, for he returned with a *bhote salam* and a bottle of gin to him who had sent for the loan of a saddle. The word *gin* in the Hindostannee language means a saddle, and as there is no name for the juice of the juniper in India, blacky thought his saheeb wanted to take a drink instead of a ride.

Several officers mounted their Arabians in camp near Baroda, and gallopped off to see the Guickwars gardens, desiring their grooms to follow. On coming into the suburbs of the city, they hired a guide, who readily undertook to conduct them. One who spoke tolerable Hindostannee had explained their object to their conductor, who seemed all intelligence, went up one street and down another, passed through a great gate, and making a full stop said, "Most noble gentlemen, there are the Guickwars gardens." Those whom he addressed stared, for they beheld a collection of tigers, lions, cheetoes, rhinoceroses, and elephants, well secured in monstrous cages. "Terrible, terrible, terrible, upon my honour," said the worthy Scotch captain, who had instructed the guide, "that I should not have remembered how like *bangon* is to *baughan*; terrible, terrible, terrible, upon my honour."

Gentle reader, while George True was languishing for Nannette, Charles Thoughtless was in possession of domestic bliss. The former was often distracted in balancing a logical account between ambition and love, when the latter was delighted by the vivacity of his young companion. An apartment had been erected in the compound for Frank Stanley, whose steady friendship and sober sense were serviceable to the young pair; and the benevolent adjutant would often drop in when he did not really want to see the regimental returns, but used this as a pretext for his coming, that he might witness the harmony and felicity of their humble dwelling. Mr. True was also a frequent looker-on; but about this period he lost his Mentor, who returned to Europe on leave of absence for the benefit of his health, and Panama with her two ayahs retired into the spicy groves of Malabar, to subsist on the little independence which, through the influence of her charms, the weakness of a good man had bestowed. The adjutancy fell to the lot of a most worthy successor; generous, brave, frank, and discerning, he made it his glory to distinguish and reward humble merit; hence Charles Thoughtless and Frank Stanley experienced a change in their immediate master, but none in the good offices of a real friend.

Soon after the departure of Captain Noble for Europe, an unexpected occurrence hastened the accomplishment of George's fate. In one of his morning visits to Mahé, he found Mr. Fortier and the family in a state of dejection, which was so unusual a sight that a tear started to his eye, when, in grasping the worthy Frenchman's hand, he said, "My dearest Sir, what can have happened to shade with sorrow the happiness I so lately witnessed?"

"Such, my child," said he, "is the alternation of human life. I have received very unpleasant news from Europe, which will oblige me to sail for England very shortly, my presence being absolutely required there; and as Mrs. Fortier's health is in a declining state, she intends to accompany me with

Nannette, and really the idea of parting with scenes and friends so long familiar to affection has saddened that enjoyment of life for which we usually evince our gratitude to Providence."

This intelligence almost petrified George; but upon recovering his faculties of speech, he opened his hopes respecting Mr. Fortier's adopted daughter, and intimated that he had wrung from her a blushing consent. Mr. Fortier frankly avowed that he thought no man in existence more worthy of Nannette, "though," said he, "she is a girl that could only love for the fine qualities of the soul." In short, Madame Fortier also expressed her high satisfaction; "for," said she, "it has been the wish of my heart to see you and Nannette happy." Mr. Fortier then apprized George that Nannette had only two thousand rupees of her own, but added that he had placed £2500 at interest, with Chase, Chinnery, and Co. of Madras, soon after her mother's death, with the intention of transferring it to his wife's namesake on her wedding-day.

"My dearest sir," replied George, "your intention was noble, but I never thought of wealth and Nannette together; she is a treasure in herself, therefore the money will serve to warm your residence in Europe, and cheer the declining health of Mrs. Fortier."

"I have enough," said he, "my generous boy," and he warmed at the thought; "but for the honour of France, my sweet Nannette shall not want pin-money. *Ab imo corde,* I rejoice in leaving her under the protection of such a husband; and you must purchase a company directly. But pardon me, the remainder of the sum at your disposal I would wish to be settled on her."

George left every arrangement to the noble-minded Mr. Fortier, who having invited the Rev. Mr. Dunsterville and Colonel Mars to Mahé, bestowed upon him his adopted child, together with his blessing, devoutly offered for their eternal happiness. A little moon of retirement had scarcely passed away, when Mrs. True consented to grace a ball proposed by George's brother officers in honour of her marriage. The mess-room was converted into a fairy scene by art and taste, and the esplanade of Cannanore exhibited an elegant variety of marquees belonging to the beauty and fashion of Malabar and Canara, who came in from the different civil and military stations on the joyous occasion. The gaiety and splendour of the scene may be conceived, but would be difficult to describe. Harmony seemed to have descended from the spheres, and the admirable cadence of a fine band was only equalled by the graceful movements of the dancers. After supper, which was served up in a hall of canvas, communicating with the ball-room, and illuminated with a profusion of variegated lights, the joys of Terpsichore were resumed, and Colonel Mars delayed so long the call for Sir Roger de Coverley, that he was prevented from having a field-day next morning. The late adjutant's spacious bungalow had been fitted up for the reception of Mrs. True, in which Madame Fortier passed a few days previous to her departure for Europe.

Cannanore is the head-quarters of the provinces of Malabar and Canara, and the station for an European regiment, with sometimes two battalions of sepoys. The fort is washed on three sides by the sea, being built on a rocky projection, and it is sufficiently strong on the land side. During the monsoon, the breakers dash against it with magnificent explosions of spray, that roar like thunder upon the rocks; and from its ramparts the cantonments, town, adjacent country, and distant ghauts, form as charming a prospect as the eye of taste need desire, particularly when the sun is rising on the mountains, and casting broad streaks of light and shade over the green masses beneath; or when, declining towards the west, he reflects his parting glory on the seeming melancholy of the scene. The immediate country is a charming variety of low hills and narrow valleys, laid out in well-watered rice grounds, and cottages and groves adorn the surface everywhere. The esplanade is skirted by officers' bungalows and gardens, their smiling neatness lending a charm to the level parades near them. These dwellings are composed of red stone, found near the surface in Malabar, which are easily cut into bricks and hardened in the air; and they are covered with cudjans, which add rural simplicity to their elegant and airy construction. The Beeby of Cannanore is a Mopla or Mahomedan, descended from Arabians who settled on this coast at an early period. Her family were of little note in the country before the purchase of this place from the Dutch; and according to report, their wealth was acquired by traffic. Since the cession of Malabar to the company, the Beeby has no political power, and only keeps a few irregular troops for the collection of her revenue derived from the land, for she pays the company a tax of four thousand rupees, and is permitted to farm her own estate. Besides these resources, she has several ships, and carries on an extensive trade; but the company's officers collect the customs, and have stations at convenient distances along the coast. In conformity to the law of inheritance in Malabar, the succession goes in the female line. The average breadth of the province is 35 miles, and its length 155; but the district of Cannanore extends not more than four miles from the sea. However, the whole coast is generally called Malabar from Cape Comorin up to Bombay.

The inhabitants consist of Namboozee, Brahmins, Nairs, Teers, Malears, Poliars, Parsees, and Moplas. The latter bury their dead, and all the rest burn the bodies, except the Parsees, who expose them to be eaten by birds of prey. The Teers are free men and cultivators of the soil; the Malears are musicians, and the Poliars are slaves. A Teer must keep at 12 paces distance from a Nair; and if a Poliar were to approach that proud race of warriors nearer than 96 paces, he might be cut down, according to custom; so that when a slave communicates with a Nair he has to strain his lungs. But there is a tribe of outcasts called Niadis, who live in the woods, and howl like dogs when they see persons approach. Refuse is generally thrown to them, upon which they feed; for them to come near any habitation would be thought so contaminating by the higher casts, that the water of the Ganges would hardly effect purification.

Bartolomeo was not far wrong in supposing, that several brothers had one and the same wife in Malabar. The most extraordinary customs prevail among the Nairs with respect to marriage, cohabitation, and inheritance. It is said there are eleven tribes of Nairs, in all of which property is divided equally among the sons and daughters of the deceased's sister, for no man knows his own child. In some of the tribes, the Nairs marry, but never cohabit with their own wives, who are at liberty to grant their favours to any male of equal or higher rank; but the Nimboory Brahmins are thought the most honourable fathers for offspring. In others, particularly the Shekarry family, the males never marry, but attach themselves to ladies belonging to the same tribe. Their sisters reside in their houses, and the children they produce in this lawful way are heirs to the property. This, though scarcely credible, is perfectly true.

The exports of Malabar are coir, cocoa-nuts, timber, rice, ghee, ginger, piece goods, cardamoms, pepper, sandal wood, turmeric, arrow root, and betel nut. Among the population, Christians have from the earliest periods been very numerous, and there are 44 Syrian or Nestorian churches, besides vast numbers established by the Portugese. Hyder Ally is said to have destroyed upwards of 60,000 Christians; but according to recent computations, there are still about 50,000 on the Malabar coast alone, besides 20,000 Jews. Within the limits before described, this province has been calculated to contain 600,000 souls, and it yields to the company about £250,000 in revenue, a considerable part of which is given in pensions to Nair chiefs, who have now no political power. The lofty barrier of the ghauts runs N. E. and S. W. along its whole extent, at the distance of from 40 to 70 miles from the sea, presenting to the voyager a country of most lovely aspect, bounded by an horizon peculiarly grand and magnificent.

CHAP. XII.

But we, who owe frail life to purer climes,
With detestation shudder at such crimes;
We start at perjury, and blush at shame,
And feel the value of unsullied fame.
See these rich, populous, expansive plains,
Who sways the sceptre o'er those fine domains?
Here no such feelings occupy the breast,
The rich are tyrants, and the poor opprest.
O! let the consequence inspire thy soul:
Britannia's merchants all these realms control.

THAT the lower classes, or great mass of mankind in India, are sunk in ignorance, slavery, vice, and superstition, is universally admitted, without at all detracting from the natural equality of the Hindoos in regard to all other human beings, for man is every where essentially the same, and becomes what the institutions of his country make him, either independent or servile. In the higher ranks of life, throughout Hindostan, perfect notions of moral purity and public spirit exist, but practice is every where wholly at variance with theory; and it being thought the interest of those in power to countenance the Brahmins in their horrible delusions, the common people are kept in a deplorable state of superstitious darkness, and have entirely lost their ancient purity of principle and guileless simplicity of manners.

Nothing therefore can be more erroneous than Dr. Robertson's opinion that the customs and institutions of India are the same now as they were in ancient times, and likely so to continue. In fact, here, as in all countries, the original religion has been split into so many sects, that some of them bear hardly the resemblance of the parent stock. In dress, equipage, furniture, adherence to tenets of faith, and conformity to ancient laws of cast, great innovations have taken place. The dress is not now as it was described by Quintus Curtius, and the casts in every village form themselves into something like freemason lodges, and prescribe rules of conduct for their own observance. A Hindoo Rajah may be now seen entertaining his European guests with ham and turkey, and doing all but eating and drinking the highest delicacies under the weight of which his table groans; while sofas, mirrors, pictures, chairs, lustres, girondoles, and sideboards, covered with massy plate, glitter in rich array, which clearly shew the effect that intercourse invariably has on prejudice.

There are, it is said, in India, ten different nations of Hindoos, professing the doctrines of Brahma, out of which about ten millions of individuals have adopted Mahomedanism, and a very considerable proportion have embraced our own inestimable faith; there are besides the Seiks, who are converts from both Brahma and Mahomed to pure deism, and the philosophers who pretend to laugh at them all. The Hindoos are divided into three great sects, each considered heterodox by the other. The followers of Brahma take, for their scriptural authority, the Veidam, which is written in the Sanscrit language, while the sacred volumes of the Budhists are composed in the Balli tongue, and those of the Jaines in Prakrit, both of which are held by the followers of the Veidam to be derivations from Sanscrit; each party firmly believes its own to be the original language in which God wrote their doctrines. Nanac, the founder of the Seiks, wrote his book called the Adi Granth, in the Guramuck character, which is a modern species of Nagari. Besides these great divisions among the Hindoos, it is said that there are twenty-one heretical sects.

Whoever instituted the Brahminical idolatry and wrote the Veidas was most consummately artful, and not only acquainted with the laws of Moses, but with the early learning of Egypt and of the West, even to Athens. No doubt he had travelled much, and on his return his experience was directed to the civilization of his countrymen, and the accomplishment of ambitious views. He taught that Brahma had created all things; he divided the people into four great natural bodies; and, to screen his own power, and that of his party the priests, he seemed to bestow all authority on the nobles or warrior cast, from whom the kings were alone to be chosen. But to reconcile the Vyasees and Soodres to their condition, he inculcated the notion, that the middling classes and dregs of society were placed in their low situation on account of sins committed in a former life, and that by conformity to prescribed rules, they might transmigrate up to the highest honour and glory; but if disobedient, that they must expect to be transformed into vile animals and hideous shapes. The four great divisions were again split into as many casts as there were callings in life, or as the pride and vanity of men suggested distinctions. Though the sons of a tailor were doomed to stitch away from one generation to another, yet they felt gratification in perceiving many degraded conditions below them; for some are held so infamous, that even a pariah, or a man who has lost cast, will not touch them. Thus each vocation in life became a society under a sort of patriarchal government. As in the code of Moses, so in the laws of Brahma, small matters were settled among the people, great ones alone were brought before the king; and to this day a similar mode of administration of justice is common, for the oldest and most venerable looking man in a village is *Cutwal*, with a court under him, to whose decision all litigants are obliged to submit their grievances. But those writers who have supposed that the government of the Rajahs was like that of a wise father, mildly presiding over a family, have greatly erred; nothing but absolute power was contemplated by the code of Brahma. It was death for a man of low cast to speak insolently to a Brahmin; and in Malabar, where the Mogul emperors never reformed the manners, or influenced customs, a peasant was cut down like a mad dog that dared to approach a warrior. Implicit obedience, and passive faith, were the indispensable conditions of existence, and to be trodden to death under the feet of elephants, or starved in cages hung near the great entrances to palaces, were common punishments for trivial omissions of ceremony.

The Brahmins, who were at liberty to exercise the functions of the sacerdotal office, or lay employments, became divided into clerical and secular orders, but both were held so sacred, even by kings, that nothing was so heinous as even to meditate the death of an individual belonging to either, he being considered as the temple of the pure essence of God; yet, by reason of worldly affections, the soul of a Brahmin was not always considered in that state; but whenever he could so abstract his thoughts from all earthly things as mentally to feel spiritual influence, he was Brahma. Thus they say it is ridiculous for a man whose soul is part of God to worship himself; and therefore idols are placed in their temples into which certain divinities are forced by strong incantations. Some of these are so sublime, that all distinctions of cast are laid aside in their presence, as at Juggurnaut, where no Hindoo will hesitate to eat from the table of the great idol. Brahmins filled all the offices in the gift of the crown, and in fact concentrated all authority so completely in themselves, that the rajahs were only like puppets. The inferior priests rose to power by practising great austerities, and imposing upon the people, whom they encouraged to mutilate and afflict the body, to perform long pilgrimages, and voluntarily to sacrifice themselves. Various modes of suicide are yet quite common, such as starvation, sitting so long in one posture that the nails of the fingers grow through the hands, and drowning in the sacred streams, besides retirement into jungles and mountains, where melancholy soon puts a period to life. While undergoing voluntary starvation, friends are permitted to feed the devotees with a little milk; but to prevent being defiled by human evacuation, a small piece of cotton at the end of a string is frequently let down into the stomach, which, it is said, brings up every particle of the milk that is not converted into blood.

It is most probable that the Brahminical fabric of deception was not constructed at once, but rose by degrees, like other piles that have withstood the destructive hand of time. According to tradition, a lawgiver named Maga, who is reported to have come from the west, revised the whole system when it had fallen into great disorder; but in its very best state, as far as we are acquainted with its principles, it was unfriendly to improvement beyond a certain degree. But it appears that if a limit be set to the progress of human ingenuity, the mental powers travel like a crab, and we accordingly find the Hindoos retrograding for centuries, till they are now in a state of comparative barbarism, with all the effeminacy of luxury which civilization has left behind. Perhaps the Brahmins foresaw that their system would enervate the people, for they never thought the Khatri cast could be destroyed, and therefore no nursery was prepared for a fresh supply of warriors; or they calculated that, in the state to which their doctrines would reduce the peasantry, whoever would be king they must necessarily be retained as priests; for although seemingly mild and passive, yet the Hindoos when roused by the Brahmins about tenets of faith, are formidable, and capable of sacrificing themselves by millions.

Thus in the foregoing brief notice of the Brahminical system, it will be seen that the passions and desires of mankind were so completely kept in check by hope and fear, that hardly any thing but harmony could take place till improvement had attained its limits. Accordingly civilization proceeded with unabated vigour for several centuries, and all the arts quickly rose to that point of improvement beyond which the institutions prohibited them from advancing. Division into tribes, sects, and parties, seems to be the general state of human societies, and history does not show us any great empire where equality reigned; but on the contrary the pride and natural coldness of men towards each other have in all ages formed lines of distinction. The effect therefore of the institution of casts in Hindostan was felt but little individually; but in a political point of view it so enfeebled the inhabitants as to render them an easy prey to every invader.

The Budhists are undoubtedly apostates from Brahminism. Budha is supposed to have been born in Bengal, and he is often called the Dhurma Rajah; but it is related of him that he travelled into Greece, and was the Minos of Crete! The Budhists are still divided into casts on the island of Ceylon, in the same manner as the Brahmins, except that the warriors take precedence of the priests. They deny the divine origin of the Veidas, and permit a great latitude to their followers in the use of animal food, though the cow is held sacred. Sacrifices and idols in their temples are prohibited, and Budha is alone worshipped as an incarnation in the Lama of Thibet; but anciently, there was a globular form in their caves and pagodas, to which, as an emblem of deity, adoration was paid.

Budha relaxed the dicipline of Brahma, but the founder of the Jaines drew the reins still tighter with respect to the care of animal life; for with them it is accounted the highest perfection of sanctity to abstain from the slaughter of any living creature. They believe that the world never was created; and that all animals have existed from eternity, and merely change their forms till absorbed into God's essence by becoming perfectly free from worldly pollution. Like the Brahmins, they are divided into four casts, and have similar ceremonies of marriage, baptism, and initiation. Their deities are the spirits of holy men, whose naked images, all in one form and posture, are seated cross-legged in their temples on a marble altar called Pursunaut. But in open pagodas they have an image of Gomata Ruja Iswara, who is represented at Kurcul in Canara thirty-eight feet high and ten feet in circumference; and there is also a colossal statue of him at Baligoli in Mysore, where a high priest still officiates, and some magnificent ruins of this sect are to be found. Nothing is believed by them but what they can perceive; they pretend to have no traditions respecting a general deluge; and as they deny that the world ever was created, their notions respecting time are uncommonly complex. They talk of 2,000,000,000,000,000 segaras, or oceans of years. Now a palya is an estimate of the time that a vast pit filled with chopped hairs would take to be emptied at the rate of one hair in a century, and a sagara is equal to a palya multipled by ten cotis of cotis, or 1,000,000,000,000,000 palyas are only one sagara.

Sir John Malcolm has given an interesting account of the Seiks in the eleventh volume of Asiatic Researches. Besides the province of Lahore, which in the reign of Aurungzebe yielded a revenue of £2,469,500, they have the whole of the Panjab, part of Multan, and most of the country between the Jumna and the Sutlege, from lat. 28° 40′ to 32° north. For a long time after their organization by Har Govind, the tenth successor of Nanac, they became exceedingly formidable to their neighbours. He arranged them with consummate skill, on the plan of a military confederation of chiefs, and inspired them with an ardent thirst for conquest. Their great council of state was held at Amritsar, over which the acalis or priests presided; and an august ceremony was instituted of eating together in the council chamber some consecrated cakes, as a testimony of harmony previous to their deliberations. The acalis are distinguished from the other Seiks by wearing blue dresses, and they are called "Immortals." But at present the chiefs are nearly all pursuing their own particular interests, having split into parties, and lost those principles of patriotism and union with which their fathers were inspired. Drunkenness prevails so much among them that it is quite impossible to transact business with a chief, except in that lucid interval between the evaporation of one debauch, and the stimulating doses taken to produce another. The meaning of the word Seik is disciple, and the initiation of a convert is the solemn devotion of his future life to steel in defence of the state. Even their very salutations were made to inspire patriotism. When two Seiks meet, one exclaims, "Wa! guruji ka khalsa!" which is, "Success to the state of the Gurri," and he is answered with a wave of the hand to the head,

"Wa! guruji ki fateh," "Victory attend the Gurri." It is easy to conceive how soon these men might be inspirited by a skilful leader and turned against their neighbours, from whom they have in fact wrested all their possessions, having been at first under Guru Nañac cooped up in the mountains.

It was not the fate of the lovely Mrs. True to enjoy her bungalow and garden at Cannanore for any great length of time. His majesty's 12th regiment, which was stationed at Seringapatam, had been attacked by the jungle fever. In a few months one third of the brave fellows belonging to that fine corps found graves in the marsh of the Cavery, and the hospital was filled with the remainder. It was ordered to the sea coast, and it fell to the lot of the regiment at Cannanore to garrison *Seringa.* When a front rank man falls beneath the enemy's fire, he who has to take his place feels a chill at seeing the blood of his comrade, but steps forward with a steady soul; and such was the feeling throughout the cantonments on the day when the order was made known.

"My dear Nannette," said George, "you can stay here till the cold season sets in on the table land."

"Nay, George, think not so coldly," replied she; "I shall be your nurse, and you will be mine. My hope is in God when with you."

The worthy Colonel Mars marched forthwith, and a little beyond Peripatam halted for the 12th to pass with the honours of a senior corps. The sight was melancholy. Their ranks were as thin as if grape-shot had cut them down by sections, and the number of doolies that followed the regiment gave a frightful idea of the surgeon's report. Upon arriving in the strong fortress of the late Tippo Saib, the corps attended the funeral of the gallant and amiable General Clarke, and a few days after the sick list began to swell. Colonel Mars, knowing the effects of air, exercise, and cheerfulness, invented a thousand agreeable expedients to keep the mind and body roving. He and the whole of the officers visited the barracks every day to ensure the most scrupulous cleanliness; but the fever baffled human skill. For two months the corps lost on an average three men daily, so that the funeral honours were suspended, lest the dead march and such frequent firing should excite melancholy in the minds of the survivors. This fever made its first appearance in an ague fit, which was followed by a burning delirium, that rapidly consumed the frame. The usual remedies proved of little avail; but it was discovered by Dr. Scarman, the scientific garrison surgeon, that if the water of the river Cavery was thrown in pails full on the patient while in the burning state, the fever would be arrested. By this providential experiment, and the wise precautions of Colonel Mars, who established a post for convalescents at Baligoli, the jungle fever was banished from Seringapatam.

Physicians supposed that this epidemic arose from the jungles and marshes in the vicinity of the garrison; but Colonel Mars sometimes thought that it was partly caused by the narrow streets of the town in the fort, and the prodigious slaughter of goats at one of the pagodas, where a constant river of blood infected the air with stench, and produced swarms of flies, and being now in command of the place, he considerably improved its salubrity. Among the officers that died was Captain Gataker, a gentleman so perfect and amiable that to know him and not to love him was impossible. Sincerely attached to him, Dr. Scarman watched his bed with affectionate care till exhausted by fatigue. An unfavourable change forced the surgeon left in charge to fly for Scarman, and arouse him from a troubled sleep. "He will die," said the assistant. "He shall not die," replied the warm-hearted Scarman, rubbing his eyes, and confirming his reply with captain Shandy's asseveration; but in this instance the angel, though he blotted out the oath with a tear, had to record the entrance of Gataker's spirit into the gates of heaven.

Previous to this period, Sir John Malcolm had left Mysore in a flourishing state. His political talents, aided by able coadjutors, and directed to the resources of the country by the financial knowledge of the Brahmin Purnea, now prime minister to the young king, formed such an admirable code for the administration of justice, the arrangement of revenue, the distribution of the forces, and the employment of the restless military spirits thrown on the public by the overthrow of Tippo, that peace and security smiled upon industry; ruined villages resounded with the chearful hum of labour; barren wastes were robed in the green livery of cultivation; the fort and town of Mysore passing from infancy, assumed the beauty and freshness of youth, and the silver waters of the Cavery were conducted over hills by art, and glittered like the current of life through the veins of a populous city. Around and in the fort of Seringapatam all was classic ground to George, Frank, and Charles. One of the officers had been long a prisoner in it, chained toCaptain now Sir David Baird; and several of the soldiers, who had fought under Lord Cornwallis in 1792, and with General Harris when the place was stormed, pointed out those spots dear to memory. "There," said one, "over those hills we rushed to storm the batteries, pouring grape with scientific skill, while his lordship cheered and waved his hat on that height within range, on the day of the battle of Corryghaut." — "Here," said another, "we crossed the river in the night-attack on the island, and in the confusion of darkness blazed away on our own divisions who had forded there; but the guides by mistake led them under that slope where we expected determined opposition from the enemy. There the brave Colonel Baillie breathed his last, poisoned in that dungeon.

Yonder the British prisoners used to be drawn up for the purpose of receiving either circumcision or a shot through the head; and within that old palace the ancient dynasty of Mysore was immured by the usurper Hyder Ally; but there were our breaching batteries, and here we entered the fort. The struggle was tremendous along that rampart, from the breastworks of which deliberate aim was taken by the Arabs; and Tippo from behind the one on your right fired several shots himself, every one of which passed through a Briton's heart. At length in that sally-port he fell fighting till the last gasp, sword in hand, and there he lay, ambition still lowering on his brow, after he was dragged from under a heap of slain." Alternate feelings of sorrow and joy agitated the souls of the three young soldiers while they surveyed these memorials of warfare, and perambulated the ramparts or fine circular road that now graces the interior, shaded with refreshing trees.

Health had begun to diffuse gaiety and hope. Neither Mrs. True nor Mrs. Thoughtless were affected by the contagion, and Charles was the only one of the trio of friends attacked. Mary watched his drooping eye; and He who sent Isaiah to Hezekiah to say, "I have heard thy prayer, I have seen thy tears," restored him when on the brink of the grave; but the worthy surgeon of his regiment did much, for instead of sending him to hospital, he attended him in the adjutant's office, and watched the progress of disease with the care and affection of a brother. Captain Dramatic determined now to exert his powers in the service of the ladies, whose smiles were the reward he aimed at for perseverance and labour almost incredible, in converting one of Tippo's public edifices into a theatre. Whoever had the pleasure of seeing him in Goldfinch will never forget his comic talents; and he who saw him, as Harlequin, vault through windows two stories high, must have been lost in admiration at his activity. All the flowers were culled from the British drama. True and Frank performed several parts with applause; but Charles, who had practised in the battle of Aughram, and whose graceful and slender figure pointed him out for the female fashionable parts, surprized all beholders in the Citizen, Poor Gentleman, Poor Soldier, and Turnpike Gate, so that Colonel Mars was heard to exclaim "*bravo, bravissimo.*" — Captain Solomon sang "You know I'm your priest" with such inimitable Irish humour, that Purnea and the young king burst their sides, and the ladies of the seraglio from behind their silken screens giggled, notwithstanding the restraints of Hindoo female education; but the fool of pantomime gaped on one occasion so widely, to swallow a monstrous pigeon-pie, from which the birds were flying away, that the government of Mysore were terrified at the idea of being swallowed with the whole theatre down such a voracious gullet; and it was with difficulty that Mr. Coles's insinuating and bland address restored sweetness of aspect to the distorted countenances under the turbans around him. Captain MacIntosh of the artillery evinced great taste in scenic painting, and Captain De Haviland, and Lieutenant Wright with their violins, sat in the orchestra, which exhibited the musical curiosity of a fine solo performed on the fiddle by Mr. Clarke, who had lost his left arm; but *labor omnia vincit,* he changed the strings, and tying the bow to the stump, fingered so well with the right hand as to command universal applause. The beautiful little theatre of Seringapatam, the motto of which was "Nil desperandum," in allusion to the difficulties overcome in its construction, was opened with a prologue, partly written by Charles Thoughtless; for Captain Dramatic having left one that he was preparing in the ward-room, Charles wrote something on the back of it about the pleasing change, from the roaring of cannons to the silver sounds of music, and from the yellow tinge of jungle fever to the applauding looks of laughing beauty. For upwards of a year the stage imparted a vivacity to the gloomy aspect of Seringa, which was crowded every month with the beauty and fashion of Bangalore and Mysore, while its own circle was very large, being the head-quarters of a king's regiment, a battalion of artillery, and three of native infantry cantoned on the island near the fort. But a soldier's life is one of variety, and a change came over the scene.

Previous to this, however, Charles had lost all hope of promotion through the interest of Captain Noble's friend in Calcutta, although he had written that Lord Lake, when leaving the country, had left his name for an ensigncy on the adjutant general's list. But Captain Dramatic now made an effort in his favour. "Thoughtless," said that kind-hearted friend, "I have written to a relation on the governor general's staff, and his interest backed by mine here with the resident will, I think, do your business; but you may be assured, I shall leave no stone unturned to serve you when an opportunity occurs." In due time an answer arrived from Bengal. "What," said he on the staff, "do you think I have influence to get an ensigncy, when I have not interest to procure for myself an apartment in the Government House?" and a little further on he lamented that the expence of postage was so heavy. Thus the cheering smile of hope proved delusive.

The Rajah of Travancore had commenced hostilities against the company, and it was to join the army of General St. Leger that the disposable force at Seringapatam marched. All the ladies were left in garrison, and George, Frank, and Charles exulted at the idea of seeing war on an extensive scale, and participating in the toils of glory. At the distance of two marches from the new Fort of Mysore, on the road leading to the Cooteady Pass, Colonel Mars received an order to return with two companies to Seringapatam; for his seniority clashed with the claim of a company's officer in Malabar, whose command gave him a local rank, which his friends at Madras foresaw would be superseded. The colonel paced his tent with fury, and no doubt vented an oath or two on the government, for a soldier has often to obey, though in his heart he curses the necessity. George, Frank, and Charles proceeded however. The country is, in many parts, well cultivated, and abounding in plantations of tobacco; but there is little else except the jungles of Wynaud to interest the traveller, for the villages are small, and there are very few inhabitants in this wild tract. But near Manantoddy, as has been noticed, the scenery is very beautiful. Peace and improvement had shed their smiles on the stockade, and some tiled bungalows and neat huts belonging to the followers gave the appearance of life to still nature in her most lovely aspect; the spotted deer were seen starting from every copse, while the peacock strutted about with a self-satisfied air, seemingly to receive the homage of admiration from chattering monkeys, jungle fowls, and paroquets, that hopped and fluttered around. Even the road after leaving Mysore, and passing Chuttenhully, prepares the mind by contrast to enjoy the beauties of Manantoddy, for on crossing the Bowally river all is sombre shade of deep green, which imparts a melancholy idea of sameness to the fancy; but at Untersunty commence those grand arches, formed naturally by the bamboos, that lend a charm to the long perspective of the road narrowing through them to a point, and impervious to the rays of the sun. After which lawns and slopes on either hand open on the pleased eye, till, on gaining the top of Manantoddy hill, the spectator instinctively stands to gaze on the beauty that fascinates him. Thence he beholds every where an endless variety of slopes, vales, and eminences adorned with trees and flowering shrubs, the whole as if scattered by the hand of taste. At the foot of the hill, westward, the Capany river is seen meandering, as if enamoured of this lovely scene, till it loses itself in the distant glades; and southward another part of the same silver stream winds in delightful maze through the valley, on the banks of which the sepoys' huts and stockade followers' bazar afford objects of interest. The distance presents hills and mountains, robed with azure on every side. To the north are the Koochepard ranges, with variegated jungle running up their faces; to the west are unconnected hillocks, undulating like waves, till they rise into the stupendous mass of Banasore, whose gigantic brow scowls on the clouds below; and to the south and east, other ranges of equally picturesque hills, all melting as it were into each other, complete as grand a panorama of natural magnificence as the pencil of an artist would desire.

Having got the guns and stores with much difficulty down the Cooteady ghaut, the force marched on to Cotapore, and next day encamped on the sea shore near Barraghurry. Two days afterwards their tents were pitched near Calicut, so famous as being the first port gained by the Portuguese; it is beautifully described in the Luciadas of Camoens, but its glory has passed away. The zamorin's palace is now a heap of ruins, and the city a melancholy shadow of what it was before Hyder Ally and Tippo destroyed its ancient splendours. Here the commanding officer of the force received orders to send off two companies of Europeans to reinforce the garrison at Cochin. Frank and Charles were doomed to share in this service, and the latter was appointed serjeant-major of the detachment. They departed at midnight, and continued all the next day along the sea shore, till they reached Panyanee, quite exhausted by the fatigue of so tremendous a march. Mr. Warden the collector was there, and furnished them with refreshments of roasted buffaloes, rice, and clean straw upon which they slept a few hours. The march was doubly fatiguing on account of the heavy sand through which they had to move; but every time the front halted for the rear, green cocoa nuts were knocked down from the trees, and their juice proved greatly refreshing. Visible traces of terror were every where to be seen;

most of the inhabitants were Christians, who hearing of the hostile preparations, and dreading the barbarity of their neighbours favourable to the cause of the Travancore and Cochin Rájahs, had fled to places of refuge, leaving their cabins and altars to their fate. It was eight o'clock in the evening when the detachment reached Panyanee, so that their situation may be conceived.

About 12 o'clock on the same night they embarked in paddimars for Cochin. But in the confusion all the provisions were put into one boat, of which the others lost company before day-light. The wind and current being adverse, Cochin was not reached till the evening of the second day of departure from Panyanee. Fortunately Moote had brought a pot of boiled rice with him from Mr. Warden's. The officers who were with Charles and Frank, having nothing but a bottle of brandy, began to eye the rice, and such is the effect of participation in occasions of danger and toil, that these gentlemen ever after remembered those with friendly regard whose rice had saved them from starvation. Some of the boats had arrived at Cochin before the one in which they were; but two of them did not come in till the day after.

Here they learned that Cochin had been attacked a short time before, but it was defended by the small force in it with spirit. Formerly it was a place of great strength, and regularly fortified; but when it was taken by the English the walls were destroyed. The town is beautifully regular, with a fine row of houses facing the sea, and along the river. Batteries had been erected on the opposite bank to cannonade it, and the houses next the river were greatly injured. Colonel Macauly, the British agent at the court of Travancore, escaped most narrowly; for the attack on Cochin was chiefly made with the intention of murdering him. When the small reinforcement arrived, all was bustle and preparation; another visit from the enemy, who had possession of Muttacherry, being expected. The place was put in the best state of defence that circumstances would admit. All the streets of the town were fortified and batteries erected in proper positions. A gun-brig was warped up the river to Muttacherry, which it battered, and so nearly destroyed, that the chief of that place, alarmed for his palaces,ubmitted. In the meantime, the army of General St. Leger had stormed the Travancore lines, beaten the rajah, and obliged him to sue for peace on any terms.

CHAP. XIII.

"O see! the town appears in smoke and blaze,
Hark! what wild shrieks affrighted mothers raise!
That fire will leave full many a native poor
To beg at some unfeeling nabob's door;
And soon, perhaps, grim death, the beggar's friend,
May spread the houseless bed, distress to end.
And then, alas! a casual passer by
Beholds a sight to shock the heart and eye:
The ghastly vulture and the jackal prowl,
To mangle human flesh, with scream and howl,
While crowds of Hindoos pass the horrid place,
Without a change of muscle in the face!"

Throughout India, for some time before the commencement of the monsoon, the atmosphere becomes heated to an extreme degree, and very high winds prevail. During the months of May and June, this agitated state of the air is severely felt in Calcutta, and destructive conflagrations from fire often desolate the native quarters of the city, where the houses are constructed of such inflammable materials, that a spark bursts forth into a blaze in a moment, and is carried like lightning along by the wind. The houses of the Europeans and rich natives, being built of brick and terraced, escape with little damage on these frightful occasions, for the course of the destructive element is so rapid that such buildings are passed before any serious impression is made on their external parts. It is melancholy to contemplate the effects of these fires. The little all of the poor natives, their furniture, cows, goats, horses, are consumed, and frequently the lives of the owners lost in vain endeavours to save their property. Yet the evil is of such a nature as not to be easily remedied, for were the huts to be removed from the town, the same destruction would attend them, as is seen in the suburbs, and all over India where the *ghurs* are made of reeds. The calamity is chiefly owing to the carelessness with which fire is handled, and what is worse, to the frequent commission of arson. From numerous trials for this horrible crime, it appears that the proprietors of the materials wilfully destroy the houses by dropping fire in different places, to ensure the demand for their property. It is extremely difficult to detect the person who first causes a fire, for the Hindoos carry charcoal with them to light their pipes.

23d Feb. 1813. A fire broke out in Mullinga, at 11 P. M., which destroyed 400 habitations.

17th March. A very destructive fire broke out in Ram Bagaun, consuming upwards of 300 huts and houses.

18th March. There was another extensive fire in Simleah.

31st ———. At 3 P. M. a destructive fire broke out behind the general hospital.

13th April 1813. A shocking fire broke out this day in Mullinga, and extended to Soorty Bagaun; two native women perished in the flames.

15th April. A little past 11 A. M. this day, one of the most shocking fires ever remembered in Calcutta was discovered in Short's Bazar; it spread towards Mirzapore, razing more than a thousand habitations; several unfortunate natives perished in the flames.

5th May. A destructive fire raged in the Cooly Bazar.

14th ——. Three violent fires spread destruction around during the last week.

18th ——. A dreadful fire destroyed many houses at Kidderpore.

But enough is said to prove the extent of this evil; and the benevolence of the government was directed at the time above mentioned to its diminution, by enabling the natives to build their huts of less inflammable materials. After these fires, the melancholy spectacle alluded to in the lines at the head of this chapter is frequently seen. But alas! it is so common all over India, that the eye becomes familiarized by habit, and feels a shock every time of less painful disgust. "I beheld," says Dr. Buchanan in his Christian Researches, speaking of Juggurnaut, "another distressing scene this morning, at the place of skulls, a poor woman lying dead, or nearly dead, and her two children by her, looking at the dogs and vultures which were near. The people passed by without noticing the children. I asked them where was their home. They said, 'they had no home but where their mother was.'" This is an afflicting spectacle; but I have beheld the dead bodies of natives, not yet cold, who had expired under the trees in the vicinity of Calcutta, mangled and torn by adjutants, while crowds of Hindoos were passing to bathe in the Ganges; and when the corpses were pointed out to their countrymen, the cold answer was, "Hum jaunta ne, sahib,—I know him not, Sir." "Oh! but remove the body and burn it."—"Mera dustoore ne, sahib, —It is contrary to custom," answered they. Hence it may be inferred, that it is the lot of no Hindoo to meet with a good Samaritan.

One effect of the institution of casts is, that no stranger will be received into the house of a Hindoo as a guest or lodger; but a remedy for this is every where to be found by travellers who make regular stages, for in every village there is a building erected at the public charge for the accommodation of wayfaring-men, and a person appointed to provide them with fire, water, and all that the place produces, at regulated prices. In some cities, these buildings are on a very large scale, and numerous, but in every town one will be found more or less convenient, according to the wealth of the place. They are called in the Carnatic *choultries*, and in most other places dhurrumsollahs, and are superintended by the cutwal, whose *peon* is in general remarkably attentive to strangers, particularly to Europeans, who often receive poultry, milk, and butter from the magistrate as a present. The Hindoos really appear to be a tender-hearted people, but their institutions have produced customs and ceremonies at which humanity revolts with horror. To eat, drink, or associate with a stranger, would subject a man of cast to be alienated and forsaken. A military man guilty of cowardice, or a lady who had prostituted her honour in this country, would not meet with a more unfavourable reception from society than a Hindoo whose pity prompted him to help a dying traveller into his house from the road-side, when he saw the vultures and jackals watching the exit of life. The Hindoo women are very charitable, and never refuse to give a thirsty stranger water, but he must drink it at the door out of his hands, into which they will pour it from a vessel, or stand over him stooping, and let it fall into his mouth; for were he to touch the pot, it would never after be used, but broken, as we destroy what has been impregnated with some filthy or noxious thing. I once by accident trod on a mat where there was an earthen dish full of rice prepared by a woman for her family dinner. Upon which she burst into loud exclamations of sorrow, broke the *chattee*, threw away the rice, and tore the mat to pieces. I was very sorry for the pain I had unconsciously occasioned, but upon giving a rupee to a pretty little child she took up in her arms and bathed with tears, she dried her eyes,looked highly pleased, and made me a salam to the very ground, saying in the sweetest tone of voice imaginable, " Bhote, bhote salam, atcha sahib, — Many, many thanks, good sir."

If the institution of casts produced such apparent disregard to the offices of humanity, it must be allowed, on the other hand, that by prescribing the most ceremonious respect to persons, it laid the foundation for a very high polish of address, with a general propensity to abject flattery. Nothing can be more insinuating than the manners of even the middling class of Hindoos. They approach a person of superior rank as if they thought him a deity. The action of their fine persons is as much according to nature as those beautiful curves adopted by Europeans, and the countenance expresses agreeable animation or dignified gravity, just according to circumstances. Their modes of salutation are various, but the most general is the *salam* with the right hand, which is brought up to the forehead, something like our military salute. At the same time the Hindoos say, "*Ram ram,*" and the Mahomedans, "*Salam alikoom.*" On meeting old acquaintances they embrace, something like what is the fashion on the continent of

Europe, by placing the arms round each other, and dropping the head first on one shoulder and then on another, as if they kissed the cheeks. But the lower class, in salamming to superiors, kiss the ground, and the middling orders on approaching Europeans of rank touch the ground with their hand, and take off their slippers, which is likewise always done on going into their temples and houses of respectability. When a Hindoo has a favour to ask, he performs his invocations to Gunesa, the god of wisdom, and visits the person on some trifling pretext to ascertain whether he is in an auspicious temper. If the opportunity be of the golden kind, time, place, and aspect conspiring, his main purpose is broached, but nothing can discompose his patience, or induce him to mar his project by obtrusiveness or precipitation. His quiet and vigilant attention may be compared to that of a cat watching for prey, who permits not a pur to awaken suspicion, ere the moment arrives for making the decisive spring. The abject manner in which the Hindoos behave to the Brahmins is extended to other superiors. Before great men they prostrate themselves and grovel in the dust. When their Rajahs pass in state, *tom toms* are beaten and *tooteries* sounded upon, while crowds pour out of the towns and villages to prostrate themselves in the dust. They moreover call themselves by every debasing name in comparison with superiors. But the prodigious shoals of pilgrims, sanyasees, fakiers, players, jugglers, mountebanks, gipseys, and buffoons, that stroll about in every quarter, may have helped to remove boorishness from among the lower orders in India. The fakiers or mendicants that visit European families, are a most curious set of beings. Their dress is generally made of pieces of English broad cloth of all colours, which they get in presents; and thus decorated they march about with all the consequential strut of peacocks, like harlequins; only that the human shape is not displayed, for they are shrouded with bags, and robed in a sort of patchwork cloak, that serves them also for a tent both day and night. The fakiers are great favourites with all the ayahs, who are credulous and listen with avidity to their marvellous stories, and frequently persuade their mistresses to admit them as fortune-tellers, to predict the children's *nusseebs*. On such occasions, it is something more than ludicrous to witness the art of the flatterer, and to mark how successfully he insinuates himself into the good graces of every one; for the whimsical grimaces and contortions with which he at first endeavours to attract notice subside, when that object is gained, into refinement of address. He appears struck dumb by the beauty of madam and her *bavas*. With apparent rapture, he expatiates on the colour of her darling's eyes and hair, in which there may be a diversity that all natives wonder at without any affectation. The fakiers never calculate on exciting charity by a display of want or bodily infirmity, but gain their object in a much surer way by putting on the merriest faces in the world, and laughing people out of their money.

About the time that hostilities commenced in Travancore, the chief of Alleppee had barbarously murdered two serjeants, a drummer, and twenty-five rank and file, belonging to his majesty's 12th regiment. This unfortunate party were on board a paddimar, on their way to Quilon, when they touched at Alleppee in stress of weather, not being aware of any danger. It is said, that their muskets being first secured by a stratagem, the men were overpowered, their arms and legs broken, and their mutilated bodies thrown into the back water. To punish this atrocious act, a strong detachment, formed from the force at Cochin, proceeded under Major Westbury of the 17th N. I. to that place, with such secrecy and expedition that the barbarian was taken by surprize, and Charles and Frank saw him hanged next morning on a high gallows, near the spot where he had caused the brave fellows belonging to the 12th to be drowned.

On their return to Cochin, they visited Muttacherry. Part of the town is built in the European style, and inhabited by white Jews. The Rajah's palace is a large old building, with a great gate, in the porticos of which were several iron cages, containing human beings who had committed crimes, and were thus exposed to strike terror into all beholders. The sentries over them were dressed like sepoys, and having been so lately enemies, looked grimly at the two friends, who surveyed with emotion the emaciated naked bodies of the criminals, hastening fast to the common fate of man. They were loaded with chains, and the cages were just large enough to allow them to lie down, but the height was only sufficient for them to sit erect. Every rib could be counted. Misery, despair, and anguish were depicted on their countenances. Their complexions were of a deadly hue. They extended their fleshless hands for charity. "Whatever were your crimes," said Frank, "your sufferings have redeemed them," and he distributed what he had amongst them. "Here," said Charles, "may the God who comforts the afflicted, support you," and he emptied his purse into their palms. Cochin was the first fort that the Portuguese built in India; and so many of the natives were converted to Christianity along the coast, that there is hardly a pagoda to be seen. The bishop has one hundred parish churches in his diocese.

The Rajah of Cochin has no external political power, all his foreign affairs being negociated by the British government. Although he is a prince in the little district over which he presides, and has a small military force of his own to enforce the payment of revenue, yet in all other points of view, he is merely a tenant under the company, and pays them for his advantages nearly three lacks of rupees a year. In all respects, the King of Travancore is in a similar situation, having no power beyond the confines of his own dominions, a great part of the revenue of which is paid to the Madras government. Travancore is now about one hundred and forty miles in length by forty in breadth, and the king has his court at Trivandapatam. Formerly the territory of the rajah was very trifling; but an European, named Eustacheus de Lanoy, having disciplined the army of Travancore, conquests were made from other Malabar chiefs, and fortified lines constructed, which are, however, no security against the invasion of a well-organized force. The rajah is himself the greatest merchant in his dominions, and the only exporter of betel nut, pepper, and ginger; but in short he has nearly a monopoly of every thing by which money can be made.

The war being now over in Travancore, the two companies, to which Charles and Frank were attached, proceeded to join their regiment then with the army, and having passed through Cranganore, formed the desired junction at Karkante. At the former place St. Thomas is said to have landed when he arrived from Arabia to convert the Indians. The Archbishop of Cranganore has forty-five churches under him: the city exhibits some indications of former splendour, but it is now the shadow of a shadow. It was once the Jerusalem of the Indian Jews, who landed here soon after the second destruction of the temple, and received a grant of it, with some of the surrounding territory, from the king of the country, A. D. 490. Here they continued for about one thousand years, under seventy-two governors; but discord having arisen, war ensued, and they mutually destroyed each other, till they became a prey to a Malabar warrior, who entered Cranganore with his army, and put all before him to the sword. Such as escaped his fury, fled to Muttacherry, where they built a town, and have since increased very considerably, having now two synagogues. Many of their women are exceedingly fair and beautiful. But the black Jews having come into the country many centuries before, and mixed with the natives, can hardly now be distinguished from other inhabitants of Malabar. Not far from Cranganore is the oldest Syrian church in Travancore, named after St. Thomas. In the interior these establishments are very numerous, for the Portuguese, who exercised great cruelty over these ancient Christians on the sea coast, never penetrated into the woods, where the pure, simple religion of our Saviour now exists in an unadulterated state.

At what precise period the Syrian Christians came to Malabar is uncertain, but when Vasco de Gama arrived in 1503, they had above one hundred churches and a Christian king; and for thirteen hundred years before, they enjoyed a succession of bishops appointed by the patriarch of Antioch, one of whom, named Mar Joseph, was sent to Lisbon a prisoner. They have only two sacraments, baptism and the Lord's supper; they invoke no saints, have no images, and do not believe in purgatory. Their churches are built of the red stone before noticed, and are like old village churches in England. The priests wear a loose white vest, with a cap of coloured silk hanging behind, which gives a venerable air to their fine persons. Their bishop wears a vestment of red silk, with a large golden cross suspended from his neck. They all go barefooted, and wear beards down to their girdles, many of which are as white as snow, and heighten the imposing and venerable aspect of their wrinkled foreheads. Their last king was named Beliarte. He resided at Diamper, where Archbishop Menezes, from the inquisition at Goa, convened 150 Syrian clergy in 1599, and burned their books, while he marched round in procession, chaunting a song of triumph. The pope endeavoured to extirpate them. His vicar was established at Verapoli, where there is a college for twenty students, who are instructed in the Latin and Syrian languages, and he has sixty-four churches under him, besides nearly as many under the Bishop of Quilon, so that the number of Christians in southern Malabar is prodigious.

A demonstration of the force having been made over Travancore, in the course of which many parts of the interior were seen, the regiment to which

Frank and Charles belonged was sent to Cannanore, to replace the 12th at Quilon. The ghauts form an entire chain along Travancore and all Malabar, except near Paniany, where there is a sort of opening, from which the river of that name takes its rise. Paniany, which stands on the south side of it, is a place of great consequence, being the residence of the chief priest of the Moplas, who have here about forty mosques. The woods of Travancore produce cardamoms, wild cinnamon, and frankincense, with abundance of fine teik that grows up the sides of the ghauts, from which it is hauled into the rivers and conducted to the coast for ship-building. Having reached Cannanore, Charles, full of anxiety to see Mary, obtained leave, and accompanied by Moote, who carried his camp equipage, set off for Seringapatam, which he reached in four days, though distant 110 miles from Cannanore.

Mysore is 210 miles in length by 140 in breadth, and it is a sort of terrace about 3000 feet above the level of the sea, so that its climate is remarkably fine. The grape, peach, and strawberry, with nearly all the common vegetables of Europe, flourish near Seringapatam. The mutton is as fine as it is in Bengal. On the east, there is a lofty chain of ghauts, which rise near the river Kisthna, and support this fine table land, rising in many parts into firm mountains. This is more particularly the case with the masses of granite composing the western ghauts, which are covered with black earth, producing perpetual verdure, and are clothed nearly to their summits with teik, often 100 feet high; along them grows also the precious sandal wood, which is monopolized by the company, while on the eastern mountains there is hardly any timber, but every where the bare rock appears. Beyond these ghauts, the south-west and north-east monsoons have little influence; therefore Mysore is a country of showers nearly at all seasons. It abounds in iron ore, of which great quantities are exported, notwithstanding the simple and clumsy manner in which the works are carried on. Having been so long the theatre of war, and subjected to invasions of the most devastating kind, it is supposed that at present there are not more than two and a half millions of inhabitants, only seventeen thousand of whom are Mahomedans. The revenue of the Mysore Rajah, exclusive of seven lacks of *pagodas* paid to the company, is said to amount to about 2,500,000 pagodas, a great part of which is annually laid out in improvements. All the rivers in Mysore, the chief of which is the Cavery, have their sources in the ghauts generally speaking in the Coorg. From the remains of enclosures, and the traces of former irrigation, it would appear that the country was once cultivated like a garden, and under the present mild government it will soon be restored to the same state. The company have possession only of the island of Seringapatam, about four miles in length by one and a half broad; the fort occupying about a mile of that space, together with the cantonments of Bangalore, which is a most important station, being the eastern key of Mysore. Seringapatam is a place of great sanctity, and within the fort is the great temple of Shri Runga or Sheva, from whom it derived its name. The ancient Mysore family date their descent from Chrishna, and account theirs the most ancient race of Hindoo princes. Besides the temple of Shri Runga, there are two others of great antiquity, and the processions are equal in grandeur to many others in India, being attended generally by 100,000 spectators, 20,000 of whom still reside on the island, though great numbers have removed to the new city.

There are no public edifices of consequence, except the palaces, and they are gloomy looking buildings in the fort; but the Laul Baug and Dowlat Baug, garden residences of Tippo, are extremely elegant and airy. It is a pity to see the latter going to decay, but the former is kept in order at the public expence, and it ought to be so, if merely to preserve the Hindoo paintings on its external surface; among which, Colonel Baillie's defeat forms a conspicuous ornament near the great entrance, under the front viranda. The tumbrils are represented in the act of blowing up, while the Mysore cavalry are rushing on the little British square, and the effect of the discharges of grape is shown by lanes through the dense masses of horse, on every side urged on by others, seen gallopping forward in countless numbers. Nearly all the trades, casts, and religious ceremonies are depicted on the walls, reminding the classical scholar of Dido's palace. There is only one great mosque in Seringapatam, the minarets of which are very high, and from them there is a fine prospect of the country, which, though much higher than the Cavery, is watered from that river, its stream being forced into canals by prodigious embankments of huge stones, over which, during the rainy season, the roar is tremendous. The garrison is supplied with water conducted over a curious bridge, formed on stone pillars. But the greatest object of interest on the island is Hyder's mausoleum, the pillars of which are black marble; and the expence of keeping up the Mahomedan ceremonies over the tombs of Tippo, &c. costs the company 2000 pagodas per month.

Seringapatam having proved a very pleasant station, Charles took leave of it finally with some regret. He and Frank had become freemasons in the lodge there belonging to the Madras artillery, and many a pleasant evening was spent under the vine arches in its garden, where, on the evening of St. John's day, a ball was given with a grand supper, yielding to those present as much happiness as ever circulated at a court banquet. But he had to take a friendly farewell of the brethren, and retrace his steps to Cannanore. On his way, he had time to see those spots which had been the scenes of contest during the advance of the Bombay army to join Lord Cornwallis, and around Sedasur he beheld the ground still white with human bones. The jungles of the Coorg were passed without seeing either a tiger or elephant. Nearly all the inhabitants are Nairs. Being a region of great natural strength, it is not surprising that its rajah was able to make a brave stand against Hyder Ally. Guards are stationed at the gates that form the western and eastern entrances, and a close bamboo hedge runs along the frontiers. The soldiers wear quilted gowns and turbans, are armed with swords, matchlocks, creeces, and targets, and have a very warlike aspect.

CHAP. XIV.

"But lo! along the Hoogly cast your eyes,
And mark the smoke there curling to the skies.
Ah! heard you not an agonizing cry?
Perhaps now virgin innocence must die;
Led to her husband's blazing funeral bier,
For *suttee!* O disgusting e'en to hear!"

The Hindoo women are as faithful and excellent wives as any in the whole world. Husbands having the power by law of depriving them of privileges held sacred in this country, the influence of those charms of tenderness and person, with which the Almighty has enriched the female form to fascinate and fix the fickle heart of man, is their only security. They are educated in the belief that life is given them but for a husband's happiness, and that it is their duty to die with him. "It is proper," says the Gentoo law, "for a woman, after her husband's death, to burn herself in the fire with his corpse. Every woman who thus burns herself shall remain in paradise with her husband three *crores* and fifty *lacks* of years by destiny. If she cannot burn, she must in that case preserve an inviolable chastity: if she remain always chaste, she goes to paradise; and if she do not preserve her chastity, she goes to hell." But the woman who does not burn herself in the pile with her husband is deprived of her rights. She becomes the *halalcore* of the family, doomed to perform the vilest offices of an outcast from society.

Gentle, meek, passively obedient, and actively engaged in anticipating the wants, wishes, and peculiarities of her husband, a Hindoo wife sees, feels, hears, and understands but for him. Bound in marriage when an infant, he to whom she was betrothed by her father was her *nusseeb*, and should he die even before consummation, she would burn the charms of virgin innocence with him on the pile. The affection of that celebrated lady who, when asked what sort of a person the young conqueror was, whose generosity had restored her to the bosom of her family, answered she did not know, because she had no eyes but for her husband, was not more genuine than the tenderness of many a Hindoo wife. This is evident from the fact, that thousands of Hindoos who could afford to have several wives, marry but one, who must possess great merit to fix the heart of such a luxurious being, in regard to the fair sex, as a native of India.

The passion of love being thought most likely to jar with the lines of distinction drawn by the institution of casts, the ceremonies respecting marriages and the intercourse of the sexes were framed to meet the case. Contracts are formed when the bride and bridegroom are children; and if the husband likes not his lot, he may keep a seraglio of beauties selected from any tribe. It does not appear that the Hindoo ladies in ancient times were secluded, for in the dramatic pieces they are represented as performing parts in public affairs, as in Europe, and Parvardi is fabled as going round the world in search of her husband. It is supposed that the Mahomedans in a great measure introduced the custom of cooping up women in seraglios, which at present only prevails among the higher classes, the females among the lower orders being as much exposed here as in any country on the globe. Husbands and wives hardly ever walk out together, for the Hindoos have no idea of taking air and exercise. When business obliges them to go from home, the wife walks a little way behind the husband, and follows with the most respectful and sedate deportment. The females of many villages go down, according to custom, to the wells for water in the cool of the day, and a more interesting scene cannot be witnessed than to pass on such occasions, and behold groups of happy creatures, seemingly as merry as grigs, surrounded by chubby children, which are all naked, with the exception of a silver ornament suspended at the waist.

It is really melancholy to think that a custom should be supported for ages, by millions of men, which deprives children of their mother when it is the will of Providence to call away the father. Can any thing be more affecting than to see a lady in the bloom of life, decked with flowers, arrayed in all her jewels, perfumed and painted, led round the funeral pile of her husband, amidst the exulting shouts of a crowd, to be consumed by blazing faggots, upon which oil is thrown? In some parts of the Carnatic, a pit is made, and the widow leaps into the flames, or is thrown in by the Brahmins. But in most other places she takes the dead body in her arms, kisses it, and places the head on her bosom, as she sits down in a hollow made in the funeral pile. A procession then goes round it, great shouts are raised, and it is set on fire. If the blaze spreads properly, pain is over in a few moments, for the smoke produces suffocation; but the fire is sometimes so bad, that the legs and arms are roasted before life is extinct. But what fortitude it requires on the part of the victim, to see the preparations, to go through the ceremonies, to distribute presents, all which she is expected to do with ease and satisfaction. The Roman lady who shewed her husband how to die, and presented him with the dagger reeking from her own heart, exhibited not an example of greater magnanimity than that of a Hindoo wife performing suttee.

The sacrifice of human life in this way is enormous, for sometimes great numbers of concubines perform suttee, in common with the wives of a deceased great man. In the year 1803, it was ascertained that two hundred and seventy-five wives were burned with their dead husbands within thirty miles of Calcutta; and in 1804, one hundred and fifteen suttees were performed near the city. Allowing two millions of Hindoos within the circle of this estimate, and seventy millions for the number of natives in India who observe that ceremony, the annual loss of lives is little short of seven thousand. On the 12th of September 1807, near Barnagore, three miles from Calcutta, the body of a Koolin Brahmin named Kristo Deb Mookergee, who died at the age of ninety-two, was burned. He had left twelve wives, three of whom were burned with him. One was a venerable lady, having white locks. Being unable to walk from age, she was placed upon the pile by the Brahmins. The two others were young, and one of them was very beautiful. The old lady was placed on one side of the body, and the two others on the opposite side, when an old Brahmin, the eldest son of the deceased, set the pile on fire, which was instantly in a blaze, amidst the shout of Brahmins, and din of tom toms and tooteries, which drowned the dying cries of the victims. "The Koolin Brahmins," says Dr. Buchanan, "are the purest, and marry as many wives as they please. Hindoos think it an honour to have a Koolin Brahmin for a son-in-law. They sometimes have great numbers of wives. Rajeb Bonnerjee, of Calcutta, has forty, Raj Chunder Bonnerjee forty-two, Ramrajee Bonnerjee fifty, and Birjod Bookerjee, of Bisrampore, now dead, had ninety."

Many efforts have been indirectly made, by the British authorities in India, to arrest this horrible practice, and no doubt with success in the vicinity of stations; but no public act has hitherto been issued for its prohibition. The Hindoos knowing, however, the detestation in which this custom is held by Europeans, now take care to perform suttees in as secret a manner as possible, for in several instances, ladies have been saved, and rescued by force from the flames. A princess was once prevailed upon, by a British officer high in command, to live for the sake of her only son: a considerable time afterwards, in soliciting some advantage for him, she wrote thus: "When you recollect that I am his mother, and that you prevailed upon me to dishonour myself for his sake, you will cease to be offended at my soliciting this favour for him. You forced a duty upon me which does not belong to our sex; if I fail in the execution of it, I shall be the reproach of all who are allied to me; if I succeed, and this country flourish, my offence may be forgotten: my happiness depends upon you; on mine depends that of many. Consider this and determine." But when the Mahomedans were in power they prevented suttee by an exercise of their authority; and it is said, that if the Marquis of Wellesley had continued in India he would have abolished it altogether, as he did the sacrifice of children at Saugur, where twenty-three persons were drowned in the month of January 1801. His lordship by an order in council declared the practice to be murder, punishable by death. The law entitled

"A regulation for preventing the sacrifice of children at Saugur and other places," was instituted on the 20th August 1802.

Although the practice of secluding females from society did not in ancient times prevail in Hindostan, still in the most civilized periods they were held in a state of degradation and slavery. According to law, it requires the testimony of four women to prove what two men substantiate. By the institutes of Menu, women are pronounced so mutable in temper, so unsettled in affection, so perverse in nature, that owing to their passion for men, be they guarded ever so well, they soon become alienated from their husbands. The Veidam is denied to them; therefore they have no law, nor knowledge of expiatory texts, and must be as foul as falsehood. Yet their conduct is constantly to be so sedate and decorous, that they are not to laugh without covering the face with a veil. Adultery is death, and speaking to or sitting on the same couch with a strange man is adultery. Barrenness and the birth of female children are causes for divorcement. Yet Abu Talib Khan, in his vindication of the liberties of Asiatic women, labours to prove that their condition in point of happiness is superior to that in which the females of Europe are placed. He says, that they can see the male relatives of their husbands and fathers, and their old neighbours, domestics, &c. at meals; that they can visit their female friends in palankeens and close carriages, and can have musicians, dancers, and actors, so that in point of society they are not worse than ladies in London, who have to keep their doors shut all day. Wives by a subsequent marriage are not equal in rank to those by a first marriage, nor are they admitted into the society of particular ladies. But he acknowledges, who knew it well, that "it is easier to live with two tigresses than two wives." Teazing a husband is considered an essential quality of beauty; for if she does not teaze him, her charms soon lose their brilliancy in his eyes.

The shaddee or marriage ceremony is very expensive and gorgeous. This is one of the pageants upon which all the Hindoos expend vast sums. Those of the lower orders parade about the town or village in palankeens, on horses, or even on bullocks, just as their circumstances permit. In some tribes dowries are given, and in others the bride is purchased. She remains with her mother 'till maturity, when another pageant takes place in conveying her home; but it is said that the mothers connive at stolen interviews before this second ceremony is permitted.

In conformity to Mr. Fortier's advice, Lieutenant True had sent in his name for purchase, but it requires something more than money to obtain rapid promotion to a company in the British army; and not having particular interest at the Horse Guards, he was obliged to wait for an opportunity in his own corps, or some other regiment in India. He was, however, cheered with hope, and having the interest of a large fund at command, his circumstances were easy, and a smiling little boy now began to charm his vacant moments, by traces of intellectual vivacity. Mrs. True shewed particular attention to Mary, in every way consistent with their difference of rank, and often called with her husband at the office to see the little Emma, who was just six months younger than their Edward. But one morning, after the tappal came in, a sensation of despondence ran through the cantonment, in consequence of a rumour that a great house of agency at Madras had stopped payment, and the next day George received authentic information that those to whom Nannette's fortune had been entrusted were absolutely beggars, having by their failure injured almost every military man on the presidency of Fort St. George.

"Confusion," said Frank Stanley.—"Who can depend on dame Fortune?" ejaculated Charles Thoughtless.

"Well, George," said Nannette, with a brow of care and a lip of joy, "I shall not break my heart about money when I am so rich in having you and Edward." But a tear fell on the cherub cheek which she kissed and pressed to her bosom.

"It will enable me, Nannette, to show how little I ever thought of you and fortune together." But the mournful look he cast towards his laughing son proved that he knew the value of what he had lost.

Peace and plenty at this time gave cheerfulness to the aspect of Malabar. Charles and Frank made many an excursion in the vicinity of the cantonments to witness the tranquil habits of the peasantry, and see their huts covered with melons, pumpkins, and cucumbers, while their pepper vine and plantain topes peeped through the tall cocoa-nut trees around their peaceful habitations. The climate of Malabar is friendly to human life; cooled by alternate breezes from the sea and land, the air is not near so hot as in many parts of the interior much further from the line, and the vast fall of rain tempers, during the monsoon, the most burning part of the year. Game is very plentiful; the partridge, quail, snipe, rabbit, hare and fox, with other varieties abound, and the whole coast is as pleasant a station for military men as any in the country. But a civil war was on the point of deluging the plains of the Carnatic. Sir G. H. Barlow, the governor of Madras, in carrying into effect certain reductions of allowances to the company's officers according to the wishes of the court of directors, had roused a spirit of discontent in the army, which the commander in chief, General M'Dowal, seemed to foment and countenance, while he professed to support government in his place as a member of council. Many of the officers at the head of the company's troops at this time were men of great talent, and they calculated upon being able, by combination, to force the governor to comply with their views. He was unfortunately of a temper of mind ill-suited to carry harsh and unpopular measures with such generous spirits. In short, he found himself unable to govern either the commander in chief or the army, and the king's regiments were forced to level their bayonets against the company's, and dislodge the European officers who were removed from their corps, while their places were supplied by drafts from his majesty's service. But before this was effected some blood had been spilled near Seringapatam, and Colonel Mars had displayed an energy and judgment in securing the fort of Cannanore, and disorganizing the plans in Malabar and Canara, which called forth the approbation of those in power. The commander in chief resigned, and was lost on the passage home, and the governor was soon after removed, while all the officers were restored to their regiments, and very few examples made; it being the general opinion that if the one leader had possessed the spirit of young Cyrus, and the other that of Clearchus, the Madras army never would have had to regret that the violence of passion led them to meditate the destruction of that authority which they were armed to support.

Charles had now nearly began to despair of the promotion which he once expected. Captain Noble had made kind enquiries after his protegé in his letters, but gave no hint that he had a prospect of serving him. However, a change was on the point of taking place when he least expected it; for the adjutant came into the office one day, and with a smiling countenance said, "Thoughtless, I have for some time been exerting myself to promote your interest, and I think, I know at present of a situation that would suit you well." Charles was of course all attention, and expressed his humble thanks. He then made a few observations on the difficulty which a married ensign would have to encounter. "But," said he, "if you prefer it, I can now most probably get you into a sepoy battalion to act as adjutant; and should you be displaced by the return of the officers, the commander in chief would make it a point of promoting you." At length, after several circumlocutions, Charles enquired what the situation was. But instead of an answer, he received such a flattering description of the advantages that he closed with the offer without further hesitation. The adjutant then informed him that he was to be an assistant in a classical school on a very extensive scale in Calcutta. — "Good God, sir," said Charles, "are you jesting with your humble servant; I am a self-taught man, know comparatively nothing of the Latin language, and feel myself even deficient in the grammatical use of my mother tongue." — "Oh, but," answered he, "you possess great application and strong retentive powers; you are young, and the gentleman to whom you are going is perhaps one of the best qualified in the world to bring you forward; and let me also assure you, that the progress you have made in literature, without those advantages which others usually receive, gives you a double claim to consideration."—He bowed very low, on being thus complimented by so good a judge, for Charles had his share of vanity. The adjutant proceeded further into particulars, and informed him that the gentleman in question had been educated at Oxford, was a clergyman of the church of England, and after expatiating largely on his virtues—"in short," said he, "I am his son." —Application was soon after made to the commander in chief for permission to discharge Charles on the ground that he had been offered an advantageous situation in Calcutta, was a very deserving man of a respectable family, and had a wife and child to support. In due course, an answer was received from the military secretary granting the request, on condition of producing a certificate from government sanctioning him to settle in India. He was accordingly granted a furlough to proceed to Calcutta for that purpose, and an opportunity soon occurred.

One of the *beeby*'s ships was about to sail for the Hoogly, and the negociation for a passage introduced him to the lady of Cannanore, for she made the bargain herself: she was of small stature, with a stoop from age, but her eyes were keen and piercing. His conference with her was conducted by Naswangee a parsee, who had a shop in the outer viranda of the beeby's palace. This part, which faces the street, is made into shops and let to merchants, for she loses no means of amassing wealth. It was in Naswangee's shop that he stood and communicated with her ladyship through the iron bars of a window. On paying one hundred and fifty rupees, he procured an order to be received on board the semidammy, and prepared to take leave of his patron the adjutant. For this purpose he spent nearly the whole night in composing a morsel in verse :

The exile doomed in foreign lands to roam,
And quit for life his dear parental home,
With many a sigh relinquishes the shore,
And friends who make each sigh felt ten times more.
Fondly his eye each parting object views,
His tongue repeats a thousand fond adieus ;
When far away, his heart with friendship burns,
And fancy to familiar scenes returns.
So I, till life's dull ocean is passed o'er,
Till earth-born feelings touch the soul no more,
While memory's pencil paints the scene behind,
Will turn to thee my ever grateful mind.
Adieu! adieu! thou friend most truly dear,
We part, the thought excites a painful tear ;
But on my heart remains engraved thy name,
Which heaven preserve for honour, wealth, and fame!

"And now, Frank," said Charles, "I have only one wish left, and that is to see you promoted ; for confusion to me, but I feel sore at leaving you a step behind me."

"Why, Charles," replied he, "I have just been

informed that I might make my fortune by marriage. Colonel Brilliant's houses at Seringapatam and Tellichery have been offered to me, with the colonel's pretty mistress, a French girl, for he is going home, and wishes to provide her with a husband, who is to be made a conductor, and stationed on this coast."

"And you had to bear the insult of such a proposal," said Charles.

"Yes, confusion to me, but I must swallow it; for Colonel Brilliant's rank protects him."

"He is a married man too, and has several fine daughters at home, with whom his lady remained," said Charles. "I am surprized at him."

"Such is the morality of India," replied Frank; "and confusion to me, if any thing that can be conceived need surprize us. But here is a letter just arrived from my mother: — Miss Sarah is still as when I left home, and she makes frequent enquiries about me. If I could get an ensigncy—"

"The moment I save money enough," answered Charles, "you shall have one. Let hope be your guiding star."

Having sent a copy of the farewel lines to the adjutant, and presented another to Frank, who accompanied him to the beach, he embarked with Mary and Emma, and sailed down the coast to Alleppeé, where the vessel was to take in the remainder of her cargo of coir, a material which is converted into cordage and cables of a very serviceable kind, having the property of never rotting in water. The crew on board the semidammy, which was an English-built ship purchased by the beeby, were mussulmen, and natives of the Persian gulf, a region producing skilful seamen and bold pirates. They were strong and active sailors, of an Arabian cast of features, and they most strictly conformed to all the ceremonies prescribed by the Koran. At sun-rise and sun-set every day each man, on his mat spread on the deck, uttered his prayers aloud with numerous prostrations, and the name of Alla and Mahomed resounded from every part of the vessel. At night the watch below, seated on mats round the knockáda before his cabin door, heard the Koran read, and sang hymns in praise of the Most High. The regularity observed by all was worthy of observation, and formed a complete contrast to the voyage from Madras, as well as from England, during which the sailors were flogged almost every day for misconduct. The knockada was very attentive to Thoughtless and his family, sending them every day presents of figs, dates, raisins, almonds, and preparations of spiced rice and sweetmeats, which, with dried fish, plantains, and vegetable curries, constituted their diet. They did not use vinous or spirituous liquors of any kind.

The voyage was made nearly all the way in sight of the coast; having left Cannanore soon after the monsoon, the vessel reached the sand heads in twenty-one days, being wafted by delightful breezes, without a squall to interrupt the beauty of the scene. Nothing occurred to excite an apprehension of danger, except a report that a French privateer was cruizing off the coast of Malabar, and the appearance of a dead whale drifting down the Bay of Bengal, which at a distance seemed very formidable. A pilot having come on board, in eight days more the semidammy was at anchor near Calcutta, and Charles prepared to go on shore, delighted with the banks of the Hoogly, which presented an endless variety of stately buildings, beautiful gardens, plantations, lawns, and meadows.

He soon found the residence of his employer, and was pleased with him and every thing. He was one of the most noble looking Irish gentlemen his eyes had ever rested upon. His venerable age, for he was upwards of sixty, gave peculiar interest to the dignity of his person. Dressed in black, and powdered with care, he handed Mary up to his drawing-room with an air of grandeur that struck Thoughtless with awe. Every thing was in readiness for their reception; the accommodations were excellent, being on a scale of liberality much beyond expectation, and the most generous solicitude was expressed to supply omissions. His son had not exaggerated, when he stated that his father's academy was a large one. It consisted of about seventy pupils, forty of whom were boarders.

The house was superb, and the school-room so spacious, that all the assistants and scholars were under the master's eye; and there was a large punko, by which, in the hot season, the air was kept pleasantly cool. A look from this venerable man had the effect of producing silence and attention; yet he was all mildness, seldom using a harsh word or inflicting punishment.

At first this reverend man merely directed the attention of Charles to the discipline of the school. Two of his assistants were anabaptists; and Thoughtless was soon assailed by their zeal in the cause of conversion, and assured that in his present state he was as one of the damned. But being both very worldly-minded and discontented men, their success in making converts must have been very limited. One was the classical assistant. He soon complained to Charles that his salary was too small, and intimated that it was his intention to set up a school for himself, roundly insinuating that he could turn the leaves of the classics over with more rapidity than his employer, into whose private history he entered with some very uncharitable inuendoes respecting the weaknesses of human nature, from which this amiable man was not altogether free. The other assistant, a person of plain education, was just competent to teach reading, writing, and common arithmetic. He was a converted man, being, as he thought, under the influence of the spirit. He had, when in a graceless state, attempted to commit suicide, but was unsuccessful in the moment of action, having only blown away part of his head, which gave his countenance an awful expression. He was now a sort of preacher, visiting the diseased in mind and body, and consoling them with exceedingly long prayers. In expounding the Scripture, he often got into depths far beyond his capacity, and expressed his perplexity in groans. Anxious to be placed as master over a baptist charity school then about to be established, he sought every opportunity of shewing his zeal and ability to the mission at Serampore, from whom he expected the situation; and I really believe he considered himself unfortunate in labouring in an unfruitful vineyard; for he must have been sincere, as he frequently, with tears in his eyes, lamented his failure in not being able to convert the master of the school from the wicked path to the road of grace.

Thoughtless was however charmed with the manners of his master, to whom he explained the great deficiency and inaccuracy of his education, and the fear he entertained that he should be found an incapable assistant. The master was kind enough to express a contrary opinion. "You are anxious to acquire a knowledge of Latin," said he, "and I know not a more certain way of learning that fine language than by teaching it." Charles looked at him with astonishment. "You will understand the truth of what I tell you hereafter," said he;

"there is nothing more correctly true, than that by teaching we learn. — Your grammar class, by constantly repeating their lessons, will impress them on your memory; and any difficulty you meet I shall explain. Every evening we will look over together the subjects for the following day, and thus prevent you from either falling into mistakes or exposing yourself."

In a few months he had the Eaton Latin Grammar by heart — Erasmus, Eutropius, and Cornelius Nepos, with Clark's Introduction, at command. He soon read Justin, Ovid, Virgil, Horace, and, having familiarized himself with the Latin classics, began to learn Greek. In short, his employer wrote to his son that Charles was of more use than all his other assistants; but expressed some apprehensions that he would kill himself by intense study both night and day.

CHAP. XV.

"From such a land who longs not to depart,
That has within his breast a feeling heart?
Yes, every one should hail the happy day,
When Gunga's bosom bears him far away.
Yet many linger on the torrid shore
For wealth, 'till wealth can comfort life no more."

Many of the ceremonies, rites, sacrifices, penances, and practices of the brahminical idolatry fill the breast of a christian, soon after his arrival in India, with horror and disgust, which imperceptibly wear away; and if he have kept no record of those first impressions, he ceases to remember them, and regards that which is so common as not to surprize him, as in no way interesting to the rest of mankind. With what we are familiar ourselves, we often think others perfectly acquainted; and this propensity of the mind to give to the world what is new instead of what is old, shews the importance to every traveller of keeping a journal, and taking notes on the first view of things. In the foregoing pages many allusions have been made to the shocking sights every where to be seen over India of voluntary mutilations and excruciating sufferings. Volumes might be filled, if the various temples in the interior were described; but the writer, having only space for a few remarks, must refer the reader for more copious information to Buchanan, Tennant, and other authors, who have faithfully pourtrayed scenes in India.

The pagoda of Juggurnaut is situated on the Bay of Bengal, 300 miles S. W. of Calcutta. Such numbers of pilgrims die on their way thither, that for fifty miles round the country is white with human bones. Hundreds of old people travel thousands of miles every year to die there, some of them measuring the whole way with their bodies, others journeying on the broad of their backs, and several tumbling head over heels. Thousands of dogs, jackals, and vultures live on the bodies of the dead, and the adjutants are so tame as to approach and gape with horrid expectation at the living. The shouts raised by the continuous multitude constantly gaining sight of the temple from all quarters are awful. For several miles round it is like a vast encampment, and sometimes great numbers are killed by the rush of the multitude towards the great gates. Seated on a throne, between his brother and sister Boleram and Shubudra, appears the idol, made of a block of wood, having a frightfully large visage painted black, with arms of gold and gorgeous apparel. On the walls and gates of the temple are indecent figures, cut in stone, upon which both sexes look with satisfaction. During the great festivals, the idols are paraded about in pagodas made of wood, ninety feet high, fixed on carriages with sixteen wheels, and drawn by men with cables, while the axletrees are often red with the blood of devotees of both sexes, that throw themselves beneath to be crushed to death; their bodies are carried away by *hurries* and thrown into the Golgotha, to be eaten by obscene animals. The stench of this place is dreadful, and on every side the senses are disgusted by the squalid and ghastly presence of the famished pilgrims. Devotees with clotted hair and painted naked bodies are everywhere seen practising their self-tortures; and the exhalations from human ordure would infect the air, were it not that the filth serves as food to the brahminy bulls, which roam about in great numbers.

One hundred thousand souls are constantly around Juggurnaut, and their shouts are appalling when the idol is brought out, at which time the multitude, having green palms in their hands, fall down and worship. Then the procession advances, preceded by elephants and dancing girls and buffoons, while upwards of one hundred Brahmins are writhing their bodies into lascivious contortions in the different virandas belonging to each story of the artificial pagoda, that moves along glittering with tinsel and adorned with hundreds of flags, streamers and ensigns, the air resounding with the noise of tomtoms, tooteries, and bands of music. The priests sing and shout, sometimes telling the people that the god is pleased and smiles; at others, that he will not move, and frowns 'till he is gratified with more blood; while approbation at their indecent gestures, and their gross contortions of body, is expressed in yells of sensual delight. It takes £200 worth of broad cloth to cover the rutt or carriage, and the expences of the idol are £8,702 per annum, a large portion of which is for dancing girls, who are prostitutes belonging to the temple. His table costs £4,514 a year. But there are other Juggurnauts in several places, and the practices at Ishera near Calcutta, and at the temple of Kalli and elsewhere, are of a similar description. At the former place, which is near Serampore, the baptist missionaries may be seen preaching in the vicinity of those horrible scenes, while crowds are amusing themselves in laughing at these worthy men.

In some tribes the female children are destroyed, and wives purchased from other casts, and this unnatural custom is supposed to have originated in pride. The Jerajahs, Jaits, and Rajkumars practise infanticide, and the mother herself is commonly the executioner, either by putting some opium into the infant's mouth, or drawing the umbilical cord over the face. Colonel Walker, when political agent in Guzerat, investigated the matter by desire of Governor Duncan, whose humanity prompted him to aim at its abolition. It had been a custom there for 2000 years, and Broach or Barygaza is mentioned by very ancient authors as its chief seat. According to calculation, 300 children were murdered annually in Kattywar and Kutch. Colonel Walker's correspondence with the chiefs of those countries is extremely interesting, and fully detailed in the records of the times, but particularly in Moore's Hindoo Infanticide. He entreated many of them to let their daughters live, and at first received positive refusals and insulting letters. A curious one from Futteh Mahomed, to whom he wrote, in addressing the Row of Booge-Booge, is all I can insert. "It is notorious that since the avatara of Shri Chrishna, the Jerajahs, who are descended from the Jadoos, have, during a period of 4,900 years, been accustomed to kill their daughters; and it has no doubt come to your knowledge that all of God's creation, even the mighty emperors of Hindostan, besides all others, the conductors of the affairs of this world, have preserved friendship with this court, and never acted in this respect unreasonably. But you, who are an *amir* of the great sircar, the honourable company, having written to me on the subject, I have felt much uneasiness, for it does not accord with your good character. This *durbar* has always maintained friendship with the honourable company; and notwithstanding this, you have acted so unreasonably in this respect, that I am much distressed. No one has, until this day, wantonly quarrelled with this court, who has not in the end suffered loss. Do not again address me on this subject." Nevertheless Colonel Walker did persevere, and at length by publicly discussing and exposing the enormity of the practice, many of the supporters were led to abhor infanticide; and although Governor Duncan had only received a cold approval from his superiors, he had the satisfaction of saving many thousands of infants by his spirited and benevolent interference through Colonel Walker. The supreme government acknowledged that his plan was worthy of humanity; but added, "the speculative success of it cannot be considered to justify the prosecution of measures which may expose to hazard the essential interests of the state." Yet it is probable that no speculation in India ever raised the British character so high in the estimation of the natives; for many of the mothers came some years afterwards to Colonel Walker's tent in Kattywar, and placed their female children in his hands with all natural marks of affection, emphatically calling their little ones *his children*. Public opinion, however, was still adverse to the preservation of them, for the little ones in many instances were disguised as boys. The innocent creatures appeared ashamed of acknowledging their sex, and assured Colonel Walker that they were not girls, calling on their fathers with infantine simplicity to corroborate their assertions.

But infanticide, suttee, pilgrimage, and self-torture destroy not more lives than the secret practices of the Brahmins, who stop at no atrocity to gain their ends. For money they will arrest the course of justice, and screen the murderer from the laws. The blood of a Brahmin being sacred, the offence of causing it to be shed is considered by every Hindoo as the most frightful of all crimes, subjecting the soul of the perpetrator to tortures of the severest kind in the lowest hell; therefore the priests, when obstacles oppose their desires, often murder their wives and children, and mutilate themselves. The practice of dhurnea is very general in Hindostan Proper. A Brahmin, upon being paid, will place himself opposite the door of a person whom he wishes to compel to the adoption of some measure contrary to his interest, either to stay a prosecution, or pay an unjust debt, and starve himself should the man not comply, or he will threaten to cut off his leg or arm, and sprinkle the blood on his house. Few things are impossible to the Brahmins when they use this instrument of terror. Another mode of dhurnea is to place a cow or an old woman on a pile of faggots, and threaten to burn the one or other unless the thing desired be granted. No crime subjects the Brahmins to the punishment of death; and it is easy to conceive into what horrible acts the passions and desires of human nature lead these men thus placed beyond the reach of capital punishments.

Soon after the arrival of Thoughtless in Calcutta, he applied to government through the chief secretary's office for permission to settle in India, and expected a favourable answer, but to his surprise he received a flat refusal, and was referred to the Court of Directors. Their sanction being thought, however, a matter of course, Colonel Mars permitted him to remain in Calcutta, and the adjutant congratulated him on the prospect of continuing on pay so much longer in the regiment. In short, all things seemed fortunate, for the classical assistant having realized his intention of setting up a school for himself, Charles succeeded to his situation.

The scholars were generally speaking half-casts, the sons of Europeans by country-born mothers, with some Armenians and Hindoos. Many of the half-casts were of dark complexions, but of most excellent capacity, with very generous dispositions and affectionate hearts. It is to be regretted that some plan has not been devised to employ them for the advantage of their country, as they labour at present under illiberal exclusion from the army, navy, and civil service, which makes them discontented subjects. Lord Valentia, when in India, wished to send them all to England (vol. 1. p. 241.), which was a singular expedient for remedying the evils to be apprehended from their increase. There are many very worthy men in that large body of subjects that now come under the name of half-casts, and the number and respectability of the whole entitle them to very great consideration. For many years after Charles left Calcutta, he corresponded with his pupils, some of whose letters are very creditable to both their head and heart.

The two following are given as specimens, the first being in answer to a complimentary note, written from Bombay on his marriage.

MY DEAR SIR, Calcutta, 10th April 1817.

The receipt of your letter of the 13th ultimo has afforded me infinite pleasure, and your pleasing congratulations I accept with particular satisfaction.

In your welfare I have ever felt greatly interested, from a sense of the obligations I owe to you; and I rejoice extremely at your success in promoting yourself so favourably, which must alone be ascribed to that singular industry, perseverance, activity, and wonderful talent which have ever so conspicuously marked your character.

Correspondence is my delight, but from want of leisure, owing to my numerous avocations, my friends have hitherto been neglected; I embrace notwithstanding eagerly your invitation, from a conviction that a correspondent of your acknowledged capacity must prove to me edifying. In so saying, permit me to assure you that I mean no compliment, but pay a just tribute to that individual who has contributed so much to the formation of my understanding.

I shall begin with informing you of the changes which have occurred since your departure, and other matters that I presume will be deemed both interesting, and connected in some measure with your-

self. * * * * * * * *
* * * * * * * * *
* * * * * * * * *

The seizure of the Ernaud at Bombay, for want of a plantation bond, agreeably to an act of Parliament passed 200 years ago, and her final condemnation by the court of admiralty at that presidency, greatly alarmed the mercantile community, and for a time arrested commercial speculations in this quarter. The matter was jointly brought before the supreme court by a body of the merchants of this settlement, and happily decided in their favour, after the most eloquent discussion, which took place on the occasion. Doubts are still entertained as to any alteration made in the mind of the Recorder of Bombay, whose court is as competent in its power as the supreme court, and who must either candidly avow his error, or continue fixed in his resolution, and seize every ship in the same predicament as the Ernaud; because the decision of the supreme court, from being directly opposite to his own ideas of the case, arraigns his ability as a judge, and the big wigs here have noticed with some degree of severity, the conduct of the Recorder as wholly unwarrantable in the sanction of a measure which would operate seriously to the prejudice of the mercantile body in India, by discouraging speculation, a circumstance by which great loss would result to the honourable company, in the reduction of revenue. "Who shall decide when doctors disagree?" Opinion is divided of course on this important question. The lawyers at Bombay think with their recorder; those here follow the judges. But the judge at Bombay has three opinions against him, and he is too candid a man to persevere in error, after the conviction of truth has flashed upon his understanding. The affair has seriously lowered the rate of interest, from the immense quantity of money in the market, owing to a great commercial intercourse, which existed between the neighbouring settlements, having been in a great measure obstructed.

For my present situation, I am obliged to Mr. Palmer, who appointed me assistant in the marine registry office, an institution lately established, under the immediate countenance and patronage of the government, by the merchants, for the better providing ships and vessels with registered Asiatic sailors, and for protecting them from the many impositions and abuses to which both owners and seamen were subject under the old system. The rules and regulations which have been framed into bye-laws widely differ from those of the ghaut syrangs, (a class of men equal to the kidnappers of Hǒlland and crimps of England, who study nothing but their own vile interest), in the reduced ingress which they allow, compared to the former usage. In the carrying of such an ordinance into effect, the most violent opposition was experienced; for the syrangs, foreseeing that the new arrangement would blast their wicked prospects, exerted their powerful influence over the seamen; but the perseverance, zeal, and diligence exercised by the officers attached to the department, defeated resistance, and successfully attained the desired object.

In the hope that you will continue to evince your friendly consideration, I shall take leave of you, trusting that your family enjoy good health; and with cordial wishes for your prosperity,

I remain, my dear sir,
Yours very faithfully,
G. R.

MY DEAR SIR, Calcutta, Oct. 10th 1817,

Judging that my long silence will excite surprize, I am induced, with a view to expel from your mind any unfavourable impression which it may have made, to explain the cause, by recounting to you the recent disasters which befel my family, since I last had the pleasure of addressing you.

The first unhappy event was the dangerous illness of Mrs. R., who, being attacked by the pestilence raging here, was nearly carried off by it. She has at length unexpectedly recovered after lingering for a period of six weeks on the brink of the grave. The next serious occurrence was my father's bed-room being struck with lightning a little after midnight, when he was asleep. Fortunately it did him no injury, nor did it hurt any person in the house. His escape is considered particularly miraculous and providential, as his bedstead was not a foot distant from the window frame through which, and the archway over it, the lightning penetrated, entering the terrace of the house, which some of the neighbours had an opportunity of observing, appeared all in a blaze. The premises suffered considerable injury, and the window frames, venetians, and glass sashes were broken. After this I was obliged to go up the river for change of air with Mrs. R. to re-establish her health; and these events will, I trust, plead sufficiently for the delay which has occurred in acknowledging your very friendly and interesting letters of the 21st May and 2d June.

The opportunity afforded me of evincing my attachment to your interests, by promoting vigorously the object of your wishes conveyed to me in the last paragraph of your letter now before me, is particularly gratifying, as to support your undertakings under any circumstances is and ever will be an object of my most anxious solicitude. * *

* * * * * * * * *

* * * * * * * * *

Mortality in Calcutta and its adjacent provinces is very great. The police report of deaths within its jurisdiction states from two to three hundred people falling victims to the cholera morbus every day.

The merchants of Calcutta have obtained the sanction of government for erecting an exchange here, and purpose building it at their expence on that space of ground between the Bankshall and the river.

We expect soon to be gratified with the launch of the line of battle ship, built by the merchants of the settlement to set at rest the competition between the Calcutta and Bombay builders, by sending this grand specimen to England as an eastern offering to his majesty's navy at prime cost, deducting the profits of the voyage home, for she is to carry a valuable cargo.

Accept the assurances of my respectful regard and esteem, and believe me to remain with much sincerity,

My dear sir,
Your very constant friend,
G. R.

The proprietor of the school was of a very liberal and hospitable disposition, and he had a party of friends every week to dinner, as well to let the boys see company as to give celebrity to his seminary. Charles was exceedingly happy, having gained his entire esteem, and looking forward to the agreeable prospect of being perfected by him in both the Latin and Greek languages. But this felicity was not long to continue. Cards of invitation were sent out for a ladies' party which had to be countermanded, for this valuable man was taken ill with an inflammation in his liver, which baffled all medical skill, and in one month he was laid in his grave. He bore the greatest pain with fortitude and hope. Charles hardly ever quitted his bed-side. Indeed he was nearly distracted at the prospect of losing him, and no grief could be more sincere than his, for he had all to lose by his death.

This venerable man belonged to a highly respectable family in the south of Ireland, and had taken his degree as master of arts. From the interest of his connexions he soon obtained a good living as a clergyman; but being of a gay and extravagant turn he fell into embarrassments, and came out in the suite of Lord Macartney to the Cape of Good Hope, where a situation under government was obtained for him by his lordship, thence proceeding to China. Soon after, however, the Cape was given up to the Dutch and he lost his place, upon which he came out to India in search of patronage. Notwithstanding his ability, elegance of manners, and introduction to men in power, he was unsuccessful, and at length became so entangled by debts to sircars that to avoid a gaol he removed to Chandernagore under French protection, where a widow with some cash was unable to resist his captivating addresses, and surrendered herself without much ceremony. She was a pretty brunette, with all the vivacity of her nation, and several fine children were the fruits of this unfortunate connexion. With the little fund which she possessed, he freed himself from the sircars in Calcutta, and established a school which promised much wealth. She resided at Chandernagore, and he generally paid her a visit on Saturday; but she came to town occasionally, and he did not scruple to seat her at his table. When his malady increased to an alarming degree he became exceedingly anxious that his condition should be kept a secret from her, for, said he, "she will come here and prevent me from dying in peace." All precautions were unavailing. She came bathed in tears. Night and day she kept ringing in his ears the desolate state of herself and children, till he executed a deed of two shares he held in the Laudable Society. After this she appeared easy, and no sooner was the breath out of his body than she began to remove every thing, and having sent several trunks off before her to the boat, she soon followed in all the silent majesty of woe. Soon after, a judgment bond creditor took charge of the house, and the seal of the supreme court was affixed to the doors. When Charles saw the remains of this respected man laid in the grave, he looked at Mary and his children with a heart ready to break, for he saw nothing but disappointment on earth. But the sun of his prosperity, which seemed to have sunk for ever below the horizon, rose again with greater splendour.

The parents of many of the boarders resided on the west coast of Sumatra, in Poulo Penang and at Manilla, and the houses of agency in Calcutta who had charge of them looked with a favourable eye upon Thoughtless as a fit person to carry on the concern. But of this he was not aware except by the non-removal of the scholars; and having no funds of his own to purchase furniture, &c. he considered the attempt on his part to continue such an establishment as quite hopeless. However, upon consulting with those patrons of the academy with whom he was intimate, one of them offered to join him in the undertaking, as soon as he perceived that it might turn out a profitable speculation, and in his first generous impulse he offered Charles one half of the school, a deed of which he thoughtlessly deferred accepting, being well pleased with other conditions which were thrown in with great seeming liberality. This gentleman was a half-cast, who possessed many good qualities, with a very vigorous mind and amazing activity. He purchased the school furniture, plate, books, maps, globes and orreries, and circulated a card intimating to his friends and the public that, in compliance with a wish expressed by the late reverend proprietor of the seminary, he had determined to support the institution, which would be conducted under Charles Thoughtless the head assistant, and he pledged himself for attention to the morals, comforts, and progress in literature of the pupils. The school now went on successfully for a year, and the public examination exhibited such proofs of pleasing improvement, accompanied with the distribution of so many prize medals of silver and gold, that the parents were delighted. Upon which Charles feeling his situation an uncertain one, pressed the execution of the deed of copartnership, but the gentleman would now only part with one-third of the school, which Thoughtless deemed it best to accept, although he had to pass his bond for fifteen hundred rupees, the price fixed on that part of the concern, without the furniture.

Meanwhile Charles had become a member of a masonic lodge, and in regard to society and comfort his situation was improving. He now kept his buggy and palankeen, and appeared on the course or in Fort William every evening among the fashionables. But his partner now entered upon the speculation of setting up a circulating library, and became desirous of parting with the school, for which purpose he entered into a treaty with another extensive schoolmaster, from whom he was to receive a very considerable sum for the transfer of the pupils, and Charles was to be handed over, not as a partner but an assistant; for this gentleman having been unfortunate in a former connexion of that nature, determined never again to risk the consequences of a copartnership with any one, and he had accordingly made a promise on that head to his wife. Thoughtless, who had felt his consequence as a proprietor, declined all offers in any other shape, although they were very liberal, and so the negociation ended.

His partner in school-keeping, however, had in the meantime established a printing-office and newspaper, as well as a circulating library, and having so many irons in the fire he felt desirous of selling the academy to Thoughtless. Terms being agreed upon, an attorney was instructed to prepare the necessary documents, and Charles considering himself fixed, took a lease of the house in his own name. But some time after his partner either fearing he should never be paid the sum agreed upon, or being offended with something which had occurred, wished to cancel the negociation and reoccupy his place as manager of the funds of the school. As Thoughtless had never touched one penny of the profits, the whole having gone to pay off his debt for the first purchase, he determined to keep possession. The other stormed and brought the attorney's clerk to threaten him with an action; but an accommodation took place, and Charles on passing his bond for two thousand rupees became sole proprietor of the school, but not of the furniture. This was a point of great distress, for his late partner a few days after sent for the tables and chairs, which would have left him awkwardly situated had it not been for a circumstance which then occurred.

A celebrated mathematical proficient, who held a situation under the paymaster-general, had involved himself in tribulation with government by starting extraordinary questions respecting the affairs of the nation, and had embroiled himself with his employer by preferring charges against him, which a committee pronounced not demonstrated. He lost his place, worth £100 per mensem, and purchased a school which he called the Polite Academy. The prospectus of this undertaking was a very curious production, for it ridiculed the idea of classical learning in India, and yet enforced its arguments by quotations from Ovid. It consisted of four closely printed pages, which Dr. Talib, who attended the school in his capacity of surgeon, had freed from solecisms, and garnished with fulminating concords. But practice is often at variance with theory. Mr. Philomath had not been long teaching algebra before he sighed for a classical partner, and Thoughtless was summoned from Virgil by a shake of the durwan's bell to receive his visit in dashing buggy on that identical subject. "I have no idea," said he, after explaining his business, "that we should form a junction on any other terms than those of perfect equality, my house being admirably suited; the only condition I make is that you join me, all the rest I leave to yourself." Charles thanked him for his offer, but declined it. However, when his late partner sent for the furniture, he got into his buggy, closed with Mr. Philomath, and removed with his pupils, there being a clause of surrender in his lease on paying two months rent, the premises being taken at three hundred rupees per month.

For some time things went on most flourishingly, and the profits were very great; but additions had to be made to the house that swallowed up a considerable part; and it being in the nature of man that as his means increase so do his wants, Charles was able to save nothing; but, on the contrary, continued not only indebted to his former partner but to his present one seventeen hundred rupees, being the amount of one half the moveables, for which he had passed his note of hand. Dr. Talib was editor of one of the newspapers, there being seven at that time in Calcutta; and finding that Charles had a taste for poetry as well as prose, he paid him much attention. Of a very eccentric genius, Dr. Talib sometimes formed tangents from the common sphere of intellect; and about this time he was labouring indefatigably to prove that Adam had addressed Eve in the Arabic language. The literati of the college of Fort William being of opinion that Sanscrit was the mother tongue, war commenced, and Hocus Pocus with Hugo Pocus opened their batteries on Talib and Philo-Talib, but were so bespattered with paper bullets and covered with smoke, that they retired leaving the field to the latter, who turned their arms against Anthony Apposite esquire, and forced him behind his entrenchments, where he lay like a porcupine with a quill pointed in every direction. Great learning was displayed on the part of the college, and some ingenuity on the side of Talib; but the former questioned his profundity in Arabic lore, and accused him of being a plagiarist on such plausible grounds, that it required all his effrontery to parry such home-thrusts. As to Philo, he came in for his share, and he was rebuked for having given Greek and Latin quotations at random from French authors, instead of their originals.

The masonic lodge to which Charles belonged at first consisted chiefly of the tradesmen in the Cossitollah; but a rage for this mystery having taken possession of the civil and military ranks, many of them joined it, and Dr. Talib became the master, while Mr. Philomath officiated as secretary. The harmonic spirit of masonry, however, was not sufficient to preserve brotherly love in such a heterogeneous mixture; for the civil and military brethren, considering themselves as belonging to a different sphere, were shocked by the vulgarity of the plebeians, who, in return, black-balled the candidates proposed by them, and prevented the introduction of their friends; for, according to a public bye-law in every lodge, should two black balls be found in the ballot for a new member, he is rejected without enquiry; if only one, reasons are to be assigned and investigation had on the subject. Dr. Talib was at the head of the patricians, and Mr. Philomath led the lower orders, when a schism took place. A candidate was proposed, and black-balled as usual; but Dr. Talib being determined to carry his point, assembled his forces on the next night and made a speech, in which he signified the resolution of the majority to proceed in the initiation of the rejected by open force. All the plebeians quitted the lodge; but it was suggested, after the doors had been secured by Mr. Philomath, that Dr. Talib might remove the warrant, and accordingly it was proposed to return for the purpose of guarding that document, without which no lodge could assemble. But the tyler with a drawn sword obstructed the passage. "Cut him down," said one, "with his own weapon." "You may kill me," replied the young civilian very firmly, "but till then, you do not pass here." However, after the business was concluded, they returned into the lodge and found the warrant cut out of the frame. It was then hinted that Dr. Talib had it on his person, and an effort was made to recover the instrument. Philomath, followed by his troops, entered the supper room where the patricians were handling their knives and forks; "I charge you," said he to the master, "with having stolen the warrant," and he extended his hand towards Talib's breast. "Touch me," cried he, grinning most alarmingly, while his loud voice echoed through the green room, "and through your body this shall go," and the knife was raised in air. "And through your body this shall go," shouted all the legion rising from the table; but Philomath retreated in grand style, with his front to danger, though he fully expected a facer from a pupil of

Crib, who followed him down the hall shewing the attitudes of science to his companions, who burst their sides with laughter, and quaffed their claret with supreme delight. Counsellors Strettel and Fergusson were fee'd, and the law restored the warrant.

In the meantime years were passing away.—Colonel Mars and the adjutant had returned to England. Mr. True's interest had been unsuccessfully exerted for Frank Stanley, who still remained in *statu quo*, with the expectation that his regiment would be ordered to England; dreading which, George, who was now the father of three children, had exchanged into the 65th at Bombay, and accompanied that corps to the Isle of Rodriquez, and thence to the Mauritius, which General Abercromby captured with little loss, as well as the island of Bourbon, which was ably reduced by Colonel Keating. Upon his return to Bombay, he served on the expedition to the Persian Gulf and in Guzerat, where by the accidental rencounter with Robert Gordon, faithfully recorded at the opening of these sketches, he discovered the aspect of hope smiling in the distance. The adjutant who had succeeded Charles's friend, was also disposed to serve him, and the commanding officer perceiving that an answer from the Court of Directors was a visionary expectation, permitted himself to be prevailed upon to recommend Thoughtless to Sir

George Nugent for an ensigncy, which he might resign and thus free himself from the army; but Sir George, upon enquiry, finding that Charles was doing well, and that he had conducted himself quietly in Calcutta, authorized his discharge, which was accordingly sent to him with due formality. He of course thought he had done with the army for ever, and laid his shoulder to the oar with all his strength. He had acquired some little celebrity as a man of letters, written some prologues and fugitive pieces in the Vakeel and the papers of the day. But having formed an acquaintance with Tom Paine, esq. proprietor of the Grecian circus, who pressed him much to tread the stage as an amateur, he felt desirous of exhibiting his dramatic talents, yet as his partner was of opinion that it might not tend to the reputation of the school, he relinquished his intention. His astonishment was however considerable at finding some time afterwards that Mr. Philomath was determined to perform at the new theatre, of which he had become a proprietor. Charles attended on that night chiefly for the purpose of seeing my Lord Westmorland; but Philomath happening to make some very uncourtly advances towards the throne of his sovereign, and to appear as if he were star-gazing, received a volley of suppressed disapprobation, which so completely confounded him that he bade adieu to the Chouringhee company for ever. It must be owned, however, that Prince Henry was at home, and that Falstaff could not be in better hands.

Mr. Paine, of the Grecian circus, was a great curiosity, being an admirer of Utopian felicity, and the innocence of human nature. His affairs were very unprosperous; and the theatre, which he had erected at much expence, was a losing concern. He was in debt; and every effort he made to extricate himself only involved him the more. Charles felt a strong inclination to serve him. "Paine," said he, one day soon after Philomath had appeared as a nobleman, "I am now at liberty to take a part. Get up an easy comedy, or two farces; let the characters be well cast, permit no one to choose his own part, and I will answer for it you will please the audience, and draw public attention to your theatre." To this he agreed. But Dr. Talib at that time was possessed with the notion that nature had formed him for the part of Hamlet, and he persuaded Paine to attempt that most difficult undertaking. Ophelia was performed by a dark lifeless half-cast, whose face had to receive such a coat of white-wash that all expression was destroyed. But the doctor, in contemplating his own success, forgot all necessary combination, fully confident that he should electrify the house, and turn observation to himself alone. To ensure this, he stamped and stared, acted the very madman, clenched his fist in the face of the quiet

Ophelia, and groaned so tremendously, that when he came to give the instructions to the players, and talked of o'erstepping the modesty of nature, an ironical peal of applause continued for an hour, with loud fits of unrestrained laughter; but he went on and finished the part, attributing the disapprobation to the rancour of his enemies, rather than to his own misconception of the character. In short, he insisted on re-acting it, and an audience was obtained by a gratuitous distribution of tickets. Charles acted the part of Horatio, and obtained much applause in the critiques written on the occasion; but the consequences were disastrous to him, for his partner and he could never agree afterwards, and at last came to such an open rupture, that the former placed the note for 1,700 rupees in the hands of an attorney, that Charles might be immediately arrested. Mr. Squeezehim had the politeness to apprize Thoughtless, that unless the cash was instantly paid, a writ would issue forthwith. He was greatly puzzled; but having heard of the princely conduct of John Palmer, esquire, one of the most noble-minded merchants that ever breathed, he wrote him a short note, simply stating the circumstance, and adding one or two observations on the singular mode of vengeance to which his partner had resorted. This note was accompanied by a copy of the school accounts, by which Charles had a balance of outstanding debts due to him, to the amount of 3,000 rupees. Mr. Palmer said in reply, that he had not looked at the accounts, for he thought no man who could write such a simple note would attempt to deceive him, and that he had sent a check for the sum claimed to Mr. Squeezehim's office. Philomath, being thus foiled, would not receive the money, so the check was returned to the generous Mr. Palmer, and an indelible impression of gratitude was made on the heart of Charles Thoughtless. In consequence of the above affair, he sold his share of the academy, and cleared 10,000 rupees, besides freeing himself from all incumbrances; but he was restricted from exercising the profession of a schoolmaster, for five years, in or near the city of Calcutta.

Having now some money for the first time in his life, Charles thought of his promise to Frank Stanley: he wrote to his uncle, making enquiries about his father with an offer of assistance, and his heart warmed at the idea of sending a pair of shawls to his grandmother. But being out of employment he made an effort to return to the army, and waited on Sir William Grant Keir, with whom he was slightly acquainted, who received him with all his wonted benevolence. He recollected the circumstance of Charles's name having been left on his list, for he was adjutant-general, and gave him a note of introduction to the military secretary, couched in very handsome terms. Charles having delivered it, waited nearly a month for an answer;

his impatience then became extreme, and he wrote in on the subject, but received a reply that filled him with despair, for it was that they never made promises in the commander-in-chief's office ; upon which Charles took a bold and decisive step. He wrote a short memorial to the Marquis of Hastings, simply stating his services and recommendations, with an observation, expressing his confidence that his lordship could penetrate his feelings, and would attribute his seeming boldness to the proper cause. The noble marquis instantly directed him to be gazetted, and the assistant military secretary, pleased with the steps he had taken, and the papers he produced, most kindly gave him the choice of any regiment in which ensigncies were then vacant, so that he got into the same corps with his friend Mr. True.

CHAP. XVI.

"Come ye, who shun the folly of the East,
Nor court pale midnight at her gorgeous feast;
Who run from tom toms rattling at the gate,
And view no *poojahs* crowding by in state;
Who shun the great *mohorum*'s annual show,
And seldom to the grandest *nantches* go,
With me depart, though I have little wealth,
To humble competence and joyous health.
Within a narrow circle are confined
Man's real wants, when wisdom curbs the mind."

THE great Indian drums called tom toms are of a demi-globular form, and of prodigious size, covered with the skins of buffaloes, stretched on their strong frame work to a great degree of tension; upon these, men rattle away with clubs, as if struggling between life and death. It is not easy to conceive the mighty noise which these drums produce, and their constant thundering in the temples is increased by sounding long brass horns, trumpets, and gongs, while bells and cymbals are heard at intervals, with the shrill piercing tones of wind instruments like small clarionets. In the processions the tom toms of largest size are borne on carriages purposely made, and others are carried about on camels and elephants, with several men beating them, as if the world depended for safety on their exertions. These annual ceremonies in Calcutta are called Poojahs, and during their celebration the idols are drawn about in splendid artificial pagodas, made of bamboo frame work, similar to the great carriage of Juggurnaut. During the continuation of the Doorga poojah, which occupies several days, the rich natives of Calcutta vie with each other in giving splendid nantches for three nights, to which Europeans are invited by printed cards, couched in the most polite terms. Temporary buildings are erected for this display of eastern profusion, in which vast sums are annually spent; and at some of the nantches I have seen two hundred persons sit down to a sumptuous supper, where champagne circulated like water, and the richest ices were melted in the most costly liquors. These grand supper rooms were lighted with a profusion of chandeliers and wax tapers under Indian table shades, while the brilliancy was reflected by countless mirrors, and the atmosphere cooled by punkoes, tatties, and jets d'eau; artificial wildernesses breathed forth perfumes, and endless varieties of flowers called to recollection the scenes of Arabian story. Of these suppers the Hindoos will not of course partake; but they enter the apartment, congratulate the guests, and see that the European tavern-keepers employed to prepare them provide every thing on a liberal scale. Previous to the time at which these supper rooms are suddenly thrown open as if by enchantment, the crowds of company are entertained in a great amphitheatre by dancing girls, bands of music both European and native, tumblers, jugglers, actors and pantomimes, forming an assemblage which, from the costume of so many different nations, is like a great fancy ball. Perfumes and flowers are distributed, and sweetmeats handed about. Some sit and look at the dances, while others promenade round the virandas, to view the household gods, hundreds of whom are placed in conspicuous situations, some half elephant and man, others with numerous heads and arms, here quite naked, there sumptuously arrayed. The apartments of the Hindoo ladies look down upon this great amphitheatre, and from a gallery these recluses may be seen peeping through lattice work on the *tomasha* below. European ladies, on the evenings of the Doorga poojah, are asked to visit the female part of the family, whom they have always found apparently happy and full of curiosity. Many of them sing very sweetly, and play well on instruments, something like guitars. A native band of music consists of these instruments, and others like clarionets, with cymbals and kettle drums, which produce very wild, pleasing, and melancholy harmony, but most of the favourite airs of the higher class are Persian. The dancing girls are gorgeously dressed, and covered with ornaments. Their dances consist of sudden transitions; the movement is sometimes so slow that one would think they were falling asleep, then by a change of the music it is all life, and exhibits the most rapid succession of violent action. Now they take up their robe and fold it into various shapes — then they let it go, so that while they turn round like a top, this garment forms a circle resembling a peacock's tail, and this circulation is continued so long that it excites the wonder of every beholder.

In Calcutta, the great Hindoo annual festival is held in October, and it is soon followed by the Mahomedan mohorum, a ceremony that takes place in commemoration of the death and sufferings of Hossen and Hassen, the sons of Ally. You are aware perhaps, gentle reader, that the Moslems are divided into two great sects, called Sheeas and Soonnees; the former are the followers of Ally, and consider Abboo Becker, Omar, and Othman usurpers; the latter are disciples of Abboo Becker, and do not reverence the memory of Hossen and Hassen; but there are not many of that sect in India. After the death of Ally who succeeded Othman, Moveeyah the governor of Syria mounted the throne, and Hassen was poisoned by the treachery of his wife; but in the reign of Yezeed, the son of the usurper, Hossen endeavoured to recover his birthright, when he was killed in the plain of Kirbullaw. The mohorum is instituted to celebrate this tragedy, and the Sheeahs go into mourning on the occasion, and form processions with the bodies of Hossen and Hassen, in which war horses covered with wounds, a mock fight, wonderful lamentations, howling, beating of the breast, and uproar, are the leading features. The bodies having been waked in artificial mosques, called Imambarahs and Tabooses, made of frame work covered with tinsel, are on the day of the funeral procession thrown into a tank with great ceremony. But indeed these scenes have been so often the theme of description, that I shall hasten to matter of more originality.

Calcutta had been a pleasant place on the whole to Charles Thoughtless, and he could not think of leaving it without regret. Although his duties were laborious, his pleasures were commensurate, for in vacation he had most agreeable trips up the Ganges, and cheerful excursions into the interior, where he contemplated with rapture the peace and plenty that smiled upon the happy peasantry of Bengal; for although sunk in idolatry and ignorance, their blooming habitations were pictures of rural felicity. Besides, he had formed several interesting friendships and acquaintances, all which were so many links in the chain of enjoyment that must be broken. When about to bid adieu, he remembered with a sigh the dances and parties, the hospitality and gaiety of Bengal; but as his health had suffered severely, he had in reality no real cause for serious sorrow.

Meanwhile George True had determined on sailing for his native land, and he was not unmindful of the poetical Robert Gordon, whose discharge he had interest to procure; and to avoid the delay of waiting for a passage he came round to Calcutta, and was rejoiced to find Charles a brother officer in the same corps. Little Edward and Emma, who had looked upon each other in infancy, now became attached friends in childhood; but to hasten over immaterial topics, a passage was obtained, Mrs. True and family, with Gordon as their attendant, went down the river in the ship, and George remained till the next tide to settle his last Indian affairs, then accompanied by Thoughtless, he proceeded to Champaul Ghaut; and the conversation there, and on the way, suggested the lines prefixed to these chapters, on the plan of the third satire of Juvenal.

The monsoon was now about to commence in Calcutta; but such was the anxiety of Ensign Thoughtless to join his regiment, that he seized the first opportunity to engage a passage for himself and family to Bombay; but a few days before he sailed, the following letter reached him from Frank Stanley.

MY DEAREST FRIEND,

I have been shewn your letter to the commanding officer in my behalf. I shall only say, that never in my whole life did I feel more pleasure than at the moment I read your offer of purchasing me a commission. In this you have acted in a manner worthy of yourself; and let me imitate the example by saying, as Euryalus did to Nisus,

"This soul contemns mere rank." What would be my reflections were I to assume an epaulette by taking the little store that may transport you with your wife and three darlings in declining health to the restoring zephyrs and green fields of your native soil? Friendship forbid it! Since it has been my happy lot to meet one whom neither time, fortune, nor place can change, may God give me gratitude to act so as to merit the inestimable blessing. Believe me, I am contented with my condition. I feel that I am respected in the regiment, and I trust that time will raise me to that situation which certain circumstances make very desirable.

Sorry I am to tell you that Captain Solomon is dead, and the tears of the regiment have watered his grave.

> "He was a man, take him for all in all,
> We shall not look upon his like again."

You remember the kind note he sent you, with a dozen of Madeira, on the day of your marriage. There is nothing new in the regiment or elsewhere that I know of worth communicating; and, confusion to me, but it is an old song to subscribe myself

Your constant friend till death,

FRANK STANLEY.

Charles shed a tear on the letter, and wrote the following lines in memory of Captain Solomon:

> Could worth, O Solomon, preserve its blaze!
> Could honour consecrate the meed of praise!

My humble pen had not preferred thy claim,
To merit's recompence — unfading fame.
When memory's retrospective pencils paint
Past images, from long secession faint,
With agonized emotion we deplore
The good, the great, among our friends no more ;
And as an exile doomed to end his life
Far from his country, children, friends, and wife,
Tries from his recollection to erase
What fond attachment prompts him to retrace,
So would the feeling heart eradicate
From memory's tablet the decrees of fate ;
But still affection turns and hugs her chain,
Though every link inflict a pang of pain.
Mute is the tongue by eloquence inspired,
Lifeless the heart by manly ardour fired,
Cold the kind hand extended at the call
Of poor humanity, that aided all.
No more his voice shall rouse the soldier's heart,
With ardent zeal to bear an active part
In the fierce fight, his honour to defend.
Ah no! in Solomon worth lost a friend!
As a fond father lovingly corrects
His little darlings, and their course directs,
So did his tender care, though wrong, reclaim
And stimulate the right to loftier aim ;
Ever attentive merit to reward,
And zealous bright examples to record,
Amongst the private ranks he sought for worth,
And thence drew modest, humble virtue forth,
That but for him had there neglected lain,
Obscured, forgot, or viewed but with disdain!
For many a heart that pants in hope of fame,
Sinks unregarded, and without a name.
O Solomon! can I forget thy aid,
Which cheered, revived, and raised me from the shade?
While memory holds, and life remains to me,
My grateful thoughts will oft recur to thee ;

Thy friends and brothers in the path to fame,
Will also cherish thy respected name.
Thy gallant son will emulate his sire,
And to thy worth successfully aspire;
As the young eagle every effort tries
His father's course to follow through the skies;
So he may learn by imitating thee,
That virtue leads to immortality!

The Pembroke, a country ship, commanded by Captain Ross, scudded away before the N. E. monsoon, which carried her through the Indian ocean southward of Dei Gracia at the rate of twelve knots an hour. Having gained the latitude of Bombay, the course was due east, and the sea soon began to assume a greenish muddy tint. Several large snakes were now seen alongside, and a hard sandy cast was got in forty-eight fathoms, from which the bank shoaled gradually till lofty mountains appeared in the horizon; night intervening, a light-house rose to view like the evening star, and at dawn next morning the green smiling point on which it stands was neared; the captain then guided the ship on well known objects till a pilot came on board. The island of Colabah was soon cleared, and the fortress and town opened on the view. Caranjar was now a-starboard, Elephanta right a-head, the anchor dropped, and the Pembroke attracted the gaze of crowds from the ramparts of Bombay. Ensign Charles Thoughtless, his wife, and three children were soon on shore, and palankeens conveyed them to Cameron's hotel.

Having reported at the brigade major's office, Charles was carried over the rocks to Old Woman's Island, and up Colabah to the quarters of Colonel Milnes, his commanding officer, by whom he was received with brief sincerity and kindness. "Orderly," said the Colonel, "tell the adjutant to step hither." "Mr. Ward," added he, when that gentleman arrived, "Mr. Thoughtless has a family; try what you can do to get a bungalow for him. I fear there is not one unoccupied on the island." On leaving the colonel, Ward most kindly offered Charles part of his quarters, but they met Lieutenants Barnes and Ottley of the corps, who understanding that the stranger had a family, offered to vacate the bungalow they occupied, saying, "Do not refuse it, Mr. Thoughtless; the rains are now nearly over, and we prefer being in our tents." His family were soon accommodated, and after introduction to the officers, his attention was directed to the standing orders; and from the adjutant's office was derived the following information, which shews how well the 65th merited the reputation of a *crack* regiment.

Memoirs.—It was one of those corps raised during the seven years' war, and first embodied in 1759. Obscurity has cast a veil over its services for three years after formation; but in 1762 it was stationed on the island of Guadaloupe, during the attack and conquest of the Havannah, and formed a part of the force under the Earl of Albemarle, who commanded on the expedition. During the American war it was employed in that country, and suffered severely at the battle of Bunker's Hill. In 1778 it was in camp at Coxheath, and detachments from it served on board Lord Howe's fleet at the relief of Gibraltar in 1782. Two years afterwards it was stationed in Dublin, and acquired great reputation for discipline, being the first regiment which, under the superintendence of Sir David Dundas, ever practised and carried to perfection the system of field exercises compiled by that officer, and since laid down as a general regulation for the whole army. In 1785 it landed at Quebec, marched to Fort Niagara, and furnished detachments to Oswega and Fort Schlosser. Detroit saw its manœuvres in the summer of 1788, and thence it supplied detachments to Michilim, Mackinac, and Fort Erie. Next year it retraced its steps to Lower Canada, till on its arrival at la Prairie, it marched to St. John's near the mouth of lake Champlain, sending detachments to Isle aux Noix, Point au Fer, and Fort Chamblée. In 1791 it was stationed at Halifax in Novia Scotia, and proceeded to Frederickston, leaving detachments at Fort Howe and Cumberland, and dispatching others to Presque Isle and the Grand Falls.

The revolutionary war having broken out in Europe, this regiment was destined to form a part of the force under the command of Sir Charles Grey and Sir John Jervis, intended to reduce the enemy's possessions in the West Indies, and it embarked at Halifax for Barbadoes. Thence it proceeded to the islands of St. Vincent and Grenada, and in the division of Major-general Thomas Dundas took Fort Trinity on the island of Martinique, and proceeded across the country through Gros Morne to attack a post called la Reduite, about three miles from St. Pierre, which was taken by storm with considerable loss. In the operations attending the capture of the islands of St. Lucie and Guadaloupe, particularly at Fort Fleur d'Epee, part of the regiment suffered severely. It was in the unfortunate force that bravely attempted soon afterwards to defend Guadaloupe against the attack of the French General Victor Hughes. Here a series of unsuccessful operations, chiefly rendered so by the dreadful mortality among the troops, ended in that emergency which obliged the force that remained to surrender at Berville camp. The regiment was now reduced to a skeleton, and commanded by a subaltern.

On its return home, it was recruited and served for some years in Scotland, after which it was sent out to the Cape of Good Hope, and proceeded some time after to Bombay, where it arrived upwards of a thousand strong, about the time when Lord Lake's army was on route to reduce Bhurtpore. It was sent to join the division of the army forming in Guzerat to co-operate with the force under his lordship, and it marched from Broach in the month of June, when the hot winds carried death in every blast. In a few days 300 men and several officers expired, twenty men sometimes falling dead in a day. The remainder shared in three unsuccessful attempts to storm Bhurtpore, and fell by sections before the discharges of grape. A remarkable instance of courage and attachment was here displayed by a grenadier. Serjeant-major Goodger was seen fighting like a lion half-way up the impracticable breach. He had received several wounds on the face and body, and his right eye was scooped out by the push of a spear. He fell to the bottom, and the retreat was sounded. After the soldiers had gained a place of cover from the murderous fire of the fort, one of the grenadiers recollected the situation of the brave serjeant-major; he flew to the spot, removed him from a heap of slain, and placing him on his back, returned to his applauding comrades with a bullet in his hip and two in the breech of him he carried. He was sumptuously rewarded, and the serjeant-major was promoted. After this the regiment shared in all the services of the Bombay army till the expedition against the Mauritius. On its return from the Isle of France, it was sent up the Persian Gulf to reduce the Joasmere pirates, and it suffered some loss at Ras el Kymer. During the passage an extraordinary spirit of daring was evinced by Lieutenant Place. He and some others were sitting one evening near an open port. The vessel was dashing before a smart breeze. "What would you do, Jem," said one, "for a friend?" — "I would jump into that roaring sea," replied he. "Ah! you only think so," answered the first. "Look here then," said Place, and out of the port he leaped head foremost. The chief mate was present, rushed on deck, and put the ship aback at the risk of the mast's going over the side. Boats were lowered, and near an hour afterwards Jem was brought on deck, having been discovered at a great distance struggling hard for life. This brings the memoir down to near the period when Thoughtless joined this excellent corps.

Of its institutions, and first, the mess. — All the unmarried officers mess together; and the married ones are honorary members, that is, they have the privilege of going to the mess when they please; but in camp, or when absent from their families, they are members in every respect. The mess fund is formed by a certain contribution from every officer when he joins the corps, and a certain additional gratuity for every grade he gains in the regiment. A quarterly committee transacts the current business, under the control of an annual committee, of which the commanding officer is president, and in aid of these governing courts there is a code of regulations to which every member has to subscribe on joining the regiment. The non-commissioned officers have a mess established and conducted on similar principles, and the friendly society of serjeants have monthly meetings. All the unmarried privates are formed into messes, and dine under the inspection of officers and non-commissioned officers. Men distinguished for bravery in action with the enemy wear a laurel wreath round the right arm, and dine together at the expence of the regiment twice a-year. In addition to the mess fund, stock purse, regimental and band funds, there are charitable and compassionate funds for the relief of widows and orphans. All the soldiers' children and boys of the corps are obliged to attend the regimental school, and the non-commissioned officers and privates are encouraged to improve. Besides the various modes of reward and punishment, such as praise, promotion, courts-martial, congee house, stoppage of liquor, and drill, there are company's courts, in which the men judge each other under sanction of the commanding officer. Prisoners for petty offences are tried by a court consisting of a corporal who sits as president, and of four privates as members, and it may be easily conceived how important this institution is in prevention of crimes; for the soldiers are censors on the conduct of one another, and feel bound as jurors to uphold the discipline and honour of their regiment.

The corps owes its present efficiency of organization chiefly to Colonel Lionel Smith, who now commands the Poonah subsidiary force. Some of his orders display great energy and vigour of mind, with an elegance and force of diction truly eloquent, while others are playfully written as if to amuse the soldiers, by whom he is feared and loved with the utmost enthusiasm. His common name among them is *Long Tom*. The following observation, made by him in declining the resignation of an officer, will convey an idea of his energetic style: "Whoever embarks in the profession of a soldier, whether as a private or an officer of high rank, must not suppose he can demand his release when he chooses; he has given himself to his country, and can only be spared from her service when circumstances permit." The gaiety of his disposition may be conceived from the order he issued on the transfer of Fort George barracks to the king's regiments:—"Fort George barracks now belong to the king, thank God for it; the regiment will take possession of them to-morrow morning," &c.

Those regulations, compiled by various colonels and commanding officers for the guidance of all ranks, and styled the standing orders of the regiment, are written in a noble spirit, of which a short extract or two will convey a sufficient notion. "Officers must endeavour to gain the esteem and confidence of their men, by a constant attention to their interests and to their wants; be careful of their health, and spare no pains in procuring them every comfort and advantage in their power; they must on no account be provoked to give them ill language, or to treat them in a manner which may degrade them in their own opinion or that of others; they must on the other hand steadily maintain the authority which is entrusted to them, by exacting from the non-commissioned officers and soldiers the greatest respect, not suffering them to answer when reprimanded, or at any time omitting the smallest compliment due to them; anxious to promote the good order and discipline of the regiment, they must convince all under their command that they are perfectly acquainted with every part of their duty; and that as they strictly adhere to it themselves, they will not suffer the smallest failure or deviation of the performance of it in others."—"Non-commissioned officers, distinguished by their talents and good conduct, may and should look forward to the highest ranks in their profession; and may be assured, that whenever occasion offers, they shall not want the interest and support of those at the head of the regiment in attaining a superior station to which their merit gives them the most honourable title."

In short, to bring this subject briefly to conclusion, soon after Charles had made himself acquainted with the interior economy of the regiment, differing from that of his old corps in many points, some in his opinion for the better and others for the worse, a review took place, after which the general rode to the centre and addressed Colonel Milnes thus: "I am much gratified with the appearance of the 65th regiment; its efficiency reflects great credit on you and your officers, and I shall have the pleasure of representing it to the commander-in-chief as fit for any service."

CHAP. XVII.

"There are who stay to advance thy solid fame,
O Albion, and perpetuate thy name,
Whose souls despise the tempting lure of spoil,
And seek but glory in the path of toil;
While many are by other motives sway'd,
To cut a dash—in tandem to parade;
In glittering curricle through crowds to force,
Or whirl in buggy gay along the course."

THAT the civil and military servants in India are as high-minded and honourable men as any other bodies in the world, may be fairly assumed. Indeed they are placed above temptation by their munificent masters the company, who enable them, by a course of integrity, to gain with certainty that glorious independence which is the legitimate aim and end of all human exertion. But numerous are the instances in which the weakness of our common nature has led to a deviation from the path pronounced by sound sense as the wisest for man. Indeed it would seem, from the records of the courts of justice in India, that some individuals have gone out with that lesson on their minds, which a Roman nobleman is said to have given to his son, when sending him into the provinces of Asia: "My boy, make a fortune if you can by honourable means, but make a fortune." Without entering into the history of such men as have distinguished themselves in India, either by disinterestedness or misconduct, it is intimated with deference, that the extravagant scale of living in Bengal plunges young men on their first arrival into such difficulties that those who fall into them become tools in the hands of artful natives. But not to dwell further on a common topic, a more interesting subject is resumed.

Soon after the review noticed at the end of the last chapter, the 65th regiment received orders to join the army forming in Guzerat for the supposed purpose of compelling Scindea to take a subsidiary force. The ladies and families of the corps were left behind, and Charles with a heavy heart embarked on board the Paraty Pursad, a paddimar commanded by Tyndal Nayla, for Broach. Some of these boats were large enough to carry a whole company, and had a comfortable half-deck and awning to screen the men from the sun. The one in which he embarked was of a small description and open, except a small part near the stern, screened in with mats for the officers. This little fleet soon cleared Malabar point. The officers enjoyed the sea breeze, their brandy pawny, books, flutes, and segars, beneath their comparatively comfortable shed, now admiring the majestic ghauts on their right, with the beautiful diversity of scenery along the shore, then casting a look on the dark blue expanse of water that closed the horizon on the left; and now roused to other feelings by the songs or stories, the laughs or jests of the merry thoughtless soldiers, who passed their time in loud mirth beneath the burning sun, amused with forfeits, the button and the tailor, and shewing how easily the human mind conforms to circumstances, and creates happiness wherever there is hope, by laughing away reflection. Seven days the paddimars kept their course along the shore, favoured by alternate breezes from the sea and land. Having passed Domas, and saluted the commodore's cruizer, they entered the Nerbuddah, the fertile banks of which fine river appeared covered with flocks of cattle, and verdant with the various productions of bountiful nature, presenting to the view a level country, with numerous topes, through which villages met the eye. The bed of the Nerbuddah, near Broach, is narrow and dangerous, from several small islands and banks that are covered at high water. On these some of the paddimars got aground, reeling over on the side when the water left them; but in the course of a tide or two, all the troops were safely landed, and encamped near the fort on the road to Baroda.

This river is considered the southern boundary of one of the three great divisions into which the hand of nature seems to have formed Hindostan. After a course of about 750 miles, nearly from the head of the Bay of Bengal, it falls into the Gulf of Cambay, not far from Broach, and all that tract between it and the Hemaleah range is called Hindostan Proper; thence the terrritory extending southward to the river Kisthna, which rises not far from Poonah in the western ghauts, and courses eastward into the Bay of Bengal, is called the Deckan; and all the rest of the continent of Asia, to the island of Ceylon, is termed the Peninsula. In the Nerbuddah are found those types of Shiva, called Solgrammas, which are sacred pebbles held in great estimation all over India; and about ten miles from Broach there is an island, in which stands that wonderful banyan-tree, so large as to shade 7,000 men under its branches. It is called the Kuveer Bur, and it is believed to have sprung up from the spot where a saint of that name interred himself alive, according to a custom in this province. The natives say it was larger 3,000 years ago than at present, part of it having been swept away by the river along with some of the island. Charles made one of a party to see this huge banyan-tree, and the cornelian beds not far from it. The tree has 350 large trunks, of the full size of oaks 100 years old, and 3,000 smaller ones, formed by branches, which take root when they touch the ground. It is upwards of 2,000 feet in circumference, and forms such a shade that the rays of the sun cannot penetrate, so that the mind can conceive nothing more refreshing than the cool zephyr playing through these long vistas upon the cheek of an European during a burning day. The cornelians and agates are found in clay, at some depth from the surface, and round spits like wells are formed by those who search for them. Guzerat, like Bengal, in this part has a rich black soil, which is free from stones.

The fort of Broach is large and irregular, surrounding a populous town. Its walls are high and thick, with towers and bastions. It was taken last in 1803 from Dowlat Row Scindeah, by Colonel Waddington, and with the district around now belongs to the company. From one of its high towers, Charles obtained a pleasing view of the country, which is a plain of wonderful beauty, at this season (November) yellow with grain almost ripe for the sickle. Here his eye traced the magnificent windings of the Nerbuddah, the waters of which he saw conducted by human industry to its right and left, for purposes of irrigation; there he beheld fine plantations of tobacco, cotton, juwarree, sugar cane, grain, wheat, and many other productions. He then wandered along the mouldering parapet, and pausing at the breach by which it was stormed under General Wedderburne in 1772, he sighed as he contemplated the graves of that brave officer and his numerous fellow soldiers at the bottom of it. Descending from the walls, he traversed the town, and visited the mosques and pagodas, conforming to the wishes of the Mussulmen and Hindoos by taking off his boots, that he might not profane those sanctuaries. Then he inspected the wheels and looms of the numerous cotton manufacturers, and admired the simplicity of the former, consisting of a small reel for receiving the yarn, which a woman, seated on the ground, turns with her right hand, while with her left she forms the thread. The loom consists of a reed and geers, with a small beam, upon which the warp is rolled; it is prepared in the open air, and fixed in the reed and geers, which are suspended to the roof of the *ghur*, and a hole being made in the floor, across which the beam rests, the weaver with his little shuttle sits on the other side, and draws the web, as he works it, round another small beam; thus with most simple means are fabricated the tissues which for their curiosity of texture surprise even those who employ the intricate machinery of European looms.

He afterwards visited the extensive *petah*, situated outside the walls, and saw the women of the lower orders at their domestic pursuits, grinding and pounding rice, spinning and weaving, or drawing water from the wells. The mill used is composed of two round stones, one of which is turned by the hand, and the grinding is performed by two women, according to the ancient practice alluded to in the Scriptures. For pounding, a wooden mortar and pestle are used. Among the females were several pretty figures; many of them had large ivory rings on the arms, wrists, and ancles. The teeth and eye-lashes of some are painted black, and a yellow or white streak on the forehead and between the eyes, proclaims the cast. The dress most common here is a silk or cotton spencer that embraces the body and breasts closely, with a *sauree* rolled round the waist, one end of it being brought over the shoulders and head, as in Bengal.

As the force remained several days at Broach, he sometimes met the Hindoo ladies in hackeries drawn by bullocks, ornamented with bells and rich gaudy trappings, closely covered with silk or cotton, to screen them from the gaze of the vulgar. Those of a lower order he also met, covered from head to foot with a muslin veil, mounted cross-legged on Mahratta horses, led by gora wallahs.

In the cool of each evening he rambled over the fields, and rode through the adjacent villages, admiring the beautiful yellow flowers of the cotton plant, and opening the bulbs from which they blow, containing balls of cotton about the size of a pigeon's egg, which surprise the beholder by the quantity of cotton they contain. He was struck with the mode in which the farmers irrigate their fields. Deep wells are sunk at a distance from the river, which supply vast quantities of water; a wheel is fixed to a beam on the top, over which a rope passes, tied to a very large leather bag, which is so constructed that it fills and empties itself; to this rope two bullocks are tackled on an inclined plane. The bag being thrown into the well is filled with water, and the bullocks, feeling its sinking weight, move off down the slope till their load reaches the surface, and empties itself into a channel that carries it off through the fields; then the well-taught animals march backwards up the declivity till the full bag again tells them to move down it; and thus will a pair of good bullocks, often without a driver, go on for nearly a whole day, alternately moving forwards and backwards, and keeping up by their labour a small stream, which, in its course, produces fertility. He often conversed with the farmers, most of whom could speak Hindostannee. One of them, a man of large stature, short beard, and intelligent countenance, Charles addressed on the state of the tenantry. He carried a sling in his hand, with a bag full of clay balls on his shoulder, which he whizzed with great noise, to keep birds away from his ripening corn. The field, which resembled many others in its vicinity, contained several acres in a square, surrounded by a broad green walk, planted with tamarind, mangoe, lime and jack trees, and enclosed by an excellent hedge of prickly pear. A few of his answers were in substance as follows: "In fact, every thing belongs to the company. I pay three rupees a *biggah* for the land, which is nearly as much as I can make of it, and I do what I please with it. If I fail to pay my rent, the farm is distrained or sold." He extolled the fertility of the country towards Baroda, comparing it to a garden; acknowledged that the inhabitants considered themselves more flourishing and happy under the company than they had been under the Mahratta princes, and seemed contented with his situation, though he testified a natural predilection for his former rulers, more by the shakes of his beard and the changes of his aspect than by the expressions of his cautious tongue. Charles told him of other parts of India. He did not seem inquisitive, but was familiar and politely attentive in removing thorns out of the way.

The province of Guzerat is very large, and is bounded on three sides by the Arabian sea, the gulfs of Cambay and Kutch. That part of it between the two gulfs, forming nearly an island, is called Kattywar. The whole is about 380 miles in length, and 180 in breadth. Its productions are very various, comprising nearly all those of the east, with many of the vegetables of the west. Poultry is very scarce, owing to prejudice on the part of the inhabitants, for here, as in some parts of Malabar, they are not domesticated. The cocoanut and plantain trees are scarcely to be seen in the interior. Its climate is delightful in winter; but in summer the heat is dreadful. To notice all its curiosities I have not space: let it suffice to mention the city of Ahmedabad and its rocking minarets. The forests offer to naturalists the rhinoceros, tiger, and lion, and snakes of great size. Its fields present to the sportsman variety of game, and the sacred peacock, the chattering monkey, and the parrot, are to be seen on almost every tree. In the northern parts this province is very thinly inhabited, having been nearly desolated by the famine of 1802; but the southern districts are very populous, that of Broach alone containing 262 villages, which, together with the fort and petah, have been estimated at 100,000 souls: nevertheless in the whole there are only about ten millions of people, one-tenth of whom are Mahomedans, and a considerable number Parsees, there being 3000 of that very industrious race at Broach. There are several distinct races of men in Guzerat. The Bheels, who are thieves by profession, live in the forests and eat the gum that exudes from the barbal tree; but they are not so blood-thirsty as the Coolees, the most expert rogues in the world, who go quite naked, and oil their bodies, so that, if detected, it is almost impossible to hold them, being as slippery as eels. In travelling through the country, it is only by chaining every thing to the tent-pole that property can be secured; and no house is safe, for they make holes under ground like rats. The best security is to fee the Bhauts or Charons, who are held sacred, and make a livelihood by guaranteeing safety of person and property to travellers while passing within their jurisdiction, for they take an oath to commit suicide in the event of injury or loss; and such is the superstitious veneration of the thieves for them, or rather there exists such an understanding between them, that persons under their protection are hardly ever molested.

Charons are an inferior cast of Brahmins, and most of them belong to the clerical order; but Bhauts live in many places by tillage, and near Keira there are several villages of them. In ancient times they were the bards of India; and in all the noble families of Guzerat there are some of them domesticated, who sing the exploits of heroes. Being held sacred by the Hindoos, it is thought a horrible sin to cause their blood to be shed, or their life to be endangered; and such is the obstinacy of their nature, that they put themselves to death on very small provocation, and murder their wives and children if they meet with disappointment in their undertakings. Another curious class is the Puggies, who earn a subsistence by detecting thieves, in which calling they are particularly dexterous, and seldom fail to trace the plunder into the village to which it has been carried, and where the tribe called Grassias make a livehood by receiving stolen goods from the Bheels and Coolees. There is besides an infamous tribe called Dheeras, who live on carrion, and perform all the vile offices of humanity; their touch is considered contamination by every man of cast. It is supposed there are 50,000 thieves in Guzerat; yet there is a desperate cast, called Ungruas, who will engage for a small reward to carry money all over the country, and such is their character for intrepidity, that they are hardly ever attacked. In short, men of nearly all the casts in India are found in Guzerat. The Mahrattas over-ran this province soon after the foundation of their empire by Sevagee; but when it began to decline, a chief named Pillagee Guichwar invaded it, and in 1726 established his family at Baroda, being confirmed in his conquest some years afterwards by the Sattara Rajah. But the division of territory in the Mahratta states is so extraordinary, that no one can say this province belongs to any particular chief; for the Peishwa and Scindea have parts of it as well as the Guichwar, and sometimes one town is governed by this trio, and divided among them. The Jains are numerous here, and may be seen feeding flies with sugar and honey, and fanning the air with peacock's feathers, lest they should unconsciously kill any living creature.

Some of the customs are curious, but only one or two can be instanced. The people are extremely afraid of witches, and consider ugly old women as having power to injure them by their looks; and to deprive them of this fascination, they cut off the noses of these hapless objects of their antipathy. It is customary for devotees, when tired of life from age, or absorbed in spiritual contemplation, to dig a pit in which they may be suffocated. When great misfortune assails them, and hope is lost, a yellow dress is put on, or powder of that colour is sprinkled over the person, to indicate despair, and if not relieved the person assuming it commits suicide. The Hindoo merchants upon being unsuccessful in business light a lamp during the day, which announces the state of their affairs to all creditors, and during the examination of books and inventories of stock they do not appear, nor will they return to their houses till permission is granted by those to whom they are indebted. If the merchant proclaims himself a bankrupt in time, and acts honourably, he is generally set up again with applause, and looked upon as a man of great integrity. But of all their customs female infanticide is the most extraordinary. In modern times this abominable practice was confined to the Jerajah tribe; but anciently it was far more extensive: it is now nearly abolished, thanks to British influence. Its origin cannot be traced; but tradition says that a certain great rajah had an only daughter, so exquisitely beautiful and accomplished, that she appeared not to be a form of earth. Her father searched over the whole world in vain for a prince worthy to enjoy such an angel: he at length, by the advice of a Brahmin, put her to death, as the only expedient to prevent his blood from being debased by marriage with a common person. This gratification of his pride the Brahmins turned to their own advantage, by flattering him with the assurance that he would become immortal, in aiding them to propagate a report that the young lady was ordered by Brahma to be sacrificed to prevent her from being defiled by a mortal. Her father's descendants following his example, put their female progeny to death, saying that such was the decree of Brahma, and that no mortal was worthy of being husband to their daughters. They therefore bought female children from other tribes, and had them educated in conformity to their own customs.

Charles was recalled from one of his evening rambles by the bugles of the regiment sounding the warning for parade, and on reaching his tent the corporal handed him the orders: — "The line will march to-morrow morning at five o'clock." — A hollow square was formed on the parade, and three of the soldiers were brought to a drum-head court-martial for being absent from their lines, and for behaving in an unsoldier-like manner in a neighbouring village, to the disgrace of the European character. The court sentenced each to receive 300 lashes, but one-half was remitted by the humane commanding officer, who addressed the regiment on the enormity of armed guardians of the laws spreading terror among the peaceful peasants of the country. To some it may appear cruel to flog men on the eve of marching; but if such offences were not visited with immediate vengeance, our fine army would soon be little better than a rabble. During the performance of this melancholy duty, the regiment was surrounded by half the population of Broach and the neighbouring villages. Such a crowd conveyed an idea of the vast mass of men in India, and revived the question so often discussed, "How can so many brook to be governed by so few?"

Broach and its district yield a revenue to the company of about £200,000 per annum. All its imports and exports are taxed for the support of the pinjrapole or hospital for animals, in which, however, there are now very few patients or pensioners, besides a few fine cows, the milk of which pays amply for their keeping. There are about twenty-five societies here of the Banyan cast, all employed in trade, for the manufacture of cotton is very extensive, the water of the Nerbuddah at this place being famed for giving a delicate whiteness to the *baftas*. Great numbers of *Borahs* also repair hither for goods. They are spread all over India; and, although Mahomedans, they have the features and characteristics of complete Jews.

The line marched on the high road to Baroda, through the finest plain that can be imagined, cultivated like a garden; they encamped at Sitpaun, a village of about 200 ghurs composed of mud and covered with tiles, and inhabited chiefly by Moslems, who have two small mosques. There is no Hindoo temple, but each has in his own house a place dedicated to the particular god of the family. After breakfast, Charles was seated at his desk writing the notes of his journal — "Road good — not many inclosures — tank and well water in abundance near the village."

"Saheeb," said Ballo, for Mr. True had transferred his favourite servant to Thoughtless, and Moote had remained with Frank Stanley, "one man village from, sell to master want, one fine little boy."

"Good God!" said Thoughtless, "is it his own son, Ballo?"—"*Aw, saheeb*," answered Ballo, "this country such custom is."

Charles went out, and alas! found that Ballo's tale was true. A poor aged naked man held his little half-starved looking boy in his hand anxious about selling him. Thoughtless cast an earnest look upon him. He was gazing at his child, drawing him closer, and a tear stood in his eye. "Ballo," said Charles, "give him some rupees, and tell him not to sell his son." The poor man fell on his face and kissed the ground; he then rose and embraced his child. Thoughtless felt that riches have charms when we employ them to make our fellow-creatures happy.

The next march was to Ekeer, a village larger than the last, inhabited by rigid Hindoos, who closed their doors for fear of contamination when the line was passing.

"Saheeb," said Ballo, in the course of the day, "one soldier artillery cut belly in very much by *Bheel* with arrow bow from."

"How has that happened, Ballo?" asked Charles. But not to plague you, gentle reader, with the Hindostannee idiom, it occurred thus:—It is usual for the soldiers to sleep after a march. There were some small ravines in front of the mens tents, up which two Bheels crept; one entered a *routy*, holding in his breath, and began to load himself with canteens. A man who was wide awake let him approach near him, and though well oiled, seized him by the leg and gave the alarm; but the other Bheel had his bow bent and lodged an arrow in the matross's breast, so that his comrade escaped in the confusion caused by this circumstance. To prevent further accidents, the commanding officer placed the camp under the protection of the Charons belonging to the pagoda in the village. But the pursuit of the thieves down the ravines discovered another proof of the disgusting manners of this region; four decapitated bodies were lying in a ditch near the village, supposed to be travellers murdered by the Coolees. The sight was shocking, as vultures and Pariah dogs had half eaten them, and picked the eyes out of the heads, not far distant from their trunks.

Itoola was the next stage, and from Ekeer to it the road runs along a deep ravine nearly all the way. The country, though apparently a beautiful plain, is very much broken by torrents that have washed away the soft earth to a great depth in their course during the monsoon; but being quite dry at present, one of them is a good gun road for several miles. Another illustration of manners occurred here.

"Saheeb," said Ballo, waiting till Charles had done writing, "one bobberchee of artillery killed." — "How, Ballo?" asked Thoughtless. "One soldier call cook boy, and tell — 'Quick go, bring me one nice girl.' Bobberchee no like that business, say, 'won't go;'— soldier give kick — cook-boy run into sepoy tent — one sepoy think him thief, and wound bayonet with — doctor come, no good, bobberchee die."

The next halt was at Gamboa, a village on the river Dadar, where there are the ruins of an ancient bridge. Next day the force reached Baroda, forty miles distant from Broach, and the 65th regiment occupied part of the cantonments a mile beyond the city, near the village of Gorwa, situated in a fine plain as level as a bowling green, on which an army of 300,000 men might encamp and manœuvre. This grand parade is skirted by fine plantations of mangoe trees. The cantonments are built in the form of an encampment; and in the officers' lines there are many pretty bungalows, with gardens round them like English cottages.

Soon after the arrival of the regiment, the following orders were issued:— "The slaughter of cows, bullocks, peacocks, monkeys, or any other animal or bird, that may be contrary to the customs of this country, is positively forbidden. Neither the officers nor others are to visit the amdrew or the dewan, or have any intercourse with them or any of the Guickwar's officers, without the express permission of the resident. No officer is to travel through the country without a passport. All officers are positively forbid going within the wall that surrounds the palace without permission."

The next day Thoughtless and several of his brother officers mounted their horses for the purpose of visiting Baroda and the Guickwar's gardens. That city is a square surrounded by a high wall, whose side is about half a mile in length. It has four great gates exactly opposite each other, the streets leading from which are broad and well paved, and at their intersection a small square is formed, which is covered with a roof merely supported by pillars, as a sort of exchange and market. The houses and pagodas, both inside the walls and in the large petah or suburbs, are well constructed and worthy of observation. Many of them are painted on the outside, and display extraordinary figures of gods, monsters, beasts and fishes; but the external appearance of Hindoo dwellings conveys to an European a very gloomy idea of comfort, having but a few small windows or peep holes. The interior, however, is far better suited to a climate, where at certain seasons health and comfort can only be enjoyed by excluding the hot air. Although when seen from without the houses look like prisons, yet many of them have a little open square inside, with a tank, garden, or jet d'eau, which cools the apartments round it, while from each story a fine open viranda, in which the inmates amuse themselves during the cool of the day, gives a much more pleasing idea of real comfort in a hot climate than the Grecian structures introduced by the Europeans, not one of which, unless built on a very large scale, is cool in summer; hence the family has to fly for refuge in the heat of the day to the ground floor, or to a close room remote from the glare. The streets were crowded with people and the shops exhibited great wealth. Many of the women were beautiful and appeared gorgeously ornamented, being in attendance on a *shaddee* between two respectable families. They were escorting the happy pair through the streets in rich open palankeens, and scattering flowers and perfumes in their way, with tom toms beating, and music playing, while men and women in fantastic dresses were dancing and singing before them. The bride was a little girl about six years old with her teeth and eyelashes painted jet black, and the centre of her forehead deep yellow. She was dressed in silk embroidered with gold, and her arms, fingers, ancles, and toes were covered with rings, while her ears and nose were concealed by clusters of pearls and diamonds, and round her neck she wore triple chains of gold and precious stones. The bridegroom was about ten years old, and also very richly dressed. Attracted by this grand cavalcade, Thoughtless and his friends followed till the infant couple, the objects of such general interest, stopped at a temporary square edifice glittering with tinsel decorations, erected in the middle of one of the great streets; two of its sides were supported on pillars wreathed with flowers, while the floor was covered with shawl carpets. Here the bride's party entered, and distributed presents, perfumes, and sweetmeats among their guests. But the outside of this temple of Hymen gave a disgusting idea of public morals and taste, for it was ornamented with the most indecent Chinese pictures, with which both men and women appeared highly delighted, and gazed upon them with expressions of sensual joy. From the city Charles and his brother officers found their way to the gardens, which are not worth description. There are two royal cenotaphs ; one of which, supported by sixteen marble pillars with exceedingly small shafts, is a curiosity. The Guickwar's palaces are large gloomy buildings.

Soon afterwards the force was formed into two brigades, with a due proportion of artillery, cavalry, and pioneers, and encamped regularly in the plain, where the troops had a grand field day, and the cavalry a sham-fight, in honour of his highness Futteh Singh. The line was formed at day-light, but the prince did not appear till eight o'clock, when he was seen approaching on a lofty elephant, glittering with gold and scarlet trappings, accompanied by the resident, Mr. Carnack, and all the great native officers, mounted in like manner on elephants, preceded by a native band. Futteh Singh's numerous guards rode Mahratta horses. They were armed with pistols, swords, shields, and spears. Some of them were shewing off on the flanks in great style, managing their chargers with surprising dexterity, and wielding their lances. The Mahratta bit is very sharp; the reins, which are of cotton or silk, and as small as a bell cord, are generally fastened to the bow of the saddle, for the warrior prides himself on governing his steed without the aid of the bridle. The animal is in such dread of the sharp bit, so well broken in, and accustomed to the signals of his rider's knee and voice, that he will spring from one side to the other, leap forwards and backwards, throw himself on his haunches, and form circles by wheeling round on his hind legs with such celerity as to surprise an European; meanwhile the horseman is flourishing his spear, and changing it from hand to hand so quickly, that thought can hardly follow his movements. Some of the cavalry wear armour, but generally speaking, the dress is cotton trowsers, and a sort of gown with long sleeves, stuffed with cotton, and quilted; and their heads are protected by a thick turban, while their backs are screened by their shields.

Besides his numerous escort of cavalry, Futteh Singh had a corps of Gosains in his retinue. They were entirely naked as to clothing, having only their swords, belts, and bucklers on their bodies, which were frightfully painted; some of them were armed with matchlocks, and certainly a wilder looking body of enthusiasts never before met the eye of Charles Thoughtless. Nearly the whole male population of Baroda also accompanied their warlike prince, who, on his near approach to the British line, alighted from his elephant, and mounted an Arabian charger. His officers also mounted their horses, and leaving their guards and the crowd at a proper distance, were received with military honours, and seemed to view with deep interest and wonder the regular and combined movements of the brigades while changing positions, and firing from new and unexpected lines; then forming squares by battalions, and rapidly shewing their original fronts by the filing of grand divisions in double quick time. Meantime the 17th dragoons, under Major Seale, dashed across the plain, and skirmished so as to astonish the wondering crowd of Mahrattas, who saw their galloppers in a cloud of dust rushing to a new point, and a moment after heard their blazing fire-arms vomiting forth thunder in peals, of which the quick succession seemed the effect of magic rather than human skill. The force was commanded by Colonel Holmes of the company's service, who demonstrated a proper technical knowledge of his profession on the occasion. But nothing in cavalry tactics could exceed the science displayed by Major Seale, and those under his command; for the 17th dragoons, who are styled the death or glory boys, are in such a fine state of discipline, that they sit their horses with inimitable grace, and perform every movement with the precision of clock-work, and the rapidity of lightning.

His Highness Futteh Singh was of the middle age, rather corpulent, but on the whole a good looking man, with a penetrating eye, whose quick glances followed every thing. His dress was superb, and reminded one of the description given by Quintius Curtius, Lib. 9. Cap. 1. of a Hindoo rajah. — "Vestis erat auro purpurâque distincta, quæ etiam crura velabat: aureis soliis inseruerat gemmas: lacerti quoque et brachia margaritis ornata erant. Pendebunt exauribus insignes candore et magnitudine lapilli."

CHAP. XVIII.

" The stately palankeen will some invite,
With spreading *chattah*, bells and battons bright;
The *hookah*'s bubbling perfumed costly breath,
From golden tube with carpet spread beneath;
Rich *abdar'd* claret, sparkling cool champaign,
And devils spiced, 'till pleasure turns to pain,
Will others lure in exile to remain."

THE ease and splendour in which Europeans live in India attach many of them to the country; and for a long time after an old Indian returns home, he secretly sighs on remembering the past. His comfortable palankeen, into which he used carelessly to throw himself, and loll at ease with a book while paying visits or attending business, a silken chattah or umbrella shading him from the glare, and tinkling bells and silver sticks running before to proclaim his consequence, often recur to his mind; and the perfume of his hookah or Hindoo machine for smoking is not forgotten. The hookah consists of a glass or silver bottom filled with water, to the mouth of which is fixed a sort of grand pipe filled with a composition of tobacco and spices richly perfumed, the tube of which passes through the water, comes out at the side of the bottom, and is then called a snake, on account of its great length, and the many fanciful windings it forms before the end called the mouth-piece, either of silver or gold, reaches the smoker. This instrument has a very magnificent appearance, and is generally introduced after dinner, being placed by the hookahburdar, or servant for that express purpose, on a rich carpet, a considerable way from the table behind his master. The fumes of this scented tobacco are considered even by ladies as very agreeable, so that it is quite fashionable in India to smoke the hookah; and it may be easily conceived how alluringly pleasant the cool vapour is after circulating through such a length of tube to the palate, heated with the luxuries of the East. Allusion has been before made to the delicacies of the table; and in no country in the world can wines be made more delightfully cool than in India, by a process of refrigeration with saltpetre, at which the native servants, called abdars or water-coolers, are very expert. Servants of all work might be hired in Bengal either from the Pariahs or converted Christians; but there is a prejudice against the latter, and the former are great drunkards. The Mahomedan servants attend to cast almost like the Hindoos, although there are no such distinctions among them. A boy who does not hesitate to brush his master's coat, would not for the world touch a knife or fork or attend at table; and a maid that walks out with children, may not be disposed to wash or dress them. A civilian with a family will have perhaps 200 servants; while a magistrate here will not have ten. All the natives board themselves: their wages are very low, for living costs them little. A man will do well with five shillings a month, and such as use rice alone could purchase as much of it for two shillings as they would use in that time; the wages, therefore, given to servants may be said to rise in a sort of scale from ten to one hundred shillings a month. The reader will easily conceive how such an establishment of servants must keep back an individual, and prevent him from realizing independence. Nothing in India so much retards the progress of an adventurer towards the wished-for goal. A lieutenant there in the field has about thirty-five pounds sterling every month, and yet his establishment is so great, and his expences so heavy, that he can save nothing. But pursuing this dry subject no further, I return to the journal of Charles Thoughtless.

He very soon found the difficulty of keeping two establishments, and foresaw that the little fund he had in Calcutta would soon be exhausted. In short his mind began to assume a gloomy aspect, and he endeavoured to divert his melancholy by imitating part of the first satire of the first book of Horace:

Survey the world, and analyse the mind,
With philosophic truth, of human kind:
Then say why man to change is ever prone,
And never long contented with his own?

Whether his lot came to him by free will,
Or fell by chance, he pines and murmurs still.
"O happy merchant," oft the soldier cries,
When war's rude toil his manly spirit tries!
Loud tempest howls, the boisterous ocean roars,
Dispersed or lost, the merchant now deplores
His ships, and says, oppressed with rising fears,
"The warrior's choice much better now appears;
"He rushes boldly to the embattl'd plains,
"And in a moment death or glory gains."
The barrister aroused from bed of down,
By dull attorneys, burns his wig and gown;
And lauds the country squire, who, law opprest,
Extolls the long robe, as of garbs the best.
But each peculiar case to numerate,
Would comprehend mankind in every state:
For I when messman monthly greets my door,
Exclaim — "The worst of all is to be poor."
Yet mark, should hocus pocus deign to say,
"Presto — let each be happy his own way;
"Soldier your ledger take, merchant his sword,
"Lawyer your farm."—What! none of you a word?
Not one would change his old familiar state,
But murmur still at one another's fate.
Yet should he add "You ensign take this place,"
With smiling aspect to it I would pace.
But, not to smile when truth is to be told,
(Though oft a laughing phiz will truth unfold,)
Let us proceed the principles to scan,
That actuate the mind of every man;
One spring of action animates the whole,
Directing all with absolute control;
For he who ploughs the ocean or the soil,
Expounds the laws, or courts the warrior's toil,
Embarks his skiff on labour's troubled seas,
To gain in old age dignity and ease;
But when black clouds across his passage rise,
He drops the oar, and discontented sighs.

"Saheeb," said Ballo, "Colonel Milnes, compliments sends, speak to you want."

"Mr. Thoughtless," said the Colonel, "the staff situation now vacant is at your service. You have a large family." In this manner, gentle reader, the tone of his spirits was raised in a moment to something considerably above concert pitch, for his allowances were doubled; and after an ineffectual endeavour to express what he felt, he danced off to his tent, wrote to Mary, and entered in his journal, "what pleasure is afforded to the heart of man by imparting his joys or sorrows to a sympathising and beloved wife."

The city of Baroda is situated on a branch of the river Myhe, over which there is a tolerably good bridge; the country around is in the very highest state of cultivation, studded with numerous villages, and the vicinity of the capital is ornamented with several very handsome pagodas and costly tanks. Pillagee, as has been mentioned before, was the founder of the Guickwar family in this province. The exact amount of the government revenue is not known, but several districts have been ceded to the company, for the support of a subsidiary force, which yield the annual sum of 1,070,000 rupees, and are now in a progressive state of improvement. It may be said of the Guickwar, as of all the other subsidized princes, that he has no external political power, all his foreign affairs being transacted by the British resident, who is in fact placed at his court as the guardian of the company's interest. There are no hills to be seen from Baroda, except Powan Ghur, which is a very great curiosity, at no great distance. It is a rock rising out of the plain, to the height of 600 yards, and nearly everywhere perpendicular, so as to be inaccessible, except on the north side, and this part is fortified with five walls. On the top stands a famous pagoda, to which there are 240 steps; and there is an inexhaustible supply of water, with accommodations for a considerable garrison; nevertheless such is the effect of mortar batteries, and the spirit of British perseverance, that it was stormed in 1803, and taken without much loss from Dowlat Row Scindea.

Upon leaving Baroda, on the 13th January 1815, the force marched towards Powan Ghur, and on the second day having passed through a very fine tract of country, encamped near Gerode, distant about sixteen miles from the city. The hill fort above described stands near it, and looked formidable from the British camp. Colonel Stanhope, with the head-quarters of the 17th dragoons, joined the force at Gerode from Keira; some time afterwards the whole crossed the river Myhe, at the pass of Wankaneer, a very romantic village situated in a deep ravine on the south bank, and after a few marches halted for some time near Ballisanore, having passed Omreit, a large walled town in a very flourishing condition. Mr. Williams, the assistant resident at Baroda, accompanied by a considerable division of the Guickwar's cavalry, had also taken the field with Colonel Holmes, and they encamped near the British lines, in a circle round their commander. Ballisanore is remarkable for stupendous rocks and extensive jungles, in which the numbers of monkeys, pea fowl, and hares are prodigious; the men killed many of the latter running through the ranks, and the line of march.

It would be tedious to accompany the field force, during this bloodless campaign of several months, along the banks of the Myhe. Its object was not perfectly understood. At this time the Nepaul war was going on, and the Pindarries, supposed to be encouraged in their irruptions by Scindeah and Holkar, were ready to carry fire and sword into all our provinces, therefore armies of observation were stationed every where upon the frontiers. No country in the world can be finer than Guzerat, along the banks of the Myhe. The inhabitants live in villages, and the ghurs in many places are a sort of basket-work, covered with thatched roofs. During the evenings and mornings, the climate is delightful, but early in March the heat of the day becomes exceedingly oppressive, and hot winds prevail more or less from that time till the monsoon commences in the beginning of July. All the villages along the north bank of the Myhe appeared in a very flourishing condition, with a numerous rising generation, as timid as hares, and seemingly frightened at the very appearance of Europeans. The inhabitants are of the Grassia tribe, and seem to enjoy perfect security in their persons and property. Their fields are beautified with fruit trees, and many of them well fenced with milk hedge. The country, except in the vicinity of Konnee, is level; near that interesting place is an extensive plain, skirted by low hills, which give a pleasing variety to the scene. Every village has a sort of patriarchal government within itself, and such is the aspect of comfort in all of them, that squalid poverty seems to be quite a stranger. Several of them belong to the Peishwa. Thoughtless was delighted in his rides for eight or nine miles in all directions round the camp, to find these smiling villages in profusion. The children were playing at hobby, or formed a noisy circle round the schoolmaster, while their parents were employed in husbandry or conversation. "In travelling over this curious globe," said Charles to himself, "men are found wherever nature furnishes means for their sustenance. Often unconnected by any tie with each other, and like the vegetable substances on which they live, they seem born only to produce their like, and return to the earth whence they sprung." Game is exceedingly beautiful and plentiful here; the partridges light in coveys on the trees, hares swarm in the brushwood, deer start from every copse, foxes abound, the wild hog infests each jungle, and the tiger is as large as in Bengal. Captain Keith killed one measuring fourteen feet from the tip of his tail to the nose. The air swarms with birds of beautiful plumage. Peacocks are seen in the distance sailing along in full pride and expansion, and the alligator basks in the sun near the river, which produces several species of fish, while the elephant, camel, buffaloe, and large ox are seen grazing near the camp, and bands of girls carrying water from the wells, in some places from 200 to 300 feet deep. Numerous flocks of monkeys occupy every tree, and seem to view Europeans with full as much wonder as the inhabitants of the villages, of whom they are no way afraid. But their chatter and extraordinary leaps from branch to branch with their young ones hanging from the breast, when the line was passing, truly surprised every beholder.

In the plain of Konnee on the 27th of March, Captain Hutton of the 65th was buried. He possessed many good and amiable qualities. His liberality and hospitality verged on extravagance. Honourable, brave, and benevolent, he was a zealous friend, and an officer well instructed in the duties of his profession. Soon afterwards Colonel Holmes left the force under the command of Lieutenant-colonel Fitzsimon of the 65th regiment; but Major-general Lawrence, a venerable looking officer in the company's service, arrived in the latter end of April, and assumed charge of it. However, on the 3d of May the campaign closed. Some of the native corps marched under Colonel Barclay for Kattywar; the 17th dragoons and two sepoy battalions returned to Keira, while the 65th and two other corps crossed the Myhe at Kunpore, and reached Baroda on the 15th of that month.

Nature has been exceedingly bountiful to that part of Guzerat which the force traversed. It is equally as much entitled to the character of a garden as any part of Bengal. No country on earth looks more beautiful when harvest is approaching. Only one crop is reaped, where artificial watering is not used, but in most places two are forced. Cotton is the great article of husbandry, and nothing can be more charming to the eye than a field of it in full blow, with stripes of roses, tulips, and various flowers of which dyes are composed. In other places were fine fields of jewarry or Indian corn, with plantations of sugar cane, flax and hemp, grain on which the horses are fed in India, tobacco, and the castor-oil plant, whose broad deep green leaves are most grateful to the eye, intermixed with so many other lively tints of all colours and shades.— The mills worked by bullocks, for expressing the juices of different plants, are of the most simple construction; that for sugar cane being merely a large pestle and mortar, the former being attached to a lever moved by oxen, which go round as in a bark mill. A great noise is made in working this, for the cane has to be ground and pounded till it is quite dry, when it is expelled on one side of the mortar, while the juice flows into pans on the other to be boiled and refined. Indeed all the implements of husbandry are extremely simple and capable of vast improvement. The plough consists of a long beam and two pieces of wood nearly at right angles, which serve as the body and ploughshare; to the former a small pole is fixed for a handle. A yoke, something like three steps of a ladder, is passed over the bullocks heads, and rests on their necks; to the centre of it the beam is fixed, and one man guides the whole, holding the small handle of the plough with one hand, while with the other he manages the bullocks by screwing and twisting their tails. But a stroke or scrape of this ill-contrived plough hardly enters an inch deep in the hardened surface; and the persevering farmer has to retrace the furrow several times before he procures mould enough for his seed, which is covered in with the raking of a bush, or, if much caked, a harrow something like a short ladder is drawn over it, upon which the driver stands to break the clods with his own weight. All the offices of the spade and shovel are performed by a clumsy hoe, to work with which it is necessary for the labourer to sit on his hunkers, or almost stoop to the ground. The sickle is a short crooked knife, and the scythe is not known. They have no carts, and the hackery or common car is in many places very ill constructed. Barns are not used in India, where the weather can be depended upon with certainty; grain is therefore never stacked, but trampled out by oxen in the fields, and the straw left there in heaps; the bullocks being fed on oil-cake, and the milk buffaloes in Guzerat having abundance of green food during the whole year. Near the villages are granaries made of clay, which is baked into the shape of large barrels, with crowns like bee-hives, and the corn is secured in them, after they are smeared over with cow-dung, which keeps the white ants away. In the Carnatic, Mysore, and Malabar, where rice is the principal crop, and the fields are inundated annually, except for hill pulses, manure is very little used; but in Guzerat and Bengal it is not burned, but goes, as in other countries, to enrich the soil. The prevailing system of husbandry, however, is very defective. The peasantry have no knowledge of the benefit of succession crops, profitable fallows, old lays, and modern improvements, but go on from father to son in the regular unambitious course of humble imitation, without making an effort at innovation, for the purpose of reducing labour, saving time, or avoiding expence. Land is at different prices in Guzerat: on the sea coast it is hardly worth three rupees an acre, but in other places twelve are given; and it may be said that the scale of rent in India is from six to thirty shillings an acre, except in the vicinity of large cities, where high prices are given for gardens. The rent-roll is the great source of revenue to the government, for it all comes into the coffers of the state, except about one-tenth for collection, the prince being considered in general sole lord of the soil. Nevertheless a vast deal of land in every province is private property, either granted to individuals as *jaghires*, or to pagodas as free gifts; and it is now understood that the system of revenue introduced by Lord Cornwallis into the company's territories has established the zemindars as lords of the soil so long as they fulfil their contracts, and the farmers as tenants for ever if they perform their agreements. The potatoe thrives extremely well in Guzerat and Bengal, and is now produced extensively about Surat, for the supply of Bombay, where it appears at table with as laughing a countenance as in many parts of Ireland. Sweet potatoes and yams are very plentiful every where in India; and in Guzerat, cabbages, carrots, turnips, and nearly all common vegetables grow freely. Grapes are very rare either there or in Bengal; and the vine requires great care to make it produce at all, as it suffers greatly from the destructive effects of the hot winds. The great elevation of the Deckan and Mysore, and their freedom from hot winds, render them far more temperate and healthy than Guzerat or Bengal, notwithstanding their proximity to the tropic of Cancer.

The 65th regiment encamped, on its return to Baroda, near the cantonments, and it being expected that the corps would remain here during the monsoon, the soldiers were permitted to send for their families to Bombay; some of the officers did the same; but Thoughtless having heard so much of this dangerous climate, and being frightened at the number of graves in the European cemetery of the station, thought it best for Mary and his children to remain at the presidency. In fact, the hospital began to fill in the latter end of May, and on the fourth of June Lieutenant Barnes and thirty soldiers were struck with *coups de soleil*; six of them died of electric fevers, and several women and children also fell beneath the pestilence of the atmosphere. A shoemaker named Foster, married to a pretty interesting little Yorkshire woman, was struck next day and instantly expired. His poor wife, while attending his funeral in the evening, fainted from the closeness of the atmosphere, and was laid alongside her husband next morning, — a happy exchange if she joined him in heaven, for Thoughtless had never beheld despair more legibly written on a human face. In short, after a few days, there were only 250 men left fit for duty. But a sudden order having arrived, the force at Baroda marched for Kattywar on the 11th of June, under Colonel East, with six field pieces and three howitzers, Lieutenant Wilson being left in charge of the sick belonging to the 65th at the cantonments. Most fortunately a heavy fall of rain took place as the precursor of the monsoon, and all nature put on the livery of green.

While at Baroda, the thieves were very troublesome. Notwithstanding every precaution, they eluded the sentries, entered the lines, and carried off property out of the tents while the officers were asleep, by cutting their way through the walls of canvas. Only a short time before the return of the regiment, a fine young officer, Lieutenant Nixon of the company's service, residing in a bungalow, saw one of them in the dead of night in his bed-chamber; the light of the moon through the venetians enabled him clearly to observe the motions of the Bheel, but how he had entered was unaccountable. Nixon knew the danger of giving an alarm, and pretended to be sound asleep, in the hope that the thief would approach so near that he might seize him without danger of missing his hold. But the fellow being quite naked, with his head close shaved, had his skin so completely covered with some slippery substance, that poor Nixon made a dash at him in vain, and received so dreadful a cut on his right arm that it hung dangling by his side, while the Bheel leaped like harlequin over the side wall of the bungalow, through a small entrance he had made in the thatch. The wounded arm had to be amputated at the elbow joint.

The 65th regiment and 2d battalion of the 8th native infantry, with the artillery and pioneers, crossed the river Myhe, near Wausad, where it was much swollen by the late rain, and very nearly unfordable, though the bed at this place is broad and sandy. This river, a small stream in summer, rushes during the rains with foaming fury towards the gulf of Cambay, and has formed a deep passage, the banks being very high and craggy and broken into ravines. It appears from the banks of the Nerbuddah, as well as from those of the Myhe, that Guzerat in this part is a black rich soil to the depth of thirty or forty feet, resting on fine hard sand. Two marches brought them to the town of Petland, which is held in equal shares by the Peishwa and Guickwar; it is a populous and important place; the country around is extremely fine, and at present highly interesting, the farmers being busy manuring their fields and ploughing. Soon after the arrival of the force, a crowd of Hindoos assembled round the place where our men were slaughtering cattle, and bewailed their fate in loud lamentations. Two days afterwards the force crossed the Sabramutty, just below the junctions of the Menderi and Serri, at the village of Pallah, and encamped on its right bank near Wenta. This being one of the sacred streams, several pagodas are erected near it, and the number of devotees here from different parts of India at this time was great. Their appearance indicated uncommon self-denial; covered with ashes and the mud of the river, they were sitting in groups on the banks in the sun's glare, having placed themselves in one posture, which they were not to change till evening. It being contrary to the rules of their order to cut the hair, it is matted and reaches very nearly to the ground. One of them whom Charles examined had lost the use of the fingers of his right hand, from having kept them long closed over the thumb, and he shortly expected the nails to make their appearance at the back of his hand. The next march was to Dolka, an extensive Moorish town, exhibiting the ruins of former splendour. This district now belongs to the company, and is under the collector of Keira. Its grand mosques and tanks are now sinking under the mouldering hand of time, and the town does not contain one-third of its former inhabitants. Their complexion is almost fair; among the women, who wear trowsers and a loose gown, some appeared to be beautiful; most of them wore veils with holes made for their mouth and eyes, which gave them a very curious appearance. The vicinity of Dolka is like that of an English town, having fine broad roads, with hedge rows and gardens. After passing the desert space between the gulfs of Kutch and Cambay already described, they reached Limree, which is a large walled town with high towers, reminding the traveller of the descriptions in the history of Alexander the Great. Crowds of people covered the walls to see the force pass just under them. This town was ceded to the company, but it is governed by its own rajah, under a sort of zemindary tenure. Charles asked a respectable looking man whether the place belonged to the Peishwa or Guickwar: "Ah, sir," said he, "all here is yours;" but in such a tone that Thoughtless looked at him attentively. His face was a meek and resigned one, nor did his answer appear to be dictated either by flattery or servility, but uttered rather in a tone of despondency, with a sigh for his country ; and Charles could not help viewing his white beard and manly deportment with respectful regard. Two marches more brought Colonel East to Raunpore, where Colonel Barclay was encamped, with several guns and some European artillery, a detachment of the 17th dragoons and the Bombay native cavalry, the flank companies of the Bombay European regiment, with the first of the 5th, 7th, and 8th native infantry, pioneers, and a battering train.

While the 17th dragoons were on route to Raunpore from Keira, an interesting circumstance occurred. In crossing the Run, the Bheels having been found very troublesome, one of the Bhauts was engaged as security for the camp ; yet several thefts were committed next night, and in the morning, upon hearing that such was the fact, the Bhaut mangled himself so dreadfully with his own hand that he died in a few days.

Raunpore stands on the Bauhadre river. It presents a melancholy picture of former greatness now in ruins, and its old castle is a military post for a serjeant's party from Keira, who have charge of stores. All the towns within sight are walled, and the country presents a very warlike aspect. After leaving Powan Ghur not a hill had been seen; but two marches north of Raunpore the hills of Kattywar began to diversify the scene, and the country presented the countenance of misery, all the villages being nearly in ruins, and fine plains, bearing traces of former cultivation, reduced to a barren waste. Three days more brought the force to Wankineer, in ancient times the capital of Kattywar, situated on a fine clear river called the Mutsvee. This town is romantically situated on an island, with a chain of hills rising one over another just behind it; but the interior has nothing to engage admiration, for the streets are narrow and many parts of it are in ruins, particularly the mosques. Guzerat was long under the Moslems, having been invaded by Mahmud of Guzni, and the northern parts of it colonized at an early period, but at present it is all subject to the Guickwar and the Peishwa, though nearly every place in it is the private property of some petty chief, and its misery has been greatly increased by the frequent quarrels and rebellions that have taken place. The object of Colonel East's force was to reduce the fort of Juria, situated on the gulf of Kutch, the chief of which had refused to pay his tribute; and on this service the colonel marched with all practicable dispatch, notwithstanding the very frequent heavy falls of rain, which would have retarded the progress of a less vigorous commander. On the 17th July the force was on the right bank of the Adji, but the river was unfordable from a great fall of rain the night before; but as the flood subsided considerably during the day, the colonel in the evening gave orders for passing it, which was effected with very great difficulty, the bed of the river being dangerously rocky, and the stream so rapid that the men were in several instances carried away. No lives, however, were lost, and on the following day he approached Juria, having been joined by Captain Ballyntine the political agent, and a large body of the Guickwar's cavalry. Several days were spent in negociations, at some distance from the fort, but on the 8th of August the force encamped before it, and prepared to erect batteries. Juria is a place of considerable strength, but not a shot was fired, for the chief submitted immediately, and three days afterwards Colonel East removed his camp four miles from it to the banks of the Ooude, a fine clear stream.

On visiting the fort, Thoughtless found it a square, each of whose sides, about half a mile in extent, was defended by three towers; but the citadel or rajah's house was strongly fortified, and there were in all twenty-five guns mounted on the works. The walls round Juria are about twelve feet high and nine thick, surmounted by a parapet about six feet high and two thick, with loop holes breast high for musketry, so that the entire wall outside appears full eighteen feet in height. It is composed of soft granite, and the garrison had placed immense quantities of the same materials along the top to throw down upon their enemies. Parallel to this wall, and at about thirty paces distant outside, a rampart of earth, with a ditch, adds considerably to the strength of the place, which is capable of making a good defence. It has only two gates, and they are strongly flanked. The streets of the town are narrow, and the houses of a poor description. It is said that Suckeram, the father of the present chief, rose in the service of the Jam of Noa Nuggur to the possession of the forts of Juria and Balamba, with the territory thereunto belonging. But to enter into the history of these petty chiefs forms no part of the author's plan.

CHAP. XIX.

And kind Mnemosyne must not forget
That little syren *cheechee*, a brunette,
Like Venus from the sea, from Gunga's foam
She rose, and Loves and Graces round her roam.
She rouges sometimes with each tint from night,
In ivory sable to a roseless white;
A jet-black Cupid flaps his wing apace,
To drive musquitoes from her amorous face;
Malicious rogue! he often points his dart,
And leaves it quivering in a Briton's heart.
Enchanted he remains, with nerveless arm,
Till pale disease extracts the barbed charm.

THE half-cast ladies in Bengal are called *Cheechees*, which is a Hindostannee word, much used by them in Calcutta, equivalent to *fie! fie!* Some of these captivating fair ones are really pretty girls, in the very softest sense of that expression, and so irresistible, that many a young man sacrifices his future prospects at the altar of Hymen; for there is hardly an instance of one of these matches turning out well, the children being of a different tint of complexion from that of the father, and the mother so much attached to India as her native climate, that she can never be reconciled to the frozen latitudes of the north, to which her husband looks for his happiness in declining life. Many of the half-cast ladies are most amiable companions, possess affectionate hearts, and perform all the duties of good wives with tenderness and alacrity, but very few of them can enjoy European society; for a consciousness of being so different in appearance impresses them with a feeling of inferiority, under which they are ill at ease with our fair countrywomen; hence they shun their acquaintance, and, it is said, envy them. Their real happiness would consist in being connected by marriage with persons of the same cast; but it is a strange truth, that these girls look upon the young men of their own colour as beneath them; and at all the schools in Calcutta, where these charming nymphs are exhibited, their admirers are generally youthful Europeans. It has been before observed that their number is very great, and some idea may be formed of it from the seminaries and asylums in Calcutta, where upwards of five hundred half-cast girls, illegitimate daughters by native mothers of the higher ranks, are genteelly educated. The Bengal officers have an asylum, called the Kidderpore School, supported by subscription, for the express purpose of educating orphans of that description, who when married, with consent of the governors, to tradesmen or others of respectable character, receive portions from the institution. There is another, on a very large scale, supported by the government, for soldiers' children, who are apprenticed, provided for as servants, and portioned upon their marriage, suitably to their prospects in life. But to expatiate on this subject would be tedious; recourse is therefore had to the journal.

Colonel East did not remain long on the banks of the Ooude: he moved westerly to Dherole, on a fine clear stream where forage was plenty. The country immediately round it is highly cultivated, and the fields are well inclosed with hedges of prickly pear, while the prospect is enlivened by plantations of babaul and tamarind trees. Dherole, like all the other towns, has been half depopulated by the great famine. At this place, in the beginning of September, a violent fever broke out, and in a few days 140 men were in hospital out of 436, the total present of the 65th regiment. In three days Major Hutchings and twelve men of that corps fell victims to it, besides Lieutenant Hutchinson and Assistant-surgeon Keith of the Bombay artillery, with a great many brave fellows belonging to the 17th dragoons and to the Bombay European regiment. Officers seldom die in camp of disease in India, being sent off to the coast or to Europe for recovery; but the progress of this fever was so rapid that in thirty-eight hours its victims were lifeless. The burning brain drank the blood which seemed to flow towards it with the impetuosity of a torrent, and the head became so hot that to touch it was painful. In short, such was the consternation in camp, that Colonel East made several marches in the hope of escaping from this dreadful epidemic, and at length encamped on high ground near the village of Ballachoova, with the cool ocean just in front of the line, where the fever was arrested, after having made such havock as induced Thoughtless to write thus in his journal: "I have long endeavoured to contemplate death as the inevitable doom of man, and to be prepared to meet it in any shape with fortitude; but to terminate life this way is horrible, for all that die are torn out of their graves by jackals. O God! thou hast heretofore protected me, continue thy goodness."

Major Hutchings was sincerely esteemed by his friends: he possessed the finest qualities of person and mind, with manners so elegant that his company diffused happiness. Mild, gentleman-like, and unassuming, his urbanity created general cheerfulness, while the solidity of his understanding, and the extent of his general information, commanded the highest respect, and improved his young brother officers, by whom he was greatly beloved; but much as he was regretted, the regiment about this time experienced another loss, which was attended with melancholy circumstances of so affecting a nature, that the major was for a time forgotten.

The very day before the 65th embarked for Guzerat, the senior lieutenant had arrived from England, where he had been employed on the recruiting service for some time, having been severely wounded at the storm of Bhurtpore, and rendered unfit for a hot climate. Henry Taylor was in person all that the imagination of woman can form of loveliness in man, and during his residence in a country town in England he captivated the affections of a charming girl, possessed of such rank and fortune that her father absolutely set his face against the marriage. She was all generosity, however, and considering wealth unnecessary where her treasure was love, she became his bride, and her father disinherited her. They were happy for some time at home, but he was ordered out, and being in daily expectation of his company, he joined his regiment; and Colonel Milnes most kindly left him with the depôt, for the purpose of reconciling Mrs. Taylor, who was then in a very delicate state, to the climate. He resided on the island of Colabah, and close to his bungalow there was a *peré's* tomb, near which Mrs. Taylor one day saw a snake gliding among the grass, and her husband drew his sword to kill it. "Sir," said his servant, "do not hurt that snake; it is the spirit of the peré."—"Nonsense," said he; and with a blow he cut it in two.—"I wish no misfortune may happen to master," said the boy, in a melancholy tone. That very evening he was taken ill, and three days after he was a corpse. All the natives, of course, attributed his death to the resentment of the peré; and this unhappy circumstance confirmed them in their idle superstition. His poor wife went distracted, and her infant died. She remained in a state of derangement for several months, and was at length sent to England by the officers of the regiment to her father, who beheld the fatal effects of thwarting the affections of his only child.

At Ballachoova the sick recovered fast, but the force did not remain long there, for a sudden order arrived to march, and Colonel East moved on the 18th September, passed Juria, and on the 29th encamped near Wadwan, having passed through a country recovering from desolation. At this place the recruits that had lately arrived from England joined the regiment from Bombay, by way of Gogo, under Captain Keith, whose fate it was to find a grave in Kattywar. Wadwan belongs to the Peishwa, and among its inhabitants the Jains are very numerous. They have a temple here, with nearly one hundred figures represented in white marble. These images of holy men are exactly of the same form, and all seated in the same posture, but they are of different sizes. The dark recess in which this grand pantheon is displayed being profusely illuminated, the images having bright sparkling eyes produce such an effect on the observer at the distance where he is kept, that really the scene is awfully grand. Wadwan is a large town, and the inhabitants are a people of polished manners. Not far from hence, on the 24th of October, Serjeant Donn was buried, whose death was the eighth among the recruits lately arrived. His case was very affecting. Having brought with him his wife, a very interesting young woman, she unfortunately took the fever, and he became affected almost at the same time. It was a most melancholy sight to see this fine young couple in two doolies, near the hospital tents, quite delirious, with their little son, who was too young to be sensible of the loss he was going to sustain. The wife died in the morning, and her husband became sensible towards evening. His first question was about her, but on turning his head he saw her borne to the grave, and clasping his hands in agony, he sank down with a broken heart, and expired during the night. When Thoughtless looked at his little boy, he sighed, and repeated the following lines, written by a dear friend on a similar occasion at Seringapatam:

SONNET ON AN ORPHAN BOY IN THE EAST INDIES.

Poor orphan boy, cast on the world's wide stage,
Where vice and fraud thy inexperience wait,
Without a friend to guide thy tender age,
O! how I pity thy forlorn estate.

No parents have for thee their hopes and fears,
Left a lone orphan in thy infancy;
No mother watches o'er thy tender years,
Thou wilt receive no father's legacy.

Mourn not poor boy, for though thou art bereft
Of parents, friends, and from thy home art driven,
One kind Protector still to thee is left,
A tender Father lives for thee in heaven;
Who always was, and will be to the end,
The widow's and the helpless orphan's Friend.

In November the force was considerably increased. Colonel Johnson had charge of the quarter-master-general's department, with Lieutenant Reymon as assistant engineer: the artillery, upwards of 200 strong in Europeans, were under Major Hesman and Major Sealy, with a fine park and battering train. Lieutenant Grindley had charge of the commissariat, Captain Stannus of the adjutant-general's office, Lieutenant Crozier of the pioneers, Colonel Stanhope of the cavalry, and Colonels Milnes and Osborne of the brigades, consisting of the 65th Bombay European regiment, 1st battalion of the 7th N. I., and a flank corps formed from light companies, 1st of the 5th, 1st of the 8th, and 2d of the 8th, N. I. — in all about 7,100 men; and the object of the expedition was understood to be a visit to the Row of Booge, which diffused much pleasure throughout the camp. Thoughtless was again pleased with the appearance of his regiment on parade, for many of those left sick at Baroda had joined, and the arrivals from England replaced the brave fellows whose bodies had enriched the soil of Guzerat, so that six hundred rank and file now formed a respectable line.

On the 6th of December, the force arrived at the ancient city of Halwad, now almost a heap of ruins, and encamped near the cemetery, which is justly considered a great curiosity. The country from Wadwan seemed to be recovering from the dreadful effects of famine, but every where presented a melancholy aspect, being half depopulated, and the fine fertile plains quite a waste, covered with wolves, jackals, wild asses, hogs, and antelopes, with wild duck, partridge, quail, hare, cyrus bird, snipe, and bustard in very great abundance. The Jalliah tribe, as well as some other divisions of the rajpoot cast which inhabit this part of Guzerat, bury the urns containing the ashes of their deceased, and raise monuments in honour of distinguished persons. Everywhere over Kattywar, stones are set up with inscriptions, and warriors represented on them; and wherever suttee has been performed, a woman's arm is sculptured, with the hand held up in the manner of those prisoners in our courts who plead not guilty. Many of the mausoleums in the cemetery of Halwad are costly temples composed of hewn stone, with statues of gods and heroes in marble. Several of these are lingums, and the Brahmins that attend them are quite naked. The walls of the town, like its palaces, are mouldering to decay. Along one face of it there is a very extensive tank, now covered with weeds, affording a fine retreat for shoals of bald coots; along its banks are the tombs of many a Moslem warrior. But the palace, the walls of which once resounded with the voices of ambitious courtiers, is now tenantless; and the durbar, supported by massy pillars, which was once crowded with multitudes influenced by hopes and fears, is now an asylum for the owl and bat. Halwad stands on a bed of fine granite, a substance which more or less appears throughout Kattywar, so that the external appearance of its surface is not unlike that of Ireland in many parts. It is watered by numerous streams as clear as crystal, and such is the luxuriance of its vegetation that the grass in many places was a yard long.

From this town the force proceeded for Kutch, and made two marches to the river Puddar — first to Wantwadder, a village pleasantly situated on a stream called Bansana — and next, nearly to the Run, between Kutch and Guzerat. During this day's march they passed the ruins of a large village called Gentilly, which was a picture of wretchedness. It is situated on an eminence commanding a view of a dreary barren waste; the earth is parched and gaping in cracks, without vegetation, — on every side houses are deserted and in ruins — here and there a miserable being is seen peeping from among them. There may be twenty or thirty families remaining in this place, which appears to have once been the habitation of many thousands.

Here they found Captain M'Murdo, the political agent of the Bombay government, having with him a division of the Guickwar's cavalry to co-operate with the force, which now consisted of the 17th dragoons, 65th regiment, part of the honourable company's Bombay European regiment, a proportion of artillery, and several native battalions, altogether amounting to about seven thousand effective men. Reckoning in an eastern camp seven followers for each fighting man (an estimate rather below than above the mark), the camp exhibited to the eye a mass of fifty thousand men.

For several days the camp had been a scene of Asiatic pageant in the celebration of the mohorum. Here were seen men with their bodies painted and their faces disfigured, dancing and capering in the most grotesque attitudes, and flourishing weapons with wonderful dexterity — there girls gaudily dressed, and decorated with garlands of coloured and tinselled paper, singing and jumping; and everywhere groups of enthusiasts and buffoons, disguised in the skins of deer, sheep, goats, tigers, and buffaloes, with tinsel temples glittering like gold. But the display ended here; all the Mahomedan sepoys marched in procession to a great tank in the vicinity, and fired three rounds over the sinking remains of Hossen and Hassen.

Flamingoes, floricans, and wild asses are very plentiful. The latter appear at a distance a very beautiful sprightly animal of a slate colour, and as swift as an antelope, escaping from observation in a moment.

From this encampment all the heavy baggage and useless stores, together with the native families and some of the sick, were sent to Murree under the escort of an officer and 100 sepoys. It is inconceivable what numbers of children were produced in this force during this and part of the preceding year; each sepoy was the father of two or three. On the back of every loaded bullock might be seen a couple of little squalling naked creatures, tied there for preservation by their mothers during each march, and hundreds of native women running along with their little ones in baskets carried on their heads. After freeing the camp from every thing not indispensibly necessary, they moved to a little ruined village called Venassa, situated near the Run. From this place to the coast of Kutch the distance is about ten miles. During the monsoon, when the wind blows violently up the gulf, it presents a body of deep water, for the flow of the great tides which so much astonished the soldiers of Alexander covers the whole of it, and together with the deluge of waters down the Puddar, the bed of which is near the middle, renders it quite unfordable; but at present there was not any water on its surface, and it was as hard and level as a board within our observation. This sandy bed is almost wholly incrusted with fine salt, which in some places is so thick that it might be dug up and carted off. I can suggest no hypothesis as to the real cause of this large deposit of saline concretions. The great evaporation in hot climates enables the natives to make abundance of salt on the sea shore, by letting the water into pans made in the sand. But either the sea must be unusually impregnated with salt in the gulf of Kutch, or vast quantities of it are washed from the mountains by rivers. This incrustation of salt produces, on the space it covers, a most beautiful mirage. It appears to the eye like a placid lake of great extent studded with islands, and the shining surface gives to every little object of a different colour a seeming magnitude which the eye converts into ten thousand familiar shapes.

They found no difficulty in crossing the Run, which very nearly corresponds with the above description. In some parts, however, the guns sunk very deep in mud and quicksands, wherefore it became necessary often to change the direction, and carefully to examine the ground. Great quantities of dead fishes, quite hard and dry, were seen all over it. To an observer who gallopped out to a proper distance there could not be a finer sight than the field force as it appeared on this grand parade, actually in order to receive an enemy, and in momentary expectation of being engaged. The officers and men were in the highest spirits, the air was delightfully cool, and an infinity of objects attracted the attention of every one. "O! look at that ship in full sail," said one. — "Now for a dash at the Wagurs," said another. — "See! there they are! look what a shoal of cavalry blackens the horizon." — "What city is that?" asked a third: — "Surely those are castles, towers, parks, and groves." — "O! what a beautiful island," said a fourth. "See the cataract in yonder mountain; look at the buildings —why, there are trees — don't laugh, my dear fellow, I see them as clearly as I do your nose." — All this was deception.

When they reached the other side, no enemy appeared. Having marched on for four miles in a westerly direction, they encamped near a poor little village called Rhatra, where they found a tank of good water, which was a great relief to them, as all near the Run was brackish. The distant country appeared hilly, and the coast is just like that on the other side; many of the villages are in ruins. Charles, from his situation, had to precede the force, with the quarter-master-general's department. The inhabitants did not run away, but he never saw people more alarmed. The small village near the camp was surrounded by a hedge of prickly pear, and had a little temple. It contained a great number of inhabitants for its size. On their approach, they saw them over the hedge, running from one house to another. Curiosity induced Charles and some others to enter it, and they were met by a very respectable looking aged man with a long grey beard, seemingly deputed for that purpose. He invited them to dismount and rest on some low cots brought out, and entreated protection, begging that a guard might be placed over the village. In answer to their questions, he said, their arrival would relieve them from great misery, if they could destroy the robbers. "Sirs," said he, "we sow our land in the hope of reaping, but when our fields are ripe, they come, cut our harvest, carry it away, and leave us to starve." The women and children at first only peeped from their doors and windows, but at last they came out and salammed. It may be worthy of remark, that in the vicinity of the Run, the evenings and mornings were remarkably mild and pleasant; while at a distance, both on the approach and the departure, they proved bitterly cold. It is probable, that the heat absorbed by the sandy Run during the day, and given out at night, may produce this local temperature. It ought also to be noticed, that even at this little village suttees have been performed, for several stones are set up near it with the hieroglyphics before described; and others have men represented on them with infants in their arms, a symbol which apparently refers to the custom of infanticide. These are rude sculptures; and the figure of the idol in their temple, which is worshipped in many parts of India under the name of Hunnemaun, is equally so, for it is a monstrous monkey with a sword and buckler, in an erect posture and a threatening attitude, having a tail so long that it curls up round his head.

Before the force marched into the interior, it was necessary to have possession of some place of strength near the sea, and the fort of Anjar was considered most proper. They proceeded therefore without delay, keeping parallel to the Run, but considerably inland for forage and water, and marched in a westerly direction towards the place intended. The first halt was at Kattaria, the ruins of a large town, having moved to it through an open and pleasing country, presenting, however, few traces of culture or population. In Kattaria there are about one hundred inhabited ghurs or huts, which are surrounded with a dry stone rampart and parapet with small towers; the ruins extend a mile from it in all directions. Well-built stone houses of three stories are seen roofless and deserted, while beneath their walls, in little thatched mud hovels, the inhabitants are now sheltered. This part of Kutch has been for a long time the theatre of contests between the rajahs of Murvee and Mallia and the row of Booge Booge. In common with Kattywar, it has felt the desolating effects of famine. The climate is agreeable, and at this season may be called temperate. The inhabitants are robust, healthy, and have a bold commanding appearance. Their women are fine—even the common *riottees*, or labourers' wives, have interesting, plump, blooming, light-brown complexions, with an intelligent physiognomy, and their children are very pretty.

On proceeding, the force passed a pretty little village, near a large tank planted round with trees, from which the inhabitants had fled on hearing of their approach. They encamped at another much larger called Omrallah, where the people appeared in great consternation, the principal men having carried off their effects upon hearing that the force was going to halt there. Though the utmost care is taken to protect the defenceless inhabitants of an invaded country, still the approach of an enemy is dreadful, for the followers will plunder, if possible, at the risk of being hanged upon the trees during a march by the provost-marshal. The roads were good, the country fine, in some places jungly, or covered with thorns, which bear a delicious berry called by the natives bore, something like haws, but rounder and more acid; in other parts there were fine fields of cotton and jewarry. Every where the grass was long and luxuriant. In all the cemeteries women are represented on stones, performing suttee with their dead husbands in their arms, and others carrying infants for sacrifice. It is said that in former times not only wives were burnt with their husbands in this part, but that some of their children, servants, and concubines were also consumed with them in the same pile. Several shots were fired at the picquets, and some camels and bullocks were carried away from the foraging grounds, but no enemy openly opposed the march.

After passing a strong little fort called Chadwarrah, which the commander had deserted, the next halt was at Whound, a large town with a dry ditch, mud wall, and stone towers. This place is situated between two ranges of hills, and the valley is clothed with a fine crop of young wheat, having a beard like barley.

Their next march was to the village and tank of Punkaseer, during which they passed a strong hill fort called Budzou, and the large village of Seckra, whose mud wall was crowded with people. The inhabitants of the smaller places had deserted them on their approach, and repaired hither for greater security. Fine fields of wheat smiled around this place, and numerous stones were set up near it, with the figures of warriors sculptured rudely on them, in the attitudes of throwing the spear and wielding the sword, mounted on camels, horses and elephants. The camp at Punkaseer was pitched on a beautiful spot, a wood of baubel on one side, a large tank and pretty village on another, and elsewhere fine rich fields of wheat.

In the morning they continued their march by the left, and the Guickwar's auxiliaries, keeping a parallel line on the right flank, looked well. Their golden standards, streamers, tom toms, arms, and accoutrements were all strikingly different from the British line. The Mahratta saddles are made of cloth, and the horsemen use very small stirrups, into which they put only their toes. On reaching their ground of encampment, near a respectable town called Cheekansir, they learned that the enemy's cavalry had been there, and poisoned all the tanks and wells with wheat, impregnated with arsenic, which it was supposed would prevent the mineral from sinking and losing its deadly properties. The water in the wells was found to be highly poisonous, and orders were issued to draw none from them. Some of the followers, however, suffered before this was known; but the body of fluid in the tanks was too great to be affected by the quantity of arsenic thrown in, and carrying a supply with them, they encamped next day before Anjar without molestation, except from a few guns fired from the walls, to keep those off who approached to reconnoitre. The town appeared to be large, and it was surrounded by a high stone wall and towers.

During the night a lodgment was made, within a proper distance of the fort, among some stone pagodas that served to protect the covering party, who were not even fired upon, and by the next morning a battery, consisting of five eighteen-pounders, was erected at 450 yards distance from the S. W. face, with one for two mortars at the same distance behind. It was most singular, that Hussenmeah, who commanded here, and had a garrison of Arabs, did not open a gun on the party till the battery was nearly ready to destroy his defences. Numbers had gone down from camp to see the operations, and they were straggling about in heedless security, supposing that not a shot would be fired, when a smart cannonade commenced from the fort. Lieutenant Delaney of the 17th dragoons had his right arm shot off, and in a moment several of the lookers-on were killed. Though the batteries were not quite ready, the fire was briskly returned by their six-pounders, and two five and a half inch howitzers, from the position occupied by the covering party, and at ten o'clock both the batteries opened on this unhappy place. It was a melancholy sight on Christmas-day to see the blaze of destruction that burst over a large town, crowded with inhabitants. The shrieks of women and children, after the explosion of each shell, were dismal, and the confusion thus occasioned was seen and heard from the camp. The shells burst over the place with the greatest precision; at two o'clock it was in a blaze in several places, and about an hour after a breach was reported to be practicable. The enemy kept firing as long as they had a defence, but their towers not being calculated to stand against eighteen-pound shot, fell in crashes before every round directed at them, and long before the place was surrendered, the fire from it was completely silenced. Soon after three o'clock it was unconditionally given up, the garrison escaped, and Colonel Burr with a proper force took possession of Anjar. Seventy-four shells and 1800 eighteen-pound shot were fired against the town, besides the play of three six-pounders and two howitzers, and yet very little damage was done to the buildings, and a few only of the people were hurt.

In the evening Thoughtless and some others went to see the town, and entered it through the breach, which was quite practicable. It appeared about two miles in circumference, and in a very flourishing condition, with a wall round it about twelve feet high and six thick, on which there was a parapet two feet thick and six in height. In going through its defences, they counted thirty-eight pieces of cannon of different kinds. The population was very great, and the inhabitants salammed with great respect. Some of the women were beautiful, and indeed almost fair: they touched their heads gracefully with their hands, crying "Bullee ayah," a term of compliment which means "welcome." The houses are well-built stone buildings, tiled and white-washed, and the streets are wide and regular. There are two fine pagodas, one of which belongs to the Jains, and contains the assembly of holy images round that of the saint Pursenaut, placed on a higher throne, and twice the size of the others, which are all alike, having prodigiously large ears, being quite naked, and seated with the legs crossed under them, something like tailors, only that the feet cross exactly in the centre, and on the soles rest the hands, one in the palm of the other. These idols, as well as the altar on which they sit, are made of white marble; and one would suppose, from the cast of countenance and shape of the breast, that they were designed to represent women. They are placed in the sanctum sanctorum of the temple, or in that remote quarter over which the flag is spread. On going into this, the party had to take off their shoes. The place is constantly lighted up with brass lamps, and some of the ornaments in it are of gold. The priests seemed pleased with Charles for sketching the figures, and explained their names, which would be uninteresting to the reader. The other temple belongs to the followers of Brahma, and is dedicated to the mother of the gods, whose image is richly dressed and covered with jewels. In the gardens and groves that surround the town, there are numerous temples and monuments well worthy of observation, besides a Mussulmaun cemetery, and several neat mosques. This place communicates with the gulf of Kutch, by means of Toonia Bunder, or a wharf at a short distance, to which the gulf is navigable, and where there is a strong little fort. The possession of this place has opened the communication with Juria, Murvee, and Bombay.

Having left a garrison of 150 men at Toonia Bunder, and 220 at Anjar, the breach in which was built up, they marched for Booge Booge, in a north-west direction, through a country pretty well inhabited and cultivated, and encamped at a mountainous village called Ratnaur, about eleven miles from Anjar. Immediately after the fall of that fort, several of the chiefs of other places sent in their submission, and a vakeel arrived in camp from the row. Soon after they had pitched their camp, some chunam or chalk-pits were discovered near it, extending under ground to a vast extent. being lighted and aired by shafts like mines. The poor inhabitants had concealed their valuable property and implements of husbandry, all which the followers plundered and destroyed before they could be stopped. Some of the followers having been killed, and their cattle taken from them by the country people, two small villages were destroyed by order of the commanding officer, to warn them of the danger they incurred by resorting to hostilities against those who were inclined, as much as possible, to protect them.

Next morning the direction being changed to the eastward, the force entered the mountains, and encamped near a village called Warra, situated on a fine stream, winding through a well cultivated little valley, surrounded by wild high cliffs. The inhabitants all fled, and left their property to be plundered by the brutal and merciless followers, who unroofed the houses, and burnt the very ploughs and harrows. It was supposed that the force marched hither merely for water, there being hardly any at the last ground, and that negociations were on the point of being closed, which would render it unnecessary to proceed further. Negociations were certainly pending, but they were suddenly broken off, for in the morning the troops retraced their steps, and turning northward encamped within five miles of the capital, at a place called Sackhoud. The mountainous range through which they marched, and dragged the battering train with great difficulty, is wild, and so very strong by nature, that a brave handful of men, determined to conquer or die, might here make a noble defence. But no opposition was made. On arriving at a deserted village called Vuddar, a fine prospect opened on their view, namely, an extensive valley bordered with picturesque hills, interspersed with beautiful little villages of nicely white-washed houses, and robed with green fields of wheat and cotton. To the right, appeared a very high mount with religious temples on its summit, and to the left was Booge Booge, the towers of which, on a high hill, reflected the meridian rays of the sun. All the villages around were deserted, many of the houses unroofed, and the effects carried off. In short, Thoughtless made this note in his journal:—"Miserable cottagers!—you feel the effects of ambition and war;—you quit your homes, your temples, with your wives and infants, and fly from plunderers."

The fort of Booge Booge had a formidable appearance, being a high hill strongly fortified with walls and towers, standing in a plain, without a single command near it. If resolutely defended, there could hardly exist any hope of taking it by breach or escalade. In this encampment they remained for several days, receiving orders and counter-orders respecting the approach to invest the city and fort, while negociations were proceeding between the political agent and the row. During this time, several of them clambered to the top of a remarkable hill in rear of the camp. They calculated its height at 400 yards above the level of the plain. The ascent to it is extremely difficult, and from its top the towers of

Anjar could be seen, and the Run that separates Kutch from Scinde distinctly traced. There is a little fort on its summit, which, it is said, a robber with his gang defended till he was starved to death. This consists of a large basin for the retention of rain water, and several little dwellings now in ruins, the whole surrounded by a strong stone wall, which runs along frightful precipices.

In a few days the row acceded to the terms proposed to him. Some of these were, that Toonia Bunder and Anjar should remain in the company's hands, that he should pay the expences of the campaign, make a recompence for the destruction caused by plunder, and suppress the pirates in the gulf of Kutch. This treaty was announced by the discharge of a royal salute, and the delivery of extra batta to the troops. Complimentary visits were then exchanged between the Row and Colonel East. The monarch approached the camp about four o'clock in the afternoon, the whole line having been under arms from ten in the morning to receive him. Seventeen guns from the centre announced his arrival, and he was preceded by a considerable number of horse and foot, elephants, camels, tom toms, tooteries, flags, standards, and streamers. In the crowd appeared a remarkable personage on stilts eight feet high, wielding an enormous sword, which he managed in his exalted situation with great dexterity, flourishing it round his head, and proclaiming the titles and dignities of the Row of Kutch Booge. The king himself was seated in a rich howdah upon a large elephant, having one of his great officers of state near him, who fanned his majesty. The row was accompanied by perhaps 2000 Arabs, and nearly all the population of Booge Booge, so that the whole plain appeared one moving multitude; which when Charles surveyed, and turned his eyes upon the handful of men who brought this mass to bow the neck, excited strange thoughts in his mind. Colonel East, it is said, received his majesty with all proper ceremony, and made him and his officers rich presents in the name of the honourable company, so that the row returned to his capital seemingly well pleased. His personal appearance was not imposing; nor had he a countenance in which one could say there was expression. He appeared rather a young man, with an aspect desponding and melancholy, and not quite free from apprehension.

Next day Colonel East, accompanied by his staff and the brigadiers of the force, with a body guard from the 17th dragoons, returned the row's visit, and was received with all possible splendour. Several Bhauts sang during his stay, whose long white beards and fine voices attracted attention. Rich perfumes were profusely scattered, and presents of sabres, shields, spears, shawls, and embroidered robes were made to all that accompanied the Colonel.

Upon going to see the city of Booge Booge, Thoughtless found it situated about half a mile from the fortified hill, and surrounded by a wall like that of Anjar. The town is far from being strong. It is nearly a square, whose side may be three quarters of a mile in length. The streets are narrow and dirty; but the houses are in general strong stone buildings, intermixed with mosques, temples, and minarets. The row's palace is a very ancient gloomy pile, surrounded by a high and strong wall with towers. All the streets were crowded with the inhabitants who flocked, with every mark of curiosity on their countenances, to see the European visitors. The women appeared surprised at their appearance, and some of the children laughed, probably at the strangeness of the figures, which to them must have seemed ridiculous. Several of the women salammed, but the men in general paid no respect; and the Arabs, placed as guards about the palace, appeared stiff and inclined to insult them. The dress of the people is the same as in Kattywar, consisting of large turbans, trowsers, and a gown with a long cloth rolled round the waist; but among the men are seen many Scinds with large hairy caps, and Seiks whose turban and gown are of a different shape; there are also numerous Mussulmen, whose costume varies a little from the general Hindoo dress. Nearly all the women wore coloured chintzes. Many of the seniors have fine long white beards, and the men are large and robust. In mere physical qualities they are certainly not inferior to those by whom they have been conquered; but man is sunk or raised by the institutions to which he is subjected.

Like Anjar, the city of Booge Booge is surrounded by gardens, temples, and tanks, and numerous monuments illustrative of manners and customs. To the attentive observer, these specimens afford evidence of no common degree of taste and excellence in sculpture and architecture. Every where are seen memorials of the performance of suttee and infanticide; with commemorations of the actions of the illustrious dead, whose tombs have become objects of adoration. Some of their temples erected of cut stone, huge in size, and presenting a multitude of elaborate decorations, fill the mind with wonder. Tigers, lions, elephants, monkeys, and an endless variety of fanciful objects cut out of stone, ornament these fabrics, whose surfaces externally and internally are covered with statues of their gods. In the erection of these buildings, the Moorish and Asiatic style of architecture is blended; and the mixture of the wild pagoda with the Grecian dome forms a very beautiful whole. The mausoleum of Row Lacka, the grandfather of the present king, deserves some particular notice, on account of its magnificence, and the sacrifice of human life which it commemorates.

The interior building, on which a great dome rests, is a fifteen-sided figure, twenty-four feet in diameter, and in each angle stands a full length marble statue of a lady who performed suttee with him. They are represented in the bloom of life and beauty, richly dressed, decked out in jewels, and holding instruments of music in their hands. In the centre of the building, where the ashes are deposited, there is a marble head-stone with an inscription, and the emblematical representation of an arm ornamented with bracelets, the hand being held up in the posture already described. The execution of the whole does great credit to the artist, and the building would be considered a beautiful ornament in any city in Europe. Around the inner apartment runs a grand viranda, which, supporting smaller domes, forms the structure externally into a square, and at each angle there is a great entrance; a large stone elephant faces the magnificent flight of steps leading up to the grand portico, on the platform of which are two statues of Europeans in fantastic dresses, placed as guards. The pillars by which this viranda is sustained are extremely curious, and covered with most extraordinary figures, cut out of the solid stone. In short, the whole would command the fixed attention of any observer. But to notice separately all the curious monuments about Booge would be tedious, though not perhaps uninteresting. The mausoleums of Futteh Mahomed, a celebrated Moslem general, and of Dadagee, a saint, are rich pieces of Moorish architecture, carved and worked up with stucco to such an exquisite degree as to resemble marble. Their tombs are covered with richly embroidered stuffs, and an establishment is attached to each for the performance of ceremonies according to Mahomedan custom. The mausoleums of Mohomed Puny and Row Rudder, who, it is said, became a Mussulmaun convert, and is buried by his own particular desire near a very grand mosque in the south-west angle of the town, are also very curious objects.

Few rajahs in India can lay claim to greater antiquity than the Row of Kutch Booge. His family has continued in possession of the government of that country from time immemorial, and tradition carries their origin much farther into the depths of time than the date of the creation, according to our chronology.

CHAP. XX.

"More laudably inclined, with higher aim,
Some stay from motives above love and fame;
Such are whom God inspires with zeal and grace,
To turn from Moloch yon far-spreading race."

Few subjects can be of greater importance than the civilization of India, and the diffusion of the Christian religion throughout the East; and those zealous men deservedly stand high in public estimation, who are labouring to accomplish an object which would liberate so many millions of their fellow-creatures from slavery. It does not appear that the Hindoos were ever intolerant in religious matters, or that the native governments persecuted other men on account of being professors of a different creed. The loss of cast awaited such as failed to conform to prescribed customs, and relatives were held mutually responsible for their strict obedience to the ceremonial laws; but as converts were not received into the Hindoo church, it does not seem to have been contemplated that the members of it could change their tenets of faith: while, according to Mahomedan law, which prohibited apostacy on pain of death, and enjoined the destruction of all other religions, the Jew and Christian were permitted to settle under the protection of a rajah, as well as the Persian fire worshipper, and to adore God as their forefathers did before them without molestation. Nor does it appear that the great efforts made by the early Christians to convert the natives ever excited much persecution against them, although their success in Malabar and Ceylon was prodigious. The liberality of the Hindoos on this head cannot be doubted; and there is a letter on record from Jeswunt Singh, Rajah of Jadpore, to the Emperor Auringzebe, which places their sentiments on this head in a very amiable point of view.

"Your royal ancestor, Akber, whose throne is now in heaven, conducted the affairs of this empire in equity and firm security for the space of fifty-two years, preserving every tribe of men in ease and happiness; whether they were followers of Jesus or of David, of Moses or of Mahomed; were they Brahmins, were they of the sect of Dhariens, which denies the eternity of matter, or of that which ascribes the existence of the world to chance, they all equally enjoyed his countenance and favour; insomuch that his people, in gratitude for the indiscriminate protection which he afforded them, distinguished him by the appellation of Jugot Grow, guardian of mankind. If your majesty places any faith in those books by distinction called divine, you will there be instructed that God is the God of all mankind, not the God of Mahomedans alone. The Pagan and the Mussulman are equally in his presence. Distinctions of colours are of his ordination. It is he who gives existence. In your temples dedicated to his name, the voice is raised in prayer; in a house of images, where the bell is shaken, still he is the object of adoration. To vilify the religion and customs of other men is to set at nought the pleasure of the Almighty. When we deface a picture, we naturally incur the resentment of the painter; and justly has the poet said, 'Presume not to arraign or to scrutinize the various works of Power Divine.'"

European missionaries have therefore found but little obstruction to their labours on the part of the native governments; but the policy of the East India company has been not directly to encourage attempts, of which the avowed object is the overthrow of the institutions of Brahma; and doubtless, upon the broad principles of justice, the government of India is perfectly right in leaving the natives at full liberty to choose their own way to heaven. On the other hand, the endeavours of societies for the propagation of knowledge have been most liberally countenanced by the authorities connected with the East, both at home and abroad. The college of Fort William, founded on the 4th of May 1801, in a few years produced upwards of one hundred volumes on subjects interesting to mankind, and connected with the civilization of India, besides translating the Holy Scriptures into the Persian and Hindostannee languages, which noble undertaking was executed by Mirza Fitrut and Meer Bahader Ullee, under the superintendence of Colonel Colebrook and Dr. Hunter. Although the establishment of the college has been much reduced, yet no stop has been put to the diffusion of scriptural knowledge throughout the East, for the British baptist mission established at Serampore is going on with astonishing perseverance and success. Indeed, the uncommon erudition of the pious members of that establishment, and their wonderful proficiency in the languages of Asia, seem to proclaim how pleasing their labours are in the sight of that God, who bestowed such gifts on poor fishermen as enabled them to surpass the learning of Greece and Rome. Dr. Carey, belonging to the Serampore institution, one of the principal professors in the college of Fort William, is perfect master of Sanscrit, Mahratta, and Bengallie. Mr. Marshman is deeply versed in the Chinese language, and has translated the Ramazuna from the Sanscrit; and Mr. Ward is profoundly acquainted with several native tongues, and deeply conversant with the antiquities of India. At the mission press of Serampore, translations have been made of the Scriptures into Sanscrit, Bengallie, Orissa, Mahratta, Hindostannee, Guzerattee, Seik, Carnatta, Telinga, and Burman languages; while all the Gospels have been translated into Chinese by Messrs. Marshman, Lassar, and Morrison. In short, the Bibliotheca Biblica in Calcutta have bibles and testaments now in all the current languages spoken over India; the translations of which have been accomplished, in some instances, by converts of very great ability, whose conversion seems to have been almost miraculous. Sabat, in particular, whose knowledge of Persian and Arabic, and English, is so perfect, was, like St. Paul, a persecutor of Christians, and felt pleasure in witnessing the execution of his friend Abdalla, who embraced Christianity on reading the Scriptures at the court of the King of Caubul, and who was put to death under the most cruel tortures according to Mahomedan law. In fact, a taste for learning, and a spirit of enquiry after truth, have been diffused throughout Southern Asia, not only by the writings of Sabat, Mirza Fitrut, Meer Bahader Ullee, the Telinga Brahmin convert Ananda Razer, and others who have embraced Christianity, but also by Mahomedan philosophers, and Hindoo pundits of very extraordinary erudition. Lord Teignmouth, speaking of one of these literati, says—"Tuffussil Hossein Khan united in an eminent degree an extensive knowledge of mankind with the deepest erudition. His conversation was polite and instructive; his manners elegant and engaging; his integrity firm; his honour unimpeached. It was his great predilection for mathematical knowledge that induced him to cultivate an acquaintance with the English and with European authors; and from this source he derived that superior knowledge which so much distinguished him among his countrymen." A letter writen by him to his friend Mr. Anderson, in England, fully substantiates his Lordship's character of this extraordinary man.

" You ask me if I continue my studies as usual, or if my employment in public business has diverted my thoughts from literary pursuits? Some time ago, I employed myself a few months in reading the History of England; and chiefly with a view of acquiring a competent knowledge of the language. I have since given it up, and have been engaged in translating the Principia of Sir Isaac Newton; Thomas Simson's book on Algebra; Emerson on Mechanics; Apollonius de Sectione Rationis, translated into Latin by Dr. Halley; and a work on Conic Sections by De l'Hôpital, a Frenchman. All these books I am translating into Arabic, besides several short treatises on logarithms, curve lines, &c. Some of them I have already finished, and some more of them will soon be brought to a conclusion. In short, I continue to devote my leisure hours to these pursuits."

The first protestant mission to India was conducted by Bartholemew Ziegenbalg of the university of Halle in Germany, who, in 1707, founded a Christian church at Tranquebar. This pious man and his successors received the greatest encouragement, and George the First wrote a letter with his own hand to the mission, expressing his royal zeal in the great cause of converting the heathen, which, he said, was the ardent wish of the English nation. Such has been the success of the protestant mission in later times, that when Dr. Buchanan visited the Tanjore Christians, not long ago, he drew the most pleasing picture of their innocent manners and social dispositions. Only a few years before, the peasantry in that part were thieves by profession, but now, by the civilizing influence of Christian principles, they are industrious and valuable members of the community. "After the sermon was ended," says Dr. Buchanan, "I returned with the missionaries into the vestry or library of the church. Here I was introduced to the elders and catechists of the congregation. Among others came Sattianaden the Hindoo preacher, one of whose sermons was published in England some years ago, by the Society for Promoting Christian Knowledge. He is now advanced in years, and his black locks have grown grey. As I returned from the church I saw the Christian families going back in crowds to the country, and the boys looking at their *ollas*: what a contrast, thought I, is this to the scene at Juggurnaut! Here are found becoming dress, humane affections, and rational discourse. I see here no skulls, no self-torture, no self-murder, no dogs and vultures tearing human flesh! Here the Christian virtues are found in exercise by the feeble-minded Hindoos in a vigour and purity which will surprise those who have never known the native character but under the greatest disadvantages, as in Bengal. It certainly surprised myself; and when I reflected on the moral conduct, upright dealing, decent dress, and decorous manners of the native Christians of Tanjore, I found in my breast a new evidence of the peculiar excellence and benign influence of the Christian faith." In Ceylon also, the success of the Dutch in converting the natives was great. There are upwards of two hundred and forty church-ships on the island, with three schoolmasters to each, and it is calculated that one-third of the whole population, about five hundred thousand souls, are Christians, the whole island being estimated at one million and a half. These Christians were patronized by the Dutch government, and had a preference given to them with respect to all situations. They are employed as servants in every family there, and are found faithful and industrious, while in Bengal it is thought disreputable to have a native convert in the house.

But from the first establishment of the Portugueze, the government made it a grand object to convert the natives, and at first their success was most flattering. In their whole course in India, they have left the traces of conversion, and around the coast, from the Cape of Good Hope to Canton in China, a distance of twelve thousand miles, the Portugueze language is spoken and the cross of Christ adored. The magnificence of the churches at Goa is almost beyond belief, and there are about two hundred of them in the province, with more than two thousand priests attending them. Indeed, in the construction of the chapel of the palace at Goa, the Portugueze aimed at astonishing the natives of India, for it is built on the plan of St.Peter's at Rome, and yet this paragon of architecture does not impress the beholder with such awe as either the caves of Elephanta or Ellora; and the church of St.Dominic, decorated with paintings by Italian masters, is not by any means in my estimation so grand a specimen of sublime architecture as some of the ancient Hindoo pagodas. However, if the Portugueze failed to surpass the Hindoos in gorgeous temples, they astonished them by far exceeding their sacrifices of human life in the horrors of the inquisition, for no poojah ever exhibited any thing more frightful than an auto da fe, nor is, in all Picart's religious ceremonies, a representation nearly so affecting as the annual processions of that infernal institution formerly were. Mr. Dellon, long a prisoner in one of the dungeons, in his account of the inquisition at Goa, makes the blood run cold; and it is no wonder the natives hailed the downfal of that nation as their greatest deliverance from torture. While in his dungeon, where for two years he never saw a human face but that of his gaoler, he heard every morning for several months the shrieks of the unfortunate victims, who were undergoing "the question," and when at last he was led to the light of day, he beheld a long rank of victims drawn up against a wall, whose ghastly dress, profound silence, and stillness, caused them to resemble statues rather than living creatures. All had large wax-tapers in their hands, and many wore the cross of St. Andrew, while others had flames and demons painted about them, with high caps, upon which were devils. The great bell was tolling to call the multitudes to witness the auto da fe, and the procession moved off through the streets of Goa. Women were mixed promiscuously with the men, and as they all walked barefooted, the sharp stones wounded their feet, tender from long confinement, and caused the blood to stream, for they were marched through all the great streets, and regarded everywhere by an innumerable crowd of people, who had assembled from all parts of India to behold the spectacle. At length they were drawn up in the church of St. Francis, where the grand inquisitor and his counsellors attended on one side of the altar, and the viceroy of Goa with his court on the other, during the time a sermon was preached to those who were going to be burnt alive by faggots. Then the sentences were read, and the images of the heretics who had died in the dungeons were brought up along with their bones in small chests, with flames and demons on them. Soon after those who were condemned to the flames received a blow each on the breast, and were led off to the river to be consumed before the viceroy and his court, and vast multitudes of astonished Hindoos.

This was not the way, gentle reader, to civilize India, and to produce an affection for Christianity in the hearts of the natives, and nothing ever injured its cause in that country so much as the persecuting spirit of the Portugueze. In short, at the termination of their career in India, conversion had retrograded, and there were not so many Christians in Malabar as before they entered the country. At present many of the churches are mouldering to dust, and there is not a single parishioner to save them from oblivion. The plans of the British, for converting the natives of India, have never been suited to their customs and manners. A Hindoo when he embraces Christianity becomes an outcast, and looses all those ties that are dear to the human affections. His prejudices, formed into strong habits, prevent him from associating with other low native Christians, whom he has always viewed as *pariahs*, and there is no reception for him in European society, so that the converts made by the baptist mission in Bengal are the most wretched creatures imaginable. Among the Tanjore native Christians, however, there is a regular society, something like the admirable fellowship of the Quakers, and the effect of this fraternal union is seen in travelling through their smiling cottages and gardens, where peace, happiness, and comfort delight the eye, and where their missionaries are buried among the graves of the converts. There the women are upon an equality with the men, and collect in happy groups to sing evening hymns and perform other acts of adoration. But under the Baptist system all is dreary. The convert receives the word only, while he expects worldly comfort; and instead of being taught how to make himself happy, he is left to grope his way in the dark, over obstacles which not one in a hundred surmounts. When Nanac, the founder of the Seiks, determined to convert the Hindoos, he formed them, as they became proselytes, into societies, and enabled them to retain certain customs which were agreeable to their habits of mind; and any European missionary, who had power to act in a similar manner, might in a short time establish a territory of converted Hindoos. But the British government, for selfish and prudent reasons, will never lend their aid to a certain plan of conversion, by countenancing societies of native Christians, and apportioning lands for their settlement. Yet what could be more glorious in future ages than an historical record, that under the influence of British merchants the deserts of Guzerat were covered with smiling villages and wheat fields, by converts to Christianity, who were invited to settle there under misionaries, that gave them a foretaste of felicity in heaven, by teaching them to be contented and happy on earth. But it is time to drop these speculations.

Colonel East having accomplished the objects of government with respect to the Row of Booge Booge, the force marched eastward for the purpose of reducing a hill fort called Kund Kote, in possession of the Wagurs, for it was found that these plunderers, so far from acting conformably to his views, were in open hostility to him and his peaceful subjects. In five marches through a country such as has been described, covered with ruined villages, and in many places presenting fine fields of wheat, Colonel East encamped in sight of the enemy, whose position on the top of a high hill, surrounded by thick jungles, appeared very formidable. The towers and walls were crowded with men, and from their height the distant British line must have appeared contemptible. In the course of the afternoon, the 17th dragoons and some light field pieces cut their way through the jungle, and approached to reconnoitre the fort, the guns of which opened upon them with a tremendous roar, augmented by the echoes of neighbouring hills — and the garrison setting up wild shouts, and flourishing their matchlocks, spears, and swords, rushed out of the fort, came down the precipices, and spread themselves along the foot of the hill, from which they fired upon the cavalry, who could have cut them to pieces but for deep ravines that kept them at a distance, for the guns of the fort could not have been depressed so as to do any execution. Having made the necessary observations, a strong party, with some of the battering train, took up a proper position during the night, for the purpose of destroying the defences, in preparation for an attempt to take the place by escalade. The Wagurs kept up a constant blaze upon the working party during the night; but were terrified to such a degree that they deserted the fort, carrying off every thing with them that could be removed, so that next morning the party did not find more than thirty inhabitants in the place, who were chiefly Brahmins, that remained in some ancient temples, under the protection of their idols. The walls extend round the brow of a curious table land, on the summit of the hill, which is large enough for a town of considerable size. The houses are nearly all in ruins. It is evidently a place of great antiquity, having several curiously carved stone pagodas, now in a skeleton state, having, through the effects of the atmosphere, mouldered away, like iron gradually consumed by rust. In one of these is the god Sooragee, or the solar deity, represented with rays issuing from his head, the moon in one hand and the sun in the other, with four small figures behind him, and devils with tigers heads, each having four human hands, guarding the entrance. Some of the other idols are Hunnymaun and Gunnyput; they are rudely executed statues of marble. Numerous monuments of suttee, infanticide, and others representing warriors on horses, camels, &c. are set up around these pagodas. The fort has two gates, one easy of access, through a natural indentation in the side of the hill, the other difficult, being on the top, with a very rugged ascent, for the whole hill is nearly perpendicular up to the table land, as if the slope had been cut away by art. Yet this place is not strong, for there is another unfortified height near it, from which, according to the reports of the natives, it was once breached and taken by Futteh Mahomed.

Having put Kund Kote into the possession of the Kutch government, the force marched out of the country by way of a town called Wandia, and re-entered Kattywar on the 11th of February 1816. Among the hills in the vicinity of Booge Booge the cold was distressing at night, although the latitude of the place is not much higher than that of Calcutta; but heat and cold are not regulated solely by the scale of climate, being also influenced by localities, such as mountains, deserts, runs, and the nature of soils. The partridges of Kutch are remarkable for beautiful plumage, and such of the foxes as the sportsmen killed had black tails. Wolves are plentiful, and wild hogs in such abundance, that the gentlemen of the spear had a successful hog hunt every march; they frequently chased the wild asses, but all in vain, for they were as fleet as the wind. The women in that part of the country inhabited by the tribe called Wagurs, wear a breast cloth tied behind, generally of silk, with a long robe of cotton hung over the head, which is not part of the sauree or petticoat as in other places. The men shave the middle of the under jaw from the lip to the chin, leaving long whiskers generally very black, and a great beard hanging over the breast. They are strong fierce looking men.

Kutch Booge has the Indus on the west, the Gulf on the south, and Runs on the other quarters, which being covered with water during the monsoon, give the country at that season the character of an island. It is in length about 110 miles, and the average breadth is seventy, so that its surface contains 4,928,000 English acres, yet the population is estimated at only 1,155,000 souls. The trade of the country is very insignificant, and the row's revenue is not supposed to exceed eight lacks of rupees.

Colonel East, upon leaving the row's territories, proceeded rapidly down the northern coast of Kattywar, and reduced the Jam of Noa Nuggur to obedience, without coming to blows. The force then entered the Okamundel, for the purpose of destroying a horde of pirates that had established themselves near Dingy, and built a fort. After a continued march of sixteen days they encamped on the ist mus of Muddee, by which the Okamundel is joined to Kattywar. The scene around was wild; for the dark blue ocean roared in front, and in the rear was a fine sheet of water, communicating with the gulf of Kutch, the neck of land on which the line was pitched being not more than two hundred yards wide. In the distance to the left, were high purple mountains, and to the right the ruins of a fort and temple. Some of the followers who entered the Okamundel during the afternoon were fired upon, and one of them was wounded.

The next morning Colonel East, taking with him provisions for ten days, and leaving the battering train and commissariat on the isthmus, marched through a thick jungle, which the flank companies scoured without meeting any opposition, and encamped in sight of the towers of Dingy, near a large tank, which the enemy had filled with prickly pear, to poison the water. Several defiles which might have been defended by a handful of men, were passed without opposition; and the country is very wild, being covered with jungle almost impenetrable. An attempt was immediately made to reconnoitre the place, but it was found impracticable for cavalry to approach, the roads being all cut up and blockaded, and the jungle so thick that no entrance could be found. A strong detachment of infantry and field pieces, under Colonel Fitz Simon, were then sent out with the pioneers to cut a passage, and with much difficulty they got within gun-shot of the fort, when a fire of musketry was opened upon the advance, without their being able to see one of the assailants, who were concealed by the jungle. The soldiers began to answer the fire in all directions, and from the camp one would have imagined that a most sanguinary engagement was going on, for the roar of musketry and cannon was kept up without intermission for two hours, until nightfall obliged the detachment to return to camp. At day-light the following morning, a stronger party was pushed into the jungle, upon whom the enemy opened their fire, which was returned by a discharge of grape and fire balls, which set the forest in a blaze. The scene was awful: the conflagration spread on all sides with inconceivable fury; smoke involved every thing in confusion; the shouts from the fort were appalling, amidst the roar of artillery and the discharge of musketry, fired on all sides by the advanced guards of the detachment, who forced their way at the point of the bayonet through the openings made by the flames, and clambered over the half-finished walls, when the pirates having fled, the place was given up to plunder. They had collected heaps of booty here, which the soldiers secured. Not an inhabitant remained in the place, and only a few dead bodies were found. During the plunder of it the confusion was wonderful. Here were hundreds of camp followers loaded with grain and cloth; there the sepoys carrying away English books; and everywhere soldiers searching with eagerness for money, very little of which was found. Colonel East lost not a moment, but with his usual decision left a garrison here, and followed the pirates next morning to Dewarka, which was invested in the course of the night, but the chief of it surrendered at discretion next morning before the batteries opened.

Dewarka is a small town, surrounded by a wall and towers, delightfully situated near a charming sandy shore. The tide washes its walls, and the sea gives it a cool and cheerful aspect. The pagoda is magnificent, and of such antiquity that pilgrimages are made to it from all parts of India. According to tradition, the famous Dwaraca, the residence of Chrishna, was swallowed up by the sea; but there can be little doubt that this is the very place where the sun was worshipped with such grand and solemn ceremonials. The entrance from the sea face is by a very long and noble flight of stone steps, through a massy gate, when the whole front face breaks upon one with an indescribable effect. Its great pyramid is about 140 feet high; and the infinitely varied ornaments are such as to baffle all attempts at delineation. There are numerous subordinate temples, having flags, with representations of the sun and moon on them. In front of the large temple is the sacred place of ablution, formed naturally by a creek of the sea on a bed of fine pebbles; and in the water, which is as clear as crystal, are seen numerous sacred fishes sporting about quite tame, being accustomed to the crowds of devotees who feed them. For 400 yards along this charming sheet of water are small temples, and stone steps down to the margin, on which the Brahmins pray, make gods of clay or flour paste for those who come to wash away their sins, and sell little rings and amulets to the superstitious crowd. All the followers and sepoys gave their plunder for the trinkets of this place, as it is considered a great honour in other parts of India to have them, or bear a mark on some part of the body, pricked in with little stained instruments in a peculiar manner by the Brahmins. But the devotees go on to another sacred place called Aramra, for the purpose of being branded with a hot iron. The whole of this prodigious pile of pagodas is of carved stone; and there are gorgeously decorated images of Surragee, Ramchorgee, Tricongee, Mahada, and Cullangee. But it is said that the ancient idol of the pagoda has twice escaped from Dwarka, and cannot be persuaded to remain in the Okamundel. In a few days more were destroyed some other haunts of the pirates; and the chief of the island of Bate was obliged to send in his submission, and engage to suppress all those depredations in future. The Okamundel, like the rest of Kattywar, is half ruined, and presents a melancholy spectacle. Colonel East having left a considerable detachment in it to secure the complete extirpation of the pirates, recrossed the isthmus, and proceeded to invest the strong fort of Juanuggur, where matters were settled without coming to blows. Juanaggur is situated on the side of a high hill, skirted with close jungle, along which runs a fine plain watered by a clear stream; but there is nothing so remarkable about it as a sacred precipice to which pilgrimages were made from all parts of India by Hindoos who had lost their cast, and who, by leaping from the top of it, in the event of escaping with life, regained their station in society. There is a temple near it, which formerly supported a great number of Brahmins; but as the precipice is several hundred feet in perpendicular height, and as there are frightful rocks at the bottom, hardly any one ever escaped being dashed to pieces, and none repair hither at present but such as are anxious to part with life.

After this nothing interesting occurred except some marches of demonstration, till the field force was disorganized, and sent off by corps to different quarters. The 17th dragoons and several native regiments marched for Keira, and it was expected that the 65th would return to pass the monsoon at Baroda. In the northern parts of India the rainy season does not prevent military operations, being nothing like the monsoon in Malabar in regard to severity or constancy; hence it is by no means so extraordinary as some historians represent, that Alexander the Great should have performed his campaign in the Panjob during the rains. Kattywar is very thinly inhabited, and would support twenty times its present population. It contains several large towns, each under an independent chief; such are Poorbunder, Noanuggur, and Kambalia, besides those noticed before in the eastern part. The Jains are numerous, and they have very grand temples in Noanuggur and Kambalia. Kattywar is a country diversified with hill and dale, and watered by so many fine streams flowing from springs in a chain of hills by which it is traversed from east to west, that it might be cultivated like a garden; and indeed the southern parts of it bear traces of having been once in the very highest state of tillage known in any part of India. The natives seldom shoe their horses, though the country is rocky, yet they gallop with great velocity, and the hoof grows as hard as iron. Cairns of stones are to be seen in all directions, every traveller adding to the heap, as is done in Ireland and Scotland; and the trees also are covered with bits of cloth, from the same superstitious feeling.

Colonel East is now no more. His character was a great curiosity, in which were blended fine qualities with some defects. No man ought to be answerable for his personal formation; and therefore it did not detract from his real merit that his appearance was rather ludicrous. He was in complexion nearly as dark as a native, short in stature, and his belly prominent; hence when his adjutant-general, Captain Stannus, one of the finest looking men that Ireland has produced, stood near little Billy (for so

Colonel East was nicknamed), the contrast excited the exercise of the risible muscles of bucks belonging to the quizzical club; but the expression of the colonel's countenance, the vigour of his mind, and the decision of his character, caused every lighter emotion to be absorbed in admiration. He spoke quick, and with facility explained himself in very few words. His habits were those of a soldier, careless about himself, and busy and anxious for the good of others. Solely intent on the object he had in view, he marched upon it and gained what he wanted, while another man would have been thinking about the means. This promptitude was the strongest feature in his character, and one of the most necessary ingredients in the formation of a real soldier. He was decisive in all his measures; and after the execution had been determined upon, allowed not a moment to pass without exertion.— But he was at times so peevish and passionate, that hardly any one could approach him; and woe to the ears of the officer whom his eye detected at such periods on the line of march an inch out of his proper place. He would roar out with stentorian lungs, so as to be heard from right to left of the line. Yet he was tender-hearted and kind—beloved by the soldiers, whom he treated, as they ought to be, like children; and during the campaign there was not a single line punishment.

Thoughtless being full of anxiety to see his family after such a long absence, obtained permission to set off from Juannuggur for Bombay, with the intention of rejoining his corps at Baroda, to which station he purposed transporting Mary and his children. One of his greatest pleasures during the campaign had been in corresponding with little Emma, whose understanding began to display great strength, with all the variety of infantine simplicity; a short time before his departure from the force to see her, she had sent him some drawings of cottages and a sampler, in return for which she received the following lines on her birth-day :

Eight circling years have roll'd away,
Since the blue dawn of rosy day,
Saw thee embark to cross life's bay,
My Emma.

Pleasant so far thy trip hath been,
Nor squall nor storm has yet been seen,
But rippling waves and skies serene,
My Emma.

And may that God who bade you rise,
So fair beneath such burning skies,
Preserve thee still to glad these eyes,
My Emma.

Avoid the follies of mankind,
To other's faults seem often blind,
To every one be good and kind,
My Emma.

Despise vain pageant and parade,
We oft see misery in brocade,
And happiness in stuff arrayed,
My Emma.

Adorn with care thy opening mind,
Restrain each thought to roam inclin'd,
External things were not designed,
My Emma.

For happiness that all would buy,
For which e'en misers save and sigh,
Within our breast content must lie,
My Emma.

Look for it there with God thy guide,
And learn to view the brightest side,
Of every object down life's tide,
My Emma.

Thus wilt thou find that strength of soul,
To bear those ills beyond controul,
Religion will thy heart console,
My Emma.

And when thy skiff has reached that shore,
Where life and all its cares are o'er,
May heaven increase with thee its store,
My Emma.

But Charles had looked in vain for a letter from his uncle, and he now began to think that his friend True was no more; for his silence was unaccountable. However, by the very latest post before he started for Bombay, he had received a most satisfactory letter from George, stating that his passage had been exceedingly pleasant; that on his arrival in London, he had found his father there waiting for him with affectionate impatience, and that the meeting was indescribably felicitous. The liberality of his father had exceeded all bounds; delighted with Nannette and her fine children, he had arranged that they should all remain in London during the winter, and go over to Ireland in summer. But George had to relate what gave him the deepest sorrow, the death of Mr. Fortier; for that excellent man, whom he expected to find in London, was in his grave; Madame Fortier, soon after the removal of Napoleon to Elba, had returned to France; and Nannette, accompanied by her husband and father-in-law, had crossed the channel, visited Paris, and seen that esteemed lady in the capital. Hence arose George's delay in writing; for, said he, "I was anxious to announce to you my arrival in old Ireland, and delayed from time to time in the hope of being able to give you some certain account of your relations; if the information of my father be correct, your father has returned from America, and is in very flourishing circumstances near Dundalk, without male issue by his second marriage."

Nothing on earth could have raised the spirits of Charles higher than this information, and he wrote to his long-lost father in the full warmth of his heart. But in this consummation of his own prospects, he was not unmindful of the affairs of Frank Stanley. He had written to the commanding officer again on the subject, and engaged the interest of the worthy son of Captain Solomon in his behalf, by whom he was assured that Frank would shortly be promoted, in justice to his own great merit, and in deference to the esteem of every one in the regiment for him. Under the influence of this combination of joyous circumstances, which rendered Thoughtless half-mad, he set off for Poorbunder, in company with some other officers, and experienced a very polite reception from Captain Elwood, the political agent there, who informed them that they had just arrived in time to get a passage on board the Dheriadowlat, an armed paddimar belonging to government, going down to Bombay.

Poorbunder is a place of some importance. It belongs to Rajah Ramma Kimmejee, whose revenue is about two lacks of rupees, out of which he pays the Guickwar 30,000 in that coin per annum, and maintains the detachment stationed there belonging to the company as a small subsidiary force. The exports are cotton, elephants' teeth, and piece goods; and the imports wood, grain, dates and iron. There are no interesting public buildings, the town being of modern origin; the ancient capital called Goomty was on the top of a mountain; the rajah's residence can scarcely be called a palace, but his gardens are worthy of notice on account of several well executed statues of ladies that ornament the pillars of a very neat lodge erected in the centre of a tank, which, being shaded with fruit trees and refrigerated by so fine a body of water, is delightfully cool. The town is surrounded by a strong wall, and it is about two miles round the ramparts, on which at intervals there are high towers well urnished with cannon.

The paddimar, on board of which Thoughtless and his fellow travellers embarked, carried five guns with an excellent crew, so that they looked out for pirates with full confidence in their own strength, but nothing interesting occurred. In three days a fine breeze carried the Dheriadowlat into Bombay harbour, and Charles, after an absence of nearly two years, had the inexpressible joy of finding his family all well. Fortune seemed on this occasion to overpower him with a concurrence of the most agreeable circumstances, for on his arrival he not only heard that he was promoted to a lieutenancy, but that the regiment had received orders to embark at Gogo for the presidency, where it safely arrived a short time after him.

CHAP. XXI.

"Nay more — there are who stay, and who can blame?
They court not glory, yet they fear not shame.
Thy "*at homes*," Loudon! noble lady fair,
Those amateurs of reason stay to share,
Where taste and elegance with ease combine,
To charm each sense in man that is divine.
Such stay to see thy lovely helping hand,
Extend with pity o'er a burning land.
Soft as the silver moon's refreshing rays
Thy dewy kindness on poor blacky plays,
And cheers the drooping head that friendless lies,
And gives the heart, just sinking, hope to rise."

The Brahminical institution of casts seems to have communicated its principles to the ranks and classes of European society in India. A civilian's lady considers herself a superior being to the wife of an officer, and the latter looks down with contempt upon the partner of a country captain, who in her turn despises the shopkeeper, and frets if neglected by the merchant's wife. Society in Calcutta is therefore a formation of parties, and there is nothing like a general or liberal intercourse among Europeans. Public assemblies are unpopular; but there is no country in the world where hospitality is greater than in those casts into which the sojourners are divided. Large parties sit down every day to dinner; and during the winter, balls and suppers take place every night. Nearly all writers have noticed the fastidious attention to pride and exclusion which obtains in India, so that it would be trite and tedious to dwell upon such a hackneyed subject. "To hand a lady to table, or to her carriage," says Tennant, "is an affair which requires deep cogitation: if it be aspired to by a gentleman whose rank is unequal to the office, instead of paying a compliment he is guilty of rudeness, and commits an unpardonable offence. When the ladies take the floor to dance, the most perfect acquaintance with all that has ever been written upon heraldry would not enable you to make a satisfactory arrangement either of the ladies themselves or of their partners. Hardly a meeting formerly concluded without laying the foundation of turmoils and grievances." In short, the only general society in Calcutta is at the government house, to which every man having the rank and character of a gentleman is invited frequently, and no eulogium would be hyperbolical in describing the charming affability of the elegant Countess of Loudon to her guests, in those sumptuous yet tasteful entertainments with which that honour to Scotland cheered the monotony of exile.

It was a grand sight to Charles Thoughtless to behold, for the first time, the splendid circle of promenaders in the great hall of the government house, while fine military bands in alternate succession charmed the ear. The Marquis of Hastings and the Countess of Loudon, seated to receive their guests under the state canopy, ornamented with the spoils of the throne of Tippo, paid those winning attentions to the collecting company which are so delightful to the heart, while the judges and heads of departments were ranged on either hand in a semicircle on chairs glittering with gold. Further on, the scene resembled that of a grand fancy ball, from variety of costume and contrasts of appearance. Here were the British ladies parading with ostrich feathers waving gracefully over their temples; there the Armenian fair ones, wearing crowns sparkling with costly pearls and diamonds; and elsewhere, the dark complexioned Portugueze dame, whose sable ringlets blazed with precious gems, while the Turk, and Arabian, Chinese, and Gentoo gave interest to the diversity of military plumes and naval uniforms that moved around in countless succession, till supper was announced in the marble hall, where about eight hundred sat down to enjoy the luxuries of the East.

From the first arrival of the noble marquis in India, it seemed to be the mutual object of his lordship and his amiable countess to diffuse harmony and good will through all ranks of society. They almost immediately honoured the freemasons of Calcutta with their presence at a grand ball and supper at Moore's rooms; which entertainment, in point of magnificence and tasteful arrangement, was never surpassed in India. The illuminations on the occasion converted a dark night into brightness equal to the clearest day, and trains of artificial fire works were laid along all the principal streets of the city. At the opening of the Chouringhee theatre, the Countess of Loudon was hailed as the star of the East, in the prologue written by Dr. Wilson, a very elegant poet and oriental scholar, and well does Lady Loudon deserve the epithet, for she has been a particularly bright star to India, guiding all in the course of benevolence, condescension, charity, and love. She has been a munificent friend to all the institutions in the East for the alleviation of distress or the diffusion of knowledge; the zealous patroness of the education of the poor; the kind supporter of the widow and orphan; the unsolicited benefactress of the friendless, and a transcendant example of tenderness, morality, and religion.

During the absence of his regiment, Charles amused himself with inspecting the curiosities near Bombay, which are numerous and interesting; and soon after the return of his corps he was introduced to Sir Miles Nightengal, and saw a good deal of the society of the presidency. The style of living at Bombay, the number of servants kept, and the allowances from government, are all on a lower scale than either at Madras or Calcutta; and although the luxury of the East prevails there, yet it is only in the positive, while in Bengal it rises to the superlative degree. While at the Countess of Loudon's parties, or rather the public entertainments given to the civil and military servants at the government-house, massy plate and servants in rich livery are in profusion, the guests of Sir Evan Nepean find it difficult to get a metal spoon, and must trust to their own servants for attendance. But it must be owned, that the urbanity of Sir Evan makes amends for such want of accommodation, and the gallant old gentleman sets a good example by saluting with a kiss every beautiful woman presented to him, this being, as he jocosely says, one of the privileges of a governor.

The island of Bombay is about ten miles in length and three in breadth. It is joined to Salsettc by a vellard made across an arm of the sea; and as the latter communicates with the Koncan, the whole may now be considered as forming a part of the main land. In appearance Bombay is totally different from Calcutta or Madras, the houses being very old-fashioned buildings, covered with slates and tiles, and having curious projecting virandas, supported by pillars of wood, with which material many of them are chiefly constructed. The fortress, town, and island came into our possession upon the marriage of Charles the Second with Catherine of Portugal; but the whole has been since greatly improved and strengthened by fortifying a commanding position, now called Fort George. The strong walls of Bombay include a considerable city, with the finest docks and marine arsenal in India, and excellent barracks for several regiments; but nearly all the island may be described as a town, for in every habitable part European garden-houses meet the eye, and dwellings of various forms belonging to the natives diversify the scene. Here a Portugueze church, and there a Chinese pagoda; in one place a substantial Parsee mansion, and in another the airy fabrics of British taste, while a Jewish synagogue may be seen near the gloomy temple of Hindoo idolatry. In short, there is the same variety of costume, nationality and language, which has been noticed in describing Calcutta and Madras. The island contains about 220,000 inhabitants, 8,000 of whom are Parsees, the same number Mahomedans, and 4,000 Jews; so that when Portugueze, Armenian, and English settlers are taken into account, there is a constant feast for the eye of a stranger, without noticing the concourse of merchants from nearly all nations that continually crowd the streets. Bombay is admirably calculated for ship-building; the docks are so fine, and the tide rises so high on this coast, that a first-rate ship of war can enter them during the springs: it is to be observed also, that the Parsees are the most expert naval architects in the East, and the Minden of 74 guns was entirely constructed by them without any European superintendence. In no country in the world is there a class of more industrious, inoffensive, and worthy subjects than the Parsees. Like the Quakers, they support one another; and there is hardly such a thing on record as one of them being brought before a court of justice for the commission of crimes. The morality of their women is great, and their decency so exemplary, that among them prostitution is said to be unknown. Polygamy is not allowed, and wives are on a footing of perfect equality with their husbands; but they are of very retired habits, seldom going out except to the wells for water, and on visits to their female friends in close carriages. They perform their devotions at home, while their husbands and sons assemble at sun-rise and sun-set on the esplanade and along the sea-shore, to adore the great luminary of creation; in their worship the sun and the sea, as well as fire, are objects of adoration. Their priests have very little power, but the fathers of families are held responsible for the decent conduct of their respective households, over which they exercise a patriarchal government; and there is an inquisitorial moral authority vested in the elders to check every deviation from rectitude. They are all extremely sedate in their deportment, and so scrupulously attentive to the conduct of their daughters, that, if report may be depended upon, every aberration from virtue among them is visited with death. In their persons much attention is paid to cleanliness, but their houses are dirty: they use furniture similar to ours, and eat and drink with Europeans; but in general they are both temperate and abstemious. In short, the Parsees are a very remarkable race, humane, public spirited, and charitable, but superstitious even to childishness. Some of their customs with respect to marriage and sepulture are curious, for widows are permitted to marry only widowers; and although they bury their dead, yet the bodies are not covered with earth, but left in open tombs to be devoured by vultures. There are five of these public places of sepulture near Bombay, each constructed on the same principle; being divided into three compartments, one for men, another for women, and a third for children. The dead body, wrapped in cotton cloth, is let down into the grave, which is something like a well, and left there to be devoured, after which the bones are carefully picked up by means of a subterraneous communication, and placed in the family vault. Nearly the whole of Bombay belongs to the Parsees; they are copartners in every great commercial establishment, as well as zealous supporters of the charitable institutions; and during the great famine of 1802, their prodigious wealth was most liberally applied in relieving their starving fellow-creatures. But their conduct may be more effectually appreciated from the two following letters, written by Hormangee Bomangee, a partner in the great house of Forbes and Co., to an officer who had cut down some of his date trees;

they present an honourable example of calmness, temper, and forbearance.

It must be admitted that the officer, though unintentionally, was blameable. The case was briefly this: his wife, who was in a delicate state of health, had moved, during his absence on service, into a bungalow situated on higher ground than her own, belonging to the Parsee, having received preference of possession from a lady about to quit it, as was quite customary. Her husband having arrived, conceived that the circulation of air was impeded by some trees that grew near the windows, and he cut a few of them down, not supposing them to be either private property or of much value, and being ignorant that these trees are all let at a certain annual rent to natives, who, by making an incision in the trunk, procure from it a white juice called date toddy, which is converted into *arrack*. Hormangee Bobangee's servant having arrived with an order to desist, which he delivered in rather an uncivil manner, the officer blustered a little, and his pride prevented him from immediately acknowledging that he was wrong; but as soon as the thing was explained, the worthy Parsee dropped the matter, and his letters are demonstrative evidence of his temper and wisdom, as well as of the meek and amiable qualities of his respectable sect, which seem imbued with much of the simplicity and sober sense inculcated by Christianity. In justice to the gentleman who was so rash as to cut down the date trees, be it remembered that he had removed only four of them; but as he had also thinned the branches of a great many others round the house, the servant of Hormangee Bomangee had misrepresented and greatly exaggerated the injury done to the property of his master:—

DEAR SIR,

Having had a report from one of my gardeners that you had cut eleven date trees belonging to me, I ordered my people to see you, and to request that you would have the goodness not to do so; but as your answer has been that the trees belong to the honourable company, and that you would cut as many of them as you wanted, I therefore take the liberty to address you, and to say that the trees belong to me, and not to the honourable company, who has nothing to do with them; but even if the trees belonged to the honourable company, you ought to have applied and obtained a sanction from government before you ordered them to be cut. I also beg to add, that each tree is worth fifty rupees, at which rate I consider you responsible for such of them as you have cut.

I take this opportunity to acquaint you, that many gentlemen have resided in the house in which you are at present living, but I assure you, dear sir, that none of them has cut a single tree from my garden; and I am extremely sorry that you have done so without either applying to me for that pur pose, or getting a correct information as to the value of the trees you have cut.

I remain,
Dear sir,
Your obedient servant,
HORMANGEE BOMANGEE.

DEAR SIR,

I have just been favoured with your reply to my letter of yesterday's date, and I assure you that I am extremely sorry to find that, instead of three or four date trees which you state having ordered to be cut, you have already cut down twenty-nine; and which, at the rate I mentioned in my letter of yesterday, viz. fifty rupees for each tree, amounts to one thousand four hundred and fifty rupees.

You state in your letter now under acknowledgment, that Mrs. —— has not enjoyed good health for even a week since you have moved to my house; and this alone induced you to cut down the trees, and that it is your intention still to cut as many more as you think proper for the preservation of your health and of your family; — and that if you could get another house, you would not live a day in mine.

As to your family not enjoying good health since you moved to my house, I have to say that I heard it with great concern; but you will recollect perfectly well that you entered my house without obtaining my permission for that purpose; and although great many of the tenants that have lived in and quitted my house at Colabah have never taken charge of it without previously obtaining my permission so to do, yet none of them has cut a single tree, and almost every one of them has given me satisfaction.

As for your quitting the house, I have only to observe that you will be pleased to do so at your earliest convenience; and beg to add, that until you have got another house you may live in mine, for which I don't mean to charge any rent.

With regard to the trees you have already cut, I have to request that you will be so good as to pay me their value as soon as you can; but if you are disposed not to do so, I shall be under the necessity of having recourse to law, which I assure you, dear sir, I shall do with great regret, being the last person that wishes to adopt such measures.

I remain,

Dear sir,

Your obedient servant,

HORMANGEE BOMANGEE.

The Parsees on their first arrival in India adopted the native dress, which is in general a gown and loose trowsers, with a turban and party-coloured slippers turned up at the toes; but many of them wear rich shawl girdles, and very costly turbans of embroidered muslin, consisting of a whole web often from forty to sixty yards in length by one in breadth. The women have adopted the silk spenser, noticed in describing the female attire of Guzerat, but in other respects are like the Hindoo ladies, and equally fond of ornaments. In form and complexion, the Parsees bear a considerable affinity to Europeans. Many of them are very fair athletic men, and able to cope with most Englishmen in wrestling, which is a favourite exercise in the dock-yards of Bombay; but, according to the Parsee mode, the wrestlers stand at opposite sides of the ring, and struggle for an advantage in the grip, in which there is a great display of art and activity.

Mention has been made several times in this work of the Armenians, who, being Christians, of course differ but little from Europeans in customs and manners. They are the general merchants of India, and a highly respectable body of wealthy subjects. Their complexion is fair, and in address they are pleasing, but the Armenian costume gives them a remarkable appearance. It is, however, very becoming. The cap is of black velvet, and triangularly shaped, and the frock is generally of the same materials, but embraces the neck closely, flowing down to the knee, something like a surtout. Many of them, however, both in Calcutta and Bombay, may be said to emulate the Bond-street gentry, having assumed the English dress in all things except the cap, which is retained as a mark of national distinction. The Armenians have many churches in India, and a bishop's see subject to the controul of their patriarch, who resides near mount Ararat. In show and equipage they are exceedingly ostentatious; their ladies are covered with jewels, and wear crowns sparkling with precious gems; but they are very public spirited men, and liberal supporters of every thing that is laudable. One anecdote will not be unacceptable to those readers who have never heard of Sarkies Joannes of Calcutta. When this great Armenian merchant heard of the recovery of George the third in 1789, an event which occasioned great demonstrations of joy in India, he paid the debts of all the prisoners at that time in gaol, which so much pleased his Majesty that he sent him his picture in miniature through Lord Cornwallis, who questioned the Armenian respecting the great affection evinced by him for the King of England whom he had never seen. "I have, my lord," replied he, "lived under his government for near thirty years; it has never injured me; but on the contrary, always afforded its protection: and this, with industry on my part, has enabled me to accumulate a very plentiful fortune."

The fishery for pamphlets and bombaloes at the mouth of Bombay harbour affords employment to great numbers of the natives, who are strong and vigorous men, though not so tall and muscular as the inhabitants of Bengal. Their boats are much like those used in the Hoogly; some of them are made of strong planks well secured, with benches across for the rowers, and a mast or two of bamboo, to which they attach sails of various descriptions, sometimes even of mat; others badly constructed, and stitched together with the fibres of the cocoa-nut. Many of these boats are merely canoes cut out of large trees, with planks stitched round to make them roomy. The boatmen go nearly naked, seldom wearing more than a *langutty*, and a cloth round the head. No fish is of more delicious flavour than pamphlet. It is in shape and size something like whiting, but as hard as salmon, and as tender as trout; this, like the mangoe fish, might induce an epicure to undertake an Indian voyage, like the famous Quin, who is said to have resolved on a trip to Bombay for the purpose of eating it in perfection, when death interposed to make him a morsel for worms.

Bombay light-house is situated upon the point of the island of Colabah which runs down between the harbour and False Bay, into whose rocky bosom it is very dangerous for ships to enter. Colabah is about two miles in length, and in some places not a quarter of a mile in breadth. It is separated from Bombay by a rocky bed, which is dry at low water, but through it the tide rushes with such fury, that a raft secured by a cable, chained to each shore, upon which it works backwards and forwards, cannot cross during the springs. Government have erected barracks on this healthful spot for a battalion of artillery and two king's regiments, and several gentlemen have very handsome garden-houses, to which they retire after their official business in the fort. Immediately after the monsoon, Colabah is a perfect emerald isle, for the natives raise vegetables on every foot of it, the soil being very friendly to nearly all common productions. The Bombay onion is so mild and well-flavoured that it is used at table like the potatoe, which is also in as fine perfection as need be desired. Cooled and refreshed by a constant alternation of land and sea breezes, the climate is delightful for several months in the year, at all hours, except during the lull which takes place between the daily changing of the wind from the ocean to the shore. At this time no breath of air ruffles the glass-like bosom of the bay, and such Europeans as are in a declining state of health feel the utmost depression of spirits, and a difficulty in respiration truly distressing. Colabah is one of the liveliest places in India. Curiosity is constantly roused by the arrival of ships from all parts of the world; it being calculated that upwards of two hundred enter Bombay harbour and depart from it in a year. A gun is fired as soon as a ship appears in sight from the signal-post at the light-house, when a pilot is dispatched to her, and the course being made known by telegraph, conjecture is busy as to whence she comes, till the flag is hoisted that announces the country to which the stranger belongs. Free traders from Europe had, for some time before Charles left India, so completely glutted Bombay with every article, that the price was far below prime cost. Cotton from Guzerat is the great article of export; the annual shipment to China and Europe being often 85,000 bales of 375lbs. each in the course of a year. Sugars, and precious stones, particularly cornelians and agates, are also received from that province for exportation; pepper, coir, and cocoa-nuts from Malabar; spices and gems from Ceylon; pearls from Arabia; rich carpets from Turkey, and shawls from Cashmere; with piece goods and grain from various places, which are generally paid for in specie, as the imports of European articles, such as iron and other metals, mirrors and chandeliers, clocks, watches, mathematical instruments, broad cloths and blankets, with hams, cheese, wines, and malt liquors, are not considerable. The latter four articles are used only by European residents, but the natives retail them, and carry off investments to the military stations in the interior. All the other articles are used by many of the natives, who find our broad cloth and blankets very comfortable in the northern parts of India. Some of the Hindoos are good watch-makers, and a few have science enough to prize our mathematical instruments, but all the rich are fond of mirrors, chandeliers, and girandoles. Their glass, leather, woollens, and in short all Indian manufactures, except muslins, shawls, chintzes, and silks, are greatly inferior to ours; and such is the effect of English machinery that cotton can now be imported from Hindostan, converted into piece goods, equal to the muslins and baftahs of Guzerat and Dacca, and sent back to India, so as to undersell the merchandize of the natives in their own markets.

Till lately the territorial revenue of the Bombay presidency did not support the civil, marine, and military establishments; but nearly the whole resources of the Peishwa have, in consequence of the late war, become vested in that government, so that a large surplus now remains. All the establishments have been considerably increased; the army of Bombay is now 30,000 strong, and the marine consists of fifteen ships of war. Law is administered by a recorder's court, consisting of one judge, three barristers, and eight attornies, with Mahomedan and Hindoo establishments of native courts similar to those of Calcutta and Madras.

Bombay Castle, a place of considerable strength, being the citadel of the fortress, is converted into a fine arsenal. The government house, though not on a magnificent scale, is comfortable and airy, and the same may be said of the church, which is an antiquated looking piece of architecture. All the other public buildings within the fort are not such as to call forth comparison with those of Calcutta, nor yet do they sink below respectability. At some distance from the fortress, in the finest part of the island, is situated the governor's country seat, which was originally intended for a college by its founders, the Jesuits. It is a spacious building, and surrounded by fine plantations and gardens. Among the private mansions worthy of notice, Belvidere House is remarkable for its fine situation, close to the bay, and for the grand prospect it commands. It was the residence of the beautiful Mrs. Draper, the Maria of Sterne's platonic affection. Her husband was a civilian of rank, but unhappy in not being the object of her love. Her elopement from his splendid residence was somewhat romantic, for it is said that after having persuaded a dashing captain in the navy to convey her to England on board his vessel, she was so closely watched that she had to escape by means of a ladder of ropes suspended from her bed-chamber viranda, which enabled her at once to jump into the boat and into the arms of her new protector.

Life may be gaily passed at Bombay. The races exhibit much beauty and fashion, together with many a well contested heat for the annual cup of the club. There are masonic, sans souci, literary and bobbery hunt societies, and the gentlemen of the settlement make the yearly circuit of the island with much ceremony and parade. The word *bobbery* in the Hindostannee language signifies noise, and the members of the bobbery hunt are true to their designation, spreading wherever they go the loud tones of well-tuned uproar. They wear a green uniform, with a jackal or pariah dog on the button, and their sport consists in hunting that animal all over the island, which is much infested with them; after which they sit down in Bobbery Hall to regale on the luxuries of the East. St. Patrick's day is kept up at this presidency, and every where in India, with great spirit. There is a neat theatre where civil and military amateurs sometimes produce the popular performances of the day in excellent style. The frequent assemblies given at the government house also enliven society, and there are always a number of pretty girls, fresh from Europe, who, as it is humorously said, make their appearance there, not to receive a kiss from the governor, but to get husbands. All young ladies, without exception, were saluted by Sir Evan Nepean, who seemed to believe, with a great physician, that the balmy breath of female youth would be useful in prolonging life. Pretty girls, who go out to India with relations in the civil or military service, are sure of forming eligible matches. Upon going into the interior to cantonments or stations, they shine like the evening star without a competitor, and are worshipped as perfect goddesses, being fanned sometimes by four or five lovers, and escorted by a whole regiment of dragoons. As to general society at Bombay, it is just as at the other presidencies, and everywhere else, composed of a heterogeneous mixture of taste and vulgarity, simplicity and ostentation, truth and insincerity, wisdom and folly. Mrs. Graham, in her travels, has been pleased to point out differences in the manners and characteristics of the Europeans of the three grand divisions of India, which, it is presumed, a longer residence in the country, and more accurate observation, would have shewn to be illusory. This lady, and also Lord Valentia, have been faithful in describing the curiosities in and about Bombay, so that I shall omit the minute detail into which the journal of Mr. Thoughtless enters on the subject, and merely transcribe part of what he says respecting the caves of Elephanta.

The island of Elephanta is small; it may be described as a large rock of granite rising abruptly in Bombay harbour. It is clothed to its summit with jungle, and there are some small nooks or valleys where a few natives cultivate patches of soil, and cocoa-nut plantations. In the highest part of it are found the caves, and the ascent to them is rugged and difficult. The island takes its name from the figure of a monstrous elephant, hewn out of the rock at the bottom of the hill; time has worn away the prodigious legs or pillars of the mass, yet the huge ponderous body, now broken and lying in pieces, still strikes beholders with wonder. Commencing at a convenient place near the top, which seems to have been judiciously chosen, the caves penetrate into the solid rock to an amazing extent, all seemingly wrought by the labour of the chisel. Large square pillars are left, at intervals, to support the massy roof; and on entering the great cave, which is well lighted by means of a large entrance, and by outlets at different places round the conical top, the perspective of these rows of columns, in long retiring order, with statues of giants and monstrous idols peeping from behind them, really strikes the beholder with awe. This principal excavation is about 120 feet square, and in a remote part of it the enormous triad is placed, which is justly considered one of the wonders of the East. It consists of one body and three heads, representing Brahma, Vishnu, and Sheva, with their appropriate symbols. Each face is five feet in length, finely proportioned, and in the highest state of preservation. Many of the fables related in Hindoo mythology are represented in this cave on the living rock. In viewing these surprising specimens of ancient proficiency in the art of sculpture in India, the astonishment is chiefly excited by the noble boldness of design, for the finishing is but coarse; yet it must be acknowledged that many of the female figures have an exquisite elegance, an indescribable airy contour, which could be given solely by the hand of purest taste. Few of the statues are now in a perfect state, and many of them were so offensive to modesty that they have been disfigured. The Portugueze having carried away numerous specimens of sculpture, and mutilated others, the caves were considered as profaned, and desecrated, and are now entirely deserted by the Brahmins. To prevent the total destruction of these celebrated remains of antiquity, government has caused a wall to be erected across the great entrance, and a house has been built near it for a serjeant, who, with a guard of sepoys, has charge of them, and whose business it is to show them to strangers. There are several smaller excavations near the large one; and the caves of Salsette and Kenneri are nearly as remarkable as those of Elephanta, for they contain gigantic figures twenty feet high. In wandering over these ruins of ancient magnificence, Charles felt that a vast mass of population must have once been congregated in their now silent precincts. These wonderful specimens of art do not reveal to us the age in which they were produced, or the names of the artists. One of the caves of Kenneri was converted, by the Portugueze jesuits, into a church and monastery, but all is now tenantless, and the resort of bats and hyænas. Fine tanks, lingum temples, carved images of deities, magnificent flights of steps, and the labour of an age in rock and marble, are all desolate; and these mournful mutations impress the sensitive heart with a kindred feeling of melancholy.

It was not the fortune of the 65th regiment to remain long on the green island of Colabah, for in the month of October 1816, it was ordered to relieve the 2d battalion 56th regiment, then serving with the Poonah subsidiary force, and about to be disbanded in consequence of peace in Europe. From the preparations making at this time to destroy the Pindarries, it was fully expected that the division under Colonel Smith at Seroor would immediately take the field; therefore all the families of the 65th regiment were again advised to remain at Bombay, and Thoughtless had once more the prospect of a long separation from his wife and children.

CHAP. XXII.

"And ye, my loved associates, should I go
To winter's regions of eternal snow,
His shivering hand that chills the icy pole,
Can never stop the current of my soul.
The blood may freeze, the pulse may cease to beat,
The heart may lose the glow of vital heat,
But intellect will with affection burn,
And memory, while she lives, to you will turn;
For in my soul whatever scion grows
Of virtue, she to your example owes."

ON the 12th October 1816, Thoughtless marched with the regiment from Colabah to the New Bunder, all the officers having sent their horses round by way of Tannah. The day was oppressively hot. Here the 65th embarked in open boats to cross the bay to Panwell, a considerable village situated in the Koncan, on the main road to Poonah. In passing Bombay and the fine islands of Elephanta, Salsette, and Tannah, the scenery was remarkably grand. About four o'clock they entered the Pen river, which has its source in the ghauts, and is broad and deep during flood-tide; but being a little too late, the boat in which Charles was embarked grounded about nightfall, a mile below the Bunder, at Panwell; and Tudor, Thompson, Faden, and he, with their men, were obliged to land and march to the camp. This they found a most laborious and difficult undertaking, for the night was exceedingly dark, and being unable to procure a guide, they wandered along the bed of the river, sometimes up to the middle in mud, and proceeded four miles ere they were challenged by the sentries around the camp. However, as the baggage had been sent off the day before, they found the tents pitched, and their servants ready with refreshments. Thoughtless soon fell into a sound sleep, forgetting by this gift of bountiful providence, the sorrow of his late separation, and all the cares of life. Having slept with his tent open on account of the heat, he beheld, on awaking, the sun rise in glorious beauty over a hill, and he sprung from his couch to contemplate a most romantic scene of curious nature around. Hills and mountains near and distant, of most fantastic shapes, formed the horizon on every part of its circle. The camp was pitched close to a large tank in Paddy fields, near the river, which was almost dry. The village of Panwell, a collection of Indian huts constructed of bamboos, mud, and other simple materials, and thatched with the leaves of the cocoa-nut tree, was at no great distance. It is a poor place, but being one of general resort to and from Bombay and Poonah, it is a station for a detachment of sepoys, and has a small tavern kept by a Portugueze, for the accommodation of travellers. The natives were fishing the large tank with nets. Those who held the nets swam in with them, and remained stationary in a proper part of the mass of water, while great numbers of men and women, nearly naked, plunged in around them, forming a wide circle. They then began to beat the water with their arms and legs, making at the same time as great a noise as possible, and gradually approaching the nets, which were held extended, so that the frightened fishes leaped into them in amazing numbers, and were instantly entangled among the snares fixed for them in the net-work.

At Panwell they buried private William Melling, who died of suffocation from heat and fatigue, or perhaps from grief, for he had left behind him his wife, a little interesting woman, and his child, whom Charles saw at the Bunder, crying most bitterly. Three marches brought them to the head of the Bore ghaut, and they encamped close to the romantic little village called Condulla, consisting of a few ghurs, near which there is a magnificent tank, made by order of Nanna Furnese. That tract of country through which they passed, is, like Malabar and Canara, exceedingly fine, consisting of hill and dale, and watered by numerous streams, while from it rises abruptly that stupendous wall of mountains the Ghauts. They passed the villages of Conallah, Parawah, Chouck, Kunnapoor, Hull, and Capolly, all pleasantly situated, and watered by tanks or by mountain streams, which are seen during the monsoons tumbling over the ghauts in grand cascades, and rolling their waters with unfordable impetuosity towards the ocean; at present they flowed with an agreeable prattle over their meandering and pebbly beds. Capolly is situated in a nook just under the high cliffs of mountains that seem to rise above the skies. On each side of it is a mighty ridge or natural wall of solid rock, extending for several miles; and the little valley, or indentation, in which the village stands, seems as if permitted by providence to conduct man to the only practicable pass in this vicinity across the ghauts.

The Bore ghaut is difficult in some places, but by no means so high or rugged as the Poodicherrum and Cooteaddy. It is impossible to do any thing like justice to a lusus naturæ so extraordinary as the scene around the camp at Condulla. There was infinite variety, with the most sublime beauty and order, amidst seeming confusion: glens of amazing depth; precipices, impending rather than perpendicular; cataracts of many hundred feet, though at this season merely the beds of these cascades were to be seen; fantastic rocks and hills, assuming every conceivable form; mountains clothed to their summits with lofty trees, and beautifully variegated foliage, exhibiting every gradation of tint, from the softest yellow to the darkest green; the grand depth of shade, and the lucid contrast; the warmth and animation of every part just after the refreshing monsoon; the fine cool bracing air, flowing in invigorating currents through the chasms in the high overhanging rocks, with the forts of Lowghur and Esapour in sight,—formed an *ensemble* which no language can describe.

Fine fertile valleys run off from the ghauts into the plains of the Deckan. It has been before explained, that this grand division of India extends from the river Nerbuddah to the Kisthna, and comprises the provinces of Kandeish, Dowlutabad, Visiapour, G̃olconda, and part of Berar. The village of Karlle, near which the first halt was made, is small, but pleasingly situated in a mangoe grove, and very famous on account of the caves in its neighbourhood. Thoughtless and many others clambered up the mountain to see the celebrated one, which is supposed to have been dedicated to the worship of Buddah; though according to the common report it was constructed by the Jains. It is situated, with several smaller excavations, on the summit of a mountain of granite, and the ascent to it is difficult. There is a fine platform of about one hundred feet square cut out of the rock before the great entrance to the vestibule of the temple, which is arched, and supported by a row of pillars on each side. The effect is very grand, the inner temple being about 130 feet in length and fifty broad, without any figures or statues; but in the vestibule the walls are covered with mythological representations in basso relievo on the rock; and before the gate are pillars twenty-four feet high, and eight in diameter, with lions on the capitals remarkably well sculptured. This temple is similar to one among those of Kenneri, except that the roof is of wood and the dimensions much larger. The roof, which seems to have been put up long after the excavation was made, and to have been constructed to support the rocky arch which was giving way, is very curiously carved. The cave was half full of devotees, and tents were pitched in a nook on the side of the hill for the accommodation of the Brahmins belonging to a small modern Bowannee pagoda near it, which is now the object of veneration, while the magnificent structure is neglected, and believed to be haunted by devils. Great numbers of cripples and diseased persons had, however, taken shelter in the latter, in the hope of receiving relief from the idol in the small one, to which pilgrimages are made; and many women were offering gifts and prayers for children. In short, the great platform was like a fair, and the Brahmins were reaping the benefit of native credulity.

Thence to Seroor by way of Poonah, there are at regular stages comfortable bungalows for travellers, built by a subscription of the civil and military gentlemen belonging to the subsidiary force. From the head of the ghauts to the vicinity of Poonah they made three marches. They passed several villages and the town of Tulligaum, near which there is a remarkably fine tank and a mangoe tope, under the refreshing shade of whose trees the regiment encamped. They crossed the rivers Endrane and Powna, branches of the Beema, which receives all the small contributions to the Kisthna in this part. The prospect from the camp on the heights overlooking the Peishwa's capital was interesting. Daporé lay on one hand, while on the other extended the city of Poonah, its fertile plain watered by the Moota and Moola rivers, with a lofty round hill rising near it, on whose summit stands the temple of Parbutta the wife of Sheva, and high hill forts in the distance; the whole scene exhibiting a pleasing diversity of upland and dale. Daporé was the cantonment of the Peishwa's brigade, commanded by Major Forde, and officered by Europeans, the men being sepoys disciplined and appointed like the company's troops. Next day they encamped on the left bank of the Beema, which is one of the great arms of the Kisthna. The towns and villages in the vicinity of Poonah are built of stone and lime, and the houses covered with tiles, but they are generally surrounded by mud walls that give them a dull appearance.

From Koragaum on the Beema they reached Seroor in two marches. It is forty miles north of Poonah, the intervening country being hilly but tolerably cultivated. Seroor, at this time the head-quarters of the subsidiary force, is situated on the right bank of the Gore river, which falls into the Beema. The immediate approach to it is barren and unprepossessing, but this forbidding aspect serves to heighten the agreeable effect of the gardens and bungalows, which, peeping from among cypress trees, suddenly break upon the view from the heights just over the cantonments. At this station, long celebrated for gaiety and pleasure, they found a great number of very handsome houses, a neat little theatre, a racket-court, and a race-course. The officers of the 65th were regaled with a sumptuous breakfast, which awaited their arrival at Captain Ledwick's, of the company's service, who commanded in the absence of Colonel Smith. He was returning with the field force from the banks of the Godavery, where it had been guarding the passes from Kandish in the hope of intercepting the Pindarries. In the meantime Thoughtless had an opportunity of looking about him. The regularity of the various cantonments in India gives them a very cheerful appearance. They all retain the plan of a camp; indeed they have risen from encampments, the soldiers having been permitted to build huts of such materials as the place afforded for better shelter than tents during the rainy season, and the officers to erect bungalows instead of their marquees. In the course of time the temporary buildings of the former were converted by government into barracks, and the bungalows by individual labour and expence became private property, being surrounded by handsome gardens, lawns, and plantations, beautified with the plants, shrubs, fruits, and vegetables of Europe as well as of Asia, while the dwellings themselves were enriched with furniture, paintings, and hangings. The proprietor of a handsome bungalow, on quitting the station, found no difficulty in selling his house and improvement either to a brother officer of the regiment which relieved his corps, or to a native, who made the purchase for the purpose of charging rent for it in future. In rear of the lines where the bazar had stood, native towns arose in the same gradual way, and where the artillery park was, substantial stores and magazines were built for the reception of trains and ammunition. The vine flourishes in the Deckan with great luxuriance, and the grapes produced at Seroor are large and delicious. Fine peaches, apricots, leechies, figs, pine apples, oranges, lemons, citrons, melons, pumpkins, mangoes, plantains, and all the fruits of the East, grow here with native richness; and the mulberry, strawberry, and nearly all the vegetable tribe common in the gardens of Europe, reach maturity in this fine soil and climate. The winter is as cold as the autumn in England; but the summer, just before the commencement of the monsoon, is so dreadfully hot, that tender plants then require to be covered from the sun, and demand much attention. But in July the rain falls, and spring commences; and in September, when the monsoon is over, the crops are sown, and the whole country is in full bloom during December and January; rice, jewarry, wheat, cotton, grain, oil plant, sugar cane, tobacco, and hemp grow freely in this soil. Cotton is not produced to any great extent, but all the other articles are cultivated largely; and the whole vicinity of Seroor at this time in tillage appeared to be in a most flourishing state.

Colonel Smith soon came in with the 56th regiment, and a considerable part of the force. Charles was struck with his martial air; he was of large stature, with a fine penetrating aspect, and the polished address of a highly educated man of the world. The second battalion 56th was shortly after its return reviewed preparatory to its disorganization. This fine corps had its 8th and light companies armed with rifles and clothed in green, and their skilful evolutions gave an interesting diversity to the correct manœuvres of the battalion, which fixed all beholders with admiration. On this occasion Colonel Smith in his orders bestowed the highest praise on Colonel Kingscote, the officers and men of this crack regiment. "In a system of discipline which that excellent officer," said he, "laid down, his Majesty's regulations have been always carefully preserved; every individual has been perfectly instructed in his part; and the strictest scrutiny into its interior order, or the most watchful eye on its field movements, would equally find it a beautiful battalion, at once perfect, cheerful, and zealous in all its duties to their country. There is no language of praise or thanks Colonel Smith could feel to be too strong in describing the merits of such a corps." These praises, though strong, were by no means hyperbolical, for this regiment was so completely organized that the system pervaded the very looks of the men, and every one was a guardian placed over the conduct of his comrade. It was like a piece of fine clockwork or mechanism, in which every part moved with perfect regularity. But this great attention to systematic order was in some things carried to ridiculous lengths. For instance, a detachment composed of a non-commissioned officer from each company, with the serjeant-major at their head, ranged themselves round the mess-table every evening immediately after the cloth was removed, and each man making a grand salute by regular signal, with the right hand presented an order-book held in the left to that officer behind whose chair he stood, who after reading returned the book, which was given to another, so that every one was supposed to peruse general, division, and regimental orders at dinner. After the books were replaced in the left hand, the serjeant-major gave another signal, and the whole saluted, faced, and marched in file after their superior round the table, and out at the door. There is no accounting for the whims and fancies of men. Colonel Smith himself, when in command of the 65th regiment, was systematic even to the expulsion of whiskers from his corps, deeming it easier to shave the face to the tip of each ear, than to raise a crop of hair where nature never intended one to grow; but on the subject of exhibiting orders, he was diametrically opposite in his arrangement to Colonel Kingscote. He permitted no non-commissioned officer to enter the mess-room of the 65th while the officers were at dinner. If it was necessary to communicate orders to any one at table, a mess-waiter informed the officer that he was wanted, and he withdrew to receive the message.

Immediately after the review, volunteering commenced, and a great part of the men enlisted into the 65th regiment. All discipline in the two corps for a few days was lost, and upwards of sixteen hundred men became complete bacchanalians, for canteens were opened on the parades to enable them to spend the bounty with all possible expedition. The scene was one of great confusion. Here were some parading with drums beating up for recruits, and there others running about mad from the effects of intoxication, while the plain was strewed as if after a battle with men dead drunk. Colonel Smith was carried by the soldiers all round the cantonments on their shoulders, and fell several times from the reeling machine that supported his manly fabric; all this he bore with good-nature, and by his fascinating affability so replenished the ranks, that his regiment, from being one of the weakest, was raised to the full numerical force of a strong corps. The rifles were transferred to the 65th, and two of the companies were soon arrayed in green. But after such disorganization it required some time to restore the regiment to perfect discipline; and as it was expected to remain at Seroor, a treaty being on the eve of conclusion with Scindea and Holkar, under whose secret influence it was supposed the Pindarries were acting, the families came up from Bombay. The amateurs were preparing to entertain the ladies with theatricals, and balls and parties were circulating pleasure around, when a sudden order interrupted the amusements, and called the force to the frontiers of the district under Colonel Smith's command, extending from the right bank of the Godavery to the left of the Kisthna. They accordingly moved northward, leaving the families and sick at Seroor, and after three marches encamped near Ahmednuggur, a strong fortress built by Auringzebe, and one of the company's posts, forty miles distant from the cantonments on the road to Jaulna. In these marches they crossed the Gore river, now quite fordable, and passed the villages of Herigney, Ranjangaum, Auckulneer, and several others, in a miserable state of dilapidation, having suffered extremely from the famine of 1802. The country is rude and in many parts barren, but in others covered with crops of grain, which at this season, the latter part of December, was in the blade, and had a fine appearance.

Ahmednuggur is situated in a grand plain covered with plantations of fruit trees, and watered by the river Suna, which is distributed over it by means of aqueducts composed of hard cement; many of them are now choked up, but they serve to commemorate the once prosperous state of this immense garden. The fort is a mile in circumference, built of stone, with a ditch forty yards broad and sixteen feet deep. There are several interesting ruins in it of Moorish architecture, but they are crumbling to dust. The breach made by Sir Arthur Wellesley is still partly open, but not practicable, for the place surrendered to him after the storm of the Petah, which is a large town surrounded by a high wall, with several mosques. The interior has become, however, nearly a heap of ruins, and exhibits an impressive monument of the revolutions in human affairs. Lady Hood, when here, caused to be placed in the wall, near the gate which was stormed, a black marble slab, with an inscription commemorating the fate of Captain Mackenzie, of the 78th regiment, and the officers who fell in the assault. About four miles from Ahmednuggur, situated on a hill, there is a monument ninety feet high, sacred to the memory of Salabut Khaun, one of Auringzebe's generals; and a mile distant from the fort there is a small ruined palace, in the centre of an extensive and beautiful tank; it reminds the beholder of those imaginary edens which poets delight to describe, being surrounded by a fine garden planted with fruit trees, and laid off in broad walks. Charles gazed upon the scene with a mixed sensation of delight and pain.

After advancing four marches northward, they encamped near the large walled town of Pooltamba, now nearly in ruins, though finely situated on the river Godavery, which receives all the streams in this quarter of the Deckan. Part of the country passed over was very fine, particularly about Bellapore, a considerable town on the Pera river, which is a large branch of the Godavery. The plain around it was covered with ripening jewarry, and the farmers' men were seated on trees in the fields, keeping off the crows from the grain, which they did by uttering most frightful cries. Other extensive tracts were covered with jungle, inhabited by antelopes in immense herds, wild hogs, bustards, and hyenas. The bed of the Godavery in this part of its course is about 300 yards broad, but at this season it was quite fordable. This fine river rises in the ghauts, crosses Dowlutabad and Golconda from west to east, and falls into the bay of Bengal. At Pooltamba they learned that Major Lushington, with the 4th Madras native cavalry, had overtaken a large body of the Pindarries and cut seven hundred of them to pieces with the loss of some men and of Captain Dark, who was run through the body by a spear. This corps marched seventy-six miles in fifteen hours, and the hurkaru who brought the dispatch to Colonel Smith travelled 118 miles in thirty-four hours.

The colonel stationed his force in brigades along the Godavery, in sight of the passes through the mountains into Kandeish, and they were for several months constantly sending out light parties after the Pindarries, who were plundering the country in all directions. Near the towns along the river, the fine fields of badgery, dholl, grain, and oil plant appeared all in a deplorably ruined state; but the one half of the country was uninhabited, except by antelopes, wild boars, and tigers. The force had several grand hog hunts along the river, in one of which Major Campbell of the company's service was killed. His horse's foot, during the chase, got entangled in one of the cracks made by the sun in the earth, and the major was thrown and dragged along till beaten to death against the ground. He was buried near the village of Bursair, on a hill, and a monument was raised there by his brother officers to record his memory, for he was a brave and most worthy character. They had fine sport in fox hunting, bustard and partridge shooting, and in bringing down antelopes with the rifle, for their greyhounds were not able to look at them, and except when a fawn happened to be in the herd, no dog could get near one of them. Their marches and counter-marches extended along the Godavery, almost from its source to Dowlutabad; and upon gaining sight of the hill fort of that town, various parties were formed from camp to see it and the caves of Ellora. Thoughtless availed himself of one of these parties to visit them.

About four o'clock in the morning Wilson, Booth, Thomson, and he, started from camp near Peepelgaram. On the road they met some friends returning, whose report considerably damped their expectations of pleasure, for it appeared that they had been fired upon by Bheels during the night; but being well-armed, the party proceeded, and a little further fell in with a detachment of the 3d N. I. under Lieutenant Shaw, who very politely gave them a guard of sepoys. Besides their head servants, they had a camel and hoont wallah to carry their canteens, with breakfast and dinner apparatus, together with their mussauls, couch wallahs, and gora wallahs, so that they were now too formidable to be apprehensive of danger from mere robbers. They halted for breakfast at a ruined village about half-way. The dhurrumsullah was large and comfortable. It had in one part of it a stone statue of Hunnymaun, with a very long tail, and near the idol there was a lingum. An old man, whose shrunk shanks could scarcely support his emaciated body, was, when they alighted, busily employed in anointing with oil and vermillion the face and body of Hunnymaun, whom he approached with evident marks of respect and devotion, salamming to the very ground. About one o'clock they reached the caves, distant from camp about twenty-two miles.

The mountain in which they are is of semicircular form, and in extent about two thousand yards. It is approached from the west through a well-watered and beautifully shaded plain, on which numerous ruins indicate the former magnificence, population, and cultivated state of this part of the Deckan. The large walled town of Cassebeara is in a flourishing situation, and the only one which Thoughtless had seen to the north of Poonah that did not excite those feelings of pity which naturally arise on beholding the ruins of what once abounded with life, and all things interesting to humanity. A little further on are the ruins of the city of Ellora, the walls of which are yet in a state of good order, while the interior offers nothing but a melancholy picture of abandonment, not containing now one fortieth of its former population. Here they were met by a Brahmin, who conducted them up to the caves. Although curiosity had been sufficiently excited to anticipate something beyond measure wonderful, yet on this occasion the reality by far exceeded what Thoughtless had imagined. It is idle to attempt the description of these caves; indeed a volume might be filled with what must be here compressed into a page, for they contain the whole history of the Hindoo mythology.

Great numbers of Brahmins live in these caves upon the presents made by devotees, pilgrims, and strangers attracted hither by curiosity. The one who conducted them was very communicative and lively. According to his account, he had also attended Lady Hood through them, and he was so loud in praising her ladyship's generosity, that they soon discovered his eulogy to be a *ruse* to work upon their liberality. He gave them all the information in his power on the subject of the history and formation of the caves; but they soon perceived that he knew no more than themselves, for he assured them very gravely, that the mountain had been thus excavated five thousand years ago by the gods, during the nights of six months; and that previous to this wonderful work of the heavenly powers, the world had existed many thousands of years. From authentic information it would appear that these stupendous excavations were completed about one thousand years ago, some time before the Mahomedan invasion, when the Brahminical system of idolatry was in the zenith of its splendour. There are also good grounds for supposing that they were intended for colleges, in which the priests could reside and teach all the ceremonies of their mythology. No wonder that the ignorant should credit any story, however fabulous, respecting monuments of art so amazing as to strike the most enlightened beholder with wonder and awe.

The mountain is a solid mass of exceedingly fine granite, about four hundred feet above the level of the plain. Along the face of this, there are eight principal caves, and about twenty small ones, some of which are not worth notice. Among the large caves there is one like Elephanta, and another resembling Karlee, but by far exceeding either of them in magnificence, variety, and extent. A pagoda one hundred feet high is here cut out of the solid rock. Thousands of colossean figures, fourteen feet high, ornament the walls, and the mountain seems to be supported by gigantic pillars, on which the regular orders of architecture are displayed, together with that curious style of decoration so common over Asia. All the stages of human life are here represented as faithfully as by the pen of Shakespeare. The infant puking, the father and mother in the bloom of health and beauty, then decrepid with age and infirmity, and again the pithless skeletons of their former selves. A miser is seen upwards of ten feet high, with his children and wife, and an old woman grasping his legs, and imploring charity, with starvation on their countenances, while a thief is stealing away bags of money from behind the shivering hard-hearted wretch, who seems to be spurning away those who are kneeling before him for aid. In one place are represented the struggles between the gods and the giants to secure the sea of butter; in another the thirty thousand millions of divinities flying to the assistance of Brahma, Vishnu, or Shevah. Here the metamorphoses of these brothers, and there the history of their amours, with the battle at the feast of the king of the mountains, and ten thousand other most extraordinary combats and stories, all vividly bodied forth on the solid rock, and finished with all the art of sculpture, in such fine proportions that even severe criticism must look with complacency upon the minute correctness, elegance, and indescribable grace displayed in the more remarkable specimens.

In extent, some of the caves are wonderful. The largest, which is called Khylas or Paradise, is in length 245 feet, and in breadth 143. In effecting this vast excavation the chisel seems to have been the only instrument used, therefore the labour and perseverance, time and expence, must have been very great. The Brahmins conduct strangers over the whole to the greatest advantage, the last shewn exceeding all the former in grandeur and extent. Some of them are of three stories, communicating with each other by a flight of magnificent stairs, and each story having a grand viranda, supported by beautiful pillars running along its front. On going into the lowest one, the stranger is surprised; the next astonishes him; but the last confounds him, for it still surpasses the others. The interior of every cave is lighted with great art and taste, imparting, by its well-contrived remoteness from glare on the one hand and darkness on the other, that fine effect to the statuary which an artist would delight to produce in his exhibition room.

The great stone pagoda before noticed has thousands of figures both within and without, in basso relievo, together with innumerable separate statues, representing the conquest of Ceylon by the gods, and many other pieces of history in the Hindoo mythology. This pagoda is cut out of solid stone, and there is between it and the scarped rock a considerable space. Under the latter, there are a viranda and galleries, in which fifty giants stand as guards round the temple, with symbols denoting their exploits. The height of the scarp is ninety feet, and from the galleries the pagoda appears as if it had been placed on the backs of elephants, tigers, and lions, and as if its weight were crushing these furious looking animals to death, for only the heads, legs, and part of their bodies appear outside. Many of the other caves are equally wonderful.

The party spent the whole day and a great part of next morning among these caves, for they could hardly satisfy their curiosity. In going through them they saw many old Brahmins, and cripples lying on low cots, or on mats spread on raised parts of the floor; but these devotees (except such as expected charity) hardly raised their heads to notice them, being so much accustomed to strangers. Some of the Brahmins had long white beards, and a very venerable benevolent aspect and appearance, as if freed from all worldly care; others were emaciated, looking as if in torture, covered with ashes, having their hair matted in a most filthy looking manner, and being scarcely able to open their eyes from the quantity of dirty paint smeared over their faces. Upon returning, the visitors found the table laid, and every thing in order for dinner in a small round pagoda, near the great cave called Khylas, which was large enough to hold all their couches, and upon a carpet being spread on the floor, they really felt most comfortable after the fatigue of the day. Their pick-nick was excellent; Captain Wilson had claret and cherry bounce, Thomson had Hodson's pale ale, Booth produced fine old madeira, and Charles had humble port wine. These, with a good dinner, soon made them frolicksome, and as the seeming lethargy of the Brahmins in the caves attracted their observation, they determined on rousing them from their slumber. Accordingly they discharged their pistols in the air, reloaded with blank cartridge, and fired away with all possible rapidity. But very few of the Brahmins came near them, for most of those philosophers were completely absorbed in the contemplation of heavenly things.

The next day they rode over the mountain to Dowlutabad, about eight miles distant from the caves, by a road which is in many parts difficult. On the terrace of the mountain, there is a very extensive tank, covered with wild duck and teal, and a large walled Moorish town called Roza, with a tomb sacred to the memory of Aurungzebe, in which the natives believe that a part of him is interred, as other parts are supposed to be at Aurungabad,

Ahmednuggur, and elsewhere. The road on approaching Dowlutabad, by way of Kakusdullah, where there is a great manufactory of paper, is cut out of a mountain, and well paved; this must have been a work of considerable labour. The ruins of this ancient city, once distinguished for its opulence, (*Dowlut* signifying *rich*, and *abad* being merely the generic term for city) are several miles in circumference, and the surrounding wall is still in good order, though the interior is a heap of rubbish, the few inhabitants that remain near it having erected habitations at some distance. The water for the supply of this place was conducted from a large reservoir, formed in a valley between two mountains, by a mound of solid masonry run across, and was distributed by means of pipes to all parts of the city.

One of the curiosities in the Deckan is the hill fort of Dowlutabad, in which the Nizam has a garrison. It is cut out of the solid rock, and apparently impregnable, for the perpendicular height of each face is about ninety feet, and it has a wet ditch thirty feet broad and twenty deep. From the capital of the scarp, the hill shelves up to a point so gradually, that even if the besiegers could mount the first perpendicular, their labour would be little more than commenced. The hill itself may be about three hundred and fifty feet high from the base, and is cut nearly into a square. It is quite a shell, the fort being excavated out of it, with tanks for the retention of water, and winding stairs and passages that astonish those who examine its interior. These excavations were made before the invention of gunpowder, and the immense body of solid stone cut away was transported from its original situation to various parts of the fort, by the tedious means of human labour.

Aurungabad was, during the Moorish empire, the capital of the Deckan. It is a very extensive city, situated within eighteen miles of the caves of Ellora, and about 260 miles N. E. of Bombay. Even in its present state of decay, the numerous mosques and the ruins of former magnificence, give it an air of grandeur. It is the station of a British political agent, and the head-quarters of several battalions of the Nizam's army, disciplined and clothed like sepoys, and commanded by European officers, either lent by the company, or deriving rank and pay from the government of Hyderabad. Captain Sydenham exercises the functions of a general under the Nizam, and is commander-in-chief of that part of his army organized on our system of tactics. The Nizam has his court at Hyderabad, the capital of Golconda, situated on a branch of the river Kisthna, 352 miles N. E. of Madras. The fortress of Golconda is only six miles from the city, to which it is joined by a famous wall of communication. This fort is on the summit of a conical hill, and is deemed impregnable. In 1687, when Aurungzebe conquered the Deckan, it fell into his hands by treachery. The celebrated diamond mines now hardly produce revenue enough to pay the expence of working them. Near them there are mines of salt, and fine iron for sword blades; and the vicinity of Hyderabad produces calicoes and chintzes of the most curious and complicated workmanship in India.

The nature of this work renders it impossible to enter minutely into the history of provinces, or to detail the splendid military achievements of British arms in the Deckan; for these particulars I refer to Waring's History of the Mahrattas, to Dow's History of Hindostan, and to Orme's Account of the Military Transactions in India.

Upon his return to the force, Charles was ordered to proceed to Bombay on duty. From Nagamtan on the river Godavery to Bombay, the distance is two hundred and forty miles, by way of Toka and Hewrah, two military posts of some importance, which form a chain of communication between Ahmednuggur and Jaulnah, where the principal part of the Nizam's subsidiary force is cantoned, and thence the line is prolonged to Nagpore, the station of another considerable division of the Madras army, being the subsidiary with the Rajah of Berar. As the high road to Bombay, by way of Seroor and Poonah, was reported perfectly safe for travellers, Charles was not furnished with a guard, and passed over this tract merely accompanied by his servants, and a camel to carry what was necessary. He found a comfortable dhurrumsallah in every town where it was necessary to halt, and the inhabitants evinced a disposition to treat him with kindness and respect. Nearly all the towns are in a state of decline, exhibiting the ruins of former population, and surrounded with high walls for the protection of the little that remains. In most of the dhurrumsallahs, there is a rude stone figure of Hunnymaun, over which the natives throw oil or water frequently, and place before it offerings of nice cakes, which are immediately carried off by poor half-starved looking boys. The people approach the images of Hunnymaun with all possible respect, taking off their shoes and salamming very low. It is in thus traversing a country, without martial parade or anything to draw off the attention of the natives from their occupations and amusements, that one has the most interesting opportunities of seeing them in their real character; and as Charles was curious on this point, he often went out of his way for the purpose of noticing what chance might reveal to his observation. Those travellers are perfectly correct who have reported that the Hindoos make feasts for flies of sugar and honey, and watch them while feeding with great satisfaction. It is no less true that they carry grain of various descriptions into the fields, and place it near every ant hillock which lies in their way, as a provision for these little animals. In short, their tenderness for every species of animated matter is almost incredible, and can only be accounted for on the principle of the doctrine of transmigration.

With many of the natives of different ranks, casts, and degrees of intelligence, he had long conversations. Some of them appeared hardly to have common ideas on subjects even within their observation; others were well informed, and possessed of vigorous minds; several were exceedingly inquisitive, and more inclined to ask than to answer questions, and not a few were full of acute remarks on various subjects, talking of our great power and extensive sway in the country. These would screw their right fore-finger into the left closed hand, and exclaim with a most significant expression of countenance, and a loud smack of the lips, that we had pushed ourselves in *so* to the Deckan, the Koncan, Guzerat, the Carnatic, and Bengal, and that they were all our own now. "Ah sir," said one of them to him, "it is nonsense to call this gaum or town Scindea's, and that the Peishwa's; for they are all nothing but tenants of the English."

Both during his march to Bombay and his return to the force by a different route, he was forcibly struck with the discontent manifested by the natives in regard to our occupation of the country. It was also quite apparent that the Peishwa's troops were fired with hatred, and the impression on his mind was that an explosion would shortly take place. In fact, this did occur soon after, and the state of public feeling which he had observed in the country was occasioned by the secret designs of the Mahratta chiefs, who were preparing their subjects at this time for war, and circulating false reports respecting the views and encroachments of the honourable company. But in short Mr. Elphinston the British resident at Poonah had observed such warlike preparations and dispositions on the part of the Peishwa, that he thought it necessary to direct the force to march for the capital, and Thoughtless met his regiment on its route thither, with the rest of the army, having very narrowly escaped a body of Pindarries who passed him. By an accident his servants had separated from him and taken another and nearer road, so that upon their arrival in camp it was supposed that the Pindarries had cut him and a small escort of sepoys to pieces; therefore upon his arrival he was congratulated as one risen from the dead by his warm-hearted companions. The body of plunderers that passed in the vicinity of his march was pursued by Major Smith of the first battalion 14th native infantry, and nearly destroyed after a march of four successive days and nights over a distance of 150 miles. Such a march for infantry was considered very great, and it was noticed handsomely in orders. "Colonel Smith never troubles the troops with idle praise; he hopes therefore that the sincerity with which he applauds the steady perseverance, the cool judgment and military skill of Major Smith upon this occasion, and the conspicuous exertions of the officers and soldiers under him may prove the more acceptable."

This arduous service was performed in the month of May, which is the hottest season in the Deckan. Trimbuckgee Danglae, who was at the head of these Pindarries, had been one of the Peishwa's principal chiefs; and in consequence of determined hostility to the English, evinced more particularly by the murder of the Guickwar's minister at Punderpore, had been confined in the fort of Tannah, near Bombay, from which he effected his escape. It was believed that the Peishwa himself had countenanced the murder of the Guickwar's shasti, and an investigation of the affair became imperative on the part of the British government, then in close alliance with the chief of Guzerat. The Peishwa disavowed the act, and gave up the author, as he said, to justice, on condition that his life should be spared. Sufficient care was not taken of him in the fort of Tannah, and he made his escape through a closet which communicated with a stable; and while the sentinel stood waiting for his return he passed the gate, it is said, in the disguise of a gora wallah. He soon gained the mountains, and raised a considerable party amongst his vassals and adherents, which was daily increasing by the accession of Pindarries, under which denomination he with his force for some time traversed the country. The Peishwa gave it out that the vast military preparations making by him were for the purpose of crushing this daring chief; but his good faith and sincerity were suspected, and it was afterwards found that he viewed Trimbuckgee's operations with hope and complacency. The force advanced to Poonah, and Mr. Elphinstone compelled the Peishwa to explain his views and enter into a new treaty with the Honourable Company which was thought to be more secure and advantageous than the former.

The city of Poonah is of modern construction, and not entitled to much notice. It is well watered by the Moota and Moola, which form a junction near it. The Peishwa's palaces and gardens are objects of curiosity; the former exhibit a display of eastern grandeur, and are also furnished with costly articles of European manufacture. Some of the rooms are completely wainscotted with British mirrors, and the ceiling is hung with gorgeous chandeliers — a profusion of time-pieces, mathematical instruments, and globes decorated the apartments, which were furnished also with costly velvet beds, and the richest carpets. The streets of the city are broader in general than those of other native towns, and exhibit the appearance of vast wealth. There are several pagodas; but these, being of modern construction, are not objects of great veneration, and the Brahmins of Poonah make annual processions to Punderpore on the Beena, and to Sattara on the Kisthna, where there are sacred temples of great antiquity. The plain in which Poonah stands is like a garden, and the scenery very fine, having the ghauts in the distance. The city lies under a high range of mountains, with several romantic hill forts in sight, and near its walls is the round and steep natural mount on which the Parbutty is situated. Poonah is not of great extent or of imposing appearance. In point of strength it is not worthy of much consideration; but its great wealth and the sacred nature of its government, the Peishwa being a Brahmin, give it a preponderance among the Mahratta states.

Peishwa was the title of the prime minister under the Sattara Rajah, who is the legitimate sovereign of all the possessions belonging to the Poonah government; but about a century ago, one of the ancestors of Badgé Row, the present Peishwa, induced the reigning rajah either by coercion or persuasion to retire from the cares of the throne. Being a Brahmin, it was unlawful for the usurper to assume the title of rajah, and he continued to govern under that of Peishwa, making the subjects believe that the resignation of the monarch was a voluntary act. Indeed a sham ceremony of showing the successor of Sevagee, the founder of the Mahratta empire, annually to his subjects, was always kept up, although it is well known that the Sattara Rajah is a close prisoner, and surrounded by the Peishwa's creatures. The survivors of this venerably ancient family consist of the rajah, his mother, and his two brothers, who were at this time confined in the almost inaccessible fort of Sattara, situated sixty miles south of Poonah. After this usurpation, the Peishwa removed his seat of government to Poonah, then beginning to flourish, and there it has since continued. The city has never been fortified, and is only surrounded by slight walls that would keep off a sudden attack of cavalry; for the government of Poonah depend for protection, in any emergency, upon the strength of a strong hill fort called Poorundar, about eighteeen miles distant.

Both Poonah and Sattara are situated in the ancient kingdom of Viziapour, which was overthrown by the Moguls, and finally ruined by Aurungzebe. The vast and curious remains of the once mighty city of Sattara are about 130 miles S. E. of Poonah, and still strike the beholder with wonder and surprise, being upwards of fifteen miles in circumference. After the ruin of this mighty kingdom, and the decline of the Mogul power, the Mahrattas who inhabited the mountains rose into notice under Sevagee, and Sattara was long their capital. Since the battle of Paniput this empire has declined, and it may now be said that the only chief who has any thing like independence is Scindea. Lord Valentia has described the dusserah and the etiquette of the Poonah court so minutely, that it is unnecessary to say any thing on those subjects, more particularly as the Poonah government is now no more. The Hon. Mr. Elphinstone resided in an extensive range of buildings erected in the sungum or fork of the rivers Moota and Moola, within a stone's throw of the city of Poonah. This most learned and ingenious gentleman kept an open table for all European officers who passed the residency, and welcomed them with eastern magnificence and British hospitality. The cantonments for the Poonah division of the subsidiary force were also near the city, and formed a beautiful display of elegant cottages and bungalows, surrounded by gardens in the European style, filled with the various fruits of the Deckan, overtopped with cypress trees that imparted a majestic grandeur to the scene.

Soon after the political arrangements had been concluded which called for the presence of the army, the force returned to Serroor to be cantoned during the approaching monsoon. The amateurs marshalled their theatrical columns, and entertained the ladies, who had been left almost in solitude, with some excellent specimens of farcical humour. Balls and suppers were not wanting, so that gaiety and festivity, sweetened by the recollection of late deprivations, everywhere prevailed. But scarcely had the rains subsided, and the jockey club found the course fit for the annual races, when the force again took the field, and resumed their station on the banks of the Godavery. The Mahratta states had now assumed a very warlike appearance. The Marquis of Hastings was moving with a vast force upon Scindea. Holkar's government was suspected; the rajah of Berar was little to be depended upon, and the Peishwa appeared ready to break faith if opportunity offered. In these circumstances, a very active campaign being apprehended, proper preparations were made to meet an approaching storm, which soon began to rage, as will be seen in the next chapter.

CHAP. XXIII.

"But look! the tide now ebbs — hark!—splash of oars—
I leave thee, and these long frequented shores.
My fondest hope — O may it not be vain!
Is soon, my friend, to press thy hand again.
Once more, the *dandies* call, farewell! adieu!
And Gunga bore him swiftly from my view.
The stormy ocean soon will roar between —
Perchance till death has clos'd life's busy scene!"

Instead of immediately pursuing the course of events in the Deckan, we find it necessary to bring up collateral matter, which has fallen considerably in arrear. The regiment to which Frank Stanley belonged had at length received orders to return home, and it was drafted at Tritchinopoly. Frank accompanied the head-quarters to Madras, where, a very short time before he embarked for Europe, his long promised promotion took place, and he was raised to that rank in life by his merit which he had so long signally deserved. Although love smiled before him in the prospect, and hope beckoned him from the white cliffs of his native land, yet he left India with a sorrowful heart, and his farewell letter bore evident marks of melancholy: — "I am much concerned to say, my dearest friend, that this will be the last time I shall write to you in India, for the ship is arrived from Bengal, and we go on board to-morrow morning. I have been waiting in anxious expectation some time past for a letter from you, but I am greatly afraid I shall be obliged to leave the country without one. Notwithstanding the pleasing prospect before me, I cannot account for the reason, but I do not feel half so much pleasure in leaving India as I expected I should; perhaps leaving you behind, and a chance of never seeing you more, is partly the cause. I suppose you have heard of the death of Colonel E—— and Lieut. S——, who are much regretted by the whole regiment. Poor fellows, they were preparing to go home the day before they died. To see men cut off in the prime of life, after a few days illness, almost makes me indifferent about my future prospects, for 'we know not to-day what to-morrow may bring forth.' I had the good fortune the other day to receive a very affectionate letter from my mother; she is well, and anxiously waiting to see me, so is the old squire, and if I may trust a mother's love, so is Miss Sarah. Pray have you heard again from your father? I shall go to Ireland shortly after I get home to see him, and should have liked to be the bearer of a letter from you, with a ring or some token of your affection. Having some fine elephants' hair, I shall get one made in England, and deliver it to him in your name, for I am sure you will send me a note of introduction to the old gentleman. Please to present my kind respects to

Mrs. T—, and I hope this will find her and all your little ones in good health; and I pray God you may enjoy every blessing this world can give together.

> ' She who her lovely offspring eyes
> With tender hopes and fears,
> O bless her with a mother's joys,
> But spare a mother's tears.'

"Do, my excellent friend, let me hear from you at all opportunities, it will be my greatest consolation. We expect to put in at the Cape; if so, I will send you a letter. But should I not receive one from you in two or three months after my arrival in England, I shall conclude something has happened. I must now bid you a long adieu! and something tells me I shall never have the pleasure of seeing you any more. For all past favours I have nothing to return you but my unfeigned thanks, and may the Almighty bless and prosper you and Mrs. T—. Go whither I may, you will always possess the entire esteem and affection of your constant friend till death."

A tear had been dropped on this letter by the writer, and it was wet with another from the reader, for Charles sighed at the probability that they should never meet again in this world. His own health was in a most delicate state from long residence in the climate, and he laboured under an affection of the liver; but although he had received the most pressing invitation from his father to return home, yet he could not in honour quit the force on leave of absence during the war, when it was expected that every officer should keep at his post so long as he was able to stand. He was, however, cheered by the prospect of soon following his friend to the renovating breezes of his native climate, for a probability existed that by the vast preparations then making the Marquis of Hastings would force the native powers into his measures without striking a blow. Some other circumstances had also elevated Charles's spirits to a high degree. His old benefactor, Captain Noble, had returned to India to insure his majority, and had written to Thoughtless in the most friendly terms, assuring him that his greatest satisfaction almost through life had been the reflection of having assisted his merit in its dawn, which had since advanced him to the station in life that he so well deserved. He had also received letters from his father, and from his friend George True, who was now a captain on half-pay residing on his paternal estate, which quite delighted him. The former breathed the most ardent anxiety to see him, and the latter described every thing in the most enchanting colours; for when we are pleased and happy within ourselves, all the world seems robed in smiles.

"With emotions of joy," said Charles's father, in his first letter, "which I am unable to describe, I received your letter of the 3d June. Thank God that my son is yet living; that his father has been spared after various fatigues, dangers, and troubles by sea and land: I shall deem it the best gift of Providence to receive a long absent son, his wife, and little offspring, with all that tender parental affection which the human heart can possess." He then went on to describe the success he had met with in the United States, and the affluence in which he lived in his native country. "You, my dear Charles," continued he, "are my only son; but I have three daughters by a second marriage, smart lively girls, the eldest has a striking resemblance of you, and the mother says that she is the pet on that account. Providence has been kind in giving you a happy inclination to improve your mind. You well know that my embarrassments were the cause of your having been left with your grandmother and uncle, for an unfortunate copartnership ruined my affairs, and forced me to quit my native country. We have both been successful in overcoming the persecution of fortune, thank God; I hope that we have both done with her hard gusts, that we shall have a happy meeting in this country, and that my dear dear son's presence will aid, cheer, and comfort me in my declining years. Therefore, my dear Charles, come hither with your family as soon as possible; thank God I am able to make a handsome provision for you; in short, I shall gladly share to the last shilling with you. But what is fortune to health? and yours is impaired. The thought fills me with anxiety. Your grandmother and aunt in Dublin are dead. My mother died last October, good old lady; she was pleasingly affected on hearing your former letter read. I am now in the fifty-fourth year of my age, and enjoy good health. I am still fond of music, and keep my violin and flute in good order, and sometimes play for the children, who dance well. Since your letter arrived they have had much chat about your little ones, and I assure you my wife will be most happy to see you all. 'Tis astonishing to observe the affectionate anxiety manifested by your sisters to make friends of your children." In another letter this affectionate parent entered into further particulars with so much warmth of feeling that Thoughtless determined upon giving up his prospects in the army, and going home with his family as soon as he could do so with honour. "My dear and only son," said his father, "nothing in this world ever afforded me such a degree of satisfaction as the receipt of your letters, assuring me that you are still in the land of the living, and affording hopes that I may soon have the pleasure of seeing you, your wife and dear little offspring; but I feel uneasy that your health is impaired: exert yourself to come to this country, your debilitated constitution will be renewed, and by God's permission, I expect and hope to see you an ornament to society in my declining years, to fill my place and fall into my connections. I reside in the country, ten miles from Dundalk, during vacation, but I have a house in Dublin, and one in Dundalk also, where I intend to fix you and family, for I spend nearly half my time in it, being a lively improved country town, situated in one of the best parts of Ireland. Thank God you have escaped the pestilential climate of Guzerat, and now breath the elevated air of the Deckan. Most undoubtedly you have been and will be happy in the choice you have made; a good wife is the greatest blessing a man can have in this sublunary life. You seem to possess a disposition suited to domestic happiness, but your situation in the army deprives you of the real enjoyments to be attained in that way.—The feelings of a man leaving his wife and family, perhaps never to see them again, at a few hours warning, to take the field against a formidable enemy, and the fatigues, troubles, and deprivations incident thereto, must torture even the bravest officer living. I can have but a faint idea of the state of mind induced by such emotions; but I think a military life ill calculated to ensure the comfort of a wife and family, which must be the object of every honourable man who has elevation of soul sufficient to prefer the happiness of his partner to his own. I sincerely recommend you, as soon as you can consistently with honour, to make arrangements and return to your native country. It is my intention to make you an allowance fully adequate to support yourself and family genteelly, till in the course of nature you will succeed to my income, which, without exaggeration, is eight hundred per annum. I am sure that after having served your king and country so many years, it will be easy for you to retire to the half-pay. When you have arrangements made for leaving that country, let me know when you expect to arrive in London, and I shall meet you there. My dear son, my happiness in a great measure depends on your existence, and having you and your sweet little family near me would smooth my passage through the declining part of life. My health is, and has been for years, very good — my weight eighteen stone, though I ride a great deal on horseback, and rise very early — my wife and children all join me in prayers for your safety and speedy arrival. May God bless you, Mary, and your dear little children, is the fervent ejaculation of your affectionate father." When Thoughtless made known the change in his prospects to his friends and companions, particularly to his warm-hearted countryman, Adam Cuppage, "I protest," said he, "your story is just like a novel, and it would be equally interesting if you were judiciously to give it here and there a slight tint of the marvellous."

True's letters abounded with the most charming descriptions of society in the north of Ireland, particularly in the lively towns of Armagh and Newry. The elder Mr. True, with a delicacy which did him honour, had put George into possession of a small estate of his in county Down, which came into the family with his mother: he himself resided on his paternal property in county Armagh, but such a constant intercourse was kept up between the two families that hardly a day passed without some exchange of courtesy. Robert Gordon had become the confidential steward of the captain, and in course of time was appointed agent and receiver to the father and son, for which situation he was well qualified both in point of education, address, and intelligence. His love for poetry still continued, and George sent his friend Charles a description of the vicinity of his country seat, written by the author of "The Fate of Mary."

In county Down, where many a crystal rill
Adorns those meads which bleaching linens fill,
(Esto perpetua — Erin go brah)
Lies Newry, on the confines of Armagh;
Whose northern aspect, opening hill and dale,
Where peace and plenty robe each happy vale,
Through which the Bann bears off to broad Lough Neagh,
The treasures that wide ocean's depths convey;
On other sides mountainous ridges rise,
And seem as if they kissed the dewy skies,
Slievegullion towers,—the northern weather glass,
And Carlingford 'gainst Neptune leans his mass;
Along whose lofty side six miles and more,
From Newry, are a lough and charming shore,
Industry slow, and poverty have crept,
To nestle where the eagles once have slept;
For not a nook whose herbs would feed a pig,
But cheers a heart as merry as a grig.
Thy hand, good Ogle, round your rural seat,
Has formed a scene where taste may recreate:

High winding roads that cut the mountain side,
Green shady clumps which barren roughness hide;
And rich plantations, lawns and meadows, grace
The spot called Fathom — wild romantic place.
Exactly on the other ridgy side,
The lough between, rough Grinan opens wide,
Near whose broad top a sort of table land,
With little vales and slopes on either hand,
Extends; and thence a bubbling sedgy brook,
Meanders to the tide through many a nook.
Hard by a lively lodge stands on a lawn,
Whose face receives the rosy peep of dawn;
A pretty garden sweetly smiles behind,
Whose flowery shrubs perfume each zephyr kind,
Secured from the cold north's repulsive chills,
By one of Erin's friendly emerald hills;
Before the door is smiling Greenwood park,
Whose image animates the blue waves dark,
And many a breathing rose lends fragrance mild,
To summer gay, and e'en to winter wild,
Where hospitality without parade,
And elegance in classic robe arrayed
For friendship in the castle spread the board,
While sprightly dance and song their aid afford.
Old Erin too sits with the jokes and laughs,
Half mellow, and the sparkling goblet quaffs;
While blushing charity with melting eye,
Strives from the world to hide her tender sigh;
But truth perceives her gliding with full hands
Behind to poverty who sculking stands.
A little onward Hall's enriched domains,
Enliven the far spreading hills and plains;
And hound and horn, poor puss, thy life pursue,
In mimic war, slap dash, with loud halloo.
Next finely seated, further up the shore,
Where zephyrs play, and sometimes billows roar,
Is Warren Point, whose tepid summer waves
Soft silver sand in sparkling curls receives;

And bathing-lodges, dear to jocund health,
Rise all around the offspring of kind wealth ;
Till nature in her softest, wildest charms,
At sweet Rosstrevor admiration warms.

The uncertainty when he should be refreshed with the sight of those scenes of his youth, the approach of his children to that age when it was necessary, in a moral and physical point of view, for them to be sent to Europe, the departure of his earliest and dearest friend — these considerations, combined with the morbid feelings caused by hope long deferred, were beginning to prey on his mind. It is true he was surrounded by many estimable noble-minded companions, who permitted him to call them friends, and whom he esteemed as such in every sense of the word; but to his heart friendship was like a second marriage, for while he contemplated the fine qualities of his new associates, he often sighed and mentally exclaimed, "Still unlike Frank Stanley." He had lost in him his most intelligent Indian correspondent, whose letters, instead of being filled with slip-slop, abounded in interesting remarks on men and manners, and in observations on the curiosities in art and nature which he had seen in his marches through the Carnatic, and in voyaging along nearly the whole coast of Coromandel, from Adam's Bridge to Juggurnaut. He had viewed the stupendous structures raised in times beyond the range of historical record in honour of the Brahminical idols. He had surveyed with astonishment those remains of antiquity on the island of Seringham, near the mouth of the Cavery, where 40,000 Brahmins were once supported by the pilgrimages made to them. There are seven square enclosures with walls twenty-five feet high and four thick, each having four large gates and high pagodas, some of which are composed of stones thirty-three feet long and five in diameter, and the outward wall is about four miles in circumference. The pagoda of Chillambrun, near Porto Novo, is 120 feet high, built of stones forty feet long and five feet square, and covered with plates of copper, with figures of gods and animals so innumerable as to baffle description, for the whole structure is upwards of 1300 feet in length and near 1000 in breadth. But these famous monuments need not here be noticed, for all the historians of the East speak of them with wonder, and who that has directed his curiosity towards India requires to be told of the seven pagodas on the mountain of Mavalipuram near Sadras? We shall therefore turn to more original matter, of which a great quantity still before us must necessarily be compressed into a small space.

It may be said that nearly all the Deckan is inhabited by Mahrattas, for although Mahomedans are numerous in the territories of the Nizam, yet they bear no proportion to the great mass of population, which comes under the general description applicable to other parts of India. Whether the Mahrattas were the aborigines of the country, or the descendants of Persian settlers, as it has been learnedly attempted to be proved in the Asiatic Researches by Major Wilford, seems a question of little consequence. At present they are Hindoos in every respect, and the fighting casts are exceedingly brave as to individual courage. In the reign of Aurungzebe they began to be very powerful, and he fought numerous battles with them, frequently driving them back to the mountains, from which they again emerged with new spirit, and at length under Sevagee, who was general in the army of the great king of Begapore, laid the foundation of that empire which threatened at one time to subdue all the East. Its progress was arrested by the Mahomedans at the battle of Paniput; but its resources were so great in the beginning of the present century, that the revenue amounted to seventeen millions sterling, and the population to 40,000,000 of souls. The five chiefs who composed it, namely, the Peishwa, Scindea, Holkar, the Rajah of Berar, and the Guickwar, had a regular army of 300,000 men, and were able to bring three times that numerical strength into the field. Their artillery and material were truly formidable; they had founderies for guns, and manufactories for every kind of warlike stores, conducted by French engineers. Perron's brigade under Scindea was alone 40,000 strong, with 400 pieces of artillery; it was in as fine a state of order and discipline as the company's sepoys, and was armed in a similar manner, and perfectly organized on the most modern scientific principles. Holkar fought the battle of Deeg with twenty-four perfectly disciplined battalions, and 150 pieces of cannon. With such a warlike population, spread over a tract of 1000 square miles, with so many hill forts, which a handful of brave men might defend against a mighty army, the physical resources of this people were prodigious. Let any man think of all this, and at the same time reflect that a combination was forming among all the Mahomedan chiefs for the destruction of the British; that Shah Allum was about to cede Agra and Delhi to the French; that Tippo, tinctured with all the enthusiasm of the revolution, called himself citizen, and had his cannon cast with a tiger devouring the head of an Englishman; that the Grand Seignior, the King of Cabul, the Nabob of Oude, and the Nizam, were all ready, and that the Mahrattas were invited to join in the plunder of the British empire, and he will at once have a slight glance at the merit and ability of the Marquis Wellesley, who steered the vessel of his country through such a storm. He seized the French faction at Hyderabad, alarmed the Afghans by turning the Persians upon them, captured Seringapatam, beat Scindea, and drove every Frenchman out of his service, saved Poonah from plunder, while the battles of Delhi, Assaye, and Argaum added laurels to the British arms. In short, the tremendous danger that threatened our prosperity in India may be conceived, but it cannot be accurately described. The siege of Bhurtpore, which was five times assaulted, cost 3000 lives alone, chiefly British. All those ambitious chiefs, however, who aimed at our destruction and at universal empire in the East, were humbled. But under the feeble administration of the Marquis Cornwallis which followed, (for that great man seemed to have lost his energy a short time before his death, during his second government of India,) concessions that were made to Scindea, at a time when his insolence deserved correction, inspired the restless Mahrattas with confidence and hope, and laid the foundation for the late war. These feelings were continually gaining ground under the mild and conciliating administration of Lord Minto, who was continually impelled to this moderate course by an anxious wish on the part of the court of directors to preserve peace, and not to increase their territories. It appears that while the British government of India abstained most religiously from encroachment, and made impartial justice the measure and rule of their conduct, the Mahrattas and the Goorkas were meditating an extension of their power, and exciting discontent and rebellion in all the provinces within their influence under British controul.

In the meantime, the Pindarries were secretly encouraged by the Mahratta chiefs, and hordes of them annually overran the fertile plains of our provinces, and those of our immediate allies, carrying destruction along with them, and sparing neither age nor sex. From the reports in the Calcutta Gazette, it appears that they committed the most horrid excesses, "by the indiscriminate butchery of men, women, and children, bearing the latter in triumph on their spikes." No feeling mind could endure the idea of such dreadful irruptions; and the Marquis of Hastings, on assuming the government of India, directed his attention to this subject as one of the utmost importance. The Mahratta states were called upon in vain to restrain those plunderers who passed through their territories to invade the company's, and upon failing to do so, they virtually became parties to their aggressions; but although his lordship was fully aware of the hostile sentiments of the Mahratta chiefs, notwithstanding their cunning evasions and crafty subterfuges, he gave them a full opportunity of re-establishing themselves in his confidence: he signified to them, that his intentions in approaching their dominions with a British army, were only to disable the Pindarries from destroying the harmless peasantry of the defenceless villages. For this purpose his lordship took the field, and his penetrating genius, foreseeing the extensive combination that was to be overcome, he put in motion the grandest British army that the native powers ever saw. Some idea of this force may be afforded by the following extract from an officer's letter, dated Right

Bank of the Jumna, in camp, October 27th, 1817:— "We are now on our march — supposed, in the first instance, to be directed against the fortress of Gwalior, belonging to Scindea. The great object of the campaign, however, is the entire annihilation of the Pindarries. The whole of the army now in the field consists of ten divisions, each of about 10,000 men. We are advancing from the three Presidencies towards the same point, with the finest army ever perhaps heard of in India. The governor-general is with our division, which is about 13,000 strong, with sixty pieces of cannon. The camp followers of this division alone amount to 67,000. For the carriage of the baggage of our regiment, we have 40 elephants and 400 camels; every elephant has two keepers, and every two camels have one. Of us, there are 37 officers present, among whom there are 810; every horse in the regiment has two attendants, one as a groom, the other to provide grass; these alone amount to 1,400, besides 120 for the mess, and 900 for the bazar to supply the provisions; in all, for our regiment alone, about 3,500 followers, besides their wives and children. The Marquis of Hastings travels in a most princely style: he has 150 elephants and 400 camels, besides state elephants splendidly accoutred, having superb solid silver howdahs or castles on their backs. There are now actually 36 rajahs and independent chieftains, of various ranks, on their way to pay their respects to the Marquis. Some of them, indeed, are already in camp."

The Madras army was advancing under Sir Thomas Hislop, while a division of the Bombay force, commanded by Sir William Grant Kerr in Guzerat, and Brigadier-generals Doveton and Smith, with their subsidiaries in the Deckan, co-operated with his lordship in the fine dispositions made to form a grand chain round the Pindarries, leaving no hope of escape. Previous to this, as before noticed, the Peishwa had been forced to give security for his conduct, having been detected in attempts to excite the Mahratta chiefs to war, and in endeavours to corrupt the native troops. In consequence of this treacherous conduct, it was thought expedient to show him that he had something to lose in forfeiting the friendship of the East India company, whose hand had replaced him on his throne when driven into exile by Holkar. Therefore, as a deserved punishment for breach of faith, a treaty was forced upon him at the point of the bayonet. By this he ceded to the British government territories yielding a clear revenue of thirty-four lacks of rupees (being nearly the half of his gross income) or £480,000 per annum. Of this revenue, £300,000 were attached to the presidency of Bombay, and secured by the cession of that tract of the Koncan, about eighty miles in extent, lying between Demaun and Panwell. The occupation of Bassein and Jambosen, with their dependencies, was also transferred to the company, together with the Peishwa's share of tribute from Kattywar. The remaining £180,000 were appropriated to the Madras presidency, and provided for by cessions of territory in the Carnatic, together with the forts of Darwar and Kishelgur. Ahmednuggar was also ceded with 2,000 yards around it, and a considerable tract of pasture lands for the troops in the Deckan. On the part of the company, it was agreed that the subsidiary force should be augmented to 12,000 men; and with respect to the Peishwa, that he should maintain 8,000 irregular horse and foot, to be officered by Europeans.

On the good faith of this treaty, Brigadier-general Smith (for he had now local rank) marched from Seroor, leaving part of his force at Poonah, and having crossed the Godavery at Toka, encamped near the passes of Unkee Tunkee. But in a few days the non-arrival of the Bombay dawk filled every one with alarm for the safety of those at Poonah. As soon as General Smith found that all communication was actually cut off, he made forced marches back, fully assured from the above circumstance, and from the appearance of parties of Mahratta horse hovering about, that hostilities had commenced. On arriving at Seroor, they found all the cantonment in a state of apprehension. Various reports of the destruction of the detachment at Poonah having reached them, they were making active preparations against an expected attack. The hills commanding the lines were fortified, and the ladies and families had been placed for security in the theatre, which lay under a strong battery erected on one of its heights. All the roads to the cantonments were rendered impracticable for horse, and every precaution was taken that the safety of the place required. Under these circumstances the general sent all the families under a strong escort to Ahmednuggar, and proceeded immediately to Poonah.

His little force consisted of one regiment of European infantry, three battalions of sepoys, with a proportion of horse and foot artillery, a battering train, and a complement of pioneers, but unfortunately the only cavalry were a small body of irregulars under Captain Spiller, recently organized agreeably to the late treaty, for two regiments of Madras cavalry that had been attached to him were sent to reinforce General Doveton, whose division was in advance. The total effective with General Smith consisted of about 3,000 fighting men, the remainder of his force being at Poonah, Seroor, and Ahmednuggar. Previous to leaving Seroor, the enemy had appeared, and carried off some of the commissariat cattle from the vicinity. About twelve miles on the high road to Poonah, a very considerable body of horse, estimated at 5,000, appeared on the right flank. As it seemed to be their intention to cut off the commissariat, the horse artillery were wheeled to protect that department, and after receiving some shots, the enemy retired in confusion, when Captain Spiller, at the head of his irregulars, charged their rear with great gallantry, and cut several to pieces with his own hand, but in this brave dash against such superior numbers, he narrowly escaped with his life, having received a spear wound in his cheek, near the eye. On reaching the ground of encampment at Kunderpore, they found the European bungalow erected for travellers in flames, the enemy having set it on fire, and from the heights they saw their rear-guard closely engaged with the enemy, who cut through the baggage, and wounded several of the camp followers, who had left Seroor in a very straggling manner, notwithstanding orders to the contrary, and arrangements for their protection. The knapsacks of two companies of the 65th regiment were taken, and the whole loss of baggage and grain in the force was very considerable. Colonel Milnes commanded the rear-guard, and had an arduous day's march; he did not arrive till near sun-set, having been engaged with the enemy, and marching and countermarching from ten o'clock until he reached camp. The want of regular cavalry was greatly felt. The force marched next morning in much more compact order, forming a sort of hollow square round the park and baggage. Very large bodies of horse appeared on their flanks and rear, pressing closely, but the discharge of cannon from different parts of the line forced those assailants to recede with loss. Having crossed the Beema about twelve o'clock, they encamped near it. The villages were deserted and every thing belonging to Europeans was destroyed; the guard-house over the ferry boats was burnt, and the bungalow for travellers reduced to ashes. Various accounts had reached them respecting the force at Poonah. By one which they had reason to credit, the detachment had been cut to pieces, and according to another, great loss had been sustained; but it was certain that, with due allowance for native exaggeration, a serious attack had been made upon Mr. Elphinstone by the treacherous Peishwa.

When the force moved next day the enemy appeared in great strength in their front, and having posted themselves on the heights of Lonee, two low ridges through which lies the high road to Poonah, forming a kind of long pass where a good defence might be made, it was generally believed that they would fight. The summits of these ridges were covered with bodies of infantry, and the plain was black with solid divisions of Mahratta cavalry. Against these their little column boldly advanced, and the flankers and riflemen in front were sharply attacked with a fire from matchlocks, while great numbers of rockets were discharged at the line, which falling among the baggage, for a few moments caused confusion, and inflicted terrible wounds. The enemy had also some small gingals mounted on camels, which were fired from distant heights;

but the fine effect of the horse artillery that gallopped to the flanks and front as occasion required, and threw shells with great precision among them, with frequent discharges of grape, soon dispersed them. From the rapid retreats of their masses of horse when the shells broke among them, their loss seemed considerable, but knowing their opponents deficiency in cavalry, they continued all day to harass them, but without doing much injury. The fatigue and exposure to a burning sun during the day were dreadful; it was four o'clock before the force gained sight of Poonah, where they had the satisfaction of beholding the British flag, near the village of Kirkee, while the Mahratta camp extended an immense way behind the Parbutta, to avoid which it was necessary to make a detour. Soon after, however, they were met by the light battalion, and Major Cunningham's irregular horse, and about sun-set encamped near their companions, from whom they learned the particulars of an attack that had been made upon them on the 5th, by Gockla, the Peishwa's commander-in-chief.

Immediately after the departure of General Smith from Seroor, the Peishwa resumed his military preparations, and his attempts to corrupt the fidelity of the company's native troops. His highness had secretly brought into the city large bodies of Arabs from his forts, and his vassal chiefs were every day joining him with reinforcements of horse. Under these circumstances the British camp and artillery were posted advantageously near the ruined village of Kirkee, in a bend of the river which protected its flanks and rear, being very rocky with steep banks, and in that part almost unfordable.

Mr. Elphinstone, as soon as he perceived these hostile indications, pressed for satisfactory explanation, and on the morning of the 5th November, having received a most insolent answer from his highness, and observing an armed force approaching the sungum, he and his suite and guards made their escape to camp. In a few minutes the British residency was in a blaze, and all his valuable property, manuscripts, and oriental curiosities, valued at upwards of 80,000 rupees, were either plundered or consumed. At the same time the European cantonments, the beauty of which has been noticed, were set on fire and entirely destroyed, and the Peishwa's army collected in and about Poonah, estimated at 15,000 cavalry and 8,000 infantry, approached the British position in battle array. A Portuguese named Pinto, who held the rank of major in the Peishwa's service, commanded a battalion of infantry organized in the European style, and his park of artillery, consisting of 14 guns, were served by Portuguese. One of the officers described the approach of this formidable host to Thoughtless, by comparing it to the waves of an angry sea, assuring him that the divisions seemed to follow each other in endless succession as far as the eye could reach, while all the heights were covered with elephants bearing the Peishwa and his great officers of state, who came out to witness the certain destruction of the force at Kirkee.

Opposed to this, Colonel Burr of the company's service, who commanded, had only the Bombay European infantry, a detachment of recruits belonging to the 65th regiment, two battalions of sepoys, with a proportion of European artillerymen, and a detachment of irregular horse, in all about 3,000 fighting men. With this small but firm little band, he advanced to meet the shock. The attack began with a dreadful discharge of artillery on both sides, and an attempt by the enemy's infantry to make an impression on his line, which was soon followed by a tremenduous charge of their cavalry. In a body they pushed directly for the Europeans; but receiving a cool and deliberate fire, turned and forced their way through the 7th Bombay native infantry, and these brave sepoys were for some time intermixed among them, and fought nobly with their bayonets. Large masses of the cavalry got into the rear, and the engagement became very critical, depending in a great measure on the steadiness of the Europeans in the right wing, who were quite unbroken. Just at the proper moment Major Ford, who commanded the Peishwa's brigade, arrived with his men from the cantonments at Dapore, and opening a well-directed fire upon the masses of the enemy that had got into the rear, struck a panic to their hearts, which was communicated to the whole, for they retreated in the utmost confusion, leaving vast numbers of dead on the field, and never after dared to hazard a renewal of the fight.

Colonel Burr, in his report of this engagement, stated that "Mr. Elphinstone most gallantly exerted himself throughout the day in setting a distinguished example of zeal and animation to the troops." Indeed, it appeared that British valour so completely astonished the Peishwa, that he made his escape from the battle, and that it was with the greatest difficulty his commander-in-chief persuaded him from setting off direct for the fortress of Poorundar.

During this sanguinary action, for the enemy lost about five hundred men, though the casualties were on Colonel Burr's part only one officer and fifty soldiers, the ladies of this part of the force were in the village of Kirkee, which had been fortified in a temporary manner for their protection, and their situation during the agonizing suspense and tremendous fire that was kept up for a considerable time, may be more easily conceived than described.

The Peishwa's conduct roused a strong suspicion in the mind of every one, that all the Mahratta chiefs had confederated and agreed to make simultaneous attacks on the British forces in their vicinity, in the hope of destroying the army in detail; and there was reason to conclude, that nothing would prevent Scindea from supporting the common cause, but the wise and effectual measures of the Marquis of Hastings. From the blood-thirsty and treacherous manner in which the war was commenced on the part of the Peishwa, and which left him no shadow of hope for reconciliation, it was assumed that he confidently relied on the combination of which he was a part as sufficiently powerful to aninhilate the British. Every thing in his dominions within the power of his troops, that bore the name of European, was destroyed, and the houses of private individuals were razed to their very foundations. Lieutenant Vaughan of the 15th Madras N. I., and his brother of the marine service, were taken at Karlee, on their way to join the army, dragged along almost naked by their barbarous murderers to Tullygaum, where they were hanged; and the resentment of the soldiers was raised to the highest pitch, by a report that one of the brothers had been forced to execute the other. A small escort of sepoys, with Lieutenants Hunter and Morrison of the Madras corps, were also attacked on their way to join, and forced to surrender. The sepoys were cut to pieces, and the officers carried off to a strong hill fort. No doubt it was the intention to destroy them in the event of the war being successful, and indeed their lives were only spared through the remonstrances made by Mr. Elphinstone upon the murder of the Vaughans.

General Smith encamped exactly before the Mahrattas, the river Moota Moola running beween, and the village of Yellara, which is situated near the bank, under a height which was called Picket Hill, being on his side, with a fine plain extending for near a mile to the enemy's lines on the other bank. The river was, however, very rocky and difficult to pass, having deep banks, and being lined with Arabs. From the hill he had a full view of the position occupied by the Peishwa, who had the city of Poonah on his left, whence his line extended to Harris's tope, having encamped on the ground where the British cantonments had stood. His army, drawn up in front of their tents, which seemed to be two miles in length and a mile in depth, appeared prodigious; from the amazing masses and groups of horse and foot within view, it was estimated that upwards of one hundred thousand persons were assembled, and of this concourse thirty thousand were fighting men.

Thoughtless, in reflecting upon what he saw and heard, was much at a loss to account for the conduct of the Peishwa, who, considering it a hopeless undertaking again to attack Colonel Burr, nevertheless remained near Poonah in a position backed by a chain of high hills, affording no retreat but through difficult passes, while an enemy, flushed with success, and inflamed with resentment, was approaching to attack him. In short, Charles expected that the force would have been immediately led against the enemy, with the certainty of complete success; he inferred that the Peishwa had committed a fatal error by awaiting the junction of General Smith's division with that of Colonel Burr, and that after his failure at Kirkee, his real interests demanded a retreat from Poonah into the plains of the Deckan, where his numerous cavalry would have been useful in harassing a pursuing enemy, and in keeping up the spirits of his confederates. As he had not adopted this course, Charles considered that his army must be inevitably destroyed by a spirited attack on his camp in such an unfavourable situation and in such peculiar circumstances. Consequently his surprise and disappointment were great, upon witnessing the operations of General Smith after his junction with the force at Kirkee.

On the following morning, proper reconnoissances having been made, some guns were placed on Picket Hill, which swept the banks of the river with grape shot, for the purpose of enabling a party to examine the fords; but the Arabs having good cover, rendered it impossible to effect the purpose with accuracy. The whole force attempted about midnight to pass them, but it being found impracticable in the dark, the attempt, after fruitless endeavours, was abandoned. During the whole of the day there was constant skirmishing between the Arabs and riflemen, which produced a very great display of personal bravery, for the Arabs crossed the river, and several of them lost their lives in a daring attack upon Captain Clutterbuck and part of the light company of the 65th regiment. In the course of the ensuing day, the horse artillery and riflemen having cleared the banks of the river, the force was formed into two divisions, one of which, under Lieutenant-colonel Milnes, about 3 o'clock in the evening, crossed a ford near the village of Yellara, with all the field pieces, and took up a position on the bank, immediately in front of the right of the enemy's camp, notwithstanding the opposition of the whole of his infantry and Arabs, who charged several times to the very bayonets. The Peishwa's batteries kept up a tremendous cannonade on the ford and on the troops, as they were forming, which was continued until nine o'clock, all the while briskly returned by our guns. The Bombay regiment suffered a good deal, and the casualties in the division were considerable. The wounds were nearly all from cannon shot, and were terrible to behold; some of the soldiers were literally crushed to pieces by the discharge of a cannon carrying shot of one hundred pounds weight.

Colonel Milnes gained well-earned honour and praise by a display of coolness and judgment seldom surpassed. While he was crossing the river the shot flew about him like a shower of hail, yet he asked Lieutenant Farquharson, his brigade quarter-master, playfully, "What are those whistling about us?" (" And Farquharson," said Thoughtless, " do you think the Colonel had Charles the 12th in his mind at that time?" " I really do not know," replied he, " but he seemed as unconcerned as I do now.") It was reported that Colonel Milnes, after repulsing the repeated charges of the enemy, sent an aide-de-camp to General Smith for orders, and offered to take the camp with his division, but this was declined, and he was directed to bivouac on the bank of the river during the night. The other divisions lay on their arms, under Picket Hill, having sent all their camp equipage to the village of Kirkee, and before day-light next morning, they crossed the river at the sungum, and formed line on the right of Colonel Milnes, when the whole advanced to attack the Mahratta camp. Bodies of horse appeared in the front which were cleared away by a cannonade from the horse artillery. The morning was just peeping over the mountains when the British line approached the Mahratta tents, and the 65th regiment was exactly opposite to that part from which the batteries had blazed the evening before. Mr. Elphinstone, accompanied by his assistants Mr. Russel and Captain Pottinger, with General Smith and all his staff, were behind the colours. A dead silence prevailed. The dooly bearers thought they saw lighted matches in front, and ran precipitately to one flank, while our artillery fired under an impression that the enemy's guns were about to open upon them. All the staff pressed closely towards the 65th. "Gentlemen," said Major Warren, who commanded the regiment, "keep back; you are preventing me from seeing my men;" for he was as coolly attentive to the preservation of a good line as he would have been on parade, though he expected every moment to storm the batteries, at the first blaze of a cannon. "They are off," said Mr. Elphinstone. "I fear they are," said General Smith; and the smoke clearing away the light discovered that the Peishwa had fled with his army, leaving a great part of his camp standing. The distant hills were covered with his followers and baggage, but a large body of his cavalry appeared in the rear, and threatened to charge the line. The guns were turned upon them, and they wheeled in great confusion at full gallop round the right flank and escaped. General Smith pursued the fugitives across the enemy's camp to the bottom of the hills; but having no means of following them with effect, he soon returned to invest Poonah. The Mahratta camp was covered with dead and dying men, horses, and bullocks, from the effects of the cannonade the evening before, and it presented a most melancholy sight to a feeling mind. With the exception of the large unwieldy cannon before noticed, the Peishwa carried away all his guns with him, and effected his retreat over the little Bore Ghaut into the plains south of Poonah; which city, being left with only a small garrison to defend it, was surrendered in the course of the day, and the British flag was hoisted on the palace under a royal salute.

Thoughtless could not conceive what had induced General Smith to fight the battle of Poonah with one half of his force, and when the victory was gained, why he did not push on and reap all the advantages of it, instead of affording the enemy an opportunity to escape during the night. Powerful motives, no doubt, suggested the line of conduct pursued by the general, who undoubtedly possesses talent and genius. He was anxious, perhaps, to save the effusion of human blood, which might be the consequence of a rash attack upon an enemy so vastly superior in numbers. Acquainted as he was by experience with the obstinately daring courage of the Arabs, four thousand of whom were with the Peishwa, he might be justly apprehensive of the risk to be run in attacking them on ground peculiarly suited to their habits of warfare, being intersected with numerous ruins and hedges, affording them good cover; and no doubt a contest to dislodge them would have been sanguinary, urged to fight, as they would have been, by the powerful motive of securing a retreat for their master and his army. Moreover, it was the object of both Mr. Elphinstone and General Smith to preserve the city of Poonah from plunder and destruction, which a rash battle in its immediate vicinity might have occasioned. Those magnificent praises which Sir Thomas Hislop bestowed upon General Smith for "*the wisdom of his plans, the gallantry and valour displayed in their execution, and the decision and promptitude with which his attack of the enemy's lines was arranged, and their dispersion and overthrow effected by a perseverance and determined courage which have never been surpassed,*" were perhaps in every respect measured by strict justice. In their consequences, every thing conduced to the public good; but if the other Mahratta chiefs had succeeded in their treacherous designs, and formed a junction with the Peishwa, the organized state of his army, the vast treasure he had collected, and his mighty influence, address, and persuasive power might have produced very injurious results, which a more dashing mode of warfare at Poonah would have prevented. Success is not always the criterion of able conduct. To judge properly of any enterprize, it is necessary to consider not only what it effected, but also what it did not effect, and moreover to look at what might have taken place if possible events had ensued, according to the calculation of one of the contending parties. But it is really with deference, doubt, humility, respect, and on nearly all other points admiration for General Smith, that the emotions passing in the soul of Charles Thoughtless on the above occasion are here offered to professional men.

Two officers and eighty-five non-commissioned officers and soldiers were killed and wounded during these operations; but not less than 1,500 of the enemy were destroyed.

CHAP. XXIV.

Say what is man? From infancy he grows,
And as he ripens, various beauty shows—
He stores the ready and capacious mind
With what the flood of time has left behind.
But when become the Mentor of his day,
The skilful pilot of life's rocky bay,
In hoary age beneath the silent sod
He rests, till called before the throne of God.
How vain the toil to hoard up crores of wealth,
Man's cup of joy is competence and health,
In rural ease to smile dull care away,
And taste the good of every fleeting day.

After the capture of Poonah, proclamations were issued to the inhabitants, and circulated as widely over the country as possible, to counteract the inflammatory and false publications of the Peishwa. The inhabitants were taken under British protection, and assured that they would be maintained in their rights, in the possession of their property, and in the free exercise of their religious customs and ceremonies. A great deal of public property was found in Poonah, and the Peishwa's arsenal was well furnished with military stores. Prize agents were appointed to dispose of the captured property, and arrangements both civil and military were speedily made for the government and protection of the place. Lieutenant-colonel Burr, with 200 Europeans and four native battalions, was appointed to remain there in command; and the remainder of the force, consisting of the 2d Madras cavalry, which had joined from J-aulna the day after the city was taken, two European regiments, four native battalions, with horse and foot artillery and pioneers, was formed into three brigades for field service. Two guns and 300 sepoys, under Captain Watson of the Bombay establishment, were sent off to open the communication with the presidency. General Smith having learned that part of the enemy had encamped under Synghur, a detachment was sent thither on the night of the 19th, which about daylight next morning completely surprised them, and took their camp and guns under a tremendous fire from the fort of Synghur, which, however, did not injure the detachment, for the cannon could not be depressed sufficiently, and the shot flew over their heads. Prize property to a vast amount was taken, consisting of pearls and diamonds; it is supposed that the merchants of Poonah had sent their valuable articles thither for safety. Many of the soldiers enriched themselves with plunder, and during several days were carrying hats full of pearls, jewels, and gold ornaments about for sale, without knowing their real value, being anxious to exchange them for money or hoondies on Bombay, ere the prize agents should discover that they possessed such valuable plunder. Six guns and a great quantity of ammunition were taken; the former were spiked, and in blowing up the latter, Lieutenants

Willock and Johnston, of the horse artillery, with five men, were dreadfully burnt by an accident in the explosion.

The force marched in pursuit of the Peishwa on the 22d November, and on the next day, with some difficulty, the guns were got over the little Bore Ghaut; the pass being steep, would have afforded an opportunity for making a fine stand, but no enemy appeared. This range of mountains passes near Poonah from the great western chain, and continues in an easterly direction for several miles. The inhabitants are called Ramoosies, and, like the Bheels in other parts, are the aborigines, who were driven from the plains by the Mahomedan conquerors and the Mahrattas. They have ever since maintained a sort of independence, living by plunder, but observing strict honour with respect to those travellers who claim and pay for their protection in passing through this mountainous region.

Next day a halt was found necessary in order to get the baggage over the ghaut; but on the 25th, the force marched 24 miles on the road to Sattara. At about half that distance is situated the considerable town of J-ajooree, with a superb pagoda on a high rock of granite in its vicinity. This structure is of modern date, having been built by the grandfather of the great Holkar, but it is in high estimation among the Mahrattas, and is supported by a considerable revenue. Its exterior is very grand, having a flight of steps cut out of the rock near a quarter of a mile in length, over which are several curious triumphal arches placed at intervals, as distinguishing the main entrance. These arches are ornamented with figures, and connected by a row of pillars along each side, which, during the festival, are illuminated with thousands of lamps, so that all night the hill appears to the distant country quite in a blaze. Soon after passing this pagoda, the enemy's cavalry appeared in great force on both flanks; and General Smith, with the horse artillery, and the 2d, accompanied by Mr. Elphinstone and suite, and all the staff, pursued them for several miles. The body which appeared on the right suffered the general to approach within gun-shot, and they appeared drawn up in good order behind a nullah, but as soon as this obstacle was crossed, and the artillery opened upon them, they scampered off in great confusion. Some camels loaded with rockets were taken, and a few prisoners made whose horses had been killed; they stated that the Peishwa was at Sattara with 25,000 fighting men. The country through which the force marched from the little Bore Ghaut to the Nera river was uncommonly fine, with many lovely valleys in high cultivation, and in a military point of view remarkably strong by nature. The enemy pressed, during the latter part of the march, closely upon the rear and the baggage, but they were kept off by constant discharges of cannon, which induced General Smith to return with the cavalry, and the infantry were so much delayed by frequent halts, that it was night before the force crossed the bridge over the Nera, which the enemy did not attempt to destroy. About 13 miles south of the fine valley of this river a chain of ghauts runs eastward from the western mountains, through which there is a long and difficult pass at Salpee, on the high road to Sattara. Narra Punt and Napunker, two of the Peishwa's most resolute sirdars, determined to oppose General Smith at the head of this pass, and posted large bodies of cavalry on the table land, a beautiful plain, with rocket men and sharpshooters on the sides of the declivities through which the road winds. General Smith expected to be attacked here, and made judicious arrangements. He pushed forward riflemen and light infantry, and sent flanking parties along the mountains; they clambered over the cliffs and dislodged the enemy, who, however, continued from the head of the pass to rockade the line, till the horse artillery gained the summit and dispersed them. They left their dead on the field of contention, and retired slowly over a most beautiful plain bounded by hill forts, finely watered by silver streams, branches of the Kisthna, enlivened with numerous villages, and smiling with all the charms of luxuriant cultivation. The crops were now in full bloom, and it was melancholy to see the labours of the husbandman destroyed by the lords of the soil in ambitious contention. On this plain Gockla drew up several times across the road, and it was estimated that the three divisions with him were 20,000 strong, but they constantly gave way upon receiving a few shots or shells from the artillery, for they had none to return, and it was consequently a murderous warfare on their part. Yet such superiority in numbers was not without effect. They covered the whole plain, attacked in front, flank, and rear, and every five minutes forced the line to halt for the rear-guard, thus frequently forced to fire grape at them. In short, General Smith had to fight for the ground on which he encamped almost every day, till the Peishwa, retreating southward with the family of the Sattara Rajah, whose person it was his interest to have near him, got several marches in advance; but upon hearing that a British force was approaching from Darwar under General Pritzler, he left the banks of the Kisthna, and moved northward.

The scenery in the vicinity of Sattara was most enchanting. The horizon presented a more or less distant variety of hills capped with forts and crowded with men. Clear rivulets meandered through the vallies, covered with clumps of fruit trees, and charming villages built of stone and lime, neatly tiled, and without fortifications, altogether presenting an image of security and rural happiness such as would please the eye even in England. They were full of inhabitants, who were quite ready to assist either party, and the seniors came out to offer their cock and rupee to General Smith as soon as the Mahrattas had retired. The cock is laid at the feet of a conqueror as an emblem of a brave people at the mercy of their invader, and the rupee is at once an offer of tribute and a claim for protection. Both parties afforded them all possible security, and placed guards over their towns, but still they were plundered and ruined by the villanous followers of both armies, one of whom General Smith hanged in this valley for tearing the rings out of the ears and nose of a woman; one half of the vagabonds that followed the camp were flogged for robbing the gardens and sugar plantations near the line of march, and even unroofing the houses for fire-wood. Soon after passing Sattara, General Smith changed his direction, and marched on the high road to Punderpore. The enemy opposed him every day, and kept the troops exposed to the burning sun from morning till night, so that it was generally seven o'clock in the evening before their tents were pitched, and their lips and noses suffered exceeding pain from the scorching rays darting directly on their faces.

It would be tedious to detail the march from day to day, as it continued for a considerable time with little variation, the enemy making every exertion to retard the pursuit of General Smith, while he strained each nerve to overtake the Peishwa. The mode of warfare adopted by Gockla was that which it seems he ought to have chosen immediately after the failure of attack on the force at Kirkee; for by it he veteranized his cavalry, and harassed General Smith exceedingly, who often exposed himself to great danger in the skirmishes which daily occurred. On the 3d of December a post arrived from Bombay, after the force had reached the ground of encampment near Meharee, and a royal salute announced that treaties of alliance had been concluded with Dowlat Row Scindeah and Newab Meer Kaun. On the 7th they encamped near Punderpore, where the rear-guard was completely surrounded by the enemy, and General Smith, upon seeing it closely pressed, had gallopped to it with his staff, accompanied by Mr. Elphinstone and suit, escorted by a troop of the 2d cavalry, so that for some time they were separated from the line. Their danger was imminent; for, one of their guns being upset, the Mahrattas raised a loud shout and charged with spirit, but drew off again upon receiving a volley from the infantry. The general's orderly dragoon was shot. Captain Grant had a ball through his hat, and Mr. Pottinger one in his holsters. In short, Captain Hardcastle, upon being dispatched to the line for reinforcements, had to gallop for his life through the enemy, who might have destroyed the rear-guard, the general, with Mr. Elphinstone, and the whole staff of the division, if they had pressed forward when they charged. Punderpore stands on the left bank of the Beema. It is a large town, but the country around it is poor, and nearly all the villages are in ruins. The pagodas of the sacred bathing place support a great number of Brahmins. Mr. Elphinstone here received the official account of the treacherous attack made by the Rajah of Berar on the subsidiary force near Nagpore, which was fortunately repulsed by Colonel Scott, though with the severe loss, on his part, of four officers and 300 men killed and wounded.

The direction in which the Peishwa retreated enabled General Smith to continue the pursuit by way of Seroor, where he determined to leave the battering train, which greatly impeded his advance, it being necessary to cut roads for the heavy guns. Gockla opposed him at the fords of the Nera, Beema, and Gore rivers, but being without artillery he only exposed his cavalry to certain destruction, and the havock made in their dense masses by shot and shells was so great, that the ground was covered in many places with dead bodies of men and horses. On the 17th December the force reached Seroor, and the carriage cattle were so much exhausted by continued marching, that it was found necessary to change many of them. For twenty-one days they had moved at the average of fifteen miles, engaged with the enemy from morning till night. The cavalry were nearly broken down by excessive fatigue, but the infantry were in high spirits; there were very few sick in the force, and indeed the general health of the Europeans seemed much improved by this severe service and exposure to the sun. At this place the general lost no time in equipping his division as a light field force, and in pursuing the enemy northward. He marched to the westward of Ahmednuggur, and crossed the Pera river at Colaur, keeping along the left bank to Sungumneer, through a fine valley, with hills on the right, left, and front; thence to the bottom of the Warsowa Pass the country was rich in an extreme degree, studded with villages and towns, and covered with luxuriant fields of wheat, hemp, gram, sugar-cane and jewarry. Over this fine region the Peishwa's army had moved, like a flight of locusts, destroying all in their way; it was now doomed to further injury from the march of the British force.

On the table land of this chain of mountains, his highness the Peishwa had been encamped for some days, and he was joined at this place by Trimbuckgee Danglae, with a reinforcement of Arabs and Bheels. Some of the northern sirdars had also increased his ranks, and it was reported that he had with him four thousand Arabs, about the same number of other infantry, four six-pounders, and 30,000 horse. General Smith made arrangements to ascend the Warsowa ghaut, which is a long and very difficult pass that might have been easily defended. The Peishwa had broken up the roads, and it required a whole day to remove the obstacles, during which time he retreated on the high road leading to Poonah with his whole army.

General Smith knowing the difficulties of the road he had taken, pursued him with only the horse artillery, 2d cavalry, the 65th regiment, the 1st of 2d N. I. and pioneers, leaving the remainder of his force with Colonel Boles to follow leisurely, for he naturally felt some apprehension for Seroor and Poonah. About ten miles from Warsowa there is another ghaut of very difficult ascent, called Manhulla, up which the guns were dragged by the men. The town of Barramwarra is situated on the table land of this romantic mountain, and near it the Peishwa's army had encamped, and paid the last honours to the son of Gockla, a fine young man of twenty years of age. The natives assured Thoughtless that his wife, about fifteen years of age, and of great beauty, performed suttee with his body. From this town, which was in a very ruined state, Charles had a fine view of those vast ranges of ghauts, on the highest table land of which he now stood. No country in the world can be stronger for defensive warfare than this part of the Deckan. It appears as if it had been once an entire table land, though now broken into hills and ridges of rocks, as if all the soft parts had been washed away by the flood. The hills are of most fantastic shapes, many of them are isolated, and the little valleys are in full cultivation. From this height the force descended into the plain of Wuttoor, by a pass which is long and difficult. At the bottom of it there is a very neat dhurrumsallah, with a fine well for travellers, and the town of Wuttoor, situated near it, appeared in a very flourishing state. The force encamped there late in the evening of the last day in the year 1817, and Charles Thoughtless laid his weary head on his pillow, after breakfasting on beefsteaks at supper time, and uttering a soldier's short prayer: "O God, I thank thee with all my heart and soul for thy protection during the past year."

From Wuttoor to Kullum, a large town on the Gore river, the distance is twenty miles, which they marched the following day, and about two o'clock next morning proceeded through a romantic glen with several *warries* belonging to the Bheels; having crossed the Beema at the town of Keir. On approaching the fort of Chakoon the guns of it opened upon them, but they defiled out of their range and encamped near it. Serious apprehensions were now entertained that an attack had been made on Poonah, for a continued cannonade had been heard during the march from Wuttoor in that direction. Here General Smith received intelligence of the march of the second of the 1st Bombay native infantry from Seroor, by desire of Colonel Burr, to reinforce him at Poonah against the approach of the Peishwa, but this corps was intercepted at Koragaum, and nearly cut to pieces. Upon hearing a confused rumour of this disaster from the natives, General Smith marched for the scene of reported contention, and Thoughtless there beheld a most melancholy sight; the streets of the village were choked up with dead Arabs, swelled to a prodigious size by the heat of the sun, and the plain around was covered with putrifying carcases of men, horses, camels, and bullocks, so that the stench was intolerable. The soldiers were digging up the ruins of the houses for the Europeans that had been killed, thirteen of whose bodies were laid out near a grave which the pioneers were making, while the officers of the force were searching for their deceased friends. Of those who had been in the action not one remained on the spot alive to relate the particulars. All was a scene of death and desolation. The substantial stone houses were demolished by cannon shot, and many of them burning, having been set on fire seemingly in the struggle of the contending parties to possess them. In the course of the following day, General Smith received the official report of this action, which he justly pronounced in his orders on the subject to be one of the most brilliant examples of gallantry and perseverance recorded in our Indian annals. From that report, and from private accounts afterwards communicated to Thoughtless by several of the survivors, the particulars here stated were collected.

A detachment, consisting of a detail of Madras artillery and two six-pounders of the second battalion 1st Bombay native infantry about 600 strong, and 300 auxiliary horse, the whole under Captain Staunton of the company's service, marched from

Seroor for Poonah at 8 P. M. 31st December, and reached the heights overlooking Koragaum, about ten in the forenoon of the 1st January, whence the whole of the Peishwa's army, estimated 30,000 horse and eight thousand infantry, were discovered in the plain south of the Beema. To retreat before such masses of cavalry was impossible. The officers with Captain Staunton were Lieutenant Chisholm and Assistant-surgeon Wiley of the Madras artillery, Lieutenant and Adjutant Pattinson, and Lieutenant Conlon second of 1st regiment, and Lieutenant Jones of the 10th Bombay N. I., doing duty with that corps, the assistant-surgeon in charge of it Mr. Wingate, and Lieutenant Swanston in command of the auxiliary horse. These gentlemen formed a circle on the heights of Koragaum around their commander, and it was debated what course should be pursued for the preservation and honour of the detachment in the perilous situation in which they found themselves. For such a handful of men to remain in the plain was certain destruction, to retreat was equally dangerous, and only two alternatives presented the shadow of hope, for the idea of cutting their way to Poonah through the Peishwa's army was out of the question. The village of Koragaum, with several strong houses and inclosures, lay half a mile before them on the left bank of the Beema, while a strong height difficult of approach for cavalry was a little way on their right, but without water or cover for the men.

Captain Staunton moved therefore upon the village with the intention of occupying it, and had scarcely succeeded in reaching it with his detachment when he was attacked in the most determined manner by three divisions of the Peishwa's best infantry, supported by immense bodies of horse and the fire of two pieces of artillery. The enemy's troops were animated to the utmost exertions by the presence of the Peishwa on a distant height, attended by all the principal Mahratta chiefs, who flattered his highness with the prospect of witnessing the destruction of this gallant handful of British troops.

Impressed with terror at the intrepidity of the European character, the Peishwa, on seeing Captain Staunton advance down the heights of Koragaum, exclaimed to Gockla, who had offered to cross the river and attack the detachment, "They are coming to attack us!" But on perceiving that the advance guard was making towards the village, he permitted the Arabs to plunge into the Beema, and endeavour to gain possession of it before the British, and they succeeded in posting themselves in the strongest parts of it, from which it was found impossible to dislodge them, and the contest for the remainder was obstinately continued from noon till nine P. M. During that time almost every pagoda and house had been repeatedly taken and retaken, and one of the guns for several minutes was in possession of the enemy. The detachment was placed in the most trying situation at this period; nearly the whole of the artillerymen and about one-third of the infantry and auxiliary horse were killed or wounded. From the exertions which the European officers had been called upon to make in leading their men to frequent charges with the bayonet, their numbers also were diminished. Lieutenant Chisholm was no more, having fallen under several wounds. Mr. Assistant-surgeon Wingate was also killed. His right arm was broken in a charge on the Arabs, in which he and Lieutenant Conlan, who was also wounded, were made prisoners, and thrust into a pagoda of which the enemy had possession. Mr. Wingate there dressed his own arm, but a few moments after Lieutenants Swanston and Pattinson charged the Arabs, and Mr. Wingate having evinced a desire to escape was stabbed in the breast and expired, but Conlan was rescued. The two brave officers who led the men on in this desperate attempt were wounded, but Pattinson could not remain inactive while able to wield his sword, and he joined in other charges which cost him his life. Only Captain Staunton, Lieutenant Jones and Mr. Assistant-surgeon Wiley then remained, nearly exhausted, to direct the efforts of the remaining part of the force, who were almost frantic from the want of water, and the unparalleled exertions they had made throughout the day without any sort of refreshment, after a fatiguing march of twenty-six miles. But under cover of the night they were enabled to procure a supply of water, and at nine P.M. the enemy was forced to abandon the village, after sustaining an immense loss in killed and wounded.

"The British character," said General Smith, "was nobly supported throughout the whole of this arduous contest by the European officers and the small detachment of Madras artillery. The medical officers also led the sepoys to charges with the bayonet, the nature of the contest not admitting of their attending to their professional duties; and in such a struggle the presence of a single European was of the utmost consequence, and seemed to inspire the native soldiers with the usual confidence of success. At day-light on the 2d, the enemy was still in sight, but did not renew the attack, although it prevented the troops, whose ammunition was nearly expended, from receiving either a supply of that or provisions." In fact, it was the rapid march of the light division from Wuttoor which obliged the Peishwa to retreat over the little Bore ghaut, but of this the detachment at Koragaum was entirely ignorant. Upon seeing the enemy march southward, Captain Staunton considered his further advance towards Poonah impracticable. He buried his dead in the best manner possible, under the ruins of the houses which the cannonade of the enemy had destroyed, and made preparations for returning to Seroor. The tents were torn and converted into slings for the wounded soldiers, and with the aid of those who escaped, and the few bullocks and horses that remained, he marched during the night of the 2d, and reached Seroor at 12 o'clock in the forenoon of the 3d, having had no refreshment since the 31st December. He brought in nearly all the wounded, and both the guns and colours of the regiment, which the Arab chiefs had vainly hoped to present as trophies to the Peishwa; and by his brave and determined conduct deserved all the praises and honours which followed this brilliant example of noble exertion and exemplary patience under every species of privation.

Finding that the Peishwa had moved southward, in which direction General Pritzler was ready to take up the pursuit, General Smith marched for Seroor to replenish his commissariat, where royal salutes were fired on the 7th January for the battle of Maidenpore, gained by his excellency General Sir Thomas Hislop on the 21st December, over the army of Muller Row Holkar; for the battle of Nagpore, won a few days before it by Brigadier-general Doveton; and for the subsequent surrender of that city to the British troops. Here also Thoughtless learned that the Pindarries were nearly exterminated by the various attacks made upon them, and that Sir John Malcolm was following up the advantages gained with brilliant success, so that hope began to cheer him with the expectation of soon being enabled, by general peace, to return home. On the 8th January, however, information reached General Smith, that General Pritzler had turned the Peishwa, and gained some advantages by successful charges made by the 22d dragoons. He marched therefore with the light division, leaving Colonel Boles to follow with the park and stores, and continued for several weeks making moves and countermoves every day, at an average of twenty miles. The *dawks* were now beginning to arrive regularly from Bombay, and Thoughtless, on the 20th January, entered in his journal — "We have received, for the first time since October, some Bombay gazettes. The editor says in one paper, — 'The Peishwa is not, as reported, at Punderpore; but it is no matter where he is.' I wish this gentleman was marching after him as we are, and he would soon find it to be a matter of some moment." On the 22d January, they gained sight of the enemy near the town of Ogur, on the Kisthna, having marched by way of Punderpore, and made countermarches in all directions. The south of the Deckan, near the river Kisthna, is abundantly rich. Its banks are covered with towns, and the country clothed with fine crops of cotton, tobacco, wheat, sugar-cane, gram, and jewarry.

CHAP. XXV.

O truly blest, if bliss he knows,
  Who, healthful in some safe retreat,
Which simple competence bestows,
  Feels no ambition to be great.

Whose acres few and garden give,
  Nicely to trim, amusive toil;
Whose mind, philosophy to live
  Serenely on his native soil.

What if no *durwan* stand in state
  Before his lowly cottage door;
Would a *sawarry* at his gate
  Increase the joy he has in store?

General Smith had made a forced march of thirty miles to Ogur, for the purpose of surprising the Peishwa, whose army was encamped near the town on the banks of the Kisthna; but the horse artillery, cavalry, and a light battalion, formed from the flank companies of native corps, and mounted on *tattoos*, only reached the heights overlooking that fine river in time to see the clouds of dust that hovered over the retreat of the Mahrattas. The force had marched 222 miles since its last departure from Seroor, taking but one halting day to rest the cattle, nearly exhausted by continued exertion. This rapid pursuit far exceeded the Peishwa's calculation, and he felt himself sorely pressed upon all sides. Gockla, with the flower of his cavalry, was at this period around the division of General Pritzler, impeding his advance from the south, when General Smith broke in most unexpectedly before him upon his highness and the main body of his army. Chittamun Row, Napunker, and Trimbuckgee Danglae, with 12,000 horse, made a bold effort to cover his retreat on the high road to Sattara, and the next day these daring chiefs attacked the light division in front, flank, and rear, near Mirrich, with great impetuosity, cut off a non-commissioned officer's party of the light battalion, and in one of their charges, having penetrated the baggage flank, slaughtered many of the followers, and carried away some plunder, it being impossible, with such a deficiency of cavalry, to pursue the enemy in all directions. Gockla, upon being apprised of the able and unexpected manner in which General Smith had taken up the pursuit of his royal master, drew off his cavalry from their attack on General Pritzler, and making a forced march of near forty miles, fell upon the rear of the light division next day, who were pushing hard to reach Tausgaum, and were closely engaged with the other chiefs in front and flank. General Smith soon perceived, from the immense bodies of cavalry and numerous standards approaching on all sides, that the whole of the Mahratta cavalry were around him. The plain, as far as the eye could reach, was literally covered with them, and it was sufficient to excite the wonder of a spectator that such a handful of men should have dared to press forward after four times their number of infantry with guns, in the face of fifteen times their numerical strength of Mahratta cavalry, whose korrallies or flankers were individually so brave that they gallopped along the line within a few paces of the riflemen and light infantry spread round to keep off their *matchlocks*, depending for safety upon their shields and armour. But coolness and discipline will always be found irresistible opposed to any numerical superiority deficient in these essential qualifications. Gockla's men were individually brave, and he was an experienced and able general, well acquainted with our tactics, for he had fought as an auxiliary under Sir Arthur Wellesley, and seen some of the most dashing service in India; but his troops being in a disorganized state, and without that mutual dependence upon each other which discipline ensures, he never could actuate them with his own brave spirit, and they invariably deserted him in the hour of trial. He was, however, by this mode of warfare making soldiers of them. The casualties during this day's service were considerable; but the enemy lost immense numbers from the fire of grape, shells, and round shot discharged upon them nearly the whole day. They however succeeded, by their perseverance and boldness, in retarding the advance of the light division, for every thing wore so much the appearance of a general action, that the British commander at length halted in the evening at the village of Kauta, without being able to reach Tausgaum, where the enemy shewed vast masses next morning, and disputed every mile of the road to Neemluck. Here they encamped so near, and in such prodigious numbers, that the light division lay all night fully accoutred. On the following day they reached Koragaum, eighteen miles distant, notwithstanding the great efforts made by Gockla to prevent their advance.

Upon moving next morning the scene was interesting. The sun rose in beauty over the high romantic hill fort of Booserghur, below which large bodies of the enemy appeared drawn up, while their artillery rockaded the line. A large mass of them, directly in front, defiled along the left flank, and soon after another, equally numerous, passed down the right. The horse artillery and cavalry had scarcely dislodged their rocket-men, who had killed several sepoys, when an immense column appeared advancing at full gallop upon the front. A line was formed to receive them, and at this time the engagement was pretty general in every quarter. The division in front formed at the distance of five hundred yards, and stood for some time in silent awe, but raising a shout advanced again with the intention of charging the cavalry drawn up to mask the guns, which were now opened upon them by Captain Pierce with such effect, that they wheeled suddenly to the left and dispersed in the greatest confusion. From Pussasowla to Reymutpore the road winds through hills, and the vallies are broken into nullahs or ravines, and much intersected with hedges, so that the ground was unfavourable for cavalry, and the force marched on without much molestation except from rockets, which blazed upon the line from every height. But upon passing Julgaum, and entering the vale of Sattara, the enemy's whole force of cavalry appeared drawn up in columns of attack to the right, just out of cannon-shot range. Their korrallies were in every direction, sniping with the riflemen and flankers, and their rocket-boys were stationed on distant heights, showering their deadly missiles upon the line; from one of these Colonel Milnes had a very narrow escape, for his horse, on being struck by the shaft, made such violent plunges that his rider was thrown from the saddle with great violence, but fortunately arose uninjured, though two sepoys had their legs so much shattered by the same rocket that amputation was found necessary. General Smith continued his march, and Gockla, whose person was conspicuous at the head of his men, advanced also in a parallel line, for several miles. The sight was grand and interesting. He expected that General Smith would have taken the road to the left, to avoid the hill fort of Mungheer directly in front, and both columns marched upon it till their heads closed to within short cannon range. A struggle followed between the advance guards to gain the main road under the hill. The horse artillery opened a tremendous fire on the masses of cavalry, advancing at full gallop to pass under the guns of the fort, which they sustained for some time; but at length, dispirited by the numbers that were falling, they wheeled to the right in great disorder, and fled down the opposite side of the mountain. Towards evening the force encamped near the head of the Salpee Pass, down which the Peishwa had effected his retreat, having been very nearly intercepted in it by Colonel Boles and the heavy division. The enemy had sent their baggage down the Salpee after the Peishwa, and finding themselves thus cut off from the only road over the mountains in this quarter, endeavoured to pass along the bottom of the chain of ghauts, under the fort of Chunden Wunden, from which there is a communication with the main road, and they were seen about twilight advancing from among the mountains. The horse artillery, cavalry, light battalion, and flank companies were immediately dispatched to form an ambuscade, and they succeeded in forcing one division to seek safety by endeavouring to scale the mountain, on which they were directly turned. In this attempt they sustained immense loss, for the guns raked the side up which they clambered, and men and horses fell in numbers from the precipices they had gained in the vain hope of getting to the table land. But all the other divisions effected their escape under the darkness of night.

Thoughtless wrote his remarks late at night. "This," said he, "has been an interesting day's service. Before sun-rise the firing commenced. The blazing rattle of rockets, loud beyond description from the echo of the neighbouring mountains, the thunder of artillery, the bursting of shells, the cries and rout of the enemy's bodies of horse, the wild tones of their tooteries and *nagaries* urging on to the charge, the rush of our baggage to avoid the rockets, the romantic scenery of high hills on every side, the grand and steady march of 2,500 disciplined troops in the face of 30,000 Mahrattas, through this fine valley, our frequent halts and advances, announced by the bugles and drums, along the line, the flogging of followers for plundering the villages, while the *patels* were led to the general and forced to supply the commissary with grain, and were occasionally conducted back again with ropes round their necks, under a threat of death, in case of concealing provisions, are hints which may convey an idea of the scene. This fine valley, lately so beautiful, has changed its appearance. The passage of such large armies has destroyed the verdure of the fields, and many of the houses have been unroofed by the *looterers* for fire-wood. Oh! what misery the contentions of ambition generate for the humble tenants of the soil. Another ruffian was taken to-day in the act of tearing a gold-knobbed ring out of a woman's nose. Her face was covered with blood; she struggled, and he was going to cut her throat, when a *tackildar* arrested his villanous arm; he was hanged. A camp follower's wife was taken in labour on the march to-day in a nullah, and through the anxious solicitude of her husband, obtained that attendance which such a crisis demanded."

General Smith continuing the chase next day down the Salpee Pass, found that the Peishwa had escaped eastward, towards Punderpore; but before he resumed the pursuit it was necessary to replenish his store park and commissariat, and he determined moreover to avail himself of the opportunity of reinforcing his cavalry from the division of General Pritzler. Therefore having procured ammunition and grain from Colonel Boles, he re-ascended the Salpee Pass, and formed a junction at Reymutpore with General Pritzler, whose force consisted of two squadrons and the head-quarters of the 22d dragoons and 7th Madras native cavalry, an European flank battalion of eight companies from the 34th, 53d, 69th, and 84th regiments, the 1st of the 12th Madras native infantry and the Madras rifle battalion, with eight field-pieces, and a detail of artillerymen and pioneers. An efficient light force was immediately formed of the horse artillery, 22d dragoons, 2d and 7th Madras cavalry, light battalion, 65th regiment, 1st of 2d and 1st of 3d Bombay native infantry; with which General Smith determined to pursue the Peishwa. Before his departure, however, he found it expedient to take possession of Sattara, and the whole force, being joined at Koragaum by Colonel Boles and the heavy division, marched towards the ancient Mahratta capital on the 10th February 1818. They crossed the Kisthna at Maowly, a large town, with a magnificent pagoda on one bank of the river, and a handsome pavilion, belonging to the Peishwa, on the other. It is a sacred bathing place, and there are several fine flights of stone steps from the town to the water's edge. The inhabitants seemed very much alarmed, but crowded to see the force pass, after they had been furnished with tackildars to guard their property: from this place Sattara, situated on the table land of an isolated hill, has a formidable appearance. They forded the Kisthna, about fifty yards broad at Maowly, and encamped before the place of destination, in fine gardens of onions and carrots, in plantations of sugar-cane, and across fields of wheat, barley, jewarry, cotton, and dholl. The loss to the poor owners was incalculable. There was a considerable garrison in the fort of Sattara, but the *killedar* did not make a resolute defence, or he might have laughed at the efforts of General Smith for its reduction. After receiving a few shells from a mortar battery, the enemy evacuated it without returning a shot, and Thoughtless accompanied the party that took possession of a place truly wonderful, both in respect to nature and art.

Sattara stands on a hill belonging to a range, which it completely commands. The height of the fort is about three hundred yards above the plain, its length twelve hundred, and its breadth varying from three hundred to eighty at the western point. There is a table land formed by the hand of nature on the top, which is a huge rock of granite; it is cut perpendicularly all round, at an average of thirty feet. On this solid foundation the rampart is built of masonry, about eight feet high and as many broad. Numerous towers and bastions are erected round it; and there were twenty-seven guns mounted on the works, with a park well supplied with ammunition and stores. There is only one gate, exceedingly strong, but a sally-port defended by two towers opens in an opposite direction. Four fine tanks contain an abundance of water, and in short there is a small town on the summit, which, when the rajah was confined here, served as a habitation for the numerous Brahmins that surrounded him; in the centre of it a handsome house was erected for him. The petah or city of Sattara lies below in the plain under the north face of the fort; it is of great extent, and seemed rich and populous. The houses were well built of stone and lime, with good streets, and numerous gardens and orchards. The top of the hill commands a most delightful view of the valleys of Sattara, through which the Kisthna and Oomrouly meander and glitter to the eye with pleasing variety, sometimes hid beneath the rich foliage of fruit trees, and occasionally breaking forth in unexpected turns upon the sight. The British flag was hoisted under a royal salute from the camp, but after waving for a few minutes over the battlements that had long awed the Mahratta empire, it was replaced by that of the Sattara Rajah; Captain Garraway with 150 sepoys being left in charge of it; and while General Pritzler and the heavy division marched against other forts, General Smith with the light division proceeded down the Salpee Pass in pursuit of the Peishwa.

On the 19th February, after a rapid march of five days from Salpee by way of Fooltaun, a large town with magnificent pagodas, they reached Yelapore, where General Smith received information that the Peishwa was encamped at Gopalashtee, situated about thirty miles to the eastward. They marched at twelve o'clock that night, crossed the Beema at Keutalla, and about eleven o'clock next day the horse artillery and cavalry, with the staff of the force, halted on the heights overlooking the plain on which the Mahratta army was encamped; — an hour before his highness the Peishwa had thought himself in perfect safety, being assured that the British force was at a considerable distance, and his tents were struck and baggage loaded for the purpose of marching northward; — while he was in earnest conversation with his chiefs, it was announced that the English general was close upon him. When the British squadrons gained sight of the plain, they heard the tooteries and tom toms shrilly and loudly proclaiming surprise and confusion, and saw the Peishwa in rapid retreat, while Gockla with a great part of the cavalry was drawn up in line of battle across the main road; he having vowed to his highness that he would cover his retreat or lose his life. General Smith hesitated not a moment. He dispatched his staff to the different commanding officers with orders, the substance of which were that the cavalry should move down in separate columns of attack, the 22d dragoons in the centre, the 2d on the left, and the 7th on the right, while the horse artillery were directed to take up the best position according to circumstances, and at the discretion of Captain Pierce. "Thoughtless," said he, "ride to the rear, and order the light battalion up as quick as possible." Charles was not long in performing this duty, and to his surprise found the rifle companies of the 65th regiment close behind the light battalion, struggling hard to outmarch the tattoos upon which the men were mounted. Upon his return, he saw the cavalry dashing down the heights to charge Gockla in three separate columns, whose heads formed points for the formation of the line of battle. The ground was so rugged that the horse artillery could not get forward, and Charles overtook them just as the cavalry had approached within musket-shot of the enemy and formed line. Captain Pierce then used every exertion, and brought his guns into position on the right, when the line, at a round trot, made directly for the centre of the masses before it. The sight was awful, and a dead silence prevailed. Gockla had chosen his ground with great judgment, behind a nullah and other obstacles, which, he calculated, would keep back the artillery. His appearance was very formidable, the front ranks of his line having their spears couched, while the rear ranks seemed drawn up on a ridge higher than the front, armed with matchlocks. They opened a heavy fire upon the cavalry when within 150 yards of their line, which the latter did not return till they had advanced within a few paces of the Mahratta front, when the 22d dragoons discharging their pistols in the faces of the enemy, charged their centre, and the action became close and warm for a few seconds. The horse artillery, at this time on the right, could not fire; and General Smith, full of anxiety to see the cavalry close with the enemy, had gallopped into the space between the right of the 7th and the left of the guns, where he was much exposed. Gockla had a chosen body in reserve behind his left wing, for the purpose of attacking the rear or flank; and while the shock of the charge made by the 22d dragoons had forced his centre to give way, he wheeled with the greatest rapidity round his left, and passing between the guns and the right of the British line, attacked the 7th cavalry in rear with great impetuosity. General Smith was cut down, and some confusion was produced on the right;

but Major Daw, with the reserve of the 22d, charged Gockla, who was killed in this desperate but brave attempt; and now the whole of the Mahrattas fled in confusion. General Smith had received the blow of a sabre on the back of his head, but the wound was not dangerous. The slaughter of the enemy was great, and they were pursued till it was feared the horses would be blown. All the plain was strewed with their dead and wounded. The pursuit was continued. After the horses had breathed, another successful charge was made; for during the halt the chiefs had rallied their men and shown front again. In this charge the main body was overtaken, and the carnage was dreadful. The Peishwa escaped on a fleet horse; but the Sattara Rajah, his mother, and his two brothers were taken, with eleven elephants and fifty camels, some of which were loaded with treasure. Majors Daw, Doveton, and Walker preserving a fine line, and halting frequently to breathe their horses, continued the pursuit for nearly ten miles from the scene of action, and captured all the rear of the baggage of the Peishwa's army. In short, the rout and dispersion of his troops were beyond description terrific and dreadful. Thoughtless accompanied the cavalry in this course of slaughter, and saw enough to impress his mind with the most frightful image of war. The native troopers even shot unarmed palankeen boys and camp followers; but the 22d dragoons were as merciful as they were brave, and both the officers and men exerted themselves to save the prostrate foe.

Previous to this, the Peishwa becoming aware of the rapid rate at which General Smith could move, had placed his guns and infantry in forts, to enable him to march with superior celerity, so that he was completely surprised, and the result was of the greatest importance. No officer was killed in the light division, and besides the general, only Lieutenant Warren of the 22d dragoons was wounded; but 30 non-commissioned officers and soldiers were killed and wounded, with a considerable number of horses. The body of Gockla was burned in the evening, the ceremonial being accompanied with all due honours, according to the customs of his cast. His person was large, his features fine and manly, and his complexion nearly fair. He had received several wounds on his face and body, but the confusion was so great, that it could not be ascertained under whose hand he had fallen, and several inferior chiefs shared his fate around him. He wore on the morning of the action a rich dress of gold *kinkob*, with a pearl necklace, diamond ear-rings, and an ornament for the turban of immense value, which became the plunder of some of the camp followers; for the bodies of all the officers were found nearly naked upon the return of the cavalry from pursuing the enemy. It is impossible not to respect the spirit of Gockla. The judgment with which he prepared to receive General Smith was only equalled by his valour and skill in bravely endeavouring to retrieve the day, upon finding, that his centre could not withstand the charge of the 22d dragoons; and the muse of history will encircle his name with a laurel for fidelity and devotion in his country's cause.

The rescue of the Rajah of Sattara and his family from the hands of the Peishwa, gave General Smith the most lively satisfaction; for nothing could be of more importance in the present conjuncture, as the supreme government had determined to depose the usurper, and restore the rajah to some portion of the rights belonging to his ancestors. In the orders issued upon the occasion, the General warmly expressed his high sense of the meritorious and most gallant conduct of the cavalry, and his admiration of the exemplary conduct of every one engaged in the action of Ashtee. "The operations of yesterday," said he, "were necessarily confined to the cavalry; but the zeal and good conduct evinced by the whole of the troops during a period of three months of incessant marching, has been eminently conspicuous; and the brigadier-general regrets that it was impossible upon this occasion to afford them all an opportunity of meeting the enemy." This affair was truly honourable to himself, and so ruinous in its effects upon the Mahrattas, that they never dared to show their faces afterwards. Intercepted letters, from various chiefs, soon gave a picture of the desertion and the dismay consequent upon it in the Peishwa's camp. "The English general," said one, "has by this blow gained every object of his government, and rewarded his force with immense booty for the hardships they had endured for the last three months." "All the sirdars," said another, "are now endeavouring to make terms for themselves, and I am determined to withdraw from a cause which is ruined, and is involving the country in misery."

In short, the interest of the campaign here ceases. General Smith, after the sale of the prize property, returned towards Poonah, for the purpose of placing the Sattara Rajah with Mr. Elphinstone, who had remained there, having been appointed commissioner for the settlement of affairs in this part of the Deckan. The rajah now assumed all the external pomp of an eastern prince, and seated in a rich howdah on a large elephant, accompanied by his brothers and their mother, with her ladies of honour in other howdahs and rich palankeens, with flags, tom toms, tooteries, and guards, formed a pageant of no ordinary magnificence at the head of the British line. During the cool of each morning, these high personages rode richly caparisoned Mahratta horses, and only mounted their elephants in the heat of the day. The queen mother managed her horse with great dexterity, and rode, according to the custom of the ladies of her country, as gentlemen do with us. She bore the traces of great beauty, wore a rich dress of embroidered muslin, with but few ornaments; she did not conceal her face, and was both familiar and talkative with such officers as approached her. In person she appeared rather above the middle size, and her complexion was almost fair. She evinced an ardent desire to appropriate every thing that was captured to herself, for she claimed all the elephants and camels, with every fine horse and tent that she saw, as her own. Her age seemed between forty and fifty, and she had none of that timidity which one naturally supposes to belong to Hindoo ladies. In short, she appeared to be a woman possessed of much natural ability, and far greater presence of mind than the rajah, for whom she managed every thing, and he even looked to her for the answers he had to make to several questions. He appeared about 23 years of age, and his brothers something younger; but there was no great difference in their size, being all of small stature, dark complexion, and vulgar aspect, so that no person would suppose they were the children of such an intelligent, sprightly, fair woman as the queen mother. They were richly dressed in gold muslins and kinkobs, with pearl necklaces of three rows set in gold and sparkling with precious stones; their turbans and ear-rings were very costly; they wore trowsers with feet like stockings, and slippers turned up at the toes and covered with precious gems. Upon approaching towns or villages the tooteries were sounded, and the musicians, who rode on camels, began to beat their tom toms, when the inhabitants came out in crowds and prostrated themselves before their legitimate sovereign.

In this manner the force returned by easy marches, and crossed the Beema at Hingingaum, having passed the village of Tamboorna, the birth-place of Padashaw Munkisser Bow, late minister for British affairs at the court of Poonah, who till the day of his death made it the object of his life to cultivate the friendship of the English government. He made the humble spot of his birth remarkable by erecting a magnificent palace near it with fine gardens. On the 27th February they passed the large town of Barramutty, and halted next day at Moorishwar, that the rajah might return thanks to Gunputty, who has a celebrated temple here, and make presents to the Brahmins on occasion of his restoration to power. The pagodas are very magnificent and numerous, but their sanctity is not so great now as formerly; for it is believed that Gunputty forsook them, disgusted with the partiality of the Brahmins for new customs, and that this god is now incarnate at Cheechore, near Poonah. But this *avater* of Gunputty needs not be detailed, as a particular history of it is given by Lord Valentia in his Travels in India. Soon afterwards the Honourable Mr. Elphinstone arrived from Poonah to meet the rajah and escort him thither with Captain Davis and the irregular horse, and General

Smith marched for Seroor. It may here be proper to notice the most affecting circumstance of the whole campaign; twenty-two guns were fired at Boolsir for the death of her royal highness Charlotte Princess of Wales, and Thoughtless shed a tear when he reflected that rank, fortune, love, and the hope of a nation could not shield such excellence from the shaft of death; and that while her royal father's heart was torn with anguish for the irreparable loss of his only child, how little pleasure could arise from the intelligence that the British arms were successful in acquiring new and splendid conquests in the East.

General Smith only halted one day at Seroor. He proceeded northward at a rapid rate after the enemy on the road to Jaulna as far as Toka, where the march was changed to the eastward, but not long continued, for the Godavery was crossed at Rauksbone on the 18th March, and on the 28th, after prodigious marching and counter-marching, the force left their sick at Jaulna, and continued the pursuit of the Peishwa. The heat of the weather had now increased so much, that during every long march some of the men fell under coups de soleil; the thermometer stood at 109° at ten o'clock in the day, and the hospitals were soon filled with fever, liver disease, and dysentery. The Peishwa's case now became desperate. Brigadier-general Doveton was closing upon him in one direction; Colonels Adams and Scott were advancing with light divisions from other points; while General Smith was driving his highness upon them. Many of his sirdars, however, made it a point of honour to adhere to their chief in the hour of his adversity; and in the latter end of April they were surprised and cut up by Colonel Adams, who took the whole of their baggage, and all the remaining treasure of the Peishwa. Soon after which his highness surrendered himself, and received permission from his generous foes, notwithstanding all his treachery and ingratitude, to reside at Benares on a large pension.

The force now returned to Seroor, crossed the Godavery at Keir, and reached the cantonments on the 16th May, having marched since their departure thence on the 10th March 706 miles, and during the whole campaign, since their first movement from Seroor, 2,037.

In the meantime the Marquis of Hastings had returned to Calcutta, and Sir Thomas Hislop to Madras. All the hill forts belonging to the Peishwa in the Deckan and Konkan had surrendered, and Trimbuckgee Danglae had been taken prisoner by Captain Swanston at the head of a body of irregulars after a night march of sixty miles, arranged and conducted with consummate skill, by which that cunning and plotting chief was completely surprised. The 65th regiment were now suffering from the effects of fatigue and exposure to the sun; for Europeans, though they stand a hard campaign well in India, drop off rapidly on returning to quarters. But the cholera morbus, which had spread such destruction in Bengal, now travelled westward, and began to thin the ranks of the Bombay army. Many were the victims to its fury in the 65th, but Thoughtless escaped; for having now obtained leave of absence he departed for Bombay, in the hope of soon embarking with his family from the burning climate of India. Yet he could not say "*farewell*" to his valued friends without a sensation of deep regret, that cast a gloom on the cheering prospect of a return to his native land.

CONCLUSION.

No sickly clime his spirit tries,
No deadly vapours fire the brain,
Beneath the eye no comrade lies,
Whose life-blood cools the burning plain.

But rosy children course the lawn,
And sportive mazy circles form;
Whose hearts, like dew of summer dawn,
Dissolve in pity for a worm.

How bootless is the courtly smile
To him whose little ones and wife
Can melancholy quite beguile,
And strew with roses thorny life?

He who has a large family in India will find no difficulty in transporting them to England, if he have a few thousand rupees to pay for their passage. Thoughtless had a sufficient fund remaining for this purpose, and he had the good fortune to embark in an excellent vessel, of which the commander, a most worthy man, made so good use of his time, that he dropped his anchor in Table Bay exactly one month after his departure from Bombay harbour, and Charles beheld with pleasure the cloud-capt brow of the mountain that rises abruptly from Cape Town. Thence they were wafted by the steady trade-wind past St. Helena and Ascension, and in three months and twelve days after their departure from the Cape of Good Hope the passengers landed at Dover.

London being new to Charles, he remained a fortnight there, admiring the various productions of art that court the attention of the curious. At length he touched the land of his birth after an absence of seventeen years. The meeting of a father and son under such circumstances is a scene best suited to the imagination, and it is entirely omitted by him who wrote "Fifteen Years in India." Thoughtless took possession of a handsome well-furnished house in Dundalk, and he had the pleasure of seeing his friend George True, who visited him on the very day when he settled in that agreeable town. The roses and lillies of Erin bloomed on the cheeks of the lovely Nannette and her charming children; and Edward and Emma recognized in each other what fancy had been teaching them to expect. Robert Gordon, now agent to the extensive estates of Mr. True, was in the full exercise of his poetical faculties. The season of the year afforded Bob an opportunity for composition, and when Charles called to see him he had just finished the following lines, which he entitled

THE OPENING OF SPRING.

Stern winter's sky no more with tempest lowers,
To arctic climes rough Boreas steals away,
And vernal breezes and refreshing showers
Are now companions of the lengthened day.

The modest snow-drop, harbinger of spring,
Now greets the eye with robe of virgin white;
With joyful notes the birds begin to sing
At peep of dawn to hail the new-born light.

Pleased with young life, the sportive lambs are seen
Striving in mimic race with guileless mirth;
Kind nature now prepares her garb of green,
To clothe her flow'rets teeming into birth.
At this sweet season let not man be sad,
While bounteous heaven makes all around him glad.

"But," said he, "I shall not offer you this, for I intend to write a piece in commemoration of your return home." Thoughtless, however, was pleased with the concluding lines of the above stanzas, because they accorded with his feelings; and, in revisiting the scenes of his youth, he strove to repress the melancholy that arose within him by frequently repeating

"At this sweet season why should I be sad,
While bounteous heaven makes all around me glad."

All around him was gladness and joy, but every thing was new and unexpected. His habits had undergone a change of which he was not aware; and in his disappointment he at first concluded that the manners of his early companions had become deteriorated.

A few fleeting days cleared up his agitated conjectures respecting Frank Stanley, from whom he received a most satisfactory letter, stating that he was welcomed by the old squire with every sincere demonstration of joy, and that his aged mother seemed renewed with life by consummated hope, on clasping her long absent child to her maternally affectionate breast. "But," said Frank, "confusion to me, my dearest friend, if I can describe the rest.—I found that bright particular star, for so many years the north-pole of attraction to my anxious soul, in all the loveliness of matured beauty. Let the pencil of conception paint on the mind of a lover my transport at discovering that the willow had been worn for my sake. Sarah is now my wife."

To conclude:—There is every reason to hope that as much felicity as was intended to mingle in the cup of human life will be enjoyed by all the parties in question during the remainder of existence; and should the author of these humble sketches have succeeded in convincing the public that his pen has been employed in promoting the interests of morality, virtue, and religion, while he endeavoured to amuse the fancy and interest the affections of the heart, his own share of bliss will have been considerably encreased.

GLOSSARY.

ABDAR — a servant whose business it is to cool water, wine, &c.

Ayahs — maid-servants in India.

Amir — a nobleman, a lord.

Arab — the horses used by officers in India are from Arabia, and called Arabs.

Aw, saheeb — yes, Sir.

Avater — an incarnation of some deity.

Buggy — the gig, or one horse chaise, is so called in India.

Bobberchee — a cook.

Brahmins — the sacred cast in Hindostan from which the priests are selected.

Bungalow — a cottage, a name generally applied to the officers' houses near a cantonment in India.

Bheesties — men who carry water in leather bags.

Bhauts — the descendants of the ancient bards of India.

Brandy-pawny — brandy and water, the common beverage in India.

Bhote salam — best compliments.

Bavas — children.

Biggah — the third of an acre.

Borahs — hawkers, pedlars.

Baftas — piece goods made of cotton.

Brahma — the god of creation in India.

Champaul Ghaut — the name of a wharf in Calcutta.

Chattah — a large umbrella made of silk or palm leaves.

Coolies — natives in India whose business it is to carry burdens, porters.

Crore — there are one hundred lacks in a crore, and a lack is equal to 100,000, therefore a crore is ten millions.

Champo — to knead or rub the body with the hand.

Cranny — a native in Bengal who writes in an office, a clerk.

Cudjans — the leaves of the palmira and cocoa-nut trees, with which the houses are thatched.

Cutwal — the magistrate of a village or town.

Chattee — an earthen pot.

Cheechee — the Bengal half-cast ladies are nicknamed "cheechees," being a word often used by them, which in Hindostannee means "fie! fie!"

Couch wallah — a man who carries a camp cot and bedding.

Catamaran — a sort of boat used at Madras.

Dooly — a litter covered with canvas, in which sick soldiers are carried.

Dandies — the boatmen on the river Ganges are so called.

Durbar — the court of a native prince.

Durwan — a gate-keeper.

Dawks — the posts by which communication is kept up in India, post-office, letter-bag.

Fakier — a religious mendicant; properly speaking, the word is restricted to Mahomedans; but it is now generally used for beggars and enthusiasts of all descriptions in India.

Ghaut — a mountain, a hill; also a wharf, quay, or landing-place.

Ginjals — small pieces of artillery mounted on walls, or upon the backs of camels.

Goru — a spiritual guide, the confessor or family priest in India.

Ghurs — Hindoo huts or houses.

Gora wallah — a groom, horse-keeper.

Gosains — one of the divisions of Hindoo mendicant friars or enthusiasts.

Hurkarus — messengers who carry dispatches, and generally travel mounted on camels.

Hackery — the common car in India; also the covered carriage used by the natives.

Hookah — the gorgeous Indian pipe for smoking tobacco.
Havildar — a serjeant of sepoys.
Hoondee — a bill of exchange.
Hulalcore — a sweeper, a remover of filth, an outcast that performs those offices which contaminate.
Hurries — men whose business it is to remove dead bodies at Juggurnaut.
Howdah — the castle placed on the elephant for the accommodation of those who ride that animal.
Hoont wallah — a camel driver.

Jemidar — a rank in the company's military service similar to that of ensign.
Jungles — forests or uncultivated parts of the country.
Jaghires — pensions, or lands held on condition of performing certain services.

Khatri — the fighting or warrior cast.
Ka babbery ? — what noise is that?
Killedar — the commandant of a fort.
Kussum — husband.
Knockada — the captain or master of a native vessel.
Kinkob — silk embroidered with gold.

Looterers — are plunderers that follow an army in India.
Lack — a number equal to 100,000 ; a lack of rupees is £12,500.
Lingums — are temples in which barren women pray for children, and perform certain ceremonies prescribed by the Brahmins.
Langutty — a cloth which is tied round the loins.

Monsoon — the wet season in India is so called.
Matchlocks — are fire-arms discharged by means of a match instead of a flint.
Mohur — a gold coin worth sixteen rupees, or £2.
Moonshee — a teacher of languages ; generally a Mahomedan.
Mohorum — the Mahomedan annual festival in honour of Hussen and Hossen.
Mussauls — chair-boys in India.
Mussoola boat — a particular kind of boat used at Madras on account of the heavy surf on that coast.

Naik — a corporal of sepoys.

Nautchees — dancing girls.

Nusseeb — fortune, destiny, lot.

Nautch — a dance, a ball, an entertainment given in honour of some god.

Nagaries — are drums of a very large description.

Nizamut Adoulut — a native court in Calcutta, which superintends the administration of criminal law according to Hindoo and Mahomedan codes, customs, and forms.

Ollas — leaves on which the natives write with a style.

Pundit — a professor of Gentoo law, a native barrister.

Palankeen or *Palkee* — the sedan of India, carried by four men, and made so that the person in it may lie at full length.

Pagoda — the common Hindoo temples are so called; it is also a gold coin, current in many parts of India, worth 9*s*.

Parsee — the officers' head servants are in general the descendants of Persian settlers, who are called Parsees on the Bombay coast.

Punko — a large fan suspended from the ceiling to produce artificial circulation of air.

Poojah — a Hindoo procession of the *doorgas*, or idols; a festival in honour of some deity.

Paddimar — a large boat in use on the western coast of India.

Petah — the town outside a fort is so called in India.

Peré — a saint or holy Mahomedan, whose tomb is held sacred.

Patels — native officers placed over villages in some parts of India, instead of cutwals.

Rupee — a silver coin, worth 2*s*. 6*d*.

Routy — the common tents used in camp by soldiers are so called in India.

Ramram — a complimentary term of address among the Hindoos, equivalent to "good day"—"how are you."

Sepoys — native soldiers in the pay of the East India Company.

Saheeb — sir, or master; a term of respect.

Subadar — the highest rank a native officer can attain in the company's military service.

Shigrampo — a word compounded from the imperative of the Malabar verb *po*, go, and the adverb *shigram*, quick, and applied to a sort of carriage used in several parts of India.

Soubah — a title under the Great Mogul, equal to viceroy.

Salam — the Indian salutation, made by touching the forehead with the right hand.

Salam-alikoom — "peace be unto thee;" the complimentary address used by Mahomedans.

Shroff — a Hindoo banker.

Sircar — an agent who transacts money concerns; it is also applied by the natives to the British government in India.

Such bola — speak truth.

Soodres — the fourth cast, or labouring classes in India.

Sanyasee — a Hindoo religious mendicant or enthusiast.

Suttee — the ceremony of burning a wife with the dead body of her husband.

Sauree — the female dress, composed of one piece, is so called.

Shaddee — the marriage ceremony, marriage.

Sirdars — chiefs or head men.

Suwarry — the suite and equipage of a great man.

Sheva — the brother of Brahma, whose office it was to destroy what the others had created.

Sudder Dewany Adoulut — a court that superintends the administration of civil law in Bengal upon native principles.

Tank — a reservoir for water, an artificial pond.

Tatties — frames thatched with grass, upon which water is thrown to cool the air passing through them into the sitting-rooms in India.

Tiffin — the mid-day meal in India, lunch.

Topes — groves of fruit trees or others.

Teerettee — a female belonging to the Teer tribe on the coast of Malabar.

Tazzee be Tazzee — a popular song in India, called in English "Ever fresh and ever gay."

Tiek — the Indian oak is so called.

Tom toms — the common drums of India.

Tooteries — long trumpets.

Tomasha — an entertainment, a play, a merry-making, fun of any kind.

Tattoos — small country horses.

Takildar — a guard placed over a village in passing it to prevent plunder.

Viranda — a portico, or piazza (in the common acceptation of the word).

Veidam — the Hindoo Scriptures.

Vyasees — the third cast in India, composed of the middling classes.

Vishnu — the brother of Brahma and Sheva, whose duty it was to preserve what the one had made, and the other would destroy.

Warries — hamlets, small collections of huts.

Zemindars — the collectors of the rent for the government in India.

FINIS.